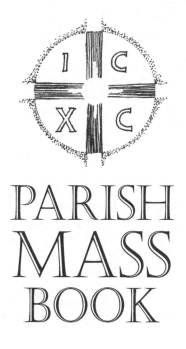

PARISH MASS BOOK

YEAR C – Volume 1

McCRIMMONS
Great Wakering Essex UK

This edition first published in 2012

Published by McCrimmon Publishing Co Ltd
10–12 High Street, Great Wakering, Essex, SS3 0EQ, UK
Telephone (01702) 218 956   Fax (01702) 216082
info@mccrimmons.com   www.mccrimmons.com

Compilation and layout
© Copyright 2012, McCrimmon Publishing Co Ltd

ISBN 978-0-85597-718-4   A5 Standard edition
ISBN 978-0-85597-719-1   A4 Large-print edition

Concordat cum Originali   Jane Porter

Nihil obstat   Rt Rev Mgr David Manson
                            Censor Deputatis, 2012

Imprimatur   + Rt Rev Thomas McMahon
                            Bishop of Brentwood

Approved for use in the dioceses of England and Wales.
Permission granted for distribution in the dioceses of Scotland and Ireland.

Acknowledgements

Excerpts from the English translation and chants of *The Roman Missal* © 2010, International Commission on English in the Liturgy Corporation (ICEL); the English translation of *General Introduction from Lectionary for Mass* © 1969, 1981, 1997, ICEL; excerpts from the English translation of *Holy Communion & Worship of the Eucharist outside Mass* © 1974, ICEL; excerpts from the English translation of *Rite of Christian Initiation of Adults* © 1985, ICEL; excerpts from the English translation of *Ceremonial of Bishops* © 1989, ICEL. All rights reserved.

Further copyright acknowledgements are found on page 4.

Project management and typesetting: Patrick Geary.

The publishers wish to express their thanks to the following for their help in the preparation of this volume: Patrick Geary, Martin Foster and Jane Porter.

Cover design: Nick Snode.

Cover illustration by The Benedictine Sisters of Turvey Abbey.
The four letters of this Christogram represent a traditional abbreviation of the Greek words for 'Jesus Christ' (i.e., the first and last letters of each of the words – 'ιHϹΟΥϹ ΧΡΙϹΤΟϹ' (Iesoùs Christòs).

Typeset in ITC Stone Serif and ITC Stone Sans.

Printed and bound by CPI Group (UK) Ltd, Croydon, CR0 4YY   I/AB

CONTENTS

MUSIC

Some music is printed in the *Order of Mass* and in the propers. A fuller set of chants for the *Order of Mass* is found in the section *Music for the Order of Mass*. Cross-references to these chants are provided in the *Order of Mass*.

Consistent with the approach used in the Altar edition of *The Roman Missal*, the music of the chants is notated in order to avoid the use of key signatures. This does not preclude the chants being sung at a different pitch. Indeed, a pitch should be chosen which is comfortable for the Priest, Deacon, reader, cantor and assembly, in order to aid full participation in the liturgy.

Copyright Acknowledgements

Scripture texts from the Jerusalem Bible, © copyright by Darton, Longman and Todd Ltd, and Doubleday and Co Inc, 1966, 1967 and 1968. Used by permission. All rights reserved.

Texts for the English translation of the Gospel readings for the Palm Sunday Procession from the Catholic Edition of the Revised Standard Version of the Bible, copyright 1965, 1966 by the Division of Christian Education of the National Council of the Churches of Christ in the United States of America. Used by permission. All rights reserved.

Psalms of the Responsorial Psalms reprinted by permission of HarperCollins Publishers Ltd. Copyright © 1963, The Grail (England) from *The Psalms: A New Translation*.

English translation of Psalms 23 and 46 on Palm Sunday of the Passion of the Lord from Copyright © 2010, Conception Abbey/The Grail, administered by GIA Publications, Inc., www.giamusic.com All rights reserved.

Music for *Memorial Acclamation D* (My Lord and my God) © copyright Tom Egan, ACCM, 1985, 2011. Used by permission. All rights reserved.

Excerpts from the English translation of the *General Instruction of the Roman Missal*, translation © 2002, International Committee on English in the Liturgy, Inc; emendations © copyright 2005, Catholic Bishops' Conference of England and Wales. All rights reserved.

Excerpts from Celebrating the Mass © copyright 2005, Catholic Bishops' Conference of England and Wales. All rights reserved.

The publishers have made every effort to seek permission from, and acknowledge correctly, the owners of copyright material contained in this volume. If any errors or omissions have been made, pardon is sought and corrections will be made in reprints.

ORDER OF MASS

ORDER OF MASS

In celebrating the Eucharist, the people of God assemble as the body of Christ to fulfil the Lord's command: 'do this in memory of me' (Luke 22:19).

At the Last Supper the Lord gathered his disciples, he spoke to them, took bread and wine, broke the bread, and gave them the Bread of life and the Cup of eternal salvation. In the Eucharist the Church to this day makes Christ's memorial and celebrates his presence in the same sequence of actions: we gather in Christ's name, in the Liturgy of the Word we listen as the word of God is proclaimed and explained, in the Liturgy of the Eucharist, we take bread and wine, give thanks, and receive the Body and Blood of Christ.

Christ is always present in his Church, particularly in its liturgical celebrations. In the celebration of Mass, Christ is really present in the very liturgical assembly gathered in his name, in the person of the minister who acts in the person of Christ, in the proclamation of his word and under the Eucharistic species. This presence of Christ under the appearance of bread and wine is called real, not to exclude other ways in which Christ is present, but because it is real *par excellence*.

cf Celebrating the Mass nn 18–19, 22;
General Instruction of the Roman Missal n 27;
Holy Communion and the Worship of the Eucharist
Outside Mass n 6.

OUTLINE OF THE ORDER OF MASS

INTRODUCTORY RITES
Opening Song
Greeting
Penitential Act
Gloria (omitted during Advent and Lent)
Opening Prayer

LITURGY OF THE WORD
First Reading
Responsorial Psalm
Second Reading
Gospel Acclamation
Gospel
Homily
Profession of Faith
Prayer of the Faithful

LITURGY OF THE EUCHARIST
Preparation of Gifts
Prayer over the Gifts

EUCHARISTIC PRAYER

COMMUNION RITE
The Lord's Prayer
Rite of Peace
Lamb of God
Holy Communion
Prayer after Communion

CONCLUDING RITES
Blessing
Dismissal

INTRODUCTORY RITES

ORDER

> *Where two or three are gathered in my name,*
> *there am I in their midst.*
> *(Matthew 18:20)*
>
> The Introductory Rites help the faithful come together as one, to establish communion and to prepare themselves properly to listen to the word of God and to celebrate the Eucharist worthily.

ENTRANCE SONG   `ALL STAND`

While the Entrance Song is sung, the Priest approaches the altar with the ministers and venerates it.

SIGN OF THE CROSS   `▷ Music p 334`

All make the Sign of the Cross as the Priest says

Priest: In the name of the Father, and of the Son, and of the Holy Spirit.
People: **Amen.**

GREETING

Priest: The grace of our Lord Jesus Christ,
and the love of God,
and the communion of the Holy Spirit
be with you all.

or

Priest: Grace to you and peace from God our Father
and the Lord Jesus Christ.

or

Priest: The Lord be with you.
People: **And with your spirit.**

A Bishop will say:

Bishop: Peace be with you
People: **And with your spirit.**

The Priest, or a Deacon, or another minister, may very briefly introduce the faithful to the Mass of the day.

PENITENTIAL ACT

Because of its emphasis on Easter and Baptism, the Blessing and Sprinkling of Water (page 62) may take place on Sundays, especially in Easter Time. When it is used it replaces the Penitential Act.

Otherwise, one of the following three forms of the Penitential Act is used. Each Penitential Act begins with the invitation to the faithful by the Priest:

Brethren (brothers and sisters), let us acknowledge our sins,
and so prepare ourselves to celebrate the sacred mysteries.

A brief pause for silence follows.

On certain days during the Church's year, for example Palm Sunday and the Easter Vigil, and during certain other celebrations, for example a Funeral Mass, Rite of Entry into the Catechumenate or Baptism, the Introductory Rites take a different form.

Penitential Act A

All: I confess to almighty God
and to you, my brothers and sisters,
that I have greatly sinned,
in my thoughts and in my words,
in what I have done and in what I have failed to do,

All strike their breast.

through my fault, through my fault,
through my most grievous fault;
therefore I ask blessed Mary ever-Virgin,
all the Angels and Saints,
and you, my brothers and sisters,
to pray for me to the Lord our God.

Penitential Act B

▷ *Music p 335*

Priest: Have mercy on us, O Lord.
People: **For we have sinned against you.**

Priest: Show us, O Lord, your mercy.
People: **And grant us your salvation.**

Penitential Act C

▷ *Music p 335*

*After the silence the Priest or another minister invokes the gracious works of the Lord
to which he invites the Kyrie eleison invocations, in sequence, as in the example below:*

Priest or minister: You were sent to heal the contrite of heart:
    Lord, have mercy.   *or*   Kyrie, eleison.
People: **Lord, have mercy.**   *or*   **Kyrie, eleison.**

Priest or minister: You came to call sinners:
    Christ, have mercy.   *or*   Christe, eleison.
People: **Christ, have mercy.**   *or*   **Christe, eleison.**

Priest or minister: You are seated at the right hand of the Father to intercede for us:
    Lord, have mercy.   *or*   Kyrie, eleison.
People: **Lord, have mercy.**   *or*   **Kyrie, eleison.**

The absolution by the Priest follows all of the options above

Priest: May almighty God have mercy on us,
forgive us our sins,
and bring us to everlasting life.

▷ *Music p 336*

All: **Amen.**

KYRIE

▷ *Music p 336*

The Kyrie, eleison (Lord, have mercy) invocations may follow:

Lord, have mercy.		Kyrie, eleison.
Lord, have mercy.		**Kyrie, eleison.**
Christ, have mercy.	*or*	Christe, eleison.
Christ, have mercy.		**Christe, eleison.**
Lord, have mercy.	–	Kyrie, eleison.
Lord, have mercy.		**Kyrie, eleison.**

GLORIA

▷ *Music p 337*

When indicated this hymn is sung or said:

All:　　**Glory to God in the highest,
and on earth peace to people of good will.
We praise you,
we bless you,
we adore you,
we glorify you,
we give you thanks for your great glory,
Lord God, heavenly King,
O God, almighty Father.**

**Lord Jesus Christ, Only Begotten Son,
Lord God, Lamb of God, Son of the Father,
you take away the sins of the world,
　　have mercy on us;
you take away the sins of the world,
　　receive our prayer;
you are seated at the right hand of the Father,
　　have mercy on us.**

**For you alone are the Holy One,
you alone are the Lord,
you alone are the Most High,
Jesus Christ,
with the Holy Spirit,
in the glory of God the Father.
Amen.**

COLLECT

▷ *Proper*

Priest:　　Let us pray.

All pray in silence for a while. Then the Priest says the Collect, to which the people respond:

People:　　**Amen.**

ALL SIT

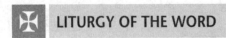

LITURGY OF THE WORD

> ## *Did not our hearts burn within us as he spoke to us and explained the Scriptures to us?*
> ### *(cf Luke 24:32)*
>
> In the Liturgy of the Word the assembly listens with hearts burning as the Lord speaks to it again and it responds with words of praise and petition.
>
> By hearing the word proclaimed in worship, the faithful again enter into the unending dialogue between God and the covenant people, a dialogue sealed in the sharing of the Eucharistic food and drink. The proclamation of the word is thus integral to the Mass and at its very centre.
>
> *Celebrating the Mass nn 19, 152*

FIRST READING   ▷ *Proper*

The reader goes to the ambo and proclaims the First Reading, while all sit and listen.

To indicate the end of the reading, the reader acclaims:

Reader: The word of the Lord.   ▷ *Music p 338*
All: **Thanks be to God.**

Following this reading, and the other readings it is appropriate to have a brief time of quiet as those present take the word of God to heart and begin to prepare a prayerful response to what they have heard.

RESPONSORIAL PSALM

The psalmist or cantor sings or says the Psalm, with the people making the response.

SECOND READING

On Sundays and certain other days there is a second reading.

To indicate the end of the reading, the reader acclaims:

Reader: The word of the Lord.   ▷ *Music p 338*
All: **Thanks be to God.**

GOSPEL ACCLAMATION   **ALL STAND**

The assembly stands for the Gospel Acclamation to welcome the Gospel.
The Gospel Acclamation may not be omitted where there is more than one reading before the Gospel.

The Gospel Acclamation is

Alleluia

ORDER

GOSPEL

The assembly remains standing in honour of the Gospel reading,
the high point of the Liturgy of the Word.

At the ambo the Deacon, or the Priest, sings or says:

Deacon or Priest: The Lord be with you.   ▷ *Music p 338*
All: **And with your spirit.**

Deacon or Priest: A reading from the holy Gospel according to N.

The Deacon or Priest makes the Sign of the Cross on the book and, together with the people,
on his forehead, lips, and breast.

All: **Glory to you, O Lord.**

At the end of the Gospel, the Deacon, or the Priest, acclaims:

Deacon or Priest: The Gospel of the Lord.
All: **Praise to you, Lord Jesus Christ.**

ALL SIT

HOMILY

The Homily is preached by a Priest or Deacon on all Sundays and Holydays of Obligation.
On other days, it is recommended.

At the end of the Homily it is appropriate for there to be a brief silence for recollection.

ALL STAND

PROFESSION OF FAITH

On Sundays and Solemnities, the Profession of Faith will follow.

In Masses that include acceptance into the order of catechumens and in ritual Masses for the election
or enrolment of names or for the Scrutinies, the Profession of Faith may be omitted.

On most occasions the form used is that of the Niceno-Constantinopolitan Creed.
However, especially during Lent and Easter Time, the Apostles' Creed (page 12) may be used.

If the Profession of Faith is not said, the Prayer of the Faithful follows.

Niceno-Constantinopolitan Creed   ▷ *Music p 339*

I believe in one God,
the Father almighty,
maker of heaven and earth,
of all things visible and invisible.

I believe in one Lord Jesus Christ,
the Only Begotten Son of God,
born of the Father before all ages.
God from God, Light from Light,
true God from true God,
begotten, not made, consubstantial with the Father;

through him all things were made.
For us men and for our salvation
he came down from heaven,

At the words that follow, up to and including 'and became man', all bow.

and by the Holy Spirit was incarnate of the Virgin Mary,
and became man.

For our sake he was crucified under Pontius Pilate,
he suffered death and was buried,
and rose again on the third day
in accordance with the Scriptures.
He ascended into heaven
and is seated at the right hand of the Father.
He will come again in glory
to judge the living and the dead
and his kingdom will have no end.

I believe in the Holy Spirit, the Lord, the giver of life,
who proceeds from the Father and the Son,
who with the Father and the Son is adored and glorified,
who has spoken through the prophets.

I believe in one, holy, catholic and apostolic Church.
I confess one Baptism for the forgiveness of sins
and I look forward to the resurrection of the dead
and the life of the world to come. Amen.

THE APOSTLES' CREED

Instead of the Niceno-Constantinopolitan Creed, the Apostles' Creed, may be used.

I believe in God,
the Father almighty
Creator of heaven and earth,
and in Jesus Christ, his only Son, our Lord,

At the words that follow, up to and including 'the Virgin Mary', all bow.

who was conceived by the Holy Spirit,
born of the Virgin Mary,
suffered under Pontius Pilate,
was crucified, died and was buried;
he descended into hell;
on the third day he rose again from the dead;
he ascended into heaven,
and is seated at the right hand of God the Father almighty;
from there he will come to judge the living and the dead.

ORDER

> I believe in the Holy Spirit,
> the holy catholic Church,
> the communion of saints,
> the forgiveness of sins,
> the resurrection of the body,
> and life everlasting. Amen.

PRAYER OF THE FAITHFUL

*Enlightened and moved by God's word, the assembly exercises its priestly function
by interceding for all humanity.*

Priest's Introduction

The Priest calls the assembly to prayer.

Intentions

As a rule the series of intentions is:

1 for the needs of the Church
2 for public authorities and the salvation of the whole world
3 for those burdened with any kind of difficulty
4 for the local community

*Nevertheless, in particular celebrations such as Confirmation, Marriage, or a Funeral, the series of
intentions may reflect more closely the particular occasion.*

The Deacon, or a Reader, announces short intentions for prayer to the assembly.

*After each intention there is a significant pause while the assembly prays,
then the response is sung or said.*

Example responses:

Deacon or Reader: We pray to the Lord.
All: **Lord, hear our prayer.**

or

Deacon or Reader: Let us pray to the Lord,
All: **Grant this, almighty God.**

or

Deacon or Reader: Let us pray to the Lord,
All: **Christ, hear us.**   *or*   **Christ, graciously hear us.**

or

Deacon or Reader: Let us pray to the Lord,
All: **Lord, have mercy.**   *or*   **Kyrie, eleison.**

After the final intention and response, there may be a period of silent prayer.

Priest's Prayer

Then the Priest says a concluding prayer to which all reply:

All: **Amen.**

ALL SIT

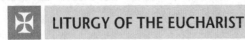

LITURGY OF THE EUCHARIST

> *Their eyes were opened and they recognised him in the breaking of bread.*
> *(cf Luke 24:30–31)*
>
> At the Last Supper, Christ instituted the Sacrifice and Paschal meal that make the Sacrifice of the cross present in the Church. From the days of the Apostles the Church has celebrated that Sacrifice by carrying out what the Lord did and handed over to his disciples to do in his memory. Like him, the Church has taken bread and wine, given thanks to God over them, broken the bread, and shared the bread and cup of blessing as the Body and Blood of Christ (cf 1 Corinthians 10:16). *Celebrating the Mass n 174*

PREPARATION OF THE GIFTS

A hymn or song may be sung, or instrumental music played during the collection, the procession, and the presentation of the gifts. If there is no music, the Priest may speak the following words aloud and the people acclaim the response at the end of each prayer.

Priest: Blessed are you, Lord God of all creation,
for through your goodness we have received
the bread we offer you:
fruit of the earth and work of human hands,
it will become for us the bread of life.

People: **Blessed be God for ever.**

Priest: Blessed are you, Lord God of all creation,
for through your goodness we have received
the wine we offer you:
fruit of the vine and work of human hands,
it will become our spiritual drink.

People: **Blessed be God for ever.**

ALL STAND

The Priest completes additional personal preparatory rites, and the people rise as he says:

Priest: Pray, brethren (brothers and sisters),
that my sacrifice and yours
may be acceptable to God,
the almighty Father.

▷ *Music p 341*

People: **May the Lord accept the sacrifice at your hands
for the praise and glory of his name,
for our good
and the good of all his holy Church.**

PRAYER OVER THE OFFERINGS

▷ *Proper*

Then the Priest says the Prayer over the Offerings, at the end of which the people acclaim:

People: **Amen.**

EUCHARISTIC PRAYER

> The Eucharistic Prayer, the centre and summit of the entire celebration, sums up what it means for the Church to celebrate the Eucharist. It is a memorial proclamation of praise and thanksgiving for God's work of salvation, a proclamation in which the Body and Blood of Christ are made present by the power of the Holy Spirit and the people are joined to Christ in offering his Sacrifice to the Father. The Eucharistic Prayer is proclaimed by the Priest celebrant in the name of Christ and on behalf of the whole assembly, which professes its faith and gives its assent through dialogue, acclamations, and the Amen. Since the Eucharistic Prayer is the summit of the Mass, it is appropriate for its solemn nature and importance to be enhanced by being sung.
>
> *Celebrating the Mass n 186*

Eucharistic Prayers I to IV are the principal prayers and are for use throughout the liturgical year. Eucharistic Prayer IV has a fixed preface and so may only be used when a Mass has no preface of its own and on Sundays in Ordinary Time. Eucharistic Prayers I to IV and Eucharistic Prayers for Reconciliation I and II are printed in full, beginning on page 18.

PREFACE DIALOGUE

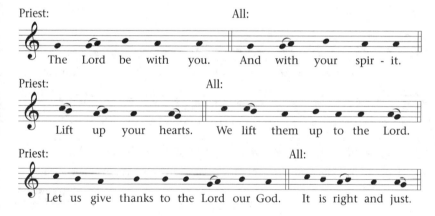

Priest: The Lord be with you. And with your spirit.

Priest: Lift up your hearts. We lift them up to the Lord.

Priest: Let us give thanks to the Lord our God. It is right and just.

Priest: The Lord be with you.
People: **And with your spirit.**

Priest: Lift up your hearts.
People: **We lift them up to the Lord.**

Priest: Let us give thanks to the Lord our God.
People: **It is right and just.**

PREFACE

The Priest continues with the Preface.

SANCTUS

The Priest concludes the Preface with the people, singing or saying aloud:

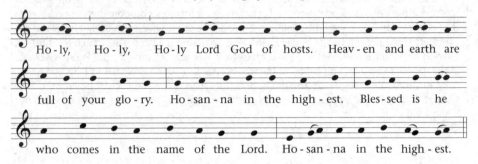

Ho - ly,   Ho - ly,   Ho - ly Lord   God   of   hosts.   Heav - en and earth are

full of your glo - ry.   Ho - san - na in the high - est.   Bles - sed is he

who comes in the name of the Lord.   Ho - san - na in the high - est.

All: **Holy, Holy, Holy Lord God of hosts.**
            Heaven and earth are full of your glory.
            Hosanna in the highest.
            Blessed is he who comes in the name of the Lord.
            Hosanna in the highest.

or

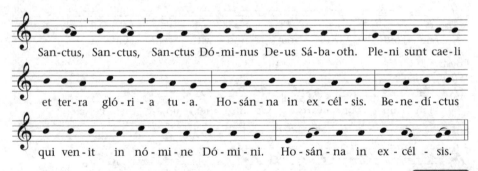

San - ctus, San - ctus, San - ctus Dó - mi - nus De - us Sá - ba - oth. Ple - ni sunt cae - li

et ter - ra gló - ri - a tu - a.   Ho - sán - na in ex - cél - sis.   Be - ne - dí - ctus

qui ven - it in nó - mi - ne Dó - mi - ni.   Ho - sán - na in ex - cél - sis.

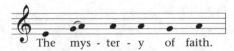

Texts for Eucharistic Prayers I to IV, Eucharistic Prayers for Reconciliation I and II and Eucharistic Prayers for use in Masses for Various Needs I to IV follow on page 18.

MEMORIAL ACCLAMATION

The Memorial Acclamation follows the words of Institution and the elevation of the host and chalice.

The Priest sings:

The mys - ter - y   of faith.

And the people continue with one of the following acclamations.

ORDER

Memorial Acclamation A

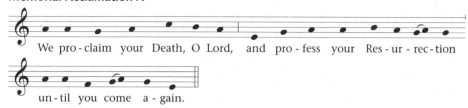

We pro-claim your Death, O Lord, and pro-fess your Res-ur-rec-tion

un-til you come a-gain.

Memorial Acclamation B

When we eat this Bread and drink this Cup, we pro-claim your

Death, O Lord, un-til you come a-gain.

Memorial Acclamation C

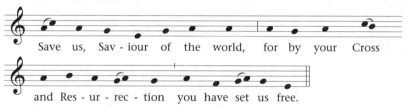

Save us, Sav-iour of the world, for by your Cross

and Res-ur-rec-tion you have set us free.

Memorial Acclamation D   *for Ireland only*

My Lord and my God.

Priest: The mystery of faith.

People: **We proclaim your Death, O Lord,**
                and profess your Resurrection
                until you come again.

or

People: **When we eat this Bread and drink this Cup,**
                we proclaim your Death, O Lord,
                until you come again.

or

People: **Save us, Saviour of the world,**
                for by your Cross and Resurrection
                you have set us free.

or for Ireland only:

People: **My Lord and my God.**

DOXOLOGY AND GREAT AMEN

At the end of the Eucharistic Prayer, the Priest takes the chalice and paten with the host and, raising both, he alone sings (or says) the Doxology. The people acclaim 'Amen'.

Priest:

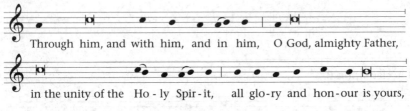

Through him, and with him, and in him, O God, almighty Father,

in the unity of the Ho - ly Spir - it,   all glo-ry and hon-our is yours,

People:

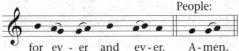

for ev - er and ev - er.   A - men.

Priest: Through him, and with him, and in him,
         O God, almighty Father,
         in the unity of the Holy Spirit,
         all glory and honour is yours,
         for ever and ever.

People: **Amen.**

▷ *page 56*

EUCHARISTIC PRAYERS

EUCHARISTIC PRAYER I

THE ROMAN CANON

On certain occasions, special forms of parts of the Eucharistic Prayer may be used.

Priest: To you, therefore, most merciful Father,
         we make humble prayer and petition
         through Jesus Christ, your Son, our Lord:
         that you accept
         and bless ✠ these gifts, these offerings,
         these holy and unblemished sacrifices,
         which we offer you firstly
         for your holy catholic Church.
         Be pleased to grant her peace,
         to guard, unite and govern her
         throughout the whole world,
         together with your servant N. our Pope
         and N. our Bishop,*
         and all those who, holding to the truth,
         hand on the catholic and apostolic faith.

---

* Mention may be made here of the Coadjutor Bishop, or Auxiliary Bishops

Commemoration of the Living

Remember, Lord, your servants N. and N.
and all gathered here,
whose faith and devotion are known to you.
For them, we offer you this sacrifice of praise
or they offer it for themselves
and all who are dear to them:
for the redemption of their souls,
in hope of health and well-being,
and paying their homage to you,
the eternal God, living and true.

Communicantes

In communion with those whose memory we venerate,
especially the glorious ever-Virgin Mary,
Mother of our God and Lord, Jesus Christ,
† and blessed Joseph, her Spouse,
your blessed Apostles and Martyrs,
Peter and Paul, Andrew,
(James, John,
Thomas, James, Philip,
Bartholomew, Matthew,
Simon and Jude;
Linus, Cletus, Clement, Sixtus,
Cornelius, Cyprian,
Lawrence, Chrysogonus,
John and Paul,
Cosmas and Damian)
and all your Saints;
we ask that through their merits and prayers,
in all things we may be defended
by your protecting help.
(Through Christ our Lord. Amen.)

Proper Forms of the *Communicantes*

*On the Nativity of the Lord
and throughout the Octave*
Celebrating the most sacred night (day)
on which blessed Mary
   the immaculate Virgin
brought forth the Saviour for this world,
and in communion with those
   whose memory we venerate,
especially the glorious ever-Virgin Mary,
Mother of our God and Lord, Jesus Christ, †

On the Epiphany of the Lord
Celebrating the most sacred day
on which your Only Begotten Son,
eternal with you in your glory,
appeared in a human body,
   truly sharing our flesh,
and in communion with those whose
   memory we venerate,
especially the glorious ever-Virgin Mary,
Mother of our God and Lord, Jesus Christ, †

On the Thursday of Holy Week at the Evening Mass of the Lord's Supper
Celebrating the most sacred day
on which our Lord Jesus Christ
was handed over for our sake,
and in communion with those
    whose memory we venerate,
especially the glorious ever-Virgin Mary,
Mother of our God and Lord, Jesus Christ,

From the Mass of the Easter Vigil until the Second Sunday of Easter
Celebrating the most sacred night (day)
of the Resurrection of our Lord Jesus Christ
    in the flesh,
and in communion with those
    whose memory we venerate,
especially the glorious ever-Virgin Mary,
Mother of our God and Lord, Jesus Christ, †

On the Ascension of the Lord
Celebrating the most sacred day
on which your Only Begotten Son,
    our Lord,
placed at the right hand of your glory
our weak human nature,
which he had united to himself,
and in communion with those
    whose memory we venerate,
especially the glorious ever-Virgin Mary,
Mother of our God and Lord, Jesus Christ, †

On Pentecost Sunday
Celebrating the most sacred day of
    Pentecost,
on which the Holy Spirit
appeared to the Apostles in tongues of fire,
and in communion with those
    whose memory we venerate,
especially the glorious ever-Virgin Mary,
Mother of our God and Lord, Jesus Christ, †

Hanc Igitur

Therefore, Lord, we pray:
graciously accept this oblation of our service,
that of your whole family;
order our days in your peace,
and command that we be delivered from eternal damnation
and counted among the flock of those you have chosen.
    (Through Christ our Lord. Amen.)

Proper Forms of the Hanc Igitur

*On Maundy Thursday
at the Evening Mass of the Lord's Supper*
Therefore, Lord, we pray:
graciously accept this oblation of our service,
that of your whole family,
which we make to you
as we observe the day
on which our Lord Jesus Christ
handed on the mysteries
    of his Body and Blood
for his disciples to celebrate;
order our days in your peace,
and command that we be delivered
    from eternal damnation
and counted among the flock
    of those you have chosen.
(Through Christ our Lord. Amen.)

*From the Mass of the Easter Vigil
until the Second Sunday of Easter*
Therefore, Lord, we pray:
graciously accept this oblation of our service,
that of your whole family,
which we make to you
also for those to whom
    you have been pleased to give
the new birth of water and the Holy Spirit,
granting them forgiveness of all their sins;
order our days in your peace,
and command that we be delivered
    from eternal damnation
and counted among the flock
    of those you have chosen.
(Through Christ our Lord. Amen.)

Be pleased, O God, we pray,
to bless, acknowledge,
and approve this offering in every respect;
make it spiritual and acceptable,
so that it may become for us
the Body and Blood of your most beloved Son,
our Lord Jesus Christ.

* On the day before he was to suffer,
† he took bread in his holy and venerable hands,
and with eyes raised to heaven
to you, O God, his almighty Father,
giving you thanks, he said the blessing,
broke the bread
and gave it to his disciples, saying:

TAKE THIS, ALL OF YOU, AND EAT OF IT,
FOR THIS IS MY BODY,
WHICH WILL BE GIVEN UP FOR YOU.

In a similar way, when supper was ended,
he took this precious chalice
in his holy and venerable hands,
and once more giving you thanks, he said the blessing
and gave the chalice to his disciples, saying:

TAKE THIS, ALL OF YOU, AND DRINK FROM IT,
FOR THIS IS THE CHALICE OF MY BLOOD,
THE BLOOD OF THE NEW AND ETERNAL COVENANT,
WHICH WILL BE POURED OUT FOR YOU AND FOR MANY
FOR THE FORGIVENESS OF SINS.

DO THIS IN MEMORY OF ME.

Memorial Acclamation

The Priest sings:

The   mys - ter - y   of   faith.

And the people continue with one of the following acclamations (overleaf):

---

* On the Maundy Thursday at the Evening Mass of the Lord's Supper, this part of the prayer begins:

On the day before he was to suffer,
for our salvation and the salvation of all,
that is today, †

Memorial Acclamation A

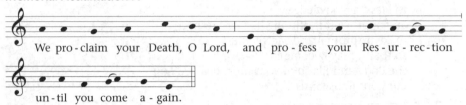

We pro-claim your Death, O Lord, and pro-fess your Res-ur-rec-tion un-til you come a-gain.

Memorial Acclamation B

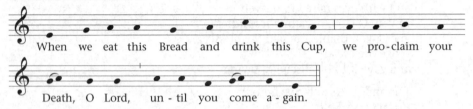

When we eat this Bread and drink this Cup, we pro-claim your Death, O Lord, un-til you come a-gain.

Memorial Acclamation C

Save us, Sav-iour of the world, for by your Cross and Res-ur-rec-tion you have set us free.

Memorial Acclamation D   *for Ireland only*

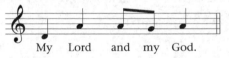

My Lord and my God.

Priest: Therefore, O Lord,
            as we celebrate the memorial of the blessed Passion,
            the Resurrection from the dead,
            and the glorious Ascension into heaven
            of Christ, your Son, our Lord,
            we, your servants and your holy people,
            offer to your glorious majesty
            from the gifts that you have given us,
            this pure victim,
            this holy victim,
            this spotless victim,
            the holy Bread of eternal life
            and the Chalice of everlasting salvation.

            Be pleased to look upon these offerings
            with a serene and kindly countenance,

and to accept them,
as once you were pleased to accept
the gifts of your servant Abel the just,
the sacrifice of Abraham, our father in faith,
and the offering of your high priest Melchizedek,
a holy sacrifice, a spotless victim.
In humble prayer we ask you, almighty God:
command that these gifts be borne
by the hands of your holy Angel
to your altar on high
in the sight of your divine majesty,
so that all of us, who through this participation at the altar
receive the most holy Body and Blood of your Son,
may be filled with every grace and heavenly blessing.
(Through Christ our Lord. Amen.)

Commemoration of the Dead

Remember also, Lord, your servants N. and N.,
who have gone before us with the sign of faith
and rest in the sleep of peace.
Grant them, O Lord, we pray,
and all who sleep in Christ,
a place of refreshment, light and peace.

(Through Christ our Lord. Amen.)

To us, also, your servants, who, though sinners,
hope in your abundant mercies,
graciously grant some share
and fellowship with your holy Apostles and Martyrs:
with John the Baptist, Stephen,
Matthias, Barnabas,
(Ignatius, Alexander,
Marcellinus, Peter,
Felicity, Perpetua,
Agatha, Lucy,
Agnes, Cecilia, Anastasia)
and all your Saints;
admit us, we beseech you,
into their company,
not weighing our merits,
but granting us your pardon,
through Christ our Lord.

Through whom
you continue to make all these good things, O Lord;
you sanctify them, fill them with life,
bless them, and bestow them upon us.

Doxology and Great Amen

At the end of the Eucharistic Prayer, the Priest takes the chalice and paten with the host and, raising both, he alone sings (or says) the Doxology. The people acclaim 'Amen'.

Priest: Through him, and with him, and in him,
         O God, almighty Father,
         in the unity of the Holy Spirit,
         all glory and honour is yours,
         for ever and ever.

People: **Amen.**

...for ev - er and ev - er.   A - men.

▷ *page 56*

EUCHARISTIC PRAYER II

This Eucharistic Prayer has its own Preface, but it may also be used with other Prefaces, especially those that present an overall view of the mystery of salvation.

On certain occasions, special forms of parts of the Eucharistic Prayer may be used.

Preface Dialogue

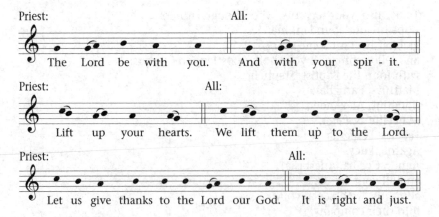

The Lord be with you.   And with your spir - it.

Lift up your hearts.   We lift them up to the Lord.

Let us give thanks to the Lord our God.   It is right and just.

Preface

Priest: It is truly right and just, our duty and our salvation,
         always and everywhere to give you thanks, Father most holy,
         through your beloved Son, Jesus Christ,
         your Word through whom you made all things,
         whom you sent as our Saviour and Redeemer,
         incarnate by the Holy Spirit and born of the Virgin.

Fulfilling your will and gaining for you a holy people,
he stretched out his hands as he endured his Passion,
so as to break the bonds of death and manifest the resurrection.

And so, with the Angels and all the Saints
we declare your glory,
as with one voice we acclaim:

Sanctus

All:

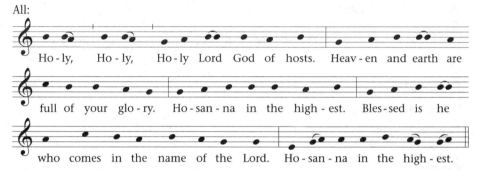

Ho-ly, Ho-ly, Ho-ly Lord God of hosts. Heav-en and earth are
full of your glo-ry. Ho-san-na in the high-est. Bles-sed is he
who comes in the name of the Lord. Ho-san-na in the high-est.

ALL KNEEL

Priest: You are indeed Holy, O Lord,
the fount of all holiness.
Make holy, therefore, these gifts, we pray,
by sending down your Spirit upon them like the dewfall,
so that they may become for us
the Body and ✠ Blood of our Lord Jesus Christ.

At the time he was betrayed
and entered willingly into his Passion,
he took bread and, giving thanks, broke it,
and gave it to his disciples, saying:

TAKE THIS, ALL OF YOU, AND EAT OF IT,
FOR THIS IS MY BODY,
WHICH WILL BE GIVEN UP FOR YOU.

In a similar way, when supper was ended,
he took the chalice
and, once more giving thanks,
he gave it to his disciples, saying:

TAKE THIS, ALL OF YOU, AND DRINK FROM IT,
FOR THIS IS THE CHALICE OF MY BLOOD,
THE BLOOD OF THE NEW AND ETERNAL COVENANT,
WHICH WILL BE POURED OUT FOR YOU AND FOR MANY
FOR THE FORGIVENESS OF SINS.

DO THIS IN MEMORY OF ME.

Memorial Acclamation

The Priest sings:

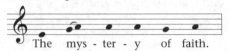

The mys - ter - y of faith.

And the people continue with one of the following acclamations:

Memorial Acclamation A

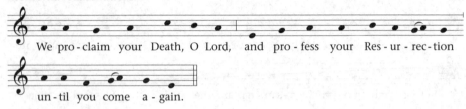

We pro - claim your Death, O Lord, and pro - fess your Res - ur - rec - tion un - til you come a - gain.

Memorial Acclamation B

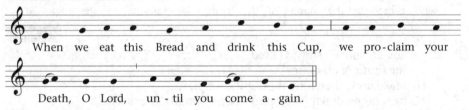

When we eat this Bread and drink this Cup, we pro - claim your Death, O Lord, un - til you come a - gain.

Memorial Acclamation C

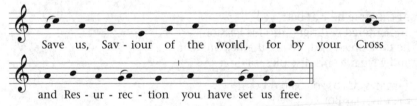

Save us, Sav - iour of the world, for by your Cross and Res - ur - rec - tion you have set us free.

Memorial Acclamation D   *for Ireland only*

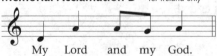

My Lord and my God.

Priest: Therefore, as we celebrate
            the memorial of his Death and Resurrection,
            we offer you, Lord,
            the Bread of life and the Chalice of salvation,
            giving thanks that you have held us worthy
            to be in your presence and minister to you.

Humbly we pray
that, partaking of the Body and Blood of Christ,
we may be gathered into one by the Holy Spirit.

Remember, Lord, your Church,
spread throughout the world,
and bring her to the fullness of charity,
together with N. our Pope and N. our Bishop *
and all the clergy.

In Masses for the Dead, the following may be added:

Remember your servant N.,
whom you have called (today)
from this world to yourself.
Grant that he (she) who was united with your Son in a death like his,
may also be one with him in his Resurrection.

Remember also our brothers and sisters
who have fallen asleep in the hope of the resurrection,
and all who have died in your mercy:
welcome them into the light of your face.
Have mercy on us all, we pray,
that with the Blessed Virgin Mary, Mother of God,
with the blessed Apostles,
and all the Saints who have pleased you throughout the ages,
we may merit to be coheirs to eternal life,
and may praise and glorify you
through your Son, Jesus Christ.

Doxology and Great Amen

At the end of the Eucharistic Prayer, the Priest takes the chalice and paten with the host and, raising both, he alone sings (or says) the Doxology. The people acclaim 'Amen'.

Priest: Through him, and with him, and in him,
           O God, almighty Father,
           in the unity of the Holy Spirit,
           all glory and honour is yours,
           for ever and ever.

People: **Amen.**

Priest: People:

...for   ev - er   and   ev - er.   A - men.

▷ page 56

* Mention may be made here of the Coadjutor Bishop, or Auxiliary Bishops

EUCHARISTIC PRAYER III

On certain occasions, special forms of parts of the Eucharistic Prayer may be used.

Priest: You are indeed Holy, O Lord,
and all you have created
rightly gives you praise,
for through your Son our Lord Jesus Christ,
by the power and working of the Holy Spirit,
you give life to all things and make them holy,
and you never cease to gather a people to yourself,
so that from the rising of the sun to its setting
a pure sacrifice may be offered to your name.

Therefore, O Lord, we humbly implore you:
by the same Spirit graciously make holy
these gifts we have brought to you for consecration,
that they may become the Body and ✠ Blood
of your Son our Lord Jesus Christ,
at whose command we celebrate these mysteries.

For on the night he was betrayed
he himself took bread,
and, giving you thanks, he said the blessing,
broke the bread and gave it to his disciples, saying:

TAKE THIS, ALL OF YOU, AND EAT OF IT,
FOR THIS IS MY BODY,
WHICH WILL BE GIVEN UP FOR YOU.

In a similar way, when supper was ended,
he took the chalice,
and, giving you thanks, he said the blessing,
and gave the chalice to his disciples, saying:

TAKE THIS, ALL OF YOU, AND DRINK FROM IT,
FOR THIS IS THE CHALICE OF MY BLOOD,
THE BLOOD OF THE NEW AND ETERNAL COVENANT,
WHICH WILL BE POURED OUT FOR YOU AND FOR MANY
FOR THE FORGIVENESS OF SINS.

DO THIS IN MEMORY OF ME.

Memorial Acclamation

The Priest sings:

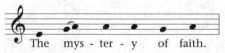

The   mys - ter - y   of   faith.

And the people continue with one of the following acclamations:

Memorial Acclamation A

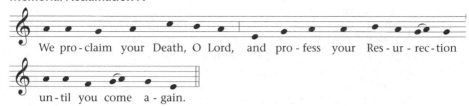

We pro-claim your Death, O Lord, and pro-fess your Res-ur-rec-tion un-til you come a-gain.

Memorial Acclamation B

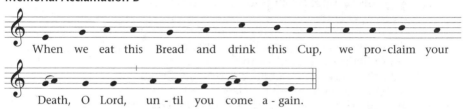

When we eat this Bread and drink this Cup, we pro-claim your Death, O Lord, un-til you come a-gain.

Memorial Acclamation C

Save us, Sav-iour of the world, for by your Cross and Res-ur-rec-tion you have set us free.

Memorial Acclamation D   *for Ireland only*

My Lord and my God.

Priest: Therefore, O Lord, as we celebrate the memorial
of the saving Passion of your Son,
his wondrous Resurrection
and Ascension into heaven,
and as we look forward to his second coming,
we offer you in thanksgiving
this holy and living sacrifice.

Look, we pray, upon the oblation of your Church
and, recognizing the sacrificial Victim by whose death
you willed to reconcile us to yourself,
grant that we, who are nourished
by the Body and Blood of your Son
and filled with his Holy Spirit,
may become one body, one spirit in Christ.

May he make of us
an eternal offering to you,
so that we may obtain an inheritance with your elect,
especially with the most Blessed Virgin Mary, Mother of God,
with your blessed Apostles and glorious Martyrs
(with Saint N.: *the Saint of the day or Patron Saint*)
and with all the Saints,
on whose constant intercession in your presence
we rely for unfailing help.

May this Sacrifice of our reconciliation,
we pray, O Lord,
advance the peace and salvation of all the world.
Be pleased to confirm in faith and charity
your pilgrim Church on earth,
with your servant N. our Pope and N. our Bishop,*
the Order of Bishops, all the clergy,
and the entire people you have gained for your own.

Listen graciously to the prayers of this family,
whom you have summoned before you:
in your compassion, O merciful Father,
gather to yourself all your children
scattered throughout the world.

† To our departed brothers and sisters
and to all who were pleasing to you
at their passing from this life,
give kind admittance to your kingdom.
There we hope to enjoy for ever the fullness of your glory
through Christ our Lord,
through whom you bestow on the world all that is good. †

In Masses for the Dead, the following may be said:
† Remember your servant N.
whom you have called (today)
from this world to yourself.
Grant that he (she) who was united with your Son in a death like his,
may also be one with him in his Resurrection,
when from the earth
he will raise up in the flesh those who have died,
and transform our lowly body
after the pattern of his own glorious body.
To our departed brothers and sisters, too,
and to all who were pleasing to you
at their passing from this life,
give kind admittance to your kingdom.

---

* Mention may be made here of the Coadjutor Bishop, or Auxiliary Bishops

There we hope to enjoy for ever the fullness of your glory,
when you will wipe away every tear from our eyes.
For seeing you, our God, as you are,
we shall be like you for all the ages
and praise you without end,
through Christ our Lord,
through whom you bestow on the world all that is good. †

Doxology and Great Amen

At the end of the Eucharistic Prayer, the Priest takes the chalice and paten with the host and, raising both, he alone sings (or says) the Doxology. The people acclaim 'Amen'.

Priest: Through him, and with him, and in him,
O God, almighty Father,
in the unity of the Holy Spirit,
all glory and honour is yours,
for ever and ever.

People: **Amen.**

Priest: People:

...for ev - er and ev - er.   A - men.

▷ *page 56*

EUCHARISTIC PRAYER IV

This Eucharistic Prayer has its own Preface which may not be replaced by another, because of the structure of the Prayer itself, which presents a summary of the history of salvation.
On certain occasions, special forms of parts of the Eucharistic Prayer may be used.

Preface Dialogue

Priest: All:

The Lord be with you.   And with your spir - it.

Priest: All:

Lift up your hearts.   We lift them up to the Lord.

Priest: All:

Let us give thanks to the Lord our God.   It is right and just.

Preface

Priest: It is truly right to give you thanks,
truly just to give you glory, Father most holy,
for you are the one God living and true,
existing before all ages and abiding for all eternity,
dwelling in unapproachable light;
yet you, who alone are good, the source of life,
have made all that is,
so that you might fill your creatures with blessings
and bring joy to many of them by the glory of your light.

And so, in your presence are countless hosts of Angels,
who serve you day and night
and, gazing upon the glory of your face,
glorify you without ceasing.

With them we, too, confess your name in exultation,
giving voice to every creature under heaven,
as we acclaim:

Sanctus

All:

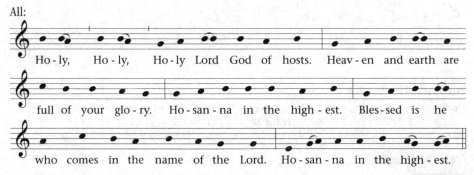

Ho-ly, Ho-ly, Ho-ly Lord God of hosts. Heav-en and earth are full of your glo-ry. Ho-san-na in the high-est. Bles-sed is he who comes in the name of the Lord. Ho-san-na in the high-est.

ALL KNEEL

Priest: We give you praise, Father most holy,
for you are great
and you have fashioned all your works
in wisdom and in love.
You formed man in your own image
and entrusted the whole world to his care,
so that in serving you alone, the Creator,
he might have dominion over all creatures.
And when through disobedience he had lost your friendship,
you did not abandon him to the domain of death.
For you came in mercy to the aid of all,
so that those who seek might find you.

Time and again you offered them covenants
and through the prophets
taught them to look forward to salvation.

And you so loved the world, Father most holy,
that in the fullness of time
you sent your Only Begotten Son to be our Saviour.
Made incarnate by the Holy Spirit
and born of the Virgin Mary,
he shared our human nature
in all things but sin.
To the poor he proclaimed the good news of salvation,
to prisoners, freedom,
and to the sorrowful of heart, joy.
To accomplish your plan,
he gave himself up to death,
and, rising from the dead,
he destroyed death and restored life.

And that we might live no longer for ourselves
but for him who died and rose again for us,
he sent the Holy Spirit from you, Father,
as the first fruits for those who believe,
so that, bringing to perfection his work in the world,
he might sanctify creation to the full.

Therefore, O Lord, we pray:
may this same Holy Spirit
graciously sanctify these offerings,
that they may become
the Body and ✠ Blood of our Lord Jesus Christ
for the celebration of this great mystery,
which he himself left us
as an eternal covenant.

For when the hour had come
for him to be glorified by you, Father most holy,
having loved his own who were in the world,
he loved them to the end:
and while they were at supper,
he took bread, blessed and broke it,
and gave it to his disciples, saying:

TAKE THIS, ALL OF YOU, AND EAT OF IT,
FOR THIS IS MY BODY,
WHICH WILL BE GIVEN UP FOR YOU.

In a similar way,
taking the chalice filled with the fruit of the vine,
he gave thanks,
and gave the chalice to his disciples, saying:

TAKE THIS, ALL OF YOU, AND DRINK FROM IT,
FOR THIS IS THE CHALICE OF MY BLOOD,
THE BLOOD OF THE NEW AND ETERNAL COVENANT,
WHICH WILL BE POURED OUT FOR YOU AND FOR MANY
FOR THE FORGIVENESS OF SINS.

DO THIS IN MEMORY OF ME.

Memorial Acclamation

The Priest sings:

The mys - ter - y of faith.

And the people continue with one of the following acclamations:

Memorial Acclamation A

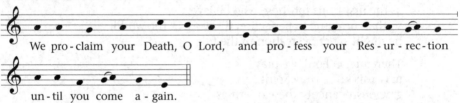

We pro - claim your Death, O Lord, and pro - fess your Res - ur - rec - tion

un - til you come a - gain.

Memorial Acclamation B

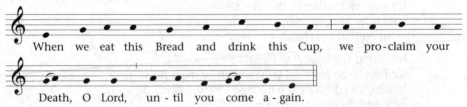

When we eat this Bread and drink this Cup, we pro - claim your

Death, O Lord, un - til you come a - gain.

Memorial Acclamation C

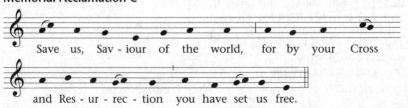

Save us, Sav - iour of the world, for by your Cross

and Res - ur - rec - tion you have set us free.

Memorial Acclamation D   *for Ireland only*

My   Lord   and   my   God.

ORDER

Priest: Therefore, O Lord,
as we now celebrate the memorial of our redemption,
we remember Christ's Death
and his descent to the realm of the dead,
we proclaim his Resurrection
and his Ascension to your right hand,
and as we await his coming in glory,
we offer you his Body and Blood,
the sacrifice acceptable to you
which brings salvation to the whole world.

Look, O Lord, upon the Sacrifice
which you yourself have provided for your Church,
and grant in your loving kindness
to all who partake of this one Bread and one Chalice
that, gathered into one body by the Holy Spirit,
they may truly become a living sacrifice in Christ
to the praise of your glory.

Therefore, Lord, remember now
all for whom we offer this sacrifice:
especially your servant N. our Pope,
N. our Bishop,* and the whole Order of Bishops,
all the clergy,
those who take part in this offering,
those gathered here before you,
your entire people,
and all who seek you with a sincere heart.

Remember also
those who have died in the peace of your Christ
and all the dead,
whose faith you alone have known.

To all of us, your children,
grant, O merciful Father,
that we may enter into a heavenly inheritance
with the Blessed Virgin Mary, Mother of God,
and with your Apostles and Saints in your kingdom.
There, with the whole of creation,
freed from the corruption of sin and death,
may we glorify you through Christ our Lord,
through whom you bestow on the world all that is good.

---

* Mention may be made here of the Coadjutor Bishop, or Auxiliary Bishops

Doxology and Great Amen

At the end of the Eucharistic Prayer, the Priest takes the chalice and paten with the host and, raising both, he alone sings (or says) the Doxology. The people acclaim 'Amen'.

Priest:	Through him, and with him, and in him,
	O God, almighty Father,
	in the unity of the Holy Spirit,
	all glory and honour is yours,
	for ever and ever.
People:	**Amen.**

Priest: People:

...for ev - er and ev - er.   A-men.

▷ *page 56*

EUCHARISTIC PRAYER FOR RECONCILIATION I

The Eucharistic Prayers for Reconciliation may be used in Masses in which the mystery of reconciliation is conveyed to the faithful in a special way, including Masses during Lent.

Although these Eucharistic Prayers have been provided with a proper Preface, they may also be used with other Prefaces that refer to penance and conversion, as, for example, the Prefaces of Lent.

| Priest: | The Lord be with you. |
| People: | **And with your spirit.** |

▷ *Music p 15*

| Priest: | Lift up your hearts. |
| People: | **We lift them up to the Lord.** |

| Priest: | Let us give thanks to the Lord our God. |
| People: | **It is right and just.** |

Priest:	It is truly right and just
	that we should always give you thanks,
	Lord, holy Father, almighty and eternal God.

For you do not cease to spur us on
to possess a more abundant life
and, being rich in mercy,
you constantly offer pardon
and call on sinners
to trust in your forgiveness alone.

Never did you turn away from us,
and, though time and again we have broken your covenant,
you have bound the human family to yourself
through Jesus your Son, our Redeemer,
with a new bond of love so tight
that it can never be undone.

ORDER

Even now you set before your people
a time of grace and reconciliation,
and, as they turn back to you in spirit,
you grant them hope in Christ Jesus
and a desire to be of service to all,
while they entrust themselves
more fully to the Holy Spirit.

And so, filled with wonder,
we extol the power of your love,
and, proclaiming our joy
at the salvation that comes from you,
we join in the heavenly hymn of countless hosts,
as without end we acclaim:

All: **Holy, Holy, Holy Lord God of hosts.**   ▷ Music p 16
          Heaven and earth are full of your glory.
          Hosanna in the highest.
          Blessed is he who comes in the name of the Lord.
          Hosanna in the highest.

Priest: You are indeed Holy, O Lord,   **ALL KNEEL**
          and from the world's beginning
          are ceaselessly at work,
          so that the human race may become holy,
          just as you yourself are holy.

          Look, we pray, upon your people's offerings
          and pour out on them the power of your Spirit,
          that they may become the Body and ✠ Blood
          of your beloved Son, Jesus Christ,
          in whom we, too, are your sons and daughters.

          Indeed, though we once were lost
          and could not approach you,
          you loved us with the greatest love:
          for your Son, who alone is just,
          handed himself over to death,
          and did not disdain to be nailed for our sake
          to the wood of the Cross.

          But before his arms were outstretched between heaven and earth,
          to become the lasting sign of your covenant,
          he desired to celebrate the Passover with his disciples.

          As he ate with them,
          he took bread
          and, giving you thanks, he said the blessing,
          broke the bread and gave it to them, saying:

Take this, all of you, and eat of it,
for this is my Body,
which will be given up for you.

In a similar way, when supper was ended,
knowing that he was about to reconcile all things in himself
through his Blood to be shed on the Cross,
he took the chalice, filled with the fruit of the vine,
and once more giving you thanks,
handed the chalice to his disciples, saying:

Take this, all of you, and drink from it,
for this is the chalice of my Blood,
the Blood of the new and eternal covenant,
which will be poured out for you and for many
for the forgiveness of sins.

Do this in memory of me.

Priest:	The mystery of faith.	▷ Music p 17
People:	**We proclaim your Death, O Lord,** **and profess your Resurrection** **until you come again.**	

or

People: **When we eat this Bread and drink this Cup,**
we proclaim your Death, O Lord,
until you come again.

or

People: **Save us, Saviour of the world,**
for by your Cross and Resurrection
you have set us free.

or for Ireland only:

People: **My Lord and my God.**

Priest: Therefore, as we celebrate
the memorial of your Son Jesus Christ,
who is our Passover and our surest peace,
we celebrate his Death and Resurrection from the dead,
and looking forward to his blessed Coming,
we offer you, who are our faithful and merciful God,
this sacrificial Victim
who reconciles to you the human race.

Look kindly, most compassionate Father,
on those you unite to yourself
by the Sacrifice of your Son,
and grant that, by the power of the Holy Spirit,
as they partake of this one Bread and one Chalice,

ORDER

they may be gathered into one Body in Christ,
who heals every division.

Be pleased to keep us always
in communion of mind and heart,
together with N. our Pope and N. our Bishop.*
Help us to work together
for the coming of your Kingdom,
until the hour when we stand before you,
Saints among the Saints in the halls of heaven,
with the Blessed Virgin Mary, Mother of God,
the blessed Apostles and all the Saints,
and with our deceased brothers and sisters,
whom we humbly commend to your mercy.

Then, freed at last from the wound of corruption
and made fully into a new creation,
we shall sing to you with gladness
the thanksgiving of Christ,
who lives for all eternity.

Priest: Through him, and with him, and in him,   ▷ Music p 18
            O God, almighty Father,
            in the unity of the Holy Spirit,
            all glory and honour is yours,
            for ever and ever.

People: **Amen.**

▷ page 56

EUCHARISTIC PRAYER FOR RECONCILIATION II

The Eucharistic Prayers for Reconciliation may be used in Masses in which the mystery of reconciliation is conveyed to the faithful In u special way, including Masses during Lent.

Although these Eucharistic Prayers have been provided with a proper Preface, they may also be used with other Prefaces that refer to penance and conversion, as, for example, the Prefaces of Lent.

Preface

Priest: The Lord be with you.   ▷ Music p 15
People: **And with your spirit.**

Priest: Lift up your hearts.
People: **We lift them up to the Lord.**

Priest: Let us give thanks to the Lord our God.
People: **It is right and just.**

Priest: It is truly right and just
            that we should give you thanks and praise,
            O God, almighty Father,

---

* Mention may be made here of the Coadjutor Bishop, or Auxiliary Bishops

for all you do in this world,
through our Lord Jesus Christ.

For though the human race
is divided by dissension and discord,
yet we know that by testing us
you change our hearts
to prepare them for reconciliation.

Even more, by your Spirit you move human hearts
that enemies may speak to each other again,
adversaries may join hands,
and peoples seek to meet together.

By the working of your power
it comes about, O Lord,
that hatred is overcome by love,
revenge gives way to forgiveness,
and discord is changed to mutual respect.

Therefore, as we give you ceaseless thanks
with the choirs of heaven,
we cry out to your majesty on earth,
and without end we acclaim:

All: **Holy, Holy, Holy Lord God of hosts.**   ▷ Music p 16
          Heaven and earth are full of your glory.
          Hosanna in the highest.
          Blessed is he who comes in the name of the Lord.
          Hosanna in the highest.

ALL KNEEL

Priest: You, therefore, almighty Father,
          we bless through Jesus Christ your Son,
          who comes in your name.
          He himself is the Word that brings salvation,
          the hand you extend to sinners,
          the way by which your peace is offered to us.
          When we ourselves had turned away from you
          on account of our sins,
          you brought us back to be reconciled, O Lord,
          so that, converted at last to you,
          we might love one another
          through your Son,
          whom for our sake you handed over to death.

          And now, celebrating the reconciliation
          Christ has brought us,
          we entreat you:
          sanctify these gifts by the outpouring of your Spirit,

that they may become the Body and ✠ Blood of your Son,
whose command we fulfil
when we celebrate these mysteries.

For when about to give his life to set us free,
as he reclined at supper,
he himself took bread into his hands,
and, giving you thanks, he said the blessing,
broke the bread and gave it to his disciples, saying:

TAKE THIS, ALL OF YOU, AND EAT OF IT,
FOR THIS IS MY BODY,
WHICH WILL BE GIVEN UP FOR YOU.

In a similar way, on that same evening,
he took the chalice of blessing in his hands,
confessing your mercy,
and gave the chalice to his disciples, saying:

TAKE THIS, ALL OF YOU, AND DRINK FROM IT,
FOR THIS IS THE CHALICE OF MY BLOOD,
THE BLOOD OF THE NEW AND ETERNAL COVENANT,
WHICH WILL BE POURED OUT FOR YOU AND FOR MANY
FOR THE FORGIVENESS OF SINS.

DO THIS IN MEMORY OF ME.

Priest: The mystery of faith.   ▷ Music p 17
People: **We proclaim your Death, O Lord,**
            and profess your Resurrection
            until you come again.

or

People: **When we eat this Bread and drink this Cup,**
            we proclaim your Death, O Lord,
            until you come again.

or

People: **Save us, Saviour of the world,**
            for by your Cross and Resurrection
            you have set us free.

or   for Ireland only:

People: **My Lord and my God.**

Priest: Celebrating, therefore, the memorial
            of the Death and Resurrection of your Son,
            who left us this pledge of his love,
            we offer you what you have bestowed on us,
            the Sacrifice of perfect reconciliation.

Holy Father, we humbly beseech you
to accept us also, together with your Son,
and in this saving banquet
graciously to endow us with his very Spirit,
who takes away everything
that estranges us from one another.

May he make your Church a sign of unity
and an instrument of your peace among all people
and may he keep us in communion
with N. our Pope and N. our Bishop *
and all the Bishops
and your entire people.

Just as you have gathered us now at the table of your Son,
so also bring us together,
with the glorious Virgin Mary, Mother of God,
with your blessed Apostles and all the Saints,
with our brothers and sisters
and those of every race and tongue
who have died in your friendship.
Bring us to share with them the unending banquet of unity
in a new heaven and a new earth,
where the fullness of your peace will shine forth
in Christ Jesus our Lord.

Priest: Through him, and with him, and in him,   ▷ *Music p 18*
O God, almighty Father,
in the unity of the Holy Spirit,
all glory and honour is yours,
for ever and ever.

People: **Amen.**

▷ *page 56*

* Mention may be made here of the Coadjutor Bishop, or Auxiliary Bishops

ORDER

EUCHARISTIC PRAYERS FOR USE IN MASSES FOR VARIOUS NEEDS

These Eucharistic Prayers have their own Prefaces which may not be replaced by another, because of the structure of the Prayers themselves.

I THE CHURCH ON THE PATH OF UNITY

Priest: The Lord be with you.   ▷ *Music p 15*
People: **And with your spirit.**

Priest: Lift up your hearts.
People: **We lift them up to the Lord.**

Priest: Let us give thanks to the Lord our God.
People: **It is right and just.**

Priest: It is truly right and just to give you thanks
and raise to you a hymn of glory and praise,
O Lord, Father of infinite goodness.

For by the word of your Son's Gospel
you have brought together one Church
from every people, tongue, and nation,
and, having filled her with life by the power of your Spirit,
you never cease through her
to gather the whole human race into one.

Manifesting the covenant of your love,
she dispenses without ceasing
the blessed hope of your Kingdom
and shines bright as the sign of your faithfulness,
which in Christ Jesus our Lord
you promised would last for eternity.

And so, with all the Powers of heaven,
we worship you constantly on earth,
while, with all the Church,
as one voice we acclaim:

All: **Holy, Holy, Holy Lord God of hosts.**   ▷ *Music p 16*
Heaven and earth are full of your glory.
Hosanna in the highest.
Blessed is he who comes in the name of the Lord.
Hosanna in the highest.

You are indeed Holy and to be glorified, O God,
who love the human race
and who always walk with us on the journey of life.
Blessed indeed is your Son,
present in our midst
when we are gathered by his love,
and when, as once for the disciples, so now for us,
he opens the Scriptures and breaks the bread.

Therefore, Father most merciful,
we ask that you send forth your Holy Spirit
to sanctify these gifts of bread and wine,
that they may become for us
the Body and ✠ Blood
of our Lord Jesus Christ.

On the day before he was to suffer,
on the night of the Last Supper,
he took bread and said the blessing,
broke the bread and gave it to his disciples, saying:

TAKE THIS, ALL OF YOU, AND EAT OF IT,
FOR THIS IS MY BODY,
WHICH WILL BE GIVEN UP FOR YOU.

In a similar way, when supper was ended,
he took the chalice, gave you thanks
and gave the chalice to his disciples, saying:

TAKE THIS, ALL OF YOU, AND DRINK FROM IT,
FOR THIS IS THE CHALICE OF MY BLOOD,
THE BLOOD OF THE NEW AND ETERNAL COVENANT,
WHICH WILL BE POURED OUT FOR YOU AND FOR MANY
FOR THE FORGIVENESS OF SINS.

DO THIS IN MEMORY OF ME.

Priest:	The mystery of faith.	▷ *Music p 17*
People:	**We proclaim your Death, O Lord,**	
	and profess your Resurrection	
	until you come again.	

or

People:	**When we eat this Bread and drink this Cup,**
	we proclaim your Death, O Lord,
	until you come again.

or

People:	**Save us, Saviour of the world,**
	for by your Cross and Resurrection
	you have set us free.

or   *for Ireland only:*

People: **My Lord and my God.**

Therefore, holy Father,
as we celebrate the memorial of Christ your Son, our Saviour,
whom you led through his Passion and Death on the Cross
to the glory of the Resurrection,
and whom you have seated at your right hand,
we proclaim the work of your love until he comes again
and we offer you the Bread of life
and the Chalice of blessing.

Look with favour on the oblation of your Church,
in which we show forth
the paschal Sacrifice of Christ that has been handed on to us,
and grant that, by the power of the Spirit of your love,
we may be counted now and until the day of eternity
among the members of your Son,
in whose Body and Blood we have communion.

Lord, renew your Church (which is in N.)
by the light of the Gospel.
Strengthen the bond of unity
between the faithful and the pastors of your people,
together with N. our Pope, N. our Bishop,*
and the whole Order of Bishops,
that in a world torn by strife
your people may shine forth
as a prophetic sign of unity and concord.

Remember our brothers and sisters (N. and N.),
who have fallen asleep in the peace of your Christ,
and all the dead, whose faith you alone have known.
Admit them to rejoice in the light of your face,
and in the resurrection give them the fullness of life.

Grant also to us,
when our earthly pilgrimage is done,
that we may come to an eternal dwelling place
and live with you for ever;
there, in communion with the Blessed Virgin Mary, Mother of God,
with the Apostles and Martyrs,
(with Saint N.: *the Saint of the day or Patron*)
and with all the Saints,
we shall praise and exalt you
through Jesus Christ, your Son.

---

* Mention may be made here of the Coadjutor Bishop, or Auxiliary Bishops

Priest: Through him, and with him, and in him,   ▷ Music p 18
O God, almighty Father,
in the unity of the Holy Spirit,
all glory and honour is yours,
for ever and ever.

People: **Amen.**

▷ page 56

II GOD GUIDES HIS CHURCH ALONG THE WAY OF SALVATION

Priest: The Lord be with you.   ▷ Music p 15
People: **And with your spirit.**

Priest: Lift up your hearts.
People: **We lift them up to the Lord.**

Priest: Let us give thanks to the Lord our God.
People: **It is right and just.**

It is truly right and just, our duty and our salvation,
always and everywhere to give you thanks,
Lord, holy Father,
creator of the world and source of all life.

For you never forsake the works of your wisdom,
but by your providence are even now at work in our midst.
With mighty hand and outstretched arm
you led your people Israel through the desert.
Now, as your Church makes her pilgrim journey in the world,
you always accompany her
by the power of the Holy Spirit
and lead her along the paths of time
to the eternal joy of your Kingdom,
through Christ our Lord.

And so, with the Angels and Saints,
we, too, sing the hymn of your glory,
as without end we acclaim:

All: **Holy, Holy, Holy Lord God of hosts.**   ▷ Music p 16
Heaven and earth are full of your glory.
Hosanna in the highest.
Blessed is he who comes in the name of the Lord.
Hosanna in the highest.

Priest: You are indeed Holy and to be glorified, O God,
who love the human race
and who always walk with us on the journey of life.

Blessed indeed is your Son,
present in our midst
when we are gathered by his love
and when, as once for the disciples, so now for us,
he opens the Scriptures and breaks the bread.

Therefore, Father most merciful,
we ask that you send forth your Holy Spirit
to sanctify these gifts of bread and wine,
that they may become for us
the Body and ✠ Blood
of our Lord Jesus Christ.

On the day before he was to suffer,
on the night of the Last Supper,
he took bread and said the blessing,
broke the bread and gave it to his disciples, saying:

TAKE THIS, ALL OF YOU, AND EAT OF IT,
FOR THIS IS MY BODY,
WHICH WILL BE GIVEN UP FOR YOU.

In a similar way, when supper was ended,
he took the chalice, gave you thanks
and gave the chalice to his disciples, saying:

TAKE THIS, ALL OF YOU, AND DRINK FROM IT,
FOR THIS IS THE CHALICE OF MY BLOOD,
THE BLOOD OF THE NEW AND ETERNAL COVENANT,
WHICH WILL BE POURED OUT FOR YOU AND FOR MANY
FOR THE FORGIVENESS OF SINS.

DO THIS IN MEMORY OF ME.

Priest: The mystery of faith.

▷ *Music p 17*

People: **We proclaim your Death, O Lord,
and profess your Resurrection
until you come again.**

or

People: **When we eat this Bread and drink this Cup,
we proclaim your Death, O Lord,
until you come again.**

or

People: **Save us, Saviour of the world,
for by your Cross and Resurrection
you have set us free.**

or   *for Ireland only:*

People: **My Lord and my God.**

Priest: Therefore, holy Father,
as we celebrate the memorial of Christ your Son, our Saviour,
whom you led through his Passion and Death on the Cross
to the glory of the Resurrection,
and whom you have seated at your right hand,
we proclaim the work of your love until he comes again
and we offer you the Bread of life
and the Chalice of blessing.

Look with favour on the oblation of your Church,
in which we show forth
the paschal Sacrifice of Christ that has been handed on to us,
and grant that, by the power of the Spirit of your love,
we may be counted now and until the day of eternity
among the members of your Son,
in whose Body and Blood we have communion.

And so, having called us to your table, Lord,
confirm us in unity,
so that, together with N. our Pope and N. our Bishop,*
with all Bishops, Priests and Deacons,
and your entire people,
as we walk your ways with faith and hope,
we may strive to bring joy and trust into the world.

Remember our brothers and sisters (N. and N.),
who have fallen asleep in the peace of your Christ,
and all the dead, whose faith you alone have known.
Admit them to rejoice in the light of your face,
and in the resurrection give them the fullness of life.

Grant also to us,
when our earthly pilgrimage is done,
that we may come to an eternal dwelling place
and live with you for ever;
there, in communion with the Blessed Virgin Mary, Mother of God,
with the Apostles and Martyrs,
(with Saint N.: *the Saint of the day or Patron*)
and with all the Saints,
we shall praise and exalt you
through Jesus Christ, your Son.

---

* Mention may be made here of the Coadjutor Bishop, or Auxiliary Bishops

Priest: Through him, and with him, and in him,   ▷ Music p 18
O God, almighty Father,
in the unity of the Holy Spirit,
all glory and honour is yours,
for ever and ever.

People: **Amen.**   ▷ page 56

III JESUS, THE WAY TO THE FATHER

Priest: The Lord be with you.   ▷ Music p 15
People: **And with your spirit.**

Priest: Lift up your hearts.
People: **We lift them up to the Lord.**

Priest: Let us give thanks to the Lord our God.
People: **It is right and just.**

Priest: It is truly right and just, our duty and our salvation,
always and everywhere to give you thanks,
holy Father, Lord of heaven and earth,
through Christ our Lord.

For by your Word you created the world
and you govern all things in harmony.
You gave us the same Word made flesh as Mediator,
and he has spoken your words to us
and called us to follow him.
He is the way that leads us to you,
the truth that sets us free,
the life that fills us with gladness.

Through your Son
you gather men and women,
whom you made for the glory of your name,
into one family,
redeemed by the Blood of his Cross
and signed with the seal of the Spirit.

Therefore, now and for ages unending,
with all the Angels,
we proclaim your glory,
as in joyful celebration we acclaim:

All: **Holy, Holy, Holy Lord God of hosts.**   ▷ Music p 16
Heaven and earth are full of your glory.
Hosanna in the highest.
Blessed is he who comes in the name of the Lord.
Hosanna in the highest.

Priest: You are indeed Holy and to be glorified, O God,
who love the human race
and who always walk with us on the journey of life.
Blessed indeed is your Son,
present in our midst
when we are gathered by his love
and when, as once for the disciples, so now for us,
he opens the Scriptures and breaks the bread.

Therefore, Father most merciful,
we ask that you send forth your Holy Spirit
to sanctify these gifts of bread and wine,
that they may become for us
the Body and ✠ Blood
of our Lord Jesus Christ.

On the day before he was to suffer,
on the night of the Last Supper,
he took bread and said the blessing,
broke the bread and gave it to his disciples, saying:

TAKE THIS, ALL OF YOU, AND EAT OF IT,
FOR THIS IS MY BODY,
WHICH WILL BE GIVEN UP FOR YOU.

In a similar way, when supper was ended,
he took the chalice, gave you thanks
and gave the chalice to his disciples, saying:

TAKE THIS, ALL OF YOU, AND DRINK FROM IT,
FOR THIS IS THE CHALICE OF MY BLOOD,
THE BLOOD OF THE NEW AND ETERNAL COVENANT,
WHICH WILL BE POURED OUT FOR YOU AND FOR MANY
FOR THE FORGIVENESS OF SINS.

DO THIS IN MEMORY OF ME.

Priest: The mystery of faith.   ▷ *Music p 17*
People: **We proclaim your Death, O Lord,**
           and profess your Resurrection
           until you come again.

or

People: **When we eat this Bread and drink this Cup,**
           we proclaim your Death, O Lord,
           until you come again.

or

People: **Save us, Saviour of the world,**
           for by your Cross and Resurrection
           you have set us free.

or   *for Ireland only:·*

People: **My Lord and my God.**

Priest: Therefore, holy Father,
as we celebrate the memorial of Christ your Son, our Saviour,
whom you led through his Passion and Death on the Cross
to the glory of the Resurrection,
and whom you have seated at your right hand,
we proclaim the work of your love until he comes again
and we offer you the Bread of life
and the Chalice of blessing.

Look with favour on the oblation of your Church,
in which we show forth
the paschal Sacrifice of Christ that has been handed on to us,
and grant that, by the power of the Spirit of your love,
we may be counted now and until the day of eternity
among the members of your Son,
in whose Body and Blood we have communion.

By our partaking of this mystery, almighty Father,
give us life through your Spirit,
grant that we may be conformed to the image of your Son,
and confirm us in the bond of communion,
together with N. our Pope and N. our Bishop,*
with all other Bishops,
with Priests and Deacons,
and with your entire people.

Grant that all the faithful of the Church,
looking into the signs of the times by the light of faith,
may constantly devote themselves
to the service of the Gospel.
Keep us attentive to the needs of all
that, sharing their grief and pain,
their joy and hope,
we may faithfully bring them the good news of salvation
and go forward with them
along the way of your Kingdom.

Remember our brothers and sisters (N. and N.),
who have fallen asleep in the peace of your Christ,
and all the dead, whose faith you alone have known.
Admit them to rejoice in the light of your face,
and in the resurrection give them the fullness of life.

---

* Mention may be made here of the Coadjutor Bishop, or Auxiliary Bishops

Grant also to us,
when our earthly pilgrimage is done,
that we may come to an eternal dwelling place
and live with you for ever;
there, in communion with the Blessed Virgin Mary, Mother of God,
with the Apostles and Martyrs,
(with Saint N.: *the Saint of the day or Patron*)
and with all the Saints,
we shall praise and exalt you
through Jesus Christ, your Son.

Priest: Through him, and with him, and in him,   ▷ *Music p 18*
O God, almighty Father,
in the unity of the Holy Spirit,
all glory and honour is yours,
for ever and ever.

People: **Amen.**   ▷ *page 56*

IV JESUS, WHO WENT ABOUT DOING GOOD

Priest: The Lord be with you.   ▷ *Music p 15*
People: **And with your spirit.**

Priest: Lift up your hearts.
People: **We lift them up to the Lord.**

Priest: Let us give thanks to the Lord our God.
People: **It is right and just.**

Priest: It is truly right and just, our duty and our salvation,
always and everywhere to give you thanks,
Father of mercies and faithful God.

For you have given us Jesus Christ, your Son,
as our Lord and Redeemer.

He always showed compassion
for children and for the poor,
for the sick and for sinners,
and he became a neighbour
to the oppressed and the afflicted.

By word and deed he announced to the world
that you are our Father
and that you care for all your sons and daughters.

And so, with all the Angels and Saints,
we exalt and bless your name
and sing the hymn of your glory,
as without end we acclaim:

All: **Holy, Holy, Holy Lord God of hosts.**   ▷ *Music p 16*
             Heaven and earth are full of your glory.
             Hosanna in the highest.
             Blessed is he who comes in the name of the Lord.
             Hosanna in the highest.

Priest: You are indeed Holy and to be glorified, O God,
who love the human race
and who always walk with us on the journey of life.
Blessed indeed is your Son,
present in our midst
when we are gathered by his love
and when, as once for the disciples, so now for us,
he opens the Scriptures and breaks the bread.

Therefore, Father most merciful,
we ask that you send forth your Holy Spirit
to sanctify these gifts of bread and wine,
that they may become for us
the Body and ✠ Blood
of our Lord Jesus Christ.

On the day before he was to suffer,
on the night of the Last Supper,
he took bread and said the blessing,
broke the bread and gave it to his disciples, saying:

TAKE THIS, ALL OF YOU, AND EAT OF IT,
FOR THIS IS MY BODY,
WHICH WILL BE GIVEN UP FOR YOU.

In a similar way, when supper was ended,
he took the chalice, gave you thanks
and gave the chalice to his disciples, saying:

TAKE THIS, ALL OF YOU, AND DRINK FROM IT,
FOR THIS IS THE CHALICE OF MY BLOOD,
THE BLOOD OF THE NEW AND ETERNAL COVENANT,
WHICH WILL BE POURED OUT FOR YOU AND FOR MANY
FOR THE FORGIVENESS OF SINS.

DO THIS IN MEMORY OF ME.

ORDER

Priest: The mystery of faith.   ▷ *Music p 17*
People: **We proclaim your Death, O Lord,**
          and profess your Resurrection
          until you come again.

or

People: **When we eat this Bread and drink this Cup,**
          we proclaim your Death, O Lord,
          until you come again.

or

People: **Save us, Saviour of the world,**
          for by your Cross and Resurrection
          you have set us free.

or   *for Ireland only:*

People: **My Lord and my God.**

Priest: Therefore, holy Father,
          as we celebrate the memorial of Christ your Son, our Saviour,
          whom you led through his Passion and Death on the Cross
          to the glory of the Resurrection,
          and whom you have seated at your right hand,
          we proclaim the work of your love until he comes again
          and we offer you the Bread of life
          and the Chalice of blessing.

          Look with favour on the oblation of your Church,
          in which we show forth
          the paschal Sacrifice of Christ that has been handed on to us,
          and grant that, by the power of the Spirit of your love,
          we may be counted now and until the day of eternity
          among the members of your Son,
          in whose Body and Blood we have communion.

          Bring your Church, O Lord,
          to perfect faith and charity,
          together with N. our Pope and N. our Bishop,*
          with all Bishops, Priests and Deacons,
          and the entire people you have made your own.

          Open our eyes
          to the needs of our brothers and sisters;
          inspire in us words and actions
          to comfort those who labour and are burdened.
          Make us serve them truly,
          after the example of Christ and at his command.

---

* Mention may be made here of the Coadjutor Bishop, or Auxiliary Bishops

And may your Church stand as a living witness
to truth and freedom,
to peace and justice,
that all people may be raised up to a new hope.

Remember our brothers and sisters (N. and N.),
who have fallen asleep in the peace of your Christ,
and all the dead, whose faith you alone have known.
Admit them to rejoice in the light of your face,
and in the resurrection give them the fullness of life.

Grant also to us,
when our earthly pilgrimage is done,
that we may come to an eternal dwelling place
and live with you for ever;
there, in communion with the Blessed Virgin Mary, Mother of God,
with the Apostles and Martyrs,
(with Saint N.: *the Saint of the day or Patron*)
and with all the Saints,
we shall praise and exalt you
through Jesus Christ, your Son.

Priest: Through him, and with him, and in him,   ▷ *Music p 18*
O God, almighty Father,
in the unity of the Holy Spirit,
all glory and honour is yours,
for ever and ever.
People: **Amen.**

▷ *page 56*

COMMUNION RITE

The eating and drinking together of the Lord's Body and Blood in a Paschal meal is the culmination of the Eucharist. The themes underlying these rites are the mutual love and reconciliation that are both the condition and the fruit of worthy communion and the unity of the many in the one.

Celebrating the Mass n 200

ALL STAND

LORD'S PRAYER

Priest: At the Saviour's command
and formed by divine teaching,
we dare to say:

All: **Our Father, who art in heaven,**
hallowed be thy name;
thy kingdom come,
thy will be done
on earth as it is in heaven.
Give us this day our daily bread,
and forgive us our trespasses,
as we forgive those who trespass against us;
and lead us not into temptation,
but deliver us from evil.

▷ *Music p 344*

Priest: Deliver us, Lord, we pray, from every evil,
graciously grant peace in our days,
that, by the help of your mercy,
we may be always free from sin
and safe from all distress,
as we await the blessed hope
and the coming of our Saviour, Jesus Christ.

All: **For the kingdom,**
the power and the glory are yours
now and for ever.

RITE OF PEACE

Priest: Lord Jesus Christ,
who said to your Apostles,
Peace I leave you, my peace I give you,
look not on our sins,
but on the faith of your Church,
and graciously grant her peace and unity
in accordance with your will.
Who live and reign for ever and ever.

All: **Amen.**

Priest: The peace of the Lord be with you always.

All: **And with your spirit.**

▷ *Music p 344*

ORDER

SIGN OF PEACE

The peace is always exchanged, though the invitation which introduces it is optional.

Deacon or Priest: Let us offer each other the sign of peace.

And all offer one another the customary sign of peace: a handclasp or handshake, which is an expression of peace, communion, and charity.

If commissioned ministers are to assist at Communion, it is desirable that they are in place on the sanctuary by the end of the exchange of peace. (Celebrating the Mass n 206)

BREAKING OF BREAD

The Priest takes the host, breaks it over the paten, and places a small piece into the chalice. Meanwhile the following is sung or said:

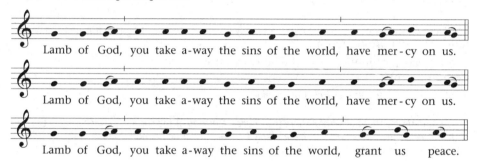

Lamb of God, you take a-way the sins of the world, have mer-cy on us.

Lamb of God, you take a-way the sins of the world, have mer-cy on us.

Lamb of God, you take a-way the sins of the world, grant us peace.

All: **Lamb of God, you take away the sins of the world,
    have mercy on us.**

   **Lamb of God, you take away the sins of the world,
    have mercy on us.**

   **Lamb of God, you take away the sins of the world,
    grant us peace.**

*The invocation may be repeated several times if the Breaking of Bread is prolonged.
The final time always ends 'grant us peace'.*

ALL KNEEL

INVITATION TO COMMUNION

After his private prayers of preparation the Priest genuflects, takes the host and, holding it slightly raised above the paten or above the chalice says aloud:

Priest: Behold the Lamb of God,   ▷ *Music p 345*
   behold him who takes away the sins of the world.
   Blessed are those called to the supper of the Lamb.
All: **Lord, I am not worthy
   that you should enter under my roof,
   but only say the word
   and my soul shall be healed.**

HOLY COMMUNION

Communion Song

The communion song begins while the Priest is receiving the Body of Christ and normally continues until all communicants have received communion.

Distribution of Communion

By tradition the Deacon ministers the chalice. Beyond this, no distinctions are made in the assignment of consecrated elements to particular ministers for distribution. (Celebrating the Mass n 211)

The communicants come forward in reverent procession. Before receiving Holy Communion standing they make a preparatory act of reverence by bowing their heads in honour of Christ's presence in the Sacrament.

The Priest, Deacon or commissioned minister of Holy Communion raises a host slightly and shows it to each of the communicants, saying:

Priest, Deacon or minister: The Body of Christ.
Communicant: **Amen.**

And the communicant receives Holy Communion.

It is most desirable that the faithful share the Chalice. Drinking at the Eucharist is a sharing in the sign of the new covenant, a foretaste of the heavenly banquet and a sign of participation in the suffering Christ. (cf Celebrating the Mass n 209)

When Communion is ministered from the chalice, the minister offers it to each of the communicants, saying:

Priest, Deacon or minister: The Blood of Christ.
Communicant: **Amen.**

And the communicant receives Holy Communion.

Period of Silence or Song of Praise

After the distribution of Communion, if appropriate, a sacred silence may be observed for a while, or a psalm or other canticle of praise or a hymn may be sung.

PRAYER AFTER COMMUNION   **ALL STAND**

Priest: Let us pray.   ▷ Proper

All pray in silence for a while, unless silence has just been observed.
Then the Priest says the Prayer after Communion, at the end of which the people acclaim:

All: **Amen.**

> *Go, make disciples of all the nations.*
> *I am with you always; yes, to the end of time.*
> *(Matthew 28:19, 20)*

The purpose of the Concluding Rite is to send the people forth to put into effect in their daily lives the Paschal Mystery and the unity in Christ which they have celebrated. They are given a sense of abiding mission, which calls them to witness to Christ in the world and to bring the Gospel to the poor.   *cf Celebrating the Mass n 217*

If they are necessary, any brief announcements to the people follow here.

BLESSING

Priest: The Lord be with you.   ▷ *Music p 346*
People: **And with your spirit.**

On certain occasions, the following blessing may be preceded by a solemn blessing or prayer over the people. Then the Priest blesses the people, singing or saying:

Priest: May almighty God bless you:
                 the Father, and the Son, ✠ and the Holy Spirit.
People: **Amen.**

In a Pontifical Mass, the celebrant receives the mitre and says:

Bishop: The Lord be with you.   ▷ *Music p 346*
All: **And with your spirit.**

Bishop: Blessed be the name of the Lord.
All: **Now and for ever.**

Bishop: Our help is in the name of the Lord.
All   **Who made heaven and earth.**

On certain occasions the following blessing may be preceded by a more solemn blessing or prayer over the people. Then the celebrant receives the pastoral staff, if he uses it, and says:

Bishop: May almighty God bless you:

making the Sign of the Cross over the people three times, he adds:

                 the Father, ✠ and the Son, ✠ and the Holy ✠ Spirit.
All: **Amen.**

If any liturgical action follows immediately, the rites of dismissal are omitted.

DISMISSAL

▷ *Music p 347*

Then the Deacon, or the Priest himself says the dismissal sentence.

Deacon or Priest: Go forth, the Mass is ended.
People: **Thanks be to God.**

or

Deacon or Priest: Go and announce the Gospel of the Lord.
People: **Thanks be to God.**

or

Deacon or Priest: Go in peace, glorifying the Lord by your life.
People: **Thanks be to God.**

or

Deacon or Priest: Go in peace.
People: **Thanks be to God.**

At the Easter Vigil, on Easter Sunday, during the octave of Easter and on Pentecost, the dismissal takes the following form:

Deacon or Priest: Go forth, the Mass is ended, alleluia, alleluia.
People: **Thanks be to God, alleluia, alleluia.**

or

Deacon or Priest: Go in peace, alleluia, alleluia.
People: **Thanks be to God, alleluia, alleluia.**

Then the Priest venerates the altar as at the beginning.
After making a profound bow with the ministers, he withdraws.

RITE FOR THE BLESSING AND SPRINKLING OF WATER

BLESSING OF WATER

After the greeting, the Priest, with a vessel containing the water to be blessed before him, calls upon the people to pray in these or similar words:

Priest: Dear brethren (brothers and sisters),
let us humbly beseech the Lord our God
to bless this water he has created,
which will be sprinkled on us
as a memorial of our Baptism.
May he help us by his grace
to remain faithful to the Spirit we have received.

And after a brief pause for silence, he continues:

Priest: Almighty ever-living God,
who willed that through water,
the fountain of life and the source of purification,
even souls should be cleansed
and receive the gift of eternal life;
be pleased, we pray, to ✠ bless this water,
by which we seek protection on this your day, O Lord.
Renew the living spring of your grace within us
and grant that by this water we may be defended
from all ills of spirit and body,
and so approach you with hearts made clean
and worthily receive your salvation.
Through Christ our Lord.

All: **Amen.**

or

Priest: Almighty Lord and God,
who are the source and origin of all life,
whether of body or soul,
we ask you to ✠ bless this water,
which we use in confidence
to implore forgiveness for our sins
and to obtain the protection of your grace
against all illness and every snare of the enemy.
Grant, O Lord, in your mercy,
that living waters may always spring up for our salvation,
and so may we approach you with a pure heart
and avoid all danger to body and soul.
Through Christ our Lord.

All: **Amen.**

or, during Easter Time

Priest: Lord our God,
in your mercy be present to your people's prayers,
and, for us who recall the wondrous work of our creation
and the still greater work of our redemption,
graciously ✠ bless this water.
For you created water to make the fields fruitful
and to refresh and cleanse our bodies.
You also made water the instrument of your mercy:
for through water you freed your people from slavery
and quenched their thirst in the desert;
through water the Prophets proclaimed the new covenant
you were to enter upon with the human race;
and last of all,
through water, which Christ made holy in the Jordan,
you have renewed our corrupted nature
in the bath of regeneration.
Therefore, may this water be for us
a memorial of the Baptism we have received,
and grant that we may share
in the gladness of our brothers and sisters
who at Easter have received their Baptism.
Through Christ our Lord.

All: **Amen.**

BLESSING OF SALT

Where the circumstances of the place or the custom of the people suggest that the mixing of salt be preserved in the blessing of water, the Priest may bless salt, saying:

Priest: We humbly ask you, almighty God:
be pleased in your faithful love to bless ✠ this salt
you have created,
for it was you who commanded the prophet Elisha
to cast salt into water,
that impure water might be purified.
Grant, O Lord, we pray,
that, wherever this mixture of salt and water is sprinkled,
every attack of the enemy may be repulsed
and your Holy Spirit may be present
to keep us safe at all times.
Through Christ our Lord.

All: **Amen.**

Then he pours the salt into the water.

SPRINKLING OF WATER

The Priest then sprinkles himself and the ministers, then the clergy and people, moving through the church, if appropriate.

Meanwhile, one of the following chants, or another appropriate song is sung.

Outside Easter Time

ANTIPHON 1   *Psalm 50:9*
Sprinkle me with hyssop, O Lord, and I shall be cleansed;
wash me and I shall be whiter than snow.

ANTIPHON 2   *Ezekiel 36:25–26*
I will pour clean water upon you,
and you will be made clean of all your impurities,
and I shall give you a new spirit, says the Lord.

HYMN   *cf 1 Peter 1:3–5*
Blessed be the God and Father of our Lord Jesus Christ,
who in his great mercy has given us new birth into a living hope
through the Resurrection of Jesus Christ from the dead,
into an inheritance that will not perish,
preserved for us in heaven
for the salvation to be revealed in the last time!

During Easter Time

ANTIPHON 1   *cf Ezekiel 47:1–2, 9*
I saw water flowing from the Temple,
from its right-hand side, alleluia:
and all to whom this water came
were saved and shall say: alleluia, alleluia.

ANTIPHON 2   *cf Wisdom 3:8; Ezekiel 36:25*
On the day of my resurrection, says the Lord, alleluia,
I will gather the nations and assemble the kingdoms
and I will pour clean water upon you, alleluia.

ANTIPHON 3   *cf Daniel 3:77, 79*
You springs and all that moves in the waters,
sing a hymn to God, alleluia.

ANTIPHON 4   *1 Peter 2:9*
O chosen race, royal priesthood, holy nation,
proclaim the mighty works of him
who called you out of darkness into his wonderful light, alleluia.

ANTIPHON 5
From your side, O Christ,
bursts forth a spring of water,
by which the squalor of the world is washed away
and life is made new again, alleluia.

PRAYER

When he returns to his chair and the singing is over, the Priest says:

Priest: May almighty God cleanse us of our sins,
          and through the celebration of this Eucharist
          make us worthy to share at the table of his Kingdom.

All: **Amen.**

The Mass continues with the Gloria.
If the Gloria is not indicated, the Mass continues with the Collect.

▷ *page 9*

PREFACES

All the Prefaces within the scope of this volume are printed here, except those specific to a given Eucharistic Prayer (e.g. the Preface of Eucharistic Prayer II).

The Prefaces are printed in the order that the celebrations occur in the propers of this volume:

Advent • Christmas Time • Ordinary Time • Lent • Triduum • Easter
then
Prefaces from the Proper of Saints and other celebrations

ADVENT

The following two Prefaces are said in Masses of Advent from the First Sunday of Advent to 16 December and in other Masses that are celebrated in Advent and have no proper Preface.

PREFACE I OF ADVENT

THE TWO COMINGS OF CHRIST

It is truly right and just,
    our duty and our salvation,
always and everywhere to give you thanks,
Lord, holy Father,
    almighty and eternal God,
through Christ our Lord.

For he assumed at his first coming
the lowliness of human flesh,
and so fulfilled the design
    you formed long ago,
and opened for us the way
    to eternal salvation,
that, when he comes again
    in glory and majesty
and all is at last made manifest,
we who watch for that day
may inherit the great promise
in which now we dare to hope.

And so, with Angels and Archangels,
with Thrones and Dominions,
and with all the hosts and Powers of
    heaven,
we sing the hymn of your glory,
as without end we acclaim:

Holy, Holy, Holy Lord God of hosts...

PREFACE II OF ADVENT
THE TWOFOLD EXPECTATION OF CHRIST

It is truly right and just,
 our duty and our salvation,
always and everywhere to give you thanks,
Lord, holy Father,
 almighty and eternal God,
through Christ our Lord.

For all the oracles of the prophets
 foretold him,
the Virgin Mother longed for him
with love beyond all telling,
John the Baptist sang of his coming
and proclaimed his presence when he came.

It is by his gift that already we rejoice
at the mystery of his Nativity,

so that he may find us watchful in prayer
and exultant in his praise.

And so, with Angels and Archangels,
with Thrones and Dominions,
and with all the hosts
 and Powers of heaven,
we sing the hymn of your glory,
as without end we acclaim:

Holy, Holy, Holy Lord God of hosts...

CHRISTMAS TIME

The following three Prefaces are said in Masses of the Nativity of the Lord and of its Octave Day, and within the Octave, even in Masses that otherwise might have a proper Preface, with the exception of Masses that have a proper Preface concerning the divine mysteries or divine Persons.

PREFACE I
OF THE NATIVITY OF THE LORD
CHRIST THE LIGHT

It is truly right and just,
 our duty and our salvation,
always and everywhere to give you thanks,
Lord, holy Father,
 almighty and eternal God.

For in the mystery of the Word made flesh
a new light of your glory has shone
 upon the eyes of our mind,
so that, as we recognize in him
 God made visible,
we may be caught up through him
 in love of things invisible.

And so, with Angels and Archangels,
with Thrones and Dominions,
and with all the hosts
 and Powers of heaven,
we sing the hymn of your glory,
as without end we acclaim:

Holy, Holy, Holy Lord God of hosts...

PREFACE II
OF THE NATIVITY OF THE LORD
THE RESTORATION OF ALL THINGS
IN THE INCARNATION

It is truly right and just,
 our duty and our salvation,
always and everywhere to give you thanks,
Lord, holy Father,
 almighty and eternal God,
through Christ our Lord.

For on the feast of this awe-filled mystery,
though invisible in his own divine nature,
he has appeared visibly in ours;
and begotten before all ages,
he has begun to exist in time;
so that, raising up in himself
 all that was cast down,
he might restore unity to all creation
and call straying humanity
 back to the heavenly Kingdom.

And so, with all the Angels, we praise you,
as in joyful celebration we acclaim:

Holy, Holy, Holy Lord God of hosts...

PREFACE III
OF THE NATIVITY OF THE LORD
THE EXCHANGE IN
THE INCARNATION OF THE WORD

It is truly right and just,
    our duty and our salvation,
always and everywhere to give you thanks,
Lord, holy Father,
    almighty and eternal God,
through Christ our Lord.

For through him the holy exchange
    that restores our life
has shone forth today in splendour:
when our frailty is assumed by your Word
not only does human mortality
    receive unending honour
but by this wondrous union we, too,
    are made eternal.

And so, in company with
    the choirs of Angels,
we praise you, and with joy we proclaim:

Holy, Holy, Holy Lord God of hosts...

THESE PREFACES ARE SAID ON MORE SPECIFIC OCCASIONS DURING CHRISTMAS TIME

PREFACE I
OF THE BLESSED VIRGIN MARY
THE MOTHERHOOD
OF THE BLESSED VIRGIN MARY

The following Preface is said on the Solemnity of Mary, the Holy Mother of God (1 January).

It is truly right and just,
    our duty and our salvation,
always and everywhere to give you thanks,
Lord, holy Father,
    almighty and eternal God,
and to praise, bless, and glorify your name
on the Solemnity of the Motherhood
of the Blessed ever-Virgin Mary.

For by the overshadowing of the Holy Spirit
she conceived your Only Begotten Son,
and without losing the glory of virginity,
brought forth into the world
    the eternal Light,
Jesus Christ our Lord.

Through him the Angels praise your majesty,
Dominions adore and Powers
    tremble before you.
Heaven and the Virtues of heaven
    and the blessed Seraphim
worship together with exultation.
May our voices, we pray, join with theirs
in humble praise, as we acclaim:

Holy, Holy, Holy Lord God of hosts...

PREFACE OF THE
EPIPHANY OF THE LORD
CHRIST THE LIGHT OF THE NATIONS

The following Preface is said in Masses of the Solemnity of the Epiphany. This Preface, or one of the Prefaces of the Nativity, may be said even on days after the Epiphany up to the Saturday that precedes the Feast of the Baptism of the Lord.

It is truly right and just,
    our duty and our salvation,
always and everywhere to give you thanks,
Lord, holy Father,
    almighty and eternal God.

For today you have revealed the mystery
of our salvation in Christ
as a light for the nations,
and, when he appeared
    in our mortal nature,
you made us new by the glory
    of his immortal nature.

And so, with Angels and Archangels,
with Thrones and Dominions,
and with all the hosts
    and Powers of heaven,
we sing the hymn of your glory,
as without end we acclaim:

Holy, Holy, Holy Lord God of hosts...

THE BAPTISM OF THE LORD

The following Preface is said on the feast of the Baptism of the Lord.

It is truly right and just,
>our duty and our salvation,

always and everywhere to give you thanks,
Lord, holy Father,
>almighty and eternal God.

For in the waters of the Jordan
you revealed with signs and wonders
>a new Baptism,

so that through the voice
>that came down from heaven

we might come to believe in your Word
>dwelling among us,

and by the Spirit's descending
>in the likeness of a dove

we might know that Christ your Servant
has been anointed with the oil of gladness
and sent to bring the good news to the poor.

And so, with the Powers of heaven,
we worship you constantly on earth,
and before your majesty
without end we acclaim:

Holy, Holy, Holy Lord God of hosts...

ORDINARY TIME

The following Prefaces are said on Sundays in Ordinary Time.

PREFACE I
OF THE SUNDAYS IN ORDINARY TIME

THE PASCHAL MYSTERY
AND THE PEOPLE OF GOD

It is truly right and just,
>our duty and our salvation,

always and everywhere to give you thanks,
Lord, holy Father, almighty
>and eternal God,

through Christ our Lord.

For through his Paschal Mystery,
he accomplished the marvellous deed,
by which he has freed us
>from the yoke of sin and death,

summoning us to the glory
>of being now called

a chosen race, a royal priesthood,
a holy nation, a people
>for your own possession,

to proclaim everywhere your mighty works,
for you have called us out of darkness
into your own wonderful light.

And so, with Angels and Archangels,
with Thrones and Dominions,
and with all the hosts
>and Powers of heaven,

we sing the hymn of your glory,
as without end we acclaim:

Holy, Holy, Holy Lord God of hosts...

PREFACE II
OF THE SUNDAYS IN ORDINARY TIME

THE MYSTERY OF SALVATION

It is truly right and just,
>our duty and our salvation,

always and everywhere to give you thanks,
Lord, holy Father,
>almighty and eternal God,

through Christ our Lord.

For out of compassion for the waywardness
>that is ours,

he humbled himself
>and was born of the Virgin;

by the passion of the Cross
>he freed us from unending death,

and by rising from the dead
>he gave us life eternal.

And so, with Angels and Archangels,
with Thrones and Dominions,
and with all the hosts
>and Powers of heaven,

we sing the hymn of your glory,
as without end we acclaim:

Holy, Holy, Holy Lord God of hosts...

PREFACE III
OF THE SUNDAYS IN ORDINARY TIME
THE SALVATION OF MAN BY A MAN

It is truly right and just,
  our duty and our salvation,
always and everywhere to give you thanks,
Lord, holy Father,
  almighty and eternal God.

For we know it belongs
  to your boundless glory,
that you came to the aid of mortal beings
  with your divinity
and even fashioned for us
  a remedy out of mortality itself,
that the cause of our downfall
might become the means of our salvation,
through Christ our Lord.

Through him the host of Angels
  adores your majesty
and rejoices in your presence for ever.
May our voices, we pray, join with theirs
in one chorus of exultant praise,
  as we acclaim:

Holy, Holy, Holy Lord God of hosts...

PREFACE IV
OF THE SUNDAYS IN ORDINARY TIME
THE HISTORY OF SALVATION

It is truly right and just,
  our duty and our salvation,
always and everywhere to give you thanks,
Lord, holy Father,
  almighty and eternal God,
through Christ our Lord.

For by his birth he brought renewal
  to humanity's fallen state,
and by his suffering cancelled out our sins;
by his rising from the dead
he has opened the way to eternal life,
and by ascending to you, O Father,
he has unlocked the gates of heaven.

And so, with the company
  of Angels and Saints,
we sing the hymn of your praise,
as without end we acclaim:

Holy, Holy, Holy Lord God of hosts...

PREFACE V
OF THE SUNDAYS IN ORDINARY TIME
CREATION

It is truly right and just,
  our duty and our salvation,
always and everywhere to give you thanks,
Lord, holy Father,
  almighty and eternal God.

For you laid the foundations of the world
and have arranged the changing
  of times and seasons;
you formed man in your own image
and set humanity over the whole world
  in all its wonder,
to rule in your name over all
  you have made
and for ever praise you
  in your mighty works,
through Christ our Lord.

And so, with all the Angels, we praise you,
as in joyful celebration we acclaim:

Holy, Holy, Holy Lord God of hosts...

PREFACE VI
OF THE SUNDAYS IN ORDINARY TIME
THE PLEDGE OF THE ETERNAL PASSOVER

It is truly right and just,
  our duty and our salvation,
always and everywhere to give you thanks,
Lord, holy Father,
  almighty and eternal God.

For in you we live and move
  and have our being,
and while in this body
we not only experience the daily effects
  of your care,
but even now possess the pledge
  of life eternal.

For, having received the first fruits
  of the Spirit,
through whom you raised up Jesus
  from the dead,
we hope for an everlasting share
  in the Paschal Mystery.

And so, with all the Angels, we praise you,
as in joyful celebration we acclaim:

Holy, Holy, Holy Lord God of hosts...

PREFACE VII
OF THE SUNDAYS IN ORDINARY TIME
SALVATION THROUGH
THE OBEDIENCE OF CHRIST

It is truly right and just,
    our duty and our salvation,
always and everywhere to give you thanks,
Lord, holy Father,
    almighty and eternal God.

For you so loved the world
that in your mercy you sent us the Redeemer,
to live like us in all things but sin,
so that you might love in us
    what you loved in your Son,
by whose obedience we have been restored
    to those gifts of yours
that, by sinning, we had lost
    in disobedience.

And so, Lord, with all the Angels and Saints,
we, too, give you thanks,
    as in exultation we acclaim:

Holy, Holy, Holy Lord God of hosts...

PREFACE VIII
OF THE SUNDAYS IN ORDINARY TIME
THE CHURCH UNITED BY
THE UNITY OF THE TRINITY

It is truly right and just,
    our duty and our salvation,
always and everywhere to give you thanks,
Lord, holy Father,
    almighty and eternal God.

For, when your children were scattered afar
    by sin,
through the Blood of your Son
    and the power of the Spirit,
you gathered them again to yourself,
that a people, formed as one
    by the unity of the Trinity,
made the body of Christ
    and the temple of the Holy Spirit,
might, to the praise
    of your manifold wisdom,
be manifest as the Church.

And so, in company with
    the choirs of Angels,
we praise you, and with joy we proclaim:

Holy, Holy, Holy Lord God of hosts...

LENT

The following Prefaces are said on Sundays in Lent especially on Sundays where a more specific Preface is not prescribed.

PREFACE I OF LENT
THE SPIRITUAL MEANING OF LENT

It is truly right and just,
    our duty and our salvation,
always and everywhere to give you thanks,
Lord, holy Father,
    almighty and eternal God,
through Christ our Lord.

For by your gracious gift each year
your faithful await the sacred paschal feasts
with the joy of minds made pure,
so that, more eagerly intent on prayer
and on the works of charity,
and participating in the mysteries
by which they have been reborn,
they may be led to the fullness of grace
that you bestow on your sons and daughters.

And so, with Angels and Archangels,
with Thrones and Dominions,
and with all the hosts
    and Powers of heaven,
we sing the hymn of your glory,
as without end we acclaim:

Holy, Holy, Holy Lord God of hosts...

PREFACE II OF LENT
SPIRITUAL PENANCE

It is truly right and just,
    our duty and our salvation,
always and everywhere to give you thanks,
Lord, holy Father,
    almighty and eternal God.

For you have given your children
    a sacred time
for the renewing and purifying
    of their hearts,
that, freed from disordered affections,
they may so deal with the things
    of this passing world
as to hold rather to the things
    that eternally endure.

And so, with all the Angels and Saints,
we praise you, as without end we acclaim:

Holy, Holy, Holy Lord God of hosts...

PREFACE III OF LENT
THE FRUITS OF ABSTINENCE

The following Preface is said in Masses of the weekdays of Lent and on days of fasting.

It is truly right and just,
    our duty and our salvation,
always and everywhere to give you thanks,
Lord, holy Father,
    almighty and eternal God.

For you will that our self-denial
    should give you thanks,
humble our sinful pride,
contribute to the feeding of the poor,
and so help us imitate you in your kindness.

And so we glorify you with countless Angels,
as with one voice of praise we acclaim:

Holy, Holy, Holy Lord God of hosts...

APPENDIX

THESE PREFACES ARE SAID ON MORE SPECIFIC OCCASIONS DURING LENT

PREFACE IV OF LENT
THE FRUITS OF FASTING

The following Preface is said in Masses of the weekdays of Lent and on days of fasting.

It is truly right and just,
    our duty and our salvation,
always and everywhere to give you thanks,
Lord, holy Father,
    almighty and eternal God.

For through bodily fasting
    you restrain our faults,
raise up our minds,
and bestow both virtue and its rewards,
through Christ our Lord.

Through him the Angels
    praise your majesty,
Dominions adore and Powers
    tremble before you.
Heaven and the Virtues of heaven
    and the blessed Seraphim
worship together with exultation.
May our voices, we pray, join with theirs
in humble praise, as we acclaim:

Holy, Holy, Holy Lord God of hosts...

THE TEMPTATION OF THE LORD

The following Preface is said on the First Sunday of Lent.

It is truly right and just,
    our duty and our salvation,
always and everywhere to give you thanks,
Lord, holy Father,
    almighty and eternal God,
through Christ our Lord.

By abstaining forty long days
    from earthly food,
he consecrated through his fast
the pattern of our Lenten observance
and, by overturning all the snares
    of the ancient serpent,
taught us to cast out the leaven of malice,
so that, celebrating worthily
    the Paschal Mystery,
we might pass over at last
    to the eternal paschal feast.

And so, with the company
    of Angels and Saints,
we sing the hymn of your praise,
as without end we acclaim:

Holy, Holy, Holy Lord God of hosts...

THE TRANSFIGURATION OF THE LORD

*The following Preface is said on the
Second Sunday of Lent.*

It is truly right and just,
    our duty and our salvation,
always and everywhere to give you thanks,
Lord, holy Father,
    almighty and eternal God,
through Christ our Lord.

For after he had told the disciples
    of his coming Death,
on the holy mountain
    he manifested to them his glory,
to show, even by the testimony of the law
    and the prophets,
that the Passion leads to the glory
    of the Resurrection.

And so, with the Powers of heaven,
we worship you constantly on earth,
and before your majesty
without end we acclaim:

Holy, Holy, Holy Lord God of hosts…

THE SAMARITAN WOMAN

*The following Preface is said on the Third Sunday of
Lent, whenever the Gospel of the Samaritan Woman
is read.*

It is truly right and just,
    our duty and our salvation,
always and everywhere to give you thanks,
Lord, holy Father,
    almighty and eternal God,
through Christ our Lord.

For when he asked the Samaritan woman
    for water to drink,
he had already created
    the gift of faith within her
and so ardently did he thirst for her faith,
that he kindled in her the fire of divine love.

And so we, too, give you thanks
and with the Angels
praise your mighty deeds, as we acclaim:

Holy, Holy, Holy Lord God of hosts…

THE MAN BORN BLIND

*The following Preface is said on the Fourth Sunday of
Lent, whenever the Gospel of the Man Born Blind is read.*

It is truly right and just,
    our duty and our salvation,
always and everywhere to give you thanks,
Lord, holy Father,
    almighty and eternal God,
through Christ our Lord.

By the mystery of the Incarnation,
he has led the human race
    that walked in darkness
into the radiance of the faith
and has brought those born in slavery
    to ancient sin
through the waters of regeneration
to make them your adopted children.

Therefore, all creatures of heaven and earth
sing a new song in adoration,
and we, with all the host of Angels,
cry out, and without end acclaim:

Holy, Holy, Holy Lord God of hosts…

LAZARUS

*The following Preface is said on the Fifth Sunday of Lent,
whenever the Gospel of the raising of Lazarus is read.*

It is truly right and just,
    our duty and our salvation,
always and everywhere to give you thanks,
Lord, holy Father,
    almighty and eternal God,
through Christ our Lord.

For as true man he wept for Lazarus his friend
and as eternal God
    raised him from the tomb,
just as, taking pity on the human race,
he leads us by sacred mysteries to new life.

Through him the host of Angels
    adores your majesty
and rejoices in your presence for ever.
May our voices, we pray, join with theirs
in one chorus of exultant praise,
    as we acclaim:

Holy, Holy, Holy Lord God of hosts…

THE PASSION OF THE LORD

This preface is said on Palm Sunday of the Passion of the Lord

It is truly right and just,
  our duty and our salvation,
always and everywhere to give you thanks,
Lord, holy Father,
  almighty and eternal God,
through Christ our Lord.

For though innocent
  he suffered willingly for sinners
and accepted unjust condemnation
  to save the guilty.

His Death has washed away our sins,
and his Resurrection
  has purchased our justification.

And so, with all the Angels,
we praise you,
  as in joyful celebration we acclaim:

Holy, Holy, Holy Lord God of hosts...

TRIDUUM

The following Preface is said in the Mass of the Lord's Supper.

PREFACE I OF THE MOST HOLY EUCHARIST
THE SACRIFICE AND THE SACRAMENT OF CHRIST

It is truly right and just, our duty and our salvation,
always and everywhere to give you thanks,
Lord, holy Father, almighty and eternal God,
through Christ our Lord.

For he is the true and eternal Priest,
who instituted the pattern of an everlasting sacrifice
and was the first to offer himself as the saving Victim,
commanding us to make this offering as his memorial.
As we eat his flesh that was sacrificed for us,
we are made strong,
and, as we drink his Blood that was poured out for us,
we are washed clean.

And so, with Angels and Archangels,
with Thrones and Dominions,
and with all the hosts and Powers of heaven,
we sing the hymn of your glory,
as without end we acclaim:

Holy, Holy, Holy Lord God of hosts...

EASTER

PREFACE I OF EASTER
THE PASCHAL MYSTERY

The following Preface is said during Easter Time. At the Easter Vigil, is said 'on this night'; on Easter Sunday and throughout the Octave of Easter, is said 'on this day'; on other days of Easter Time, is said 'in this time'.

It is truly right and just,
    our duty and our salvation,
at all times to acclaim you, O Lord,
but (on this night / on this day /
    in this time) above all
to laud you yet more gloriously,
when Christ our Passover
    has been sacrificed.

For he is the true Lamb
who has taken away the sins of the world;
by dying he has destroyed our death,
and by rising, restored our life.

Therefore, overcome with paschal joy,
every land, every people exults
    in your praise
and even the heavenly Powers,
    with the angelic hosts,
sing together the unending hymn
    of your glory,
as they acclaim:

Holy, Holy, Holy Lord God of hosts...

PREFACE II OF EASTER
NEW LIFE IN CHRIST

The following Preface is said during Easter Time.

It is truly right and just,
    our duty and our salvation,
at all times to acclaim you, O Lord,
but in this time above all to laud you
    yet more gloriously,
when Christ our Passover
    has been sacrificed.

Through him the children of light
    rise to eternal life
and the halls of the heavenly Kingdom
are thrown open to the faithful;
for his Death is our ransom from death,
and in his rising the life of all has risen.

Therefore, overcome with paschal joy,
every land, every people exults in your praise
and even the heavenly Powers,
    with the angelic hosts,
sing together the unending hymn
    of your glory,
as they acclaim:

Holy, Holy, Holy Lord God of hosts...

PREFACE III OF EASTER
CHRIST LIVING AND
ALWAYS INTERCEDING FOR US

The following Preface is said during Easter Time.

It is truly right and just,
    our duty and our salvation,
at all times to acclaim you, O Lord,
but in this time above all to laud you
    yet more gloriously,
when Christ our Passover
    has been sacrificed.

He never ceases to offer himself for us
but defends us and ever pleads our cause
    before you:
he is the sacrificial Victim
    who dies no more,
the Lamb, once slain, who lives for ever.

Therefore, overcome with paschal joy,
every land, every people exults in your praise
and even the heavenly Powers,
    with the angelic hosts,
sing together the unending hymn
    of your glory,
as they acclaim:

Holy, Holy, Holy Lord God of hosts...

PREFACE IV OF EASTER
THE RESTORATION OF THE UNIVERSE
THROUGH THE PASCHAL MYSTERY

The following Preface is said during Easter Time.

It is truly right and just,
    our duty and our salvation,
at all times to acclaim you, O Lord,
but in this time above all to laud you
    yet more gloriously,
when Christ our Passover
    has been sacrificed.

For, with the old order destroyed,
a universe cast down is renewed,
and integrity of life is restored to us in Christ.

Therefore, overcome with paschal joy,
every land, every people exults in your praise
and even the heavenly Powers,
    with the angelic hosts,
sing together the unending hymn
    of your glory,
as they acclaim:

Holy, Holy, Holy Lord God of hosts...

PREFACE V OF EASTER
CHRIST, PRIEST AND VICTIM

The following Preface is said during Easter Time.

It is truly right and just,
    our duty and our salvation,
at all times to acclaim you, O Lord,
but in this time above all to laud you
    yet more gloriously,
when Christ our Passover
    has been sacrificed.

By the oblation of his Body,
he brought the sacrifices of old to fulfilment
in the reality of the Cross
and, by commending himself to you
    for our salvation,
showed himself the Priest, the Altar,
    and the Lamb of sacrifice.

Therefore, overcome with paschal joy,
every land, every people exults in your praise
and even the heavenly Powers,
    with the angelic hosts,
sing together the unending hymn
    of your glory,
as they acclaim:

Holy, Holy, Holy Lord God of hosts...

The following two Prefaces are said on the day of the Ascension of the Lord. They may be said on the days between the Ascension and Pentecost in all Masses that have no proper Preface.

PREFACE I
OF THE ASCENSION OF THE LORD
THE MYSTERY OF THE ASCENSION

It is truly right and just,
    our duty and our salvation,
always and everywhere to give you thanks,
Lord, holy Father,
    almighty and eternal God.

For the Lord Jesus, the King of glory,
conqueror of sin and death,
ascended (today) to the highest heavens,
as the Angels gazed in wonder.

Mediator between God and man,
judge of the world and Lord of hosts,
he ascended, not to distance himself
    from our lowly state
but that we, his members,
    might be confident of following
where he, our Head and Founder,
    has gone before.

Therefore, overcome with paschal joy,
every land, every people exults in your praise
and even the heavenly Powers,
    with the angelic hosts,
sing together the unending hymn
    of your glory,
as they acclaim:

Holy, Holy, Holy Lord God of hosts...

PREFACE II
OF THE ASCENSION OF THE LORD
THE MYSTERY OF THE ASCENSION

It is truly right and just,
    our duty and our salvation,
always and everywhere to give you thanks,
Lord, holy Father,
    almighty and eternal God,
through Christ our Lord.

For after his Resurrection
he plainly appeared to all his disciples
and was taken up to heaven in their sight,
that he might make us sharers in his divinity.

APPENDIX

Therefore, overcome with paschal joy,
every land, every people exults in your praise
and even the heavenly Powers,
　　with the angelic hosts,
sing together the unending hymn
　　of your glory,
as they acclaim:

Holy, Holy, Holy Lord God of hosts...

THE MYSTERY OF PENTECOST

The following Preface is said on Pentecost Sunday.

It is truly right and just,
　　our duty and our salvation,
always and everywhere to give you thanks,
Lord, holy Father,
　　almighty and eternal God.

For, bringing your Paschal Mystery
　　to completion,
you bestowed the Holy Spirit today
on those you made
　　your adopted children
by uniting them to your Only Begotten Son.
This same Spirit, as the Church
　　came to birth,
opened to all peoples
　　the knowledge of God
and brought together
　　the many languages of the earth
in profession of the one faith.

Therefore, overcome with paschal joy,
every land, every people
　　exults in your praise
and even the heavenly Powers,
　　with the angelic hosts,
sing together the unending hymn
　　of your glory,
as they acclaim:

Holy, Holy, Holy Lord God of hosts...

PREFACES FOR OTHER OCCASIONS

MYSTERY OF MARY AND THE CHURCH

*This Preface is said on the Solemnity of The
Immaculate Conception of the Blessed Virgin Mary*

It is truly right and just,
　　our duty and our salvation,
always and everywhere to give you thanks,
Lord, holy Father,
　　almighty and eternal God.

For you preserved
　　the Most Blessed Virgin Mary
from all stain of original sin,
so that in her, endowed with the rich
　　fullness of your grace,
you might prepare a worthy Mother
　　for your Son
and signify the beginning of the Church,
his beautiful Bride without spot or wrinkle.

She, the most pure Virgin,
　　was to bring forth a Son,
the innocent Lamb
　　who would wipe away our offences;
you placed her above all others
to be for your people an advocate of grace
and a model of holiness.

And so, in company with the choirs
　　of Angels,
we praise you, and with joy we proclaim:

Holy, Holy, Holy Lord God of hosts...

MYSTERY OF
THE PRESENTATION OF THE LORD

*The following Preface is said on the feast of the
Presentation of the Lord (2 February).*

It is truly right and just,
　　our duty and our salvation,
always and everywhere to give you thanks,
Lord, holy Father,
　　almighty and eternal God.

For your co-eternal Son was presented on
　　this day in the Temple
and revealed by the Spirit
as the glory of Israel
　　and Light of the nations.

And so, we, too, go forth, rejoicing to
　　encounter your Salvation,
and with the Angels and Saints
praise you, as without end we acclaim:

Holy, Holy, Holy Lord God of hosts...

SAINT PATRICK

The following Preface is said in Ireland
on the solemnity of Saint Patrick (17 March).

It is truly right and just,
    our duty and our salvation,
always and everywhere to give you thanks,
Lord, holy Father,
    almighty and eternal God,
and to proclaim your greatness
    with due praise
as we honour Saint Patrick.

For you drew him through daily prayer
in captivity and hardship
to know you as a loving Father.

You chose him out of all the world
to return to the land of his captors,
that they might acknowledge Jesus Christ,
    their Redeemer.

In the power of your Spirit
    you directed his paths
to win the sons and daughters of the Irish
to the service of the Triune God.

And so, with the Angels and Archangels,
and with the great multitude of the Saints,
we sing the hymn of your praise,
as without end we acclaim:

Holy, Holy, Holy Lord God of hosts...

LATIN TEXTS OF THE ORDER OF MASS

CONFITEOR

Confiteor Deo omnipotenti et vobis, fratres,
quia peccavi nimis
cogitatione, verbo, opere et omissione:
mea culpa, mea culpa, mea maxima culpa.
Ideo precor beatam Mariam semper Virginem,
omnes Angelos et Sanctos,
et vos, fratres, orare pro me
ad Dominum Deum nostrum. Amen

KYRIE

Kyrie, eleison
Kyrie, eleison.

Christe, eleison.
Christe, eleison.

Kyrie, eleison.
Kyrie, eleison.

GLORIA

Gloria in excelsis Deo
et in terra pax hominibus bonae voluntatis.
Laudamus te,
benedicimus te,
adoramus te,
glorificamus te,
gratias agimus tibi propter magnam
   gloriam tuam,
Domine Deus, Rex caelestis,
Deus Pater omnipotens.

Domine Fili unigenite, Jesu Christe,
Domine Deus, Agnus Dei, Filius Patris,
qui tollis peccata mundi, miserere nobis;
qui tollis peccata mundi,
   suscipe deprecationem nostram.
Qui sedes ad dexteram Patris,
   miserere nobis.
Quoniam tu solus Sanctus,
   tu solus Dominus,
tu solus Altissimus,
Jesu Christe, cum Sancto Spiritu:
   in gloria Dei Patris. Amen.

CREDO

Credo in unum Deum,
Patrem Omnipotentem,
   factorem caeli et terrae,
visibilium omnium et invisibilium.
Et in unum Dominum Jesum Christum,
Filium Dei unigenitum,
   et ex Patre natum ante omnia saecula.
Deum de Deo, lumen de lumine,
   Deum verum de Deo vero,
genitum, non factum,
   consubstantialem Patri:
per quem omnia facta sunt.
Qui propter nos homines
   et propter nostram salutem
descendit de caelis.

Et incarnatus est de Spiritu Sancto
ex Maria Virgine; et homo factus est.

Crucifixus etiam pro nobis sub Pontio Pilato;
passus et sepultus est,
et resurrexit tertia die, secundum Scripturas,
et ascendit in caelum,
    sedet ad dexteram Patris.
Et iterum venturus est cum gloria,
    iudicare vivos et mortuos,
cuius regni non erit finis.
Et in Spiritum Sanctum,
    Dominum et vivificantem:
qui ex Patre Filioque procedit.
Qui cum Patre et Filio simul adoratur
    et conglorificatur:
qui locutus est per prophetas.
Et unam, sanctam, catholicam
    et apostolicam Ecclesiam.
Confiteor unum baptisma
    in remissionem peccatorum.
Et exspecto resurrectionem mortuorum,
et vitam venturi saeculi. Amen.

ORATE FRATRES
Orate fratres:
ut meum ac vestrum sacrificium
acceptabile fiat apud Deum
    Patrem omnipotentem.

Suscipiat Dominus sacrificium
    de manibus tuis
ad laudem et gloriam nominis sui,
ad utilitatem quoque nostram
totiusque Ecclesiae sanctae.

SURSUM CORDA
Dominus vobiscum.
Et cum spiritu tuo.

Sursum corda.
Habemus ad Dominum.

Gratias Agamus Domino Deo nostro.
Dignum et iustum est.

SANCTUS
Sanctus, Sanctus, Sanctus Dominus
    Deus Sabaoth.
Pleni sunt caeli et terra gloria tua.
Hosanna in excelsis.
Benedictus qui venit in nomine Domini.
Hosanna in excelsis.

MYSTERIUM FIDEI
Mysterium Fidei.
1 **Mortem tuam annuntiamus, Domine,**
    et tuam resurrectionem confitemur,
        donec venias.

2 **Quotiescumque manducamus panem**
        hunc
    et calicem bibimus
    mortem tuam annuntiamus, Domine,
        donec venias.

3 **Salvator Mundi, salva nos,**
    qui per crucem et resurrectionem tuam
        liberasti nos.

PATER NOSTER
Praeceptis salutaribus moniti,
et divina insitutione formati,
audemus dicere:

Pater noster, qui es in caelis:
sanctificetur nomen tuum;
adveniat regnum tuum;
fiat voluntas tua, sicut in caelo,
    et in terra.
Panem nostrum cotidianum
    da nobis hodie;
et dimitte nobis debita nostra,
sicut et nos dimittimus debitoribus
    nostris
et ne nos inducas in tentationem;
sed libera nos a malo.

Libera nos, quaesumus, Domine,
    ab omnibus malis,...
...et adventum Salvatoris nostri Iesu Christi.

Quia tuum est regnum,
et potestas, et gloria
in saecula.

AGNUS DEI
Agnus Dei, qui tollis peccata mundi:
    miserere nobis.
Agnus Dei, qui tollis peccata mundi:
    miserere nobis.
Agnus Dei, qui tollis peccata mundi:
    dona nobis pacem.

PROPER OF TIME

CONTENTS OF THE PROPER OF TIME

COMMON RESPONSORIAL PSALMS

The Responsorial Psalm should correspond to each reading and should, as a rule, be taken from the Lectionary In order, however, that the people may be able to sing the Psalm response more readily, texts of some responses and psalms have been chosen for the various seasons of the year or for the various categories of Saints. These may be used in place of the text corresponding to the reading whenever the Psalm is sung.

General Instruction of the Roman Missal n 61

The appropriate Common Responsorial Psalms are to be found at the beginning of each season.

ADVENT

ABOUT THE SEASON

Advent has a twofold character, for it is a time of preparation for the Solemnities of Christmas, in which the First Coming of the Son of God to humanity is remembered, and likewise a time when, by remembrance of this, minds and hearts are led to look forward to Christ's Second Coming at the end of time. For these two reasons, Advent is a period of devout and expectant delight.

Universal Norms on the Liturgical Year and the Calendar n 39

ABOUT THE READINGS

Each gospel reading has a distinctive theme: the Lord's coming at the end of time (First Sunday of Advent), John the Baptist (Second and Third Sunday), and the events that prepared immediately for the Lord's birth (Fourth Sunday).

The Old Testament readings are prophecies about the Messiah and the Messianic age, especially from the Isaiah.

The readings from an apostle serve as exhortations and as proclamations, in keeping with the different themes of Advent.

Introduction to the Lectionary n 93

ADVENT

COMMON RESPONSORIAL PSALMS FOR ADVENT

COMMON RESPONSE

Come and set us free, O Lord.

COMMON PSALM 1 *Psalm 24:4–5, 8–9, 10, 14 response v 1*

To you, O Lord, I lift up my soul.

1 Lord, make me know your ways.
Lord, teach me your paths.
Make me walk in your truth, and teach me:
for you are God my saviour.

2 The Lord is good and upright.
He shows the path to those who stray,
he guides the humble in the right path;
he teaches his way to the poor.

3 His ways are faithfulness and love
for those who keep his covenant and will.
The Lord's friendship is for those who revere him;
to them he reveals his covenant

COMMON PSALM 2   *Psalm 84:9–14 response v 8*

Let us see, O Lord, your mercy.

1 I will hear what the Lord God has to say,
   a voice that speaks of peace,
   peace for his people and his friends.
   His help is near for those who fear him
   and his glory will dwell in our land.

2 Mercy and faithfulness have met;
   justice and peace have embraced.
   Faithfulness shall spring from the earth
   and justice look down from heaven.

3 The Lord will make us prosper
   and our earth shall yield its fruit.
   Justice shall march before him
   and peace shall follow his steps.

 FIRST SUNDAY OF ADVENT

ENTRANCE ANTIPHON   *cf Psalm 24:1–3*

To you, I lift up my soul, O my God.
In you, I have trusted; let me not be put to shame.
Nor let my enemies exult over me;
and let none who hope in you be put to shame.

▷ *page 7*

The Gloria is omitted.

COLLECT

Grant your faithful, we pray, almighty God,
the resolve to run forth to meet your Christ
with righteous deeds at his coming,
so that, gathered at his right hand,
they may be worthy to possess the heavenly Kingdom.
Through our Lord Jesus Christ, your Son,
who lives and reigns with you in the unity of the Holy Spirit,
one God, for ever and ever.   **Amen.**

FIRST READING   *Jeremiah 33:14–16*

I will make a virtuous Branch grow for David.

See, the days are coming – it is the Lord who speaks – when I am going to fulfil the promise I made to the House of Israel and the House of Judah:

'In those days and at that time, I will make a virtuous Branch grow for David, who shall practise honesty and integrity in the land. In those days Judah shall be saved and Israel shall dwell in confidence. And this is the name the city will be called: The Lord-our-integrity.'

The word of the Lord.

Thanks be to God.

RESPONSORIAL PSALM   *Psalm 24:4–5, 8–9, 10, 14 response v 1*

> **To you, O Lord, I lift up my soul.**

1 Lord, make me know your ways.
   Lord, teach me your paths.
   Make me walk in your truth, and teach me:
   for you are God my saviour.

2 The Lord is good and upright.
   He shows the path to those who stray,
   he guides the humble in the right path;
   he teaches his way to the poor.

3 His ways are faithfulness and love
   for those who keep his covenant and will.
   The Lord's friendship is for those who revere him;
   to them he reveals his covenant

SECOND READING   *1 Thessalonians 3:12–4:2*

May the Lord confirm your hearts in holiness when Christ comes.

May the Lord be generous in increasing your love and make you love one another and the whole human race as much as we love you. And may he so confirm your hearts in holiness that you may be blameless in the sight of our God and Father when our Lord Jesus Christ comes with all his saints.

Finally, brothers, we urge you and appeal to you in the Lord Jesus to make more and more progress in the kind of life that you are meant to live: the life that God wants, as you learnt from us, and as you are already living it. You have not forgotten the instructions we gave you on the authority of the Lord Jesus.

The word of the Lord.
Thanks be to God.

GOSPEL ACCLAMATION   *Psalm 84:8*

> **Alleluia, alleluia!**
> **Let us see, O Lord, your mercy**
> **and give us your saving help.**
> **Alleluia!**

GOSPEL   *Luke 21:25–28; 34–36*

The Lord be with you.
And with your spirit.

A reading from the holy Gospel according to Luke.
Glory to you, O Lord.

Your liberation is near at hand.

Jesus said to his disciples: 'There will be signs in the sun and moon and stars; on earth nations in agony, bewildered by the clamour of the ocean and its waves; men dying of fear as they await what menaces the world, for the powers of heaven will be shaken. And then they will see the Son of Man coming in a cloud with power and great glory. When these things begin to take place, stand erect, hold your heads high because your liberation is near at hand.'

'Watch yourselves, or your hearts will be coarsened with debauchery and drunkenness and the cares of life, and that day will be sprung on you suddenly, like a trap. For it will come down on every living man on the face of the earth. Stay awake, praying at all times for the strength to survive all that is going to happen, and to stand with confidence before the Son of Man.'

The Gospel of the Lord.
Praise to you, Lord Jesus Christ.

▷ *page 11*

PRAYER OVER THE OFFERINGS
Accept, we pray, O Lord, these offerings we make,
gathered from among your gifts to us,
and may what you grant us to celebrate devoutly here below
gain for us the prize of eternal redemption.
Through Christ our Lord.   **Amen**

▷ *page 15*

Preface I of Advent, p 65.

COMMUNION ANTIPHON   *Psalm 84:13*
The Lord will bestow his bounty, and our earth shall yield its increase.

▷ *page 58*

PRAYER AFTER COMMUNION
May these mysteries, O Lord,
in which we have participated,
profit us, we pray,
for even now, as we walk amid passing things,
you teach us by them to love the things of heaven
and hold fast to what endures.
Through Christ our Lord.   **Amen.**

A solemn blessing or prayer over the people may be used.

▷ *page 59*

 # SECOND SUNDAY OF ADVENT

ENTRANCE ANTIPHON   *cf Isaiah 30:19, 30*
O people of Sion, behold,
the Lord will come to save the nations,
and the Lord will make the glory of his voice heard
in the joy of your heart.

▷ *page 7*

The Gloria is omitted.

COLLECT

Almighty and merciful God,
may no earthly undertaking hinder those
who set out in haste to meet your Son,
but may our learning of heavenly wisdom
gain us admittance to his company.
Who lives and reigns with you in the unity of the Holy Spirit,
one God, for ever and ever. **Amen.**

FIRST READING   *Baruch 5:1–9*

God means to show your splendour to every nation.

Jerusalem, take off your dress of sorrow and distress, put on the beauty of the glory of God for ever, wrap the cloak of integrity of God around you, put the diadem of the glory of the Eternal on your head: since God means to show your splendour to every nation under heaven, since the name God gives you for ever will be, 'Peace through integrity, and honour through devotedness.' Arise, Jerusalem, stand on the heights and turn your eyes to the east: see your sons reassembled from west and east at the command of the Holy One, jubilant that God has remembered them. Though they left you on foot, with enemies for an escort, now God brings them back to you like royal princes carried back in glory. For God has decreed the flattening of each high mountain, of the everlasting hills, the filling of the valleys to make the ground level so that Israel can walk in safety under the glory of God. And the forests and every fragrant tree will provide shade for Israel at the command of God; for God will guide Israel in joy by the light of his glory with his mercy and integrity for escort.

The word of the Lord.
Thanks be to God.

RESPONSORIAL PSALM   *Psalm 125 response v 3*

What marvels the Lord worked for us!
Indeed we were glad.

1   When the Lord delivered Zion from bondage,
    it seemed like a dream.
    Then was our mouth filled with laughter,
    on our lips there were songs.

2   The heathens themselves said: 'What marvels
    the Lord worked for them!'
    What marvels the Lord worked for us!
    Indeed we were glad.

3   Deliver us, O Lord, from our bondage
    as streams in dry land.
    Those who are sowing in tears
    will sing when they reap.

4   They go out, they go out, full of tears,
    carrying seed for the sowing:
    they come back, they come back, full of song,
    carrying their sheaves.

SECOND READING   *Philippians 1:4–6; 8–11*

Be pure and blameless for the day of Christ.

Every time I pray for all of you, I pray with joy, remembering how you have helped to spread the Good News from the day you first heard it right up to the present. I am quite certain that the One who began this good work in you will see that it is finished when the Day of Christ Jesus comes. God knows how much I miss you all, loving you as Christ Jesus loves you. My prayer is that your love for each other may increase more and more and never stop improving your knowledge and deepening your perception so that you can always recognise what is best. This will help you to become pure and blameless, and prepare you for the Day of Christ, when you will reach the perfect goodness which Jesus Christ produces in us for the glory and praise of God.

The word of the Lord.
Thanks be to God.

GOSPEL ACCLAMATION   *Luke 3:4, 6*

> **Alleluia, alleluia!**
> **Prepare a way for the Lord,**
> **make his paths straight,**
> **and all mankind shall see the salvation of God.**
> **Alleluia!**

GOSPEL   *Luke 3:1–6*

The Lord be with you.
And with your spirit.

A reading from the holy Gospel according to Luke.
Glory to you, O Lord.

All mankind shall see the salvation of God.

In the fifteenth year of Tiberius Caesar's reign, when Pontius Pilate was governor of Judaea, Herod tetrarch of Galilee, his brother Philip tetrarch of the lands of Ituraea and Trachonitis, Lysanias tetrarch of Abilene, during the pontificate of Annas and Caiaphas, the word of God came to John son of Zechariah, in the wilderness. He went through the whole Jordan district proclaiming a baptism of repentance for the forgiveness of sins, as it is written in the book of the sayings of the prophet Isaiah:

A voice cries in the wilderness: Prepare a way for the Lord, make his paths straight. Every valley will be filled in, every mountain and hill be laid low, winding ways will be straightened and rough roads made smooth. And all mankind shall see the salvation of God.

The Gospel of the Lord.
Praise to you, Lord Jesus Christ.

▷ *page 11*

PRAYER OVER THE OFFERINGS
Be pleased, O Lord, with our humble prayers and offerings,
and, since we have no merits to plead our cause,
come, we pray, to our rescue
with the protection of your mercy.
Through Christ our Lord.   **Amen**

▷ *page 15*

Preface I of Advent, p 65.

COMMUNION ANTIPHON   *Baruch 5:5, 4:6*
Jerusalem, arise and stand upon the heights,
and behold the joy which comes to you from God.

▷ *page 58*

PRAYER AFTER COMMUNION
Replenished by the food of spiritual nourishment,
we humbly beseech you, O Lord,
that, through our partaking in this mystery,
you may teach us to judge wisely the things of earth
and hold firm to the things of heaven.
Through Christ our Lord.   **Amen.**

▷ *page 59*

A solemn blessing or prayer over the people may be used.

THIRD SUNDAY OF ADVENT

ENTRANCE ANTIPHON   *Philippians 4:4–5*
Rejoice in the Lord always; again I say, rejoice.
Indeed, the Lord is near.

▷ *page 7*

The Gloria is omitted.

COLLECT
O God, who see how your people
faithfully await the feast of the Lord's Nativity,
enable us, we pray,
to attain the joys of so great a salvation
and to celebrate them always
with solemn worship and glad rejoicing.
Through our Lord Jesus Christ, your Son,
who lives and reigns with you in the unity of the Holy Spirit,
one God, for ever and ever. **Amen.**

FIRST READING   *Zephaniah 3:14–18*

The Lord will dance with shouts of joy for you as on a day of festival.

Shout for joy, daughter of Zion, Israel, shout aloud! Rejoice, exult with all your heart, daughter of Jerusalem! The Lord has repealed your sentence; he has driven your enemies away. The Lord, the king of Israel, is in your midst; you have no more evil to fear. When that day comes, word will come to Jerusalem: Zion, have no fear, do not let your hands fall limp. The Lord your God is in your midst, a victorious warrior. He will exult with joy over you, he will renew you by his love; he will dance with shouts of joy for you as on a day of festival.

The word of the Lord.
Thanks be to God.

RESPONSORIAL PSALM   *Isaiah 12:2–6 response v 6*

> **Sing and shout for joy**
> **for great in your midst is the Holy One of Israel.**

1   Truly, God is my salvation,
    I trust, I shall not fear.
    For the Lord is my strength, my song,
    he became my saviour.
    With joy you will draw water
    from the wells of salvation.

2   Give thanks to the Lord, give praise to his name!
    Make his mighty deeds known to the peoples,
    declare the greatness of his name.

3   Sing a psalm to the Lord
    for he has done glorious deeds,
    make them known to all the earth!
    People of Zion, sing and shout for joy
    for great in your midst is the Holy One of Israel.

SECOND READING   *Philippians 4:4–7*

The Lord is very near.

I want you to be happy, always happy in the Lord; I repeat, what I want is your happiness. Let your tolerance be evident to everyone: the Lord is very near. There is no need to worry; but if there is anything you need, pray for it, asking God for it with prayer and thanksgiving, and that peace of God, which is so much greater than we can understand, will guard your hearts and your thoughts, in Christ Jesus.

The word of the Lord.
Thanks be to God.

GOSPEL ACCLAMATION   *Isaiah 61:1 (Luke 4:18)*

> **Alleluia, alleluia!**
> **The spirit of the Lord has been given to me.**
> **He has sent me to bring good news to the poor.**
> **Alleluia!**

GOSPEL   *Luke 3:10–18*

The Lord be with you.
And with your spirit.

A reading from the holy Gospel according to Luke.
Glory to you, O Lord.

What must we do?

When all the people asked John, 'What must we do?' He answered, 'If anyone has two tunics he must share with the man who has none, and the one with something to eat must do the same.' There were tax collectors too who came for baptism, and these said to him, 'Master, what must we do?' He said to them, 'Exact no more than your rate.' Some soldiers asked him in their turn. 'What about us? What must we do?' He said to them, 'No intimidation! No extortion! Be content with your pay!'

A feeling of expectancy had grown among the people, who were beginning to think that John might be the Christ, so John declared before them all, 'I baptise you with water, but someone is coming, someone who is more powerful than I am, and I am not fit to undo the strap of his sandals; he will baptise you with the Holy Spirit and fire. His winnowing-fan is in his hand to clear his threshing-floor and to gather the wheat into his barn; but the chaff he will burn in a fire that will never go out.' As well as this, there were many other things he said to exhort the people and to announce the Good News to them.

The Gospel of the Lord.
Praise to you, Lord Jesus Christ.

▷ *page 11*

PRAYER OVER THE OFFERINGS
May the sacrifice of our worship, Lord, we pray,
be offered to you unceasingly,
to complete what was begun in sacred mystery
and powerfully accomplish for us your saving work.
Through Christ our Lord.   **Amen**

▷ *page 15*

Preface I or II of Advent, pp 65- 66.

COMMUNION ANTIPHON   *cf Isaiah 35:4*
Say to the faint of heart: Be strong and do not fear.
Behold, our God will come, and he will save us.

▷ *page 58*

PRAYER AFTER COMMUNION
We implore your mercy, Lord,
that this divine sustenance may cleanse us of our faults
and prepare us for the coming feasts.
Through Christ our Lord.   Amen.

▷ *page 59*

A solemn blessing or prayer over the people may be used.

FOURTH SUNDAY OF ADVENT

ENTRANCE ANTIPHON   *cf Isaiah 45:8*

Drop down dew from above, you heavens,
and let the clouds rain down the Just One;
let the earth be opened and bring forth a Saviour.

▷ *page 7*

The Gloria is omitted.

COLLECT

Pour forth, we beseech you, O Lord,
your grace into our hearts,
that we, to whom the Incarnation of Christ your Son
was made known by the message of an Angel,
may by his Passion and Cross
be brought to the glory of his Resurrection.
Who lives and reigns with you in the unity of the Holy Spirit,
one God, for ever and ever. **Amen.**

FIRST READING   *Micah 5:1–4*

Out of you will be born the one who is to rule over Israel.

The Lord says this: You, Bethlehem Ephrathah, the least of the clans of Judah, out of you will be born for me the one who is to rule over Israel; his origin goes back to the distant past, to the days of old. The Lord is therefore going to abandon them till the time when she who is to give birth gives birth. Then the remnant of his brothers will come back to the sons of Israel. He will stand and feed his flock with the power of the Lord, with the majesty of the name of his God. They will live secure, for from then on he will extend his power to the ends of the land. He himself will be peace.

The word of the Lord.
Thanks be to God.

RESPONSORIAL PSALM   *Psalm 79:2–3, 15–16, 18–19 response v 4*

> **God of hosts, bring us back;**
> **let your face shine on us and we shall be saved.**

1 O shepherd of Israel, hear us,
   shine forth from your cherubim throne.
   O Lord, rouse up your might,
   O Lord, come to our help.

2 God of hosts, turn again, we implore,
   look down from heaven and see.
   Visit this vine and protect it,
   the vine your right hand has planted.

3 May your hand be on the man you have chosen,
   the man you have given your strength.
   And we shall never forsake you again:
   give us life that we may call upon your name.

SECOND READING   *Hebrews 10:5–10*

Here I am! I am coming to obey your will.

This is what Christ said, on coming into the world:

You who wanted no sacrifice or oblation, prepared a body for me. You took no pleasure in holocausts or sacrifices for sin; then I said, just as I was commanded in the scroll of the book, 'God, here I am! I am coming to obey your will.'

Notice that he says first: You did not want what the Law lays down as the things to be offered, that is: the sacrifice, the oblations, the holocausts and the sacrifices for sin, and you took no pleasure in them; and then he says: Here I am! I am coming to obey your will. He is abolishing the first sort to replace it with the second. And this will was for us to be made holy by the offering of his body made once and for all by Jesus Christ.

The word of the Lord.
Thanks be to God.

GOSPEL ACCLAMATION   *Luke 1:38*

Alleluia, alleluia!
I am the handmaid of the Lord:
let what you have said be done to me.
Alleluia!

GOSPEL   *Luke 1:39–45*

The Lord be with you.
And with your spirit.

A reading from the holy Gospel according to Luke.
Glory to you, O Lord.

Why should I be honoured with a visit from the mother of my Lord?

Mary set out and went as quickly as she could to a town in the hill country of Judah. She went into Zechariah's house and greeted Elizabeth. Now as soon as Elizabeth heard Mary's greeting, the child leapt in her womb and Elizabeth was filled with the Holy Spirit. She gave a loud cry and said, 'Of all women you are the most blessed, and blessed is the fruit of your womb. Why should I be honoured with a visit from the mother of my Lord? For the moment your greeting reached my ears, the child in my womb leapt for joy. Yes, blessed is she who believed that the promise made her by the Lord would be fulfilled.'

The Gospel of the Lord.
Praise to you, Lord Jesus Christ.

▷ *page 11*

PRAYER OVER THE OFFERINGS
May the Holy Spirit, O Lord,
sanctify these gifts laid upon your altar,
just as he filled with his power the womb of the Blessed Virgin Mary.
Through Christ our Lord.   **Amen**

▷ *page 15*

Preface II of Advent, p 66.

COMMUNION ANTIPHON   *Isaiah 7:14*
Behold, a Virgin shall conceive and bear a son;
and his name will be called Emmanuel.

▷ *page 58*

PRAYER AFTER COMMUNION
Having received this pledge of eternal redemption,
we pray, almighty God,
that, as the feast day of our salvation draws ever nearer,
so we may press forward all the more eagerly
to the worthy celebration of the mystery of your Son's Nativity.
Who lives and reigns for ever and ever.   **Amen.**

▷ *page 59*

A solemn blessing or prayer over the people may be used.

 # CHRISTMAS TIME

ABOUT THE SEASON

After the annual celebration of the Paschal Mystery, the Church has no more ancient custom than celebrating the memorial of the Nativity of the Lord and of his first manifestations, and this takes place in Christmas Time.

Universal Norms on the Liturgical Year and the Calendar n 39

This solemnity of the Lord's birth [Christmas] celebrates the mystery of the incarnation by which the Word of God humbled himself to share in our humanity, in order that he might enable us to become sharers in his divinity.

Ceremonial of Bishops n 237

The ancient solemnity of the Epiphany of the Lord ranks among the principal festivals of the whole liturgical year, since it celebrates in the child born of Mary the manifestation of the one who is the Son of God, the Messiah of the Jewish people, and a light to the nations.

Ceremonial of Bishops n 240

ABOUT THE READINGS

For the vigil and the three Masses of Christmas both the prophetic readings and the others have been chosen from the Roman tradition.

The Gospel on the Sunday within the octave of Christmas, feast of the Holy Family, is about Jesus' childhood and the other readings are about the virtues of family life.

On the octave of Christmas, solemnity of the Mary, Mother of God, the readings are about the Virgin Mother of God and the giving of the holy Name of Jesus.

On the second Sunday after Christmas, the readings are about the mystery of the Incarnation.

On the Epiphany, the Old Testament reading and the Gospel continue the Roman tradition; the text for the reading from the apostolic letters is about the calling of all peoples to salvation.

On the feast of the Baptism of the Lord, the texts chosen are about this mystery.

Introduction to the Lectionary n 95

COMMON RESPONSORIAL PSALMS FOR CHRISTMAS

COMMON RESPONSE

Today we have seen your glory, O Lord.

COMMON PSALM – SEASON OF CHRISTMAS   *Psalm 97:1–6 Response v 3*

**All the ends of the earth have seen
the salvation of our God.**

1   Sing a new song to the Lord
for he has worked wonders.
His right hand and his holy arm
have brought salvation.

2   The Lord has made known his salvation;
has shown his justice to the nations.
He has remembered his truth and love
for the house of Israel.

3   All the ends of the earth have seen
the salvation of our God.
Shout to the Lord all the earth,
ring out your joy.

4   Sing psalms to the Lord with the harp,
with the sound of music.
With trumpets and the sound of the horn
acclaim the King, the Lord.

COMMON PSALM – EPIPHANY   *Psalm 71:1, 2, 7–8, 10–13 Response cf v 11*

**Before you all kings shall fall prostrate,
all nations shall serve you.**

1   O God, give your judgement to the king,
to a king's son your justice,
that he may judge your people in justice
and your poor in right judgement.

2   In his days justice shall flourish
and peace till the moon fails.
He shall rule from sea to sea,
from the Great River to earth's bounds.

3   The kings of Tarshish and the sea coast
shall pay him tribute.
The kings of Sheba and Seba
shall bring him gifts.
Before him all kings shall fall prostrate,
all nations shall serve him.

continued...

Before you all kings shall fall prostrate,
all nations shall serve you.

4   For he shall save the poor when they cry
and the needy who are helpless.
He will have pity on the weak
and save the lives of the poor.

 ## NATIVITY OF THE LORD — VIGIL MASS

25 DECEMBER
This Mass is used on the evening of 24 December.

ENTRANCE ANTIPHON   *cf Exodus 16:6–7*

Today you will know that the Lord will come, and he will save us,
and in the morning you will see his glory.

▷ *page 7*

COLLECT

O God, who gladden us year by year
as we wait in hope for our redemption,
grant that, just as we joyfully welcome
your Only Begotten Son as our Redeemer,
we may also merit to face him confidently
when he comes again as our Judge.
Who lives and reigns with you in the unity of the Holy Spirit,
one God, for ever and ever.   **Amen.**

FIRST READING   *Isaiah 62:1–5*

The Lord takes delight in you.

About Zion I will not be silent, about Jerusalem I will not grow weary, until her integrity shines out like the dawn and her salvation flames like a torch. The nations then will see your integrity, all the kings your glory, and you will be called by a new name, one which the mouth of the Lord will confer. You are to be a crown of splendour in the hand of the Lord, a princely diadem in the hand of your God; no longer are you to be named 'Forsaken', nor your land 'Abandoned', but you shall be called 'My Delight' and your land 'The Wedded'; for the Lord takes delight in you and your land will have its wedding. Like a young man marrying a virgin, so will the one who built you wed you, and as the bridegroom rejoices in his bride, so will your God rejoice in you.

The word of the Lord.
Thanks be to God.

RESPONSORIAL PSALM   *Psalm 88:4–5, 16–17, 27, 29 response cf v 2*

I will sing for ever of your love, O Lord.

1   'I have made a covenant with my chosen one;
I have sworn to David my servant:
I will establish your dynasty for ever
and set up your throne through all ages.'

2 Happy the people who acclaim such a king,
who walk, O Lord, in the light of your face,
who find their joy every day in your name,
who make your justice the source of their bliss.

3 'He will say to me: "You are my father,
my God, the rock who saves me."
I will keep my love for him always;
for him my covenant shall endure.'

SECOND READING   Acts 13:16–17, 22–25

Paul spoke of Christ, the son of David.

When Paul reached Antioch in Pisidia, he stood up in the synagogue, held up a hand for silence and began to speak: 'Men of Israel, and fearers of God, listen! The God of our nation Israel chose our ancestors, and made our people great when they were living as foreigners in Egypt; then by divine power he led them out. 'Then he made David their king, of whom he approved in these words, "I have selected David son of Jesse, a man after my own heart, who will carry out my whole purpose". To keep his promise, God has raised up for Israel one of David's descendants, Jesus, as Saviour, whose coming was heralded by John when he proclaimed a baptism of repentance for the whole people of Israel. Before John ended his career he said, "I am not the one you imagine me to be; that one is coming after me and I am not fit to undo his sandal".'

The word of the Lord.
Thanks be to God.

GOSPEL ACCLAMATION

Alleluia, alleluia!
**Tomorrow there will be an end to the sin of the world
and the saviour of the world will be our king.**
Alleluia!

GOSPEL   Matthew 1:1–25   *Shorter form (omitting oblique text): Matthew 1:18–25*

The Lord be with you.
And with your spirit.

A reading from the holy Gospel according to Matthew.
Glory to you, O Lord.

The ancestry of Jesus Christ, the son of David.

A genealogy of Jesus Christ, son of David, son of Abraham: Abraham was the father of Isaac, Isaac the father of Jacob, Jacob was the father of Judah and his brothers, Judah was the father of Perez and Zerah, Tamar being their mother, Perez was the father of Hezron, Hezron the father of Ram, Ram was the father of Amminadab, Amminadab the father of Nahshon, Nahshon the father of Salmon, Salmon was the father of Boaz, Rahab being his mother, Boaz was the father of Obed, Ruth being his mother, Obed was the father of Jesse; and Jesse was the father of King David.

David was the father of Solomon, whose mother had been Uriah's wife, Solomon was the father of Rehoboam, Rehoboam the father of Abijah, Abijah the father of Asa, Asa was the father of Jehoshaphat,

CHRISTMAS

Jehoshaphat the father of Joram, Joram the father of Azariah, Azariah was the father of Jotham, Jotham the father of Ahaz, Ahaz the father of Hezekiah, Hezekiah was the father of Manasseh, Manasseh the father of Amon, Amon the father of Josiah; and Josiah was the father of Jechoniah and his brothers. Then the deportation to Babylon took place.

After the deportation to Babylon: Jechoniah was the father to Shealtiel, Shealtiel the father of Zerubbabel, Zerubbabel was the father of Abiud, Abiud the father of Eliakim, Eliakim the father of Azor, Azor was the father of Zadok, Zadok the father of Achim, Achim the father of Eliud, Eliud was the father of Eleazar, Eleazar the father of Matthan; Matthan the father of Jacob; and Jacob was the father of Joseph the husband of Mary; of her was born Jesus who is called Christ.

The sum of generations is therefore: fourteen from Abraham to David; fourteen from David to the Babylonian deportation; and fourteen from the Babylonian deportation to Christ.

This is how Jesus Christ came to be born. His mother Mary was betrothed to Joseph; but before they came to live together she was found to be with child through the Holy Spirit. Her husband Joseph, being a man of honour and wanting to spare her publicity, decided to divorce her informally. He had made up his mind to do this when the angel of the Lord appeared to him in a dream and said, 'Joseph son of David, do not be afraid to take Mary home as your wife, because she has conceived what is in her by the Holy Spirit. She will give birth to a son and you must name him Jesus, because he is the one who is to save his people from their sins.' Now all this took place to fulfil the words spoken by the Lord through the prophet:

The Virgin will conceive and give birth to a son and they will call him Emmanuel, a name which means 'God-is-with-us'.

When Joseph woke up he did what the angel of the Lord told him to do: he took his wife to his home and, though he had not had intercourse with her, she gave birth to a son; and he named him Jesus.

The Gospel of the Lord.
Praise to you, Lord Jesus Christ.

▷ *page 11*

PROFESSION OF FAITH
All kneel at the words 'and by the Holy Spirit was incarnate.'

PRAYER OVER THE OFFERINGS
As we look forward, O Lord,
to the coming festivities,
may we serve you all the more eagerly
for knowing that in them
you make manifest the beginnings of our redemption.
Through Christ our Lord. **Amen**

▷ *page 15*

Preface I, II or III of the Nativity of the Lord, pp 66–67.

When the Roman Canon is used, the proper form of the Communicantes (In communion with those) is said, p 19.

COMMUNION ANTIPHON *cf Isaiah 40:5*
The glory of the Lord will be revealed,
and all flesh will see the salvation of our God.

▷ *page 58*

PRAYER AFTER COMMUNION

Grant, O Lord, we pray,
that we may draw new vigour
from celebrating the Nativity of your Only Begotten Son,
by whose heavenly mystery we receive both food and drink.
Who lives and reigns for ever and ever. **Amen.**

▷ *page 59*

A solemn blessing or prayer over the people may be used.

NATIVITY OF THE LORD — MASS DURING THE NIGHT

25 DECEMBER

ENTRANCE ANTIPHON *Psalm 2:7*

The Lord said to me: You are my Son.
It is I who have begotten you this day.

or

Let us all rejoice in the Lord, for our Saviour has been born in the world.
Today true peace has come down to us from heaven.

▷ *page 7*

COLLECT

O God, who have made this most sacred night
radiant with the splendour of the true light,
grant, we pray, that we, who have known the mysteries of his light on earth,
may also delight in his gladness in heaven.
Who lives and reigns with you in the unity of the Holy Spirit,
one God, for ever and ever. **Amen.**

FIRST READING *Isaiah 9:1–7*

A Son is given to us.

The people that walked in darkness has seen a great light; on those who live in a land of deep shadow a light has shone. You have made their gladness greater, you have made their joy increase; they rejoice in your presence as men rejoice at harvest time, as men are happy when they are dividing the spoils. For the yoke that was weighing on him, the bar across his shoulders, the rod of his oppressor, these you break as on the day of Midian. For all the footgear of battle, every cloak rolled in blood, is burnt, and consumed by fire. For there is a child born for us, a son given to us and dominion is laid on his shoulders; and this is the name they give him: Wonder-Counsellor, Mighty-God, Eternal-Father, Prince-of-Peace. Wide is his dominion in a peace that has no end, for the throne of David and for his royal power, which he establishes and makes secure in justice and integrity. From this time onwards and for ever, the jealous love of the Lord of hosts will do this.

The word of the Lord.
Thanks be to God.

RESPONSORIAL PSALM   *Psalm 95:1–3, 11–13 response Luke 2:11*

**Today a saviour has been born to us;
he is Christ the Lord.**

1   O sing a new song to the Lord,
    sing to the Lord all the earth.
    O sing to the Lord, bless his name.

2   Proclaim his help day by day,
    tell among the nations his glory
    and his wonders among all the peoples.

3   Let the heavens rejoice and earth be glad,
    let the sea and all within it thunder praise,
    let the land and all it bears rejoice,
    all the trees of the wood shout for joy
    at the presence of the Lord for he comes,
    he comes to rule the earth.

4   With justice he will rule the world,
    he will judge the peoples with his truth.

SECOND READING   *Titus 2:11–14*

God's grace has been revealed to the whole human race.

God's grace has been revealed, and it has made salvation possible for the whole human race and taught us that what we have to do is to give up everything that does not lead to God, and all our worldly ambitions; we must be self-restrained and live good and religious lives here in this present world, while we are waiting in hope for the blessing which will come with the Appearing of the glory of our great God and saviour Christ Jesus. He sacrificed himself for us in order to set us free from all wickedness and to purify a people so that it could be his very own and would have no ambition except to do good.

The word of the Lord.
Thanks be to God.

GOSPEL ACCLAMATION   *Luke 2:10–11*

**Alleluia, alleluia!
I bring you news of great joy:
Today a saviour has been born to us, Christ the Lord.
Alleluia!**

GOSPEL   *Luke 2:1–14*

The Lord be with you.
And with your spirit.

A reading from the holy Gospel according to Luke.
Glory to you, O Lord.

Today a saviour has been born to you.

Caesar Augustus issued a decree for a census of the whole world to be taken. This census – the first – took place while Quirinius was governor of Syria, and everyone went to his own town to be registered. So Joseph set out from the town of Nazareth in Galilee and travelled up to Judaea, to the town of David called Bethlehem, since he was of David's House and line, in order to be registered together with Mary, his betrothed, who was with child. While they were there the time came for her to have her child, and she gave birth to a son, her first-born. She wrapped him in swaddling clothes, and laid him in a manger because there was no room for them at the inn. In the countryside close by there were shepherds who lived in the fields and took it in turns to watch their flocks during the night.

The angel of the Lord appeared to them and the glory of the Lord shone round them. They were terrified, but the angel said, 'Do not be afraid. Listen, I bring you news of great joy, a joy to be shared by the whole people. Today in the town of David a saviour has been born to you; he is Christ the Lord. And here is a sign for you: you will find a baby wrapped in swaddling clothes and lying in a manger.' And suddenly with the angel there was a great throng of the heavenly host, praising God and singing:
'Glory to God in the highest heaven, and peace to men who enjoy his favour'.
The Gospel of the Lord.
Praise to you, Lord Jesus Christ.

▷ page 11

PROFESSION OF FAITH
All kneel at the words: 'and by the Holy Spirit was incarnate.'

PRAYER OVER THE OFFERINGS
May the oblation of this day's feast
be pleasing to you, O Lord, we pray,
that through this most holy exchange
we may be found in the likeness of Christ,
in whom our nature is united to you.
Who lives and reigns for ever and ever. **Amen**

▷ page 15

Preface I, II or III of the Nativity of the Lord, pp 66–67.

When the Roman Canon is used, the proper form of the Communicantes (In communion with those) is said, p 19.

COMMUNION ANTIPHON   *John 1:14*
The Word became flesh, and we have seen his glory.

▷ page 58

PRAYER AFTER COMMUNION
Grant us, we pray, O Lord our God,
that we, who are gladdened by participation
in the feast of our Redeemer's Nativity,
may through an honourable way of life become worthy of union with him.
Who lives and reigns for ever and ever. **Amen.**

▷ page 59

A solemn blessing or prayer over the people may be used.

CHRISTMAS

NATIVITY OF THE LORD — MASS AT DAWN

25 DECEMBER

ENTRANCE ANTIPHON *cf Isaiah 9:1, 5; Luke 1:33*

Today a light will shine upon us, for the Lord is born for us;
and he will be called Wondrous God,
Prince of peace, Father of future ages:
and his reign will be without end.

▷ *page 7*

COLLECT

Grant, we pray, almighty God,
that, as we are bathed in the new radiance of your incarnate Word,
the light of faith, which illumines our minds,
may also shine through in our deeds.
Through our Lord Jesus Christ, your Son,
who lives and reigns with you in the unity of the Holy Spirit,
one God, for ever and ever.   **Amen.**

FIRST READING *Isaiah 62:11–12*

Look, your saviour comes.

This the Lord proclaims to the ends of the earth: Say to the daughter of Zion, 'Look, your saviour comes, the prize of his victory with him, his trophies before him'. They shall be called 'The Holy People', 'The Lord's Redeemed'. And you shall be called 'The-sought-after', 'City-not-forsaken'.

The word of the Lord.
Thanks be to God.

RESPONSORIAL PSALM *Psalm 96:1, 6, 11–12*

**This day new light will shine upon the earth:
the Lord is born for us.**

1 The Lord is king, let earth rejoice
   the many coastlands be glad.
   The skies proclaim his justice;
   all peoples see his glory.

2 Light shines forth for the just
   and joy for the upright of heart.
   Rejoice, you just, in the Lord;
   give glory to his holy name.

SECOND READING *Titus 3:4–7*

It was for no reason except his own compassion that he saved us.

When the kindness and love of God our saviour for mankind were revealed, it was not because he was concerned with any righteous actions we might have done ourselves; it was for no reason except his own compassion that he saved us, by means of the cleansing water of rebirth and by renewing us with the Holy Spirit which he has so generously poured over us through Jesus Christ our saviour. He did this so that we should be justified by his grace, to become heirs looking forward to inheriting eternal life.

The word of the Lord.
Thanks be to God.

GOSPEL ACCLAMATION   *Luke 2:14*

Alleluia, alleluia!
Glory to God in the highest heaven
and peace to men who enjoy his favour.
Alleluia!

GOSPEL   *Luke 2:15–20*

The Lord be with you.
And with your spirit.

A reading from the holy Gospel according to Luke.
Glory to you, O Lord.

The shepherds found Mary and Joseph and the baby.

Now when the angels had gone from them into heaven, the shepherds said to one another, 'Let us go to Bethlehem and see this thing that has happened which the Lord has made known to us.' So they hurried away and found Mary and Joseph, and the baby lying in the manger. When they saw the child they repeated what they had been told about him, and everyone who heard it was astonished at what the shepherds had to say. As for Mary, she treasured all these things and pondered them in her heart. And the shepherds went back glorifying and praising God for all they had heard and seen; it was exactly as they had been told.

The Gospel of the Lord.
Praise to you, Lord Jesus Christ.

▷ *page 11*

PROFESSION OF FAITH

All kneel at the words: 'and by the Holy Spirit was incarnate.'

PRAYER OVER THE OFFERINGS

May our offerings be worthy, we pray, O Lord,
of the mysteries of the Nativity this day,
that, just as Christ was born a man and also shone forth as God,
so these earthly gifts may confer on us what is divine.
Through Christ our Lord.   Amen

▷ *page 15*

Preface I, II or III of the Nativity of the Lord, pp 66–67.
When the Roman Canon is used, the proper form of the Communicantes (In communion with those) is said, p 19.

COMMUNION ANTIPHON   *cf Zecharaiah 9:9*

Rejoice, O Daughter Sion; lift up praise, Daughter Jerusalem:
Behold, your King will come, the Holy One and Saviour of the world.

▷ *page 58*

PRAYER AFTER COMMUNION

Grant us, Lord, as we honour with joyful devotion
the Nativity of your Son,
that we may come to know with fullness of faith
the hidden depths of this mystery
and to love them ever more and more.
Through Christ our Lord. **Amen.**

▷ *page 59*

A solemn blessing or prayer over the people may be used.

 ## NATIVITY OF THE LORD — MASS DURING THE DAY

25 DECEMBER

ENTRANCE ANTIPHON   *cf Isaiah 9:5*

A child is born for us, and a son is given to us;
his sceptre of power rests upon his shoulder,
and his name will be called Messenger of great counsel.

▷ *page 7*

COLLECT

O God, who wonderfully created the dignity of human nature
and still more wonderfully restored it,
grant, we pray,
that we may share in the divinity of Christ,
who humbled himself to share in our humanity.
Who lives and reigns with you in the unity of the Holy Spirit,
one God, for ever and ever. **Amen.**

FIRST READING   *Isaiah 52:7–10*

All the ends of the earth shall see the salvation of our God.

How beautiful on the mountains, are the feet of one who brings good news, who heralds peace, brings happiness, proclaims salvation, and tells Zion, 'Your God is king!' Listen! Your watchmen raise their voices, they shout for joy together, for they see the Lord face to face, as he returns to Zion. Break into shouts of joy together, you ruins of Jerusalem; for the Lord is consoling his people, redeeming Jerusalem. The Lord bares his holy arm in the sight of all the nations, and all the ends of the earth shall see the salvation of our God.

The word of the Lord.
Thanks be to God.

RESPONSORIAL PSALM   *Psalm 97:1–6 response v 3*

**All the ends of the earth have seen
the salvation of our God.**

1   Sing a new song to the Lord
    for he has worked wonders.
    His right hand and his holy arm
    have brought salvation.

2　The Lord has made known his salvation;
　　has shown his justice to the nations.
　　He has remembered his truth and love
　　for the house of Israel.

3　All the ends of the earth have seen
　　the salvation of our God.
　　Shout to the Lord all the earth,
　　ring out your joy.

4　Sing psalms to the Lord with the harp,
　　with the sound of music.
　　With trumpets and the sound of the horn
　　acclaim the King, the Lord.

SECOND READING　*Hebrews 1:1–6*

God has spoken to us through his Son.

At various times in the past and in various different ways, God spoke to our ancestors through the prophets; but in our own time, the last days, he has spoken to us through his Son, the Son that he has appointed to inherit everything and through whom he made everything there is. He is the radiant light of God's glory and the perfect copy of his nature, sustaining the universe by his powerful command; and now that he has destroyed the defilement of sin, he has gone to take his place in heaven at the right hand of divine Majesty. So he is now as far above the angels as the title which he has inherited is higher than their own name.

God has never said to any angel: You are my Son, today I have become your father; or: I will be a father to him and he a son to me. Again, when he brings the First-born into the world, he says: Let all the angels of God worship him.

The word of the Lord.
Thanks be to God.

GOSPEL ACCLAMATION

Alleluia, alleluia!
A hallowed day has dawned upon us.
Come, you nations, worship the Lord,
for today a great light has shone down upon the earth.
Alleluia!

GOSPEL　*John 1:1–18　Shorter form (omitting oblique text): John 1:1–5, 9–14*

The Lord be with you.
And with your spirit.

A reading from the holy Gospel according to John.
Glory to you, O Lord.

The Word was made flesh, and lived among us.

In the beginning was the Word: the Word was with God and the Word was God. He was with God in the beginning. Through him all things came to be, not one thing had its being but through him. All that came to be had life in him and that life was the light of men, a light that shines in the dark, a light that darkness could not overpower.

A man came, sent by God. His name was John. He came as a witness, as a witness to speak for the light, so that everyone might believe through him. He was not the light, only a witness to speak for the light.

The Word was the true light that enlightens all men; and he was coming into the world. He was in the world that had its being through him, and the world did not know him. He came to his own domain and his own people did not accept him. But to all who did accept him he gave power to become children of God, to all who believe in the name of him who was born not out of human stock or urge of the flesh or will of man but of God himself. The Word was made flesh, he lived among us, and we saw his glory, the glory that is his as the only Son of the Father, full of grace and truth.

John appears as his witness. He proclaims: 'This is the one of whom I said: He who comes after me ranks before me because he existed before me.'

Indeed, from his fullness we have, all of us, received – yes, grace in return for grace, since, though the Law was given through Moses, grace and truth have come through Jesus Christ. No one has ever seen God; it is the only Son, who is nearest to the Father's heart, who has made him known.

The Gospel of the Lord.
Praise to you, Lord Jesus Christ.

▷ *page 11*

PROFESSION OF FAITH
All kneel at the words: 'and by the Holy Spirit was incarnate.'

PRAYER OVER THE OFFERINGS
Make acceptable, O Lord, our oblation on this solemn day,
when you manifested the reconciliation
that makes us wholly pleasing in your sight
and inaugurated for us the fullness of divine worship.
Through Christ our Lord.   **Amen**

▷ *page 15*

Preface I, II or III of the Nativity of the Lord, pp 66–67.
When the Roman Canon is used, the proper form of the Communicantes (In communion with those) is said, p 19.

COMMUNION ANTIPHON   *cf Psalm 97:3*
All the ends of the earth have seen the salvation of our God.

▷ *page 58*

PRAYER AFTER COMMUNION
Grant, O merciful God,
that, just as the Saviour of the world, born this day,
is the author of divine generation for us,
so he may be the giver even of immortality.
Who lives and reigns for ever and ever.   **Amen.**

▷ *page 59*

A solemn blessing or prayer over the people may be used.

HOLY FAMILY OF JESUS, MARY AND JOSEPH

SUNDAY IN THE OCTAVE OF THE NATIVITY OF THE LORD

When the Nativity of the Lord falls on a Sunday, this feast is celebrated
on Friday 30 December, with one reading only before the Gospel.

ENTRANCE ANTIPHON *Luke 2:16*

The shepherds went in haste,
and found Mary and Joseph and the Infant lying in a manger.

▷ *page 7*

COLLECT

O God, who were pleased to give us
the shining example of the Holy Family,
graciously grant that we may imitate them
in practising the virtues of family life and in the bonds of charity,
and so, in the joy of your house,
delight one day in eternal rewards.
Through our Lord Jesus Christ, your Son,
who lives and reigns with you in the unity of the Holy Spirit,
one God, for ever and ever. **Amen.**

There are two options for the readings before the Gospel, either of which may be used.
The first option follows. The alternative readings are found on page 106.

First Option

FIRST READING *Ecclesiasticus 3:2–6, 12–14*

Whoever fears the Lord honours his parents.

The Lord honours the father in his children, and upholds the rights of a mother over her sons. Whoever respects his father is atoning for his sins, he who honours his mother is like someone amassing a fortune. Whoever respects his father will be happy with children of his own, he shall be heard on the day when he prays. Long life comes to him who honours his father, he who sets his mother at ease is showing obedience to the Lord. My son, support your father in his old age, do not grieve him during his life. Even if his mind should fail, show him sympathy, do not despise him in your health and strength; for kindness to a father shall not be forgotten but will serve as reparation for your sins.

The word of the Lord.
Thanks be to God.

RESPONSORIAL PSALM *Psalm 127:1–5 Response cf v 1*

> **O blessed are those who fear the Lord**
> **and walk in his ways!**

1   O blessed are those who fear the Lord
    and walk in his ways!
    By the labour of your hands you shall eat.
    You will be happy and prosper.

continued...

CHRISTMAS

**O blessed are those who fear the Lord
and walk in his ways!**

2 Your wife like a fruitful vine
in the heart of your house;
your children like shoots of the olive,
around your table.

3 Indeed thus shall be blessed
the man who fears the Lord.
May the Lord bless you from Zion
all the days of your life!

SECOND READING   *Colossians 3:12–21*

Family life in the Lord

You are God's chosen race, his saints; he loves you, and you should be clothed in sincere compassion, in kindness and humility; gentleness and patience. Bear with one another; forgive each other as soon as a quarrel begins. The Lord has forgiven you; now you must do the same. Over all these clothes, to keep them together and complete them, put on love. And may the peace of Christ reign in your hearts, because it is for this that you were called together as parts of one body. Always be thankful.

Let the message of Christ, in all its richness, find a home with you. Teach each other, and advise each other, in all wisdom. With gratitude in your hearts sing psalms and hymns and inspired songs to God: and never say or do anything except in the name of the Lord Jesus, giving thanks to God the Father through him.

Wives, give way to your husbands, as you should in the Lord. Husbands, love your wives and treat them with gentleness. Children, be obedient to your parents always, because that is what will please the Lord. Parents, never drive your children to resentment or you will make them feel frustrated.

The word of the Lord.
Thanks be to God.

Alternative readings for use *ad libitum* in Year C

FIRST READING   *1 Samuel 1:20–22, 24–28*

Samuel is made over to the Lord for the whole of his life.

Hannah conceived and gave birth to a son, and called him Samuel, 'since' she said, 'I asked the Lord for him.'

When a year had gone by, the husband Elkanah went up again with all his family to offer the annual sacrifice to the Lord and to fulfil his vow. Hannah, however, did not go up, having said to her husband, 'Not before the child is weaned. Then I will bring him and present him before the Lord and he shall stay there for ever.'

When she had weaned him, she took him up with her together with a three-year-old bull, an ephah of flour and a skin of wine, and she brought him to the temple of the Lord at Shiloh; and the child was with them. They slaughtered the bull and the child's mother came to Eli. She said, 'If you please, my lord. As you live, my lord, I am the woman who stood here beside you, praying to the Lord. This is the child I prayed for, and the Lord granted me what I asked him. Now I make him over to the Lord for the whole of his life. He is made over to the Lord.'

There she left him, for the Lord.

The word of the Lord.
Thanks be to God.

RESPONSORIAL PSALM   *Psalm 83:2–3, 5–6, 9–10 response v 5*

> They are happy who dwell in your house, O Lord.

1 How lovely is your dwelling place,
   Lord, God of hosts.
   My soul is longing and yearning,
   is yearning for the courts of the Lord.
   My heart and my soul ring out their joy
   to God, the living God.

2 They are happy, who dwell in your house,
   for ever singing your praise.
   They are happy, whose strength is in you;
   they walk with ever growing strength.

3 O Lord God of hosts, hear my prayer,
   give ear, O God of Jacob.
   Turn your eyes, O God, our shield,
   look on the face of your anointed.

SECOND READING   *1 John 3:1–2, 21–24*

We are called God's children, and that is what we are.

Think of the love that the Father has lavished on us, by letting us be called God's children; and that is what we are. Because the world refused to acknowledge him, therefore it does not acknowledge us. My dear people, we are already the children of God but what we are to be in the future has not yet been revealed; all we know is, that when it is revealed we shall be like him because we shall see him as he really is.

My dear people, if we cannot be condemned by our own conscience, we need not be afraid in God's presence, and whatever we ask him, we shall receive, because we keep his commandments and live the kind of life that he wants. His commandments are these: that we believe in the name of his Son Jesus Christ and that we love one another as he told us to. Whoever keeps his commandments lives in God and God lives in him. We know that he lives in us by the Spirit that he has given us.

The word of the Lord.
Thanks be to God.

GOSPEL ACCLAMATION   *Colossians 3:15, 16*

> Alleluia, alleluia!
> May the peace of Christ reign in your hearts;
> let the message of Christ find a home with you.
> Alleluia!

or   *cf Acts 16:14*

> Alleluia, alleluia!
> Open our heart, O Lord,
> to accept the words of your Son.
> Alleluia!

CHRISTMAS

GOSPEL   *Luke 2:41–52*

The Lord be with you.
And with your spirit.

A reading from the holy Gospel according to Luke.
Glory to you, O Lord.

Jesus is found by his parents sitting among the doctors.

Every year the parents of Jesus used to go to Jerusalem for the feast of the Passover. When he was twelve years old, they went up for the feast as usual. When they were on their way home after the feast, the boy Jesus stayed behind in Jerusalem without his parents knowing it. They assumed he was with the caravan, and it was only after a day's journey that they went to look for him among their relations and acquaintances. When they failed to find him they went back to Jerusalem looking for him everywhere.

Three days later, they found him in the Temple, sitting among the doctors, listening to them, and asking them questions; and all those who heard him were astounded at his intelligence and his replies. They were overcome when they saw him, and his mother said to him, 'My child, why have you done this to us? See how worried your father and I have been, looking for you.' 'Why were you looking for me?' he replied. 'Did you not know that I must be busy with my Father's affairs?' But they did not understand what he meant.

He then went down with them and came to Nazareth and lived under their authority. His mother stored up all these things in her heart. And Jesus increased in wisdom, in stature, and in favour with God and men.

The Gospel of the Lord.
Praise to you, Lord Jesus Christ.

▷ *page 11*

PROFESSION OF FAITH

The Profession of Faith is said when this feast is celebrated on Sunday.

PRAYER OVER THE OFFERINGS

We offer you, Lord, the sacrifice of conciliation,
humbly asking that,
through the intercession of the Virgin Mother of God and Saint Joseph,
you may establish our families firmly in your grace and your peace.
Through Christ our Lord.   **Amen.**

▷ *page 15*

Preface I, II or III of the Nativity of the Lord, pp 66–67.
When the Roman Canon is used, the proper form of the Communicantes (In communion with those) is said, p 19.

COMMUNION ANTIPHON   *Baruch 3:38*

Our God has appeared on the earth, and lived among us.

▷ *page 58*

PRAYER AFTER COMMUNION
Bring those you refresh with this heavenly Sacrament,
most merciful Father,
to imitate constantly the example of the Holy Family,
so that, after the trials of this world,
we may share their company for ever.
Through Christ our Lord.   **Amen.**

▷ *page 59*

A solemn blessing or prayer over the people may be used.

SOLEMNITY OF MARY, THE HOLY MOTHER OF GOD

1 JANUARY, OCTAVE DAY OF THE NATIVITY OF THE LORD

ENTRANCE ANTIPHON
Hail, Holy Mother, who gave birth to the King,
who rules heaven and earth for ever.
or   *cf Isaiah 9:1, 5; Luke 1:33*

Today a light will shine upon us, for the Lord is born for us;
and he will be called Wondrous God,
Prince of peace, Father of future ages:
and his reign will be without end.

▷ *page 7*

COLLECT
O God, who through the fruitful virginity of Blessed Mary
bestowed on the human race
the grace of eternal salvation,
grant, we pray,
that we may experience the intercession of her,
through whom we were found worthy
to receive the author of life,
our Lord Jesus Christ, your Son.
Who lives and reigns with you in the unity of the Holy Spirit,
one God, for ever and ever.   **Amen.**

FIRST READING   *Numbers 6:22–27*

They are to call down my name on the sons of Israel,
and I will bless them.

The Lord spoke to Moses and said, 'Say this to Aaron and his sons: "This is how you are to bless the sons of Israel. You shall say to them:

May the Lord bless you and keep you.
May the Lord let his face shine on you and be gracious to you. May the Lord uncover his face to you and bring you peace."

This is how they are to call down my name on the sons of Israel, and I will bless them.'

The word of the Lord.
Thanks be to God.

CHRISTMAS

RESPONSORIAL PSALM   *Psalm 66:2–3, 5, 6, 8 response v 2*

O God, be gracious and bless us.

1   God, be gracious and bless us
     and let your face shed its light upon us.
     So will your ways be known upon earth
     and all nations learn your saving help.

2   Let the nations be glad and exult
     for you rule the world with justice.
     With fairness you rule the peoples,
     you guide the nations on earth.

3   Let the peoples praise you, O God;
     let all the peoples praise you.
     May God still give us his blessing
     till the ends of the earth revere him.

SECOND READING   *Galatians 4:4–7*

God sent his Son born of a woman.

When the appointed time came, God sent his Son, born of a woman, born a subject of the Law, to redeem the subjects of the Law and to enable us to be adopted as sons. The proof that you are sons is that God has sent the Spirit of his Son into our hearts: the Spirit that cries, 'Abba, Father,' and it is this that makes you a son, you are not a slave any more; and if God has made you son, then he has made you heir.

The word of the Lord.
Thanks be to God.

GOSPEL ACCLAMATION   *Hebrews 1:1–2*

**Alleluia, alleluia!
At various times in the past
and in various different ways,
God spoke to our ancestors through the prophets;
but in our own time, the last days,
he has spoken to us through his Son.
Alleluia!**

GOSPEL   *Luke 2:16–21*

The Lord be with you.
And with your spirit.

A reading from the holy Gospel according to Luke.
Glory to you, O Lord.

They found Mary and Joseph and the baby... When the eighth day came, they gave him the name Jesus.

The shepherds hurried away to Bethlehem and found Mary and Joseph, and the baby lying in the manger. When they saw the child they repeated what they had been told about him, and everyone who heard it was astonished at what the shepherds had to say. As for Mary, she treasured all these things and pondered them in her heart. And the shepherds went back glorifying and praising God for all they had heard and seen; it was exactly as they had been told. When the eighth day came and the child was to be circumcised they gave him the name Jesus, the name the angel had given him before his conception.

The Gospel of the Lord.
Praise to you, Lord Jesus Christ.

▷ *page 11*

PRAYER OVER THE OFFERINGS

O God, who in your kindness begin all good things
and bring them to fulfilment,
grant to us, who find joy in the Solemnity of the holy Mother of God,
that, just as we glory in the beginnings of your grace,
so one day we may rejoice in its completion.
Through Christ our Lord.   **Amen.**

▷ *page 15*

Preface I of the Blessed Virgin Mary (on the Solemnity of the Motherhood), p 53.
When the Roman Canon is used, the proper form of the Communicantes (In communion with those) is said, p 19.

COMMUNION ANTIPHON   *Hebrews 13:8*

Jesus Christ is the same yesterday, today, and for ever.

▷ *page 58*

PRAYER AFTER COMMUNION

We have received this heavenly Sacrament with joy, O Lord:
grant, we pray,
that it may lead us to eternal life,
for we rejoice to proclaim the blessed ever-Virgin Mary
Mother of your Son and Mother of the Church.
Through Christ our Lord.   **Amen.**

▷ *page 59*

A solemn blessing or prayer over the people may be used.

CHRISTMAS

SECOND SUNDAY AFTER THE NATIVITY

ENTRANCE ANTIPHON   *Wisdom 18:14–15*

When a profound silence covered all things
and night was in the middle of its course,
your all-powerful Word, O Lord,
bounded from heaven's royal throne.

▷ *page 7*

COLLECT

Almighty ever-living God,
splendour of faithful souls,
graciously be pleased to fill the world with your glory,
and show yourself to all peoples by the radiance of your light.
Through our Lord Jesus Christ, your Son,
who lives and reigns with you in the unity of the Holy Spirit,
one God, for ever and ever.   **Amen.**

FIRST READING   *Ecclesiasticus 24:1–2, 8–12*

The wisdom of God has pitched her tent among the chosen people.

Wisdom speaks her own praises, in the midst of her people she glories in herself.

She opens her mouth in the assembly of the Most High, she glories in herself in the presence of the Mighty One;

'Then the creator of all things instructed me, and he who created me fixed a place for my tent. He said, "Pitch your tent in Jacob, make Israel your inheritance." From eternity, in the beginning, he created me, and for eternity I shall remain. I ministered before him in the holy tabernacle, and thus was I established on Zion. In the beloved city he has given me rest, and in Jerusalem I wield my authority. I have taken root in a privileged people, in the Lord's property, in his inheritance.'

The word of the Lord.
Thanks be to God.

RESPONSORIAL PSALM   *Psalm 147:12–15, 19–20 response John 1:14*

The Word was made flesh,   or   **Alleluia!** *(may be repeated two or three times)*
and lived among us.

1   O praise the Lord, Jerusalem!
    Zion praise your God!
    He has strengthened the bars of your gates,
    he has blessed the children within you.

2   He established peace on your borders,
    he feeds you with finest wheat.
    He sends out his word to the earth
    and swiftly runs his command.

3   He makes his word known to Jacob
    to Israel his laws and decrees.
    He has not dealt thus with other nations;
    he has not taught them his decrees.

SECOND READING   *Ephesians 1:3–6, 15–18*

He determined that we should become his adopted sons through Jesus.

Blessed be God the Father of our Lord Jesus Christ, who has blessed us with all the spiritual blessings of heaven in Christ. Before the world was made, he chose us, chose us in Christ, to be holy and spotless, and to live through love in his presence, determining that we should become his adopted sons, through Jesus Christ, for his own kind purposes, to make us praise the glory of his grace, his free gift to us in the Beloved.

That will explain why I, having once heard about your faith in the Lord Jesus, and the love that you show towards all the saints, have never failed to remember you in my prayers and to thank God for you. May the God of our Lord Jesus Christ, the Father of glory, give you a spirit of wisdom and perception of what is revealed, to bring you to full knowledge of him. May he enlighten the eyes of your mind so that you can see what hope his call holds for you, what rich glories he has promised the saints will inherit.

The word of the Lord.
Thanks be to God.

GOSPEL ACCLAMATION   *cf 1 Timothy 3:16*

Alleluia, alleluia!
Glory be to you, O Christ, proclaimed to the pagans;
Glory be to you, O Christ, believed in by the world.
Alleluia!

GOSPEL   *John 1:1–18   Shorter form (omitting oblique text): John 1:1–5, 9–14*

The Lord be with you.
And with your spirit.

A reading from the holy Gospel according to John.
Glory to you, O Lord.

The Word was made flesh, and lived among us.

In the beginning was the Word: the Word was with God and the Word was God. He was with God in the beginning. Through him all things came to be, not one thing had its being but through him. All that came to be had life in him and that life was the light of men, a light that shines in the dark, a light that darkness could not overpower.

A man came, sent by God. His name was John. He came as a witness, as a witness to speak for the light, so that every one might believe through him. He was not the light, only a witness to speak for the light.

The Word was the true light that enlightens all men; and he was coming into the world. He was in the world that had its being through him, and the world did not know him. He came to his own domain and his own people did not accept him. But to all who did accept him he gave power to become children of God, to all who believe in the name of him who was born not out of human stock or urge of the flesh or will of man but of God himself. The Word was made flesh, he lived among us, and we saw his glory, the glory that is his as the only Son of the Father, full of grace and truth.

John appears as his witness. He proclaims: 'This is the one of whom I said: He who comes after me ranks before me because he existed before me.'

Indeed, from his fullness we have, all of us, received – yes, grace in return for grace, since, though the Law was given through Moses, grace and truth have come through Jesus Christ. No one has ever seen God; it is the only Son, who is nearest to the Father's heart, who has made him known.

The Gospel of the Lord.
Praise to you, Lord Jesus Christ.

▷ page 11

PRAYER OVER THE OFFERINGS
Sanctify, O Lord, the offerings we make
on the Nativity of your Only Begotten Son,
for by it you show us the way of truth
and promise the life of the heavenly Kingdom.
Through Christ our Lord. **Amen**

▷ page 15

Preface I, II or III of the Nativity of the Lord, pp 66–67.

COMMUNION ANTIPHON   *cf John 1:12*
To all who would accept him,
he gave the power to become children of God.

▷ page 58

PRAYER AFTER COMMUNION

Lord our God, we humbly ask you,
that, through the working of this mystery,
our offences may be cleansed
and our just desires fulfilled.
Through Christ our Lord.   **Amen.**

▷ *page 59*

A solemn blessing or prayer over the people may be used.

 # EPIPHANY OF THE LORD — VIGIL MASS

6 JANUARY
OR THE SUNDAY BETWEEN 2 JANUARY AND 8 JANUARY
This Mass is used on the evening of the day before the Solemnity.

ENTRANCE ANTIPHON   *cf Baruch 5:5*

Arise, Jerusalem, and look to the East
and see your children gathered from the rising to the setting of the sun.

▷ *page 7*

COLLECT

May the splendour of your majesty, O Lord, we pray,
shed its light upon our hearts,
that we may pass through the shadows of this world
and reach the brightness of our eternal home.
Through our Lord Jesus Christ, your Son,
who lives and reigns with you in the unity of the Holy Spirit,
one God, for ever and ever.   **Amen.**

LITURGY OF THE WORD

The readings are as for the Mass During the Day (page 115 opposite).

PRAYER OVER THE OFFERINGS

Accept we pray, O Lord, our offerings,
in honour of the appearing of your Only Begotten Son
and the first fruits of the nations,
that to you praise may be rendered
and eternal salvation be ours.
Through Christ our Lord.   **Amen.**

▷ *page 15*

Preface of the Epiphany of the Lord, p 67.

COMMUNION ANTIPHON   *cf Revelation 21:23*

The brightness of God illumined the holy city Jerusalem,
and the nations will walk by its light.

▷ *page 58*

PRAYER AFTER COMMUNION

Renewed by sacred nourishment,
we implore your mercy, O Lord,
that the star of your justice
may shine always bright in our minds
and that our true treasure may ever consist in our confession of you.
Through Christ our Lord. **Amen.**

▷ *page 59*

A solemn blessing or prayer over the people may be used.

EPIPHANY OF THE LORD — MASS DURING THE DAY

6 JANUARY
OR SUNDAY BETWEEN 2 JANUARY AND 8 JANUARY

CHRISTMAS

ENTRANCE ANTIPHON   *cf Malachi 3:1; 1 Chronicles 29:12*

Behold, the Lord, the Mighty One, has come;
and kingship is in his grasp, and power and dominion.

▷ *page 7*

COLLECT

O God, who on this day
revealed your Only Begotten Son to the nations
by the guidance of a star,
grant in your mercy,
that we, who know you already by faith,
may be brought to behold the beauty of your sublime glory.
Through our Lord Jesus Christ, your Son,
who lives and reigns with you in the unity of the Holy Spirit,
one God, for ever and ever. **Amen.**

FIRST READING   *Isaiah 60:1–6*

Above you the glory of the Lord appears

Arise, shine out, Jerusalem for your light has come, the glory of the Lord is rising on you, though night still covers the earth and darkness the peoples.

Above you the Lord now rises and above you his glory appears. The nations come to your light and kings to your dawning brightness.

Lift up your eyes and look round: all are assembling and coming towards you, your sons from far away and your daughters being tenderly carried.

At this sight you will grow radiant, your heart throbbing and full; since the riches of the sea will flow to you, the wealth of the nations come to you;

camels in throngs will cover you, and dromedaries of Midian and Ephah; everyone in Sheba will come, bringing gold and incense and singing the praise of the Lord.

The word of the Lord.
Thanks be to God.

RESPONSORIAL PSALM *Psalm 71:1–2, 7–8, 10–13 response cf v 11*

All nations shall fall prostrate before you, O Lord.

1 O God, give your judgement to the king,
to a king's son your justice,
that he may judge your people in justice
and your poor in right judgement.

2 In his days justice shall flourish
and peace till the moon fails.
He shall rule from sea to sea,
from the Great River to earth's bounds.

3 The kings of Tarshish and the sea coasts
shall pay him tribute.
The kings of Sheba and Seba
shall bring him gifts.
Before him all kings shall fall prostrate,
all nations shall serve him.

4 For he shall save the poor when they cry
and the needy who are helpless.
He will have pity on the weak
and save the lives of the poor.

SECOND READING *Ephesians 3:2–3, 5–6*

It has now been revealed that pagans share the same inheritance.

You have probably heard how I have been entrusted by God with the grace he meant for you, and that it was a revelation that I was given the knowledge of the mystery. This mystery that has now been revealed through the Spirit to his holy apostles and prophets was unknown to any men in past generations; it means that pagans now share the same inheritance, that they are parts of the same body, and that the same promise has been made to them, in Christ Jesus, through the gospel.

The word of the Lord.
Thanks be to God.

GOSPEL ACCLAMATION *Matthew 2:2*

Alleluia, alleluia!
We saw his star as it rose
and have come to do the Lord homage.
Alleluia!

GOSPEL   *Matthew 2:1–12*

The Lord be with you.
And with your spirit.

A reading from the holy Gospel according to Matthew.
Glory to you, O Lord.

We saw his star and have come to do the king homage.

After Jesus had been born at Bethlehem in Judaea during the reign of King Herod, some wise men came to Jerusalem from the east. 'Where is the infant king of the Jews?' they asked. 'We saw his star as it rose and have come to do him homage.' When King Herod heard this he was perturbed, and so was the whole of Jerusalem. He called together all the chief priests and the scribes of the people, and enquired of them where the Christ was to be born. 'At Bethlehem in Judaea,' they told him 'for this is what the prophet wrote:

And you, Bethlehem, in the land of Judah, you are by no means least among the leaders of Judah, for out of you will come a leader who will shepherd my people Israel.'

Then Herod summoned the wise men to see him privately. He asked them the exact date on which the star had appeared, and sent them on to Bethlehem. 'Go and find out all about the child,' he said 'and when you have found him, let me know, so that I too may go and do him homage.' Having listened to what the king had to say, they set out. And there in front of them was the star they had seen rising; it went forward and halted over the place where the child was. The sight of the star filled them with delight, and going into the house they saw the child with his mother Mary, and falling to their knees they did him homage. Then, opening their treasures, they offered him gifts of gold and frankincense and myrrh. But they were warned in a dream not to go back to Herod, and returned to their own country by a different way.

The Gospel of the Lord.
Praise to you, Lord Jesus Christ.

▷ *page 11*

PROCLAMATION OF MOVEABLE FEASTS

Where it is the practice, if appropriate, the moveable Feasts of the current year may be proclaimed after the Gospel.

PRAYER OVER THE OFFERINGS

Look with favour, Lord, we pray,
on these gifts of your Church,
in which are offered now not gold or frankincense or myrrh,
but he who by them is proclaimed,
sacrificed and received, Jesus Christ.
Who lives and reigns for ever and ever.   **Amen.**

▷ *page 15*

Preface of the Epiphany of the Lord, p 67.

COMMUNION ANTIPHON   *cf Matthew 2:2*

We have seen his star in the East,
and have come with gifts to adore the Lord.

▷ *page 58*

PRAYER AFTER COMMUNION

Go before us with heavenly light, O Lord,
always and everywhere,
that we may perceive with clear sight
and revere with true affection
the mystery in which you have willed us to participate.
Through Christ our Lord.   **Amen.**

▷ *page 59*

A solemn blessing or prayer over the people may be used.

BAPTISM OF THE LORD

SUNDAY AFTER 6 JANUARY
*If the Solemnity of the Epiphany is celebrated on Sunday 7 or 8 January,
the Feast of the Baptism of the Lord is celebrated on the following day (Monday),
with only one reading before the Gospel.*

ENTRANCE ANTIPHON   *cf Matthew 3:16–17*

After the Lord was baptized, the heavens were opened,
and the Spirit descended upon him like a dove,
and the voice of the Father thundered:
This is my beloved Son, with whom I am well pleased.

▷ *page 7*

COLLECT

Almighty ever-living God,
who, when Christ had been baptized in the River Jordan
and as the Holy Spirit descended upon him,
solemnly declared him your beloved Son,
grant that your children by adoption,
reborn of water and the Holy Spirit,
may always be well pleasing to you.
Through our Lord Jesus Christ, your Son,
who lives and reigns with you in the unity of the Holy Spirit,
one God, for ever and ever.   **Amen.**
or

O God, whose Only Begotten Son
has appeared in our very flesh,
grant, we pray, that we may be inwardly transformed
through him whom we recognize as outwardly like ourselves.
Who lives and reigns with you in the unity of the Holy Spirit,
one God, for ever and ever.   **Amen.**

*There are two options for the readings before the Gospel, either of which may be used.
The first option follows. The alternative readings are found on page 120.*

First Option

FIRST READING   *Isaiah 42:1–4, 6–7*
Here is my servant in whom my soul delights.

Thus says the Lord:

Here is my servant whom I uphold, my chosen one in whom my soul delights. I have endowed him with my spirit that he may bring true justice to the nations.

He does not cry out or shout aloud, or make his voice heard in the streets. He does not break the crushed reed, nor quench the wavering flame.

Faithfully he brings true justice; he will neither waver, nor be crushed until true justice is established on earth, for the islands are awaiting his law.

I, the Lord, have called you to serve the cause of right; I have taken you by the hand and formed you; I have appointed you as covenant of the people and light of the nations, to open the eyes of the blind, to free captives from prison, and those who live in darkness from the dungeon.

The word of the Lord.
Thanks be to God.

RESPONSORIAL PSALM   *Psalm 28:1–4, 9–10, response v 11*

The Lord will bless his people with peace.

1   O give the Lord you sons of God,
    give the Lord glory and power;
    give the Lord the glory of his name.
    Adore the Lord in his holy court.

2   The Lord's voice resounding on the waters,
    the Lord on the immensity of waters;
    the voice of the Lord, full of power,
    the voice of the Lord, full of splendour.

3   The God of glory thunders.
    In his temple they all cry: 'Glory!'
    The Lord sat enthroned over the flood;
    the Lord sits as king for ever.

SECOND READING   *Acts 10:34–38*
God anointed him with the Holy Spirit.

Peter addressed Cornelius and his household: 'The truth I have now come to realise,' he said 'is that God does not have favourites, but that anybody of any nationality who fears God and does what is right is acceptable to him.

'It is true, God sent his word to the people of Israel, and it was to them that the good news of peace was brought by Jesus Christ – but Jesus Christ is Lord of all men. You must have heard about the recent happenings in Judaea; about Jesus of Nazareth and how he began in Galilee, after John had been preaching baptism. God had anointed him with the Holy Spirit and with power, and because God was with him, Jesus went about doing good and curing all who had fallen into the power of the devil.'

The word of the Lord.
Thanks be to God.

CHRISTMAS

Alternative readings for use *ad libitum* in Year C

FIRST READING   *Isaiah 40:1–5, 9–11*

The glory of the Lord shall be revealed and all mankind shall see it.

'Console my people, console them,' says your God. 'Speak to the heart of Jerusalem and call to her that her time of service is ended, that her sin is atoned for, that she has received from the hand of the Lord double punishment for all her crimes.'

A voice cries, 'Prepare in the wilderness a way for the Lord. Make a straight highway for our God across the desert. Let every valley be filled in, every mountain and hill be laid low, let every cliff become a plain, and the ridges a valley: then the glory of the Lord shall be revealed and all mankind shall see it: for the mouth of the Lord has spoken.'

Go up on a high mountain, joyful messenger to Zion. Shout with a loud voice, joyful messenger to Jerusalem. Shout without fear, say to the towns of Judah, 'Here is your God.'

Here is the Lord coming with power, his arm subduing all things to him. The prize of his victory is with him, his trophies all go before him. He is like a shepherd feeding his flock, gathering lambs in his arms, holding them against his breast and leading to their rest the mother ewes.

The word of the Lord.
Thanks be to God.

RESPONSORIAL PSALM   *Psalm 103:1–2, 3–4, 24–25, 27–30 response v 1*

Bless the Lord, my soul!
Lord God, how great you are!

1 Lord God, how great you are,
   clothed in majesty and glory,
   wrapped in light as in a robe!
   You stretch out the heavens like a tent.

2 Above the rains you build your dwelling.
   You make the clouds your chariot,
   you walk on the wings of the wind,
   you make the winds your messengers
   and flashing fire your servants.

3 How many are your works, O Lord!
   In wisdom you have made them all.
   The earth is full of your riches.
   There is the sea, vast and wide,
   with its moving swarms past counting,
   living things great and small.

4 All of these look to you
   to give them their food in due season.
   You give it, they gather it up:
   you open your hand, they have their fill.

5   You take back your spirit, they die,
     returning to the dust from which they came.
     You send forth your spirit, they are created;
     and you renew the face of the earth.

SECOND READING   *Titus 2:11–14; 3:4–7*

He saved us by the cleansing water of rebirth and by renewing us with the Holy Spirit.

God's grace has been revealed, and it has made salvation possible for the whole human race and taught us that what we have to do is to give up everything that does not lead to God, and all our worldly ambitions; we must be self-restrained and live good and religious lives here in this present world, while we are waiting in hope for the blessing which will come with the Appearing of the glory of our great God and saviour Christ Jesus. He sacrificed himself for us in order to set us free from all wickedness and to purify a people so that it could be his very own and would have no ambition except to do good.

When the kindness and love of God our saviour for mankind were revealed, it was not because he was concerned with any righteous actions we might have done ourselves; it was for no reason except his own compassion that he saved us, by means of the cleansing water of rebirth and by renewing us with the Holy Spirit which he has so generously poured over us through Jesus Christ our saviour. He did this so that we should be justified by his grace, to become heirs looking forward to inheriting eternal life.

The word of the Lord.
Thanks be to God.

GOSPEL ACCLAMATION   *cf Mark 9:8*

Alleluia, alleluia!
The heavens opened and the Father's voice resounded:
'This is my Son, the Beloved. Listen to him.'
Alleluia!

or   *cf Luke 3:16*

Alleluia, alleluia!
Someone is coming, said John, someone greater than I.
He will baptise you with the Holy Spirit and with fire.
Alleluia!

GOSPEL   *Luke 3:15–16, 21–22*

The Lord be with you.
And with your spirit.

A reading from the holy Gospel according to Luke.
Glory to you, O Lord.

While Jesus after his own baptism was at prayer, heaven opened.

A feeling of expectancy had grown among the people, who were beginning to think that John might be the Christ, so John declared before them all, 'I baptise you with water, but someone is coming, someone who is more powerful than I am, and I am not fit to undo the strap of his sandals; he will baptise you with the Holy Spirit and fire.'

Now when all the people had been baptised and while Jesus after his own baptism was at prayer, heaven opened and the Holy Spirit descended on him in bodily shape, like a dove. And a voice came from heaven, 'You are my Son, the Beloved; my favour rests on you.'

The Gospel of the Lord.
Praise to you, Lord Jesus Christ.

▷ page 11

PRAYER OVER THE OFFERINGS

Accept, O Lord, the offerings
we have brought to honour the revealing of your beloved Son,
so that the oblation of your faithful
may be transformed into the sacrifice of him
who willed in his compassion
to wash away the sins of the world.
Who lives and reigns for ever and ever.   **Amen.**

▷ page 15

Preface of the Baptism of the Lord, p 68.

COMMUNION ANTIPHON   *John 1:32, 34*

Behold the One of whom John said:
I have seen and testified that this is the Son of God.

▷ page 58

PRAYER AFTER COMMUNION

Nourished with these sacred gifts,
we humbly entreat your mercy, O Lord,
that, faithfully listening to your Only Begotten Son,
we may be your children in name and in truth.
Through Christ our Lord.   **Amen.**

▷ page 59

A solemn blessing or prayer over the people may be used.

ORDINARY TIME

ABOUT THE SEASON

Besides the times of year that have their own distinctive character, there remain in the yearly cycle thirty-three or thirty-four weeks in which no particular aspect of the mystery of Christ is celebrated, but rather the mystery of Christ itself is honoured in its fullness, especially on Sundays. This period is known as Ordinary Time.

Universal Norms on the Liturgical Year and the Calendar n 43

ABOUT THE READINGS

On the Second Sunday of Ordinary Time the gospel continues to centre on the manifestation of the Lord, which Epiphany celebrates through the traditional passage about the wedding feast at Cana and two other passages from John.

Beginning with the Third Sunday, there is a semi-continuous reading of the Synoptic Gospels. This reading is arranged in such a way that as the Lord's life and preaching unfold the teaching proper to each of these Gospels is presented.

This distribution also provides a certain co-ordination between the meaning of each Gospel and the progress of the liturgical year. Thus after Epiphany the readings are on the beginning of the Lord's preaching and they fit in well with Christ's baptism and the first events in which he manifests himself. The liturgical year leads quite naturally to a termination in the eschatological theme proper to the last Sundays, since the chapters of the Synoptics that precede the account of the passion treat this eschatological theme rather extensively.

In the semicontinuous reading of Luke for Year C, the introduction of this Gospel has been prefixed to the first text (that is, on the Third Sunday). This passage expresses the author's intention very beautifully and there seemed to be no better place for it.

Introduction to the Lectionary n 105

ORDINARY

COMMON RESPONSORIAL PSALMS FOR ORDINARY TIME

COMMON RESPONSES

WITH A PSALM OF PRAISE

> **O give thanks to the Lord for he is good.**

or

> **We thank you, Lord, for the wonders of all your creation.**

or

> **O sing a new song to the Lord**

WITH A PSALM OF PETITION

> **The Lord is close to all who call him.**

or

> **Pay heed to us, Lord, and save us.**

or

> **The Lord is compassion and love.**

COMMON PSALM 1 *Psalm 18:8–11 response John 6:68; alternative response John 6:63*

Lord, you have the message of eternal life.

or

Your words, Lord, are spirit and they are life.

1 The law of the Lord is perfect,
it revives the soul.
The rule of the Lord is to be trusted,
it gives wisdom to the simple.

2 The precepts of the Lord are right,
they gladden the heart.
The command of the Lord is clear,
it gives light to the eyes.

3 The fear of the Lord is holy,
abiding for ever.
The decrees of the Lord are truth
and all of them just.

4 They are more to be desired than gold,
than the purest of gold
and sweeter are they than honey,
than honey from the comb.

COMMON PSALM 2 *Psalm 26:1, 4, 13–14 response v 1*

The Lord is my light and my help.

1 The Lord is my light and my help;
whom shall I fear?
The Lord is the stronghold of my life;
before whom shall I shrink?

2 There is one thing I ask of the Lord,
for this I long,
to live in the house of the Lord,
all the days of my life,
to savour the sweetness of the Lord,
to behold his temple.

3 I am sure I shall see the Lord's goodness
in the land of the living.
Hope in him, hold firm and take heart.
Hope in the Lord!

COMMON PSALM 3 *Psalm 33:2–9 response v 2; alternative response v 9*

I will bless the Lord at all times. *or* **Taste and see that the Lord is good.**

1 I will bless the Lord at all times,
his praise always on my lips;
in the Lord my soul shall make its boast.
The humble shall hear and be glad.

2 Glorify the Lord with me.
Together let us praise his name.
I sought the Lord and he answered me;
from all my terrors he set me free.

3 Look towards him and be radiant;
let your faces not be abashed.
This poor man called; the Lord heard him
and rescued him from all his distress.

4 The angel of the Lord is encamped
around those who revere him, to rescue them.
Taste and see that the Lord is good.
He is happy who seeks refuge in him.

COMMON PSALM 4   *Psalm 62:2–6, 8–9 response v 2*

For you my soul is thirsting, O Lord, my God.

1   O God, you are my God, for you I long;
   for you my soul is thirsting.
   My body pines for you
   like a dry, weary land without water.

2   So I gaze on you in the sanctuary
   to see your strength and your glory.
   For your love is better than life,
   my lips will speak your praise.

3   So I will bless you all my life,
   in your name I will lift up my hands.
   My soul shall be filled as with a banquet,
   my mouth shall praise you with joy.

4   For you have been my help;
   in the shadow of your wings I rejoice.
   My soul clings to you;
   your right hand holds me fast.

COMMON PSALM 5   *Psalm 94:1–2, 6–9 response v 8*

O that today you would listen to his voice!
Harden not your hearts.

1   Come, ring out our joy to the Lord;
   hail the rock who saves us.
   Let us come before him, giving thanks,
   with songs let us hail the Lord.

2   Come in; let us bow and bend low,
   let us kneel before the God who made us
   for he is our God and we
   the people who belong to his pasture,
   the flock that is led by his hand.

3   O that today you would listen to his voice!
   'Harden not your hearts as at Meribah,
   as on that day at Massah in the desert
   when your fathers put me to the test;
   when they tried me, though they saw my work.'

COMMON PSALM 6   *Psalm 99:1–2, 3, 5 response v 3*

We are his people, the sheep of his flock.

1   Cry out with joy to the Lord, all the earth.
   Serve the Lord with gladness.
   Come before him, singing for joy.

2   Know that he, the Lord, is God.
   He made us, we belong to him,
   we are his people, the sheep of his flock.

3   Indeed, how good is the Lord,
   eternal his merciful love.
   He is faithful from age to age.

ORDINARY

COMMON PSALM 7   *Psalm 102:1–4, 8, 10, 12–13 response v 8*

The Lord is compassion and love.

1   My soul, give thanks to the Lord,
    all my being, bless his holy name.
    My soul, give thanks to the Lord
    and never forget all his blessings.

2   It is he who forgives all your guilt,
    who heals every one of your ills,
    who redeems your life from the grave,
    who crowns you with love and compassion.

3   The Lord is compassion and love,
    slow to anger and rich in mercy.
    He does not treat us according to our sins
    nor repay us according to our faults.

4   As far as the east is from the west
    so far does he remove our sins.
    As a father has compassion on his sons,
    the Lord has pity on those who fear him.

COMMON PSALM 8   *Psalm 144:1–2, 8–11, 13–14 response v 1*

I will bless your name for ever, O God my King.

1   I will give you glory, O God my King,
    I will bless your name for ever.
    I will bless you day after day
    and praise your name for ever.

2   The Lord is kind and full of compassion,
    slow to anger, abounding in love.
    How good is the Lord to all,
    compassionate to all his creatures.

3   All your creatures shall thank you, O Lord,
    and your friends shall repeat their blessing.
    They shall speak of the glory of your reign
    and declare your might, O God.

4   The Lord is faithful in all his words
    and loving in all his deeds.
    The Lord supports all who fall
    and raises all who are bowed down.

SECOND SUNDAY IN ORDINARY TIME

ENTRANCE ANTIPHON   *Psalm 65:4*

All the earth shall bow down before you, O God,
and shall sing to you,
shall sing to your name, O Most High!

▷ *page 7*

COLLECT

Almighty ever-living God,
who govern all things,
both in heaven and on earth,
mercifully hear the pleading of your people
and bestow your peace on our times.
Through our Lord Jesus Christ, your Son,
who lives and reigns with you in the unity of the Holy Spirit,
one God, for ever and ever. **Amen.**

FIRST READING   *Isaiah 62:1-5*

The bridegroom rejoices in his bride.

About Zion I will not be silent, about Jerusalem I will not grow weary, until her integrity shines out like the dawn and her salvation flames like a torch.

The nations then will see your integrity, all the kings your glory, and you will be called by a new name, one which the mouth of the Lord will confer. You are to be a crown of splendour in the hand of the Lord, a princely diadem in the hand of your God; no longer are you to be named 'Forsaken', nor your land 'Abandoned', but you shall be called 'My Delight' and your land 'The Wedded'; for the Lord takes delight in you and your land will have its wedding. Like a young man marrying a virgin, so will the one who built you wed you, and as the bridegroom rejoices in his bride, so will your God rejoice in you.

The word of the Lord.
Thanks be to God.

ORDINARY

RESPONSORIAL PSALM   *Psalm 95:1-3, 7-10 response v 3*

**Proclaim the wonders of the Lord
among all the peoples.**

1   O sing a new song to the Lord,
    sing to the Lord all the earth.
    O sing to the Lord, bless his name.

2   Proclaim his help day by day,
    tell among the nations his glory
    and his wonders among all the peoples.

3   Give the Lord, you families of peoples,
    give the Lord glory and power,
    give the Lord the glory of his name.

continued...

**Proclaim the wonders of the Lord
among all the peoples.**

4   Worship the Lord in his temple.
    O earth, tremble before him.
    Proclaim to the nations: 'God is king.'
    He will judge the people in fairness.

SECOND READING   *1 Corinthians 12:4–11*

One and the same Spirit, who distributes gifts to different people just as he chooses.

There is a variety of gifts but always the same Spirit; there are all sorts of service to be done, but always to the same Lord; working in all sorts of different ways in different people, it is the same God who is working in all of them. The particular way in which the Spirit is given to each person is for a good purpose. One may have the gift of preaching with wisdom given him by the Spirit; another may have the gift of preaching instruction given him by the same Spirit; and another the gift of faith given by the same Spirit; another again the gift of healing, through this one Spirit; one, the power of miracles; another, prophecy; another the gift of recognising spirits; another the gift of tongues and another the ability to interpret them. All these are the work of one and the same Spirit, who distributes different gifts to different people just as he chooses.

The word of the Lord.
Thanks be to God.

GOSPEL ACCLAMATION   *cf John 6:63, 68*

**Alleluia, alleluia!
Your words are spirit, Lord,
and they are life:
you have the message of eternal life.
Alleluia!**

or   *cf 2 Thess 2:14*

**Alleluia, alleluia!
Through the Good News God called us
to share the glory of our Lord Jesus Christ.
Alleluia!**

GOSPEL   *John 2:1–11*

The Lord be with you.
And with your spirit.

A reading from the holy Gospel according to John.
Glory to you, O Lord.

This was the first of the signs given by Jesus: it was given at Cana in Galilee.

There was a wedding at Cana in Galilee. The mother of Jesus was there, and Jesus and his disciples had also been invited. When they ran out of wine, since the wine provided for the wedding was all finished, the mother of Jesus said to him, 'They have no wine.' Jesus said, 'Woman, why turn to me? My hour has not come yet.' His mother said to the servants, 'Do whatever he tells you.' There were six stone water jugs standing there, meant for the ablutions that are customary among the Jews: each could hold twenty or thirty gallons. Jesus said to the servants, 'Fill the jars with water,' and they filled them to the brim. 'Draw some out now' he told them 'and take it to the steward.' They did this; the steward tasted the water, and it had turned into wine. Having no idea where it came from – only the servants who had drawn the water knew – the steward called the bridegroom and said, 'People generally serve the best wine first, and keep the cheaper sort till the guests have had plenty to drink: but you have kept the best wine till now.'

This was the first of the signs given by Jesus: it was given at Cana in Galilee. He let his glory be seen, and his disciples believed in him.

The Gospel of the Lord.
Praise to you, Lord Jesus Christ.

▷ *page 11*

PRAYER OVER THE OFFERINGS

Grant us, O Lord, we pray,
that we may participate worthily in these mysteries,
for whenever the memorial of this sacrifice is celebrated
the work of our redemption is accomplished.
Through Christ our Lord.   **Amen.**

▷ *page 15*

COMMUNION ANTIPHON   *cf Psalm 22:5*
You have prepared a table before me,
and how precious is the chalice that quenches my thirst.
or   *1 John 4:16*

We have come to know and to believe
in the love that God has for us.

▷ *page 58*

PRAYER AFTER COMMUNION
Pour on us, O Lord, the Spirit of your love,
and in your kindness
make those you have nourished
by this one heavenly Bread
one in mind and heart.
Through Christ our Lord.   **Amen.**

▷ *page 59*

ORDINARY

THIRD SUNDAY IN ORDINARY TIME

ENTRANCE ANTIPHON   *cf Psalm 95:1, 6*
O sing a new song to the Lord;
sing to the Lord, all the earth.
In his presence are majesty and splendour,
strength and honour in his holy place.

▷ *page 7*

COLLECT

Almighty ever-living God,
direct our actions according to your good pleasure,
that in the name of your beloved Son
we may abound in good works.
Through our Lord Jesus Christ, your Son,
who lives and reigns with you in the unity of the Holy Spirit,
one God, for ever and ever.   **Amen.**

FIRST READING   *Nehemiah 8:2–6, 8–10*

Ezra read from the law of God and the people understood what was read.

Ezra the priest brought the Law before the assembly, consisting of men, women, and children old enough to understand. This was the first day of the seventh month. On the square before the Water Gate, in the presence of the men and women, and children old enough to understand, he read from the book from early morning till noon: all the people listened attentively to the Book of the Law.

Ezra the scribe stood on a wooden dais erected for the purpose. In full view of all the people – since he stood higher than all the people – Ezra opened the book; and when he opened it all the people stood up. Then Ezra blessed the Lord, the great God, and all the people raised their hands and answered, 'Amen! Amen!';

then they bowed down and, face to the ground, prostrated themselves before the Lord. And Ezra read from the Law of God, translating and giving the sense, so that the people understood what was read.

Then Nehemiah – His Excellency – and Ezra, priest and scribe (and the Levites who were instructing the people) said to all the people, 'This day is sacred to the Lord your God. Do not be mournful, do not weep.' For the people were all in tears as they listened to the words of the Law.

He then said, 'Go, eat the fat, drink the sweet wine, and send a portion to the man who has nothing prepared ready. For this day is sacred to our Lord. Do not be sad: the joy of the Lord is your stronghold.'

The word of the Lord.
Thanks be to God.

RESPONSORIAL PSALM   *Psalm 18:8–10, 15 response John 6:63*

**Your words are spirit, Lord,
and they are life.**

1 The law of the Lord is perfect,
   it revives the soul.
   The rule of the Lord is to be trusted,
   it gives wisdom to the simple.

2 The precepts of the lord are right,
   they gladden the heart.
   The command of the Lord is clear,
   it gives light to the eyes.

3 The fear of the Lord is holy,
   abiding for ever.
   The decrees of the Lord are truth
   and all of them just.

4 May the spoken words of my mouth,
   the thoughts of my heart,
   win favour in your sight, O Lord,
   my rescuer, my rock!

SECOND READING   *1 Corinthians 12:12–30 Shorter form (omitting oblique text): I Corinthians 12:12–14, 27*

You together are Christ's body; but each of you is a different part of it.

Just as a human body, though it is made up of many parts, is a single unit because

all these parts, though many, make one body, so it is with Christ. In the one

Spirit we were all baptised. Jews as well as Greeks, slaves as well as citizens, and one Spirit was given to us all to drink.

Nor is the body to be identified with any one of its many parts. *If the foot were to say, 'I am not a hand and so I do not belong to the body', would that mean that it stopped being part of the body? If the ear were to say, 'I am not an eye, and so I do not belong to the body', would that mean that it was not a part of the body? If your whole body was just one eye, how would you hear anything? If it was just one ear, how would you smell anything?*

Instead of that, God put all the separate parts into the body on purpose. If all the parts were the same, how could it be a body? As it is, the parts are many but the body is one. The eye cannot say to the hand, 'I do not need you,' nor can the head say to the feet, 'I do not need you.'

What is more, it is precisely the parts of the body that seem to be the weakest which are the indispensable ones; and it is the least honourable parts of the body that we clothe with the greatest care. So our more improper parts get decorated in a way that our more proper parts do not need. God has arranged the body so that more dignity is given to the parts which are without it, and so that there may not be disagreements inside the body, but that each part may be equally concerned for all the others. If one part is hurt, all parts are hurt with it. If one part is given special honour, all parts enjoy it.

Now you together are Christ's body; but each of you is a different part of it. In the Church, God has given the first place to apostles, the second to prophets, the third to teachers; after them, miracles, and after them the gift of healing; helpers, good leaders, those with many languages. Are all of them apostles, or all of them prophets, or all of them teachers? Do they all have the gift of miracles, or all have the gift of healing? Do all speak strange languages, and all interpret them?

The word of the Lord.
Thanks be to God.

GOSPEL ACCLAMATION   *Luke 4:18*

Alleluia, alleluia!
The Lord has sent me to bring the good news to the poor,
to proclaim liberty to captives.
Alleluia!

GOSPEL   *Luke 1:1–4; 4:14–21*

The Lord be with you.
And with your spirit.

A reading from the holy Gospel according to Luke.
Glory to you, O Lord.

This text is being fulfilled today.

Seeing that many others have undertaken to draw up accounts of the events that have taken place among us, exactly as these were handed down to us by those who from the outset were eyewitnesses and ministers of the word, I in my turn, after carefully going over the whole story from the beginning, have decided to write an ordered account for you, Theophilus, so that your Excellency may learn how well founded the teaching is that you have received.

Jesus, with the power of the Spirit in him, returned to Galilee; and his reputation spread throughout the countryside. He taught in their synagogues and everyone praised him.

He came to Nazara, where he had been brought up, and went into the synagogue on the sabbath day as he usually did. He stood up to read, and they handed him the scroll of the prophet Isaiah. Unrolling the scroll he found the place where it is written:

The Spirit of the Lord has been given to me, for he has anointed me. He has sent me to bring the good news to the poor, to proclaim liberty to captives and to the blind new sight, to set the downtrodden free, to proclaim the Lord's year of favour.

He then rolled up the scroll, gave it back to the assistant and sat down. And all eyes in the synagogue were fixed on him. Then he began to speak to them, 'This text is being fulfilled today even as you listen.'

The Gospel of the Lord.
Praise to you, Lord Jesus Christ.

▷ page 11

PRAYER OVER THE OFFERINGS

Accept our offerings, O Lord, we pray,
and in sanctifying them
grant that they may profit us for salvation.
Through Christ our Lord. **Amen.**

▷ page 15

COMMUNION ANTIPHON *cf Psalm 33:6*

Look toward the Lord and be radiant;
let your faces not be abashed.

or *John 8:12*

I am the light of the world, says the Lord;
whoever follows me will not walk in darkness,
but will have the light of life.

▷ page 58

PRAYER AFTER COMMUNION

Grant, we pray, almighty God,
that, receiving the grace
by which you bring us to new life,
we may always glory in your gift.
Through Christ our Lord. **Amen.**

▷ page 59

FOURTH SUNDAY IN ORDINARY TIME

ENTRANCE ANTIPHON *Psalm 105:47*

Save us, O Lord our God!
And gather us from the nations,
to give thanks to your holy name,
and make it our glory to praise you.

▷ page 7

COLLECT

Grant us, Lord our God,
that we may honour you with all our mind,
and love everyone in truth of heart.
Through our Lord Jesus Christ, your Son,
who lives and reigns with you in the unity of the Holy Spirit,
one God, for ever and ever. **Amen.**

FIRST READING   *Jeremiah 1:4–5, 17–19*

I have appointed you as prophet to the nations.

In the days of Josiah, the word of the Lord was addressed to me, saying,

'Before I formed you in the womb I knew you; before you came to birth I consecrated you: I have appointed you as prophet to the nations. So now brace yourself for action. Stand up and tell them all I command you. Do not be dismayed at their presence, or in their presence I will make you dismayed. I, for my part, today will make you into a fortified city, a pillar of iron, and a wall of bronze to confront all this land: the kings of Judah, its princes, its priests and the country people. They will fight against you but shall not overcome you, for I am with you to deliver you – it is the Lord who speaks.'

The word of the Lord.
Thanks be to God.

RESPONSORIAL PSALM   *Psalm 70:1–6, 15, 17 response v 15*

My lips will tell of your help.

1 In you, O Lord, I take refuge:
   let me never be put to shame.
   In your justice rescue me, free me:
   pay heed to me and save me.

2 Be a rock where I can take refuge,
   a mighty stronghold to save me:
   for you are my rock, my stronghold.
   Free me from the hand of the wicked.

3 It is you, O Lord, who are my hope,
   my trust, O Lord, since my youth.
   On you I have leaned from my birth,
   from my mother's womb you have been my help.

4 My lips will tell of your justice
   and day by day of your help.
   O God, you have taught me from my youth
   and I proclaim your wonders still.

SECOND READING   *1 Corinthians 12:31–13:13   Shorter form (omitting oblique text): 1 Corinthians 13:4–13*

There are three things that last: faith, hope and love; and the greatest of these is love.

Be ambitious for the higher gifts. And I am going to show you a way that is better than any of them.

If I have all the eloquence of men or of angels, but speak without love, I am simply a gong booming or a cymbal clashing. If I have the gift of prophecy, understanding all the mysteries there are, and knowing everything, and if I have faith in all its fulness, to move mountains, but without love, then I am nothing at all. If I give away all that I possess, piece by piece, and if I even let them take my body to burn it, but am without love, it will do me no good whatever.

Love is always patient and kind; it is never jealous; love is never boastful or conceited; it is never rude or selfish; it does not take offence, and is not resentful. Love takes no pleasure in other people's sins but delights in the truth; it is always ready to excuse, to trust, to hope, and to endure whatever comes.

Love does not come to an end. But if there are gifts of prophecy, the time will come when they must fail; or the gift of languages, it will not continue for ever; and knowledge – for this, too, the time will come when it must fail. For our knowledge is imperfect and our prophesying is imperfect; but once perfection comes, all imperfect things will disappear. When I was a child, I used to talk like a child, and think like a child, and argue like a child, but now I am a man, all childish ways are put behind me. Now we are seeing a dim reflection in a mirror; but then we shall be seeing face to face. The knowledge that I have now is imperfect; but then I shall know as fully as I am known.

In short, there are three things that last: faith, hope and love; and the greatest of these is love.

The word of the Lord.
Thanks be to God.

GOSPEL ACCLAMATION *John 14:5*

Alleluia, alleluia!
I am the Way, the Truth and the Life, says the Lord;
no one can come to the Father except through me.
Alleluia!

or *Luke 4:18*

Alleluia, alleluia!
The Lord has sent me to bring the good news to the poor,
to proclaim liberty to captives.
Alleluia!

GOSPEL *Luke 4:21–30*

The Lord be with you.
And with your spirit.

A reading from the holy Gospel according to Luke.
Glory to you, O Lord.

Like Elijah and Elisha, Jesus is not sent to the Jews only.

Jesus began to speak in the synagogue, 'This text is being fulfilled today even as you listen.' And he won the approval of all, and they were astonished by the gracious words that came from his lips.

They said, 'This is Joseph's son, surely?' But he replied, 'No doubt you will quote me the saying, "Physician, heal yourself" and tell me, "We have heard all that happened in Capernaum, do the same here in your own countryside."' And he went on, 'I tell you solemnly, no prophet is ever accepted in his own country.

'There were many widows in Israel, I can assure you, in Elijah's day, when heaven remained shut for three years and six months and a great famine raged throughout the land, but Elijah was not sent to any one of these: he was sent to a widow at Zarephath, a Sidonian town.

And in the prophet Elisha's time there were many lepers in Israel, but none of these was cured, except the Syrian, Naaman.'

When they heard this everyone in the synagogue was enraged. They sprang to their feet and hustled him out of the town; and they took him up to the brow of the hill their town was built on, intending to throw him down the cliff, but he slipped through the crowd and walked away.

The Gospel of the Lord.
Praise to you, Lord Jesus Christ.

▷ *page 11*

PRAYER OVER THE OFFERINGS

O Lord, we bring to your altar
these offerings of our service:
be pleased to receive them, we pray,
and transform them
into the Sacrament of our redemption.
Through Christ our Lord. **Amen.**

▷ *page 15*

COMMUNION ANTIPHON *cf Psalm 30:17–18*

Let your face shine on your servant.
Save me in your merciful love.
O Lord, let me never be put to shame, for I call on you.

or *Matthew 5:3–4*

Blessed are the poor in spirit,
for theirs is the Kingdom of Heaven.
Blessed are the meek, for they shall possess the land.

▷ *page 58*

PRAYER AFTER COMMUNION

Nourished by these redeeming gifts,
we pray, O Lord,
that through this help to eternal salvation
true faith may ever increase.
Through Christ our Lord. **Amen.**

▷ *page 59*

FIFTH SUNDAY IN ORDINARY TIME

ENTRANCE ANTIPHON *Psalm 94:6–7*

O come, let us worship God
and bow low before the God who made us,
for he is the Lord our God.

▷ *page 7*

COLLECT

Keep your family safe, O Lord, with unfailing care,
that, relying solely on the hope of heavenly grace,
they may be defended always by your protection.
Through our Lord Jesus Christ, your Son,
who lives and reigns with you in the unity of the Holy Spirit,
one God, for ever and ever.   **Amen.**

FIRST READING   *Isaiah 6:1–8*

Here I am, send me.

In the year of King Uzziah's death I saw the Lord seated on a high throne; his train filled the sanctuary: above him stood seraphs, each one with six wings.

And they cried out one to another in this way:

'Holy, holy, holy is the Lord of hosts. His glory fills the whole earth.'

The foundations of the threshold shook with the voice of the one who cried out, and the Temple was filled with smoke. I said:

'What a wretched state I am in! I am lost, for I am a man of unclean lips and I live among a people of unclean lips, and my eyes have looked at the King, the Lord of hosts.'

Then one of the seraphs flew to me, holding in his hand a live coal which he had taken from the altar with a pair of tongs. With this he touched my mouth and said:

'See now, this has touched your lips, your sin is taken away, your iniquity is purged.'

Then I heard the voice of the Lord saying:

'Whom shall I send? Who will be our messenger?'

I answered, 'Here I am, send me.'

The word of the Lord.
Thanks be to God.

RESPONSORIAL PSALM   *Psalm 137:1–5, 7–8 response v 1*

Before the angels I will bless you, O Lord.

1   I thank you, Lord, with all my heart,
    you have heard the words of my mouth.
    Before the angels I will bless you.
    I will adore before your holy temple.

2   I thank you for your faithfulness and love
    which excel all we ever knew of you.
    On the day I called, you answered;
    you increased the strength of my soul.

3   All earth's kings shall thank you
    when they hear the words of your mouth.
    They shall sing of the Lord's ways:
    'How great is the glory of the Lord!'

4   You stretch out your hand and save me,
    your hand will do all things for me.
    Your love, O Lord, is eternal,
    discard not the work of your hands.

SECOND READING   *1 Corinthians 15:1–11   Shorter form (omitting oblique text): 1 Corinthians 15:3–8, 11*

I preach what they preach, and this is what you all believed.

Brothers, I want to remind you of the gospel I preached to you, the gospel that you received and in which you are firmly established; because the gospel will save you only if you keep believing exactly what I preached to you – believing anything else will not lead to anything.

Well then, in the first place, I taught you what I had been taught myself, namely that Christ died for our sins, in accordance with the scriptures; that he was buried; and that he was raised to life on the third day, in accordance with the scriptures; that he appeared first to Cephas and secondly to the Twelve. Next he appeared to more than five hundred of the brothers at the same time, most of whom are still alive, though some have died; then he appeared to James, and then to all the apostles; and last of all he appeared to me too; it was as though I was born when no one expected it.

I am the least of the apostles; in fact, since I persecuted the Church of God, I hardly deserve the name apostle; but by God's grace that is what I am, and the grace that he gave me has not been fruitless. On the contrary, I, or rather the grace of God that is with me, have worked harder than any of the others; but what matters is that I preach what they preach, and this is what you all believed.

The word of the Lord.
Thanks be to God.

GOSPEL ACCLAMATION   *John 15:15*

Alleluia, alleluia!
I call you friends, says the Lord,
because I have made known to you
everything I have learnt from my Father.
Alleluia!

or   *Matthew 4:19*

Alleluia, alleluia!
Follow me, says the Lord,
and I will make you fishers of men.
Alleluia!

GOSPEL   *Luke 5:1–11*

The Lord be with you.
And with your spirit.

A reading from the holy Gospel according to Luke.
Glory to you, O Lord.

They left everything and followed him.

Jesus was standing one day by the lake of Gennesaret, with the crowd pressing round him listening to the word of God, when he caught sight of two boats close to the bank. The fishermen had gone out of them and were washing their nets. He got into one of the boats – it was Simon's – and asked him to put out a little from the shore. Then he sat down and taught the crowds from the boat.

When he had finished speaking he said to Simon. 'Put out into deep water and pay out your nets for a catch.' 'Master,' Simon replied, 'we worked hard all night long and caught nothing, but if you say so, I will pay out the nets.' And when they had done this they netted such a huge number of fish that their nets began to tear, so they signalled to their companions in the other boat to come and help them; when these came, they filled the two boats to sinking point.

When Simon Peter saw this he fell at the knees of Jesus saying, 'Leave me, Lord; I am a sinful man.' For he and all his companions were completely overcome by the catch they had made; so also were James and John, sons of, who were Simon's partners. But Jesus said to Simon, 'Do not be afraid; from now on it is men you will catch.' Then, bringing their boats back to land, they left everything and followed him.

The Gospel of the Lord.
Praise to you, Lord Jesus Christ.

▷ page 11

PRAYER OVER THE OFFERINGS

O Lord, our God,
who once established these created things
to sustain us in our frailty,
grant, we pray,
that they may become for us now
the Sacrament of eternal life.
Through Christ our Lord. **Amen.**

▷ page 15

COMMUNION ANTIPHON   cf Psalm 106:8–9

Let them thank the Lord for his mercy,
his wonders for the children of men,
for he satisfies the thirsty soul,
and the hungry he fills with good things.

or   Matthew 5:5–6

Blessed are those who mourn, for they shall be consoled.
Blessed are those who hunger and thirst for righteousness,
for they shall have their fill.

▷ page 58

PRAYER AFTER COMMUNION

O God, who have willed that we be partakers
in the one Bread and the one Chalice,
grant us, we pray, so to live
that, made one in Christ,
we may joyfully bear fruit
for the salvation of the world.
Through Christ our Lord. **Amen.**

▷ page 59

SIXTH SUNDAY IN ORDINARY TIME

ENTRANCE ANTIPHON *cf Psalm 30:3–4*
Be my protector, O God,
a mighty stronghold to save me.
For you are my rock, my stronghold!
Lead me, guide me, for the sake of your name.

▷ *page 7*

COLLECT
O God, who teach us that you abide
in hearts that are just and true,
grant that we may be so fashioned by your grace
as to become a dwelling pleasing to you.
Through our Lord Jesus Christ, your Son,
who lives and reigns with you in the unity of the Holy Spirit,
one God, for ever and ever. **Amen.**

FIRST READING *Jeremiah 17:5–8*

A curse on the man who puts his trust in man, a blessing on the man who puts his trust in the Lord.

The Lord says this: 'A curse on the man who puts his trust in man, who relies on things of flesh, whose heart turns from the Lord. He is like dry scrub in the wastelands: if good comes, he has no eyes for it, he settles in the parched places of the wilderness, a salt land, uninhabited.

'A blessing on the man who puts his trust in the Lord, with the Lord for his hope. He is like a tree by the waterside that thrusts its roots to the stream: when the heat comes it feels no alarm, its foliage stays green: it has no worries in a year of drought, and never ceases to bear fruit.'

The word of the Lord.
Thanks be to God.

ORDINARY

RESPONSORIAL PSALM *Psalm 1:1–4, 6 response Psalm 39:5*

**Happy the man who has placed
his trust in the Lord.**

1 Happy indeed is the man
who follows not the counsel of the wicked:
nor lingers in the way of sinners
nor sits in the company of scorners,
but whose delight is the law of the Lord
and who ponders his law day and night.

2 He is like a tree that is planted
beside the flowing waters,
that yields its fruit in due season
and whose leaves shall never fade:
and all that he does shall prosper.

continued...

**Happy the man who has placed
his trust in the Lord.**

3 Not so are the wicked, not so!
For they like winnowed chaff
shall be driven away by the wind.
For the Lord guards the way of the just
but the way of the wicked leads to doom.

SECOND READING   *1 Corinthians 15:12, 16–20*

It Christ has not been raised, your believing is useless.

If Christ raised from the dead is what has been preached, how can some of you be saying that there is no resurrection of the dead? For if the dead are not raised, Christ has not been raised, and if Christ has not been raised, you are still in your sins. And what is more serious, all who have died in Christ have perished. If our hope in Christ has been for this life only, we are the most unfortunate of all people.

But Christ has in fact been raised from the dead, the first-fruits of all who have fallen asleep.

The word of the Lord.
Thanks be to God.

GOSPEL ACCLAMATION   *cf Matthew 11:25*

**Alleluia, alleluia!
Blessed are you, Father, Lord of heaven and earth,
for revealing the mysteries of the kingdom
to mere children.
Alleluia!**

or *Luke 6:23*

**Alleluia, alleluia!
Rejoice and be glad:
your reward will be great in heaven.
Alleluia!**

GOSPEL   *Luke 6:17, 20–26*

The Lord be with you.
And with your spirit.

A reading from the holy Gospel according to Luke.
Glory to you, O Lord.

How happy are you who are poor. Alas for you who are rich.

Jesus came down with the Twelve and stopped at a piece of level ground where there was a large gathering of his disciples with a great crowd of people from all parts of Judaea and from Jerusalem and from the coastal region of Tyre and Sidon who had come to hear him and to be cured of their diseases.

Then fixing his eyes on his disciples he said:

'How happy are you who are poor: yours is the kingdom of God. Happy you who are hungry now: you shall be satisfied. Happy you who weep now: you shall laugh.

'Happy are you when people hate you, drive you out, abuse you, denounce your name as criminal, on account of the Son of Man. Rejoice when that day comes and dance for joy, for then your reward will be great in heaven. This was the way their ancestors treated the prophets.

'But alas for you who are rich: you are having your consolation now. Alas for you who have your fill now: you shall go hungry. Alas for you who laugh now: you shall mourn and weep.

'Alas for you when the world speaks well of you! This was the way their ancestors treated the false prophets.'

The Gospel of the Lord.
Praise to you, Lord Jesus Christ.

> ▷ *page 11*

PRAYER OVER THE OFFERINGS
May this oblation, O Lord, we pray,
cleanse and renew us
and may it become for those who do your will
the source of eternal reward.
Through Christ our Lord. **Amen.**

> ▷ *page 15*

COMMUNION ANTIPHON   *cf Psalm 77:29–30*
They ate and had their fill,
and what they craved the Lord gave them;
they were not disappointed in what they craved.

or   *John 3:16*

God so loved the world
that he gave his Only Begotten Son,
so that all who believe in him may not perish,
but may have eternal life.

> ▷ *page 58*

PRAYER AFTER COMMUNION
Having fed upon these heavenly delights,
we pray, O Lord,
that we may always long
for that food by which we truly live.
Through Christ our Lord. **Amen.**

> ▷ *page 59*

SEVENTH SUNDAY IN ORDINARY TIME

ENTRANCE ANTIPHON   *Psalm 12:6*
O Lord, I trust in your merciful love.
My heart will rejoice in your salvation.
I will sing to the Lord who has been bountiful with me.

> ▷ *page 7*

ORDINARY

COLLECT
Grant, we pray, almighty God,
that, always pondering spiritual things,
we may carry out in both word and deed
that which is pleasing to you.
Through our Lord Jesus Christ, your Son,
who lives and reigns with you in the unity of the Holy Spirit,
one God, for ever and ever.   **Amen.**

FIRST READING   1 Samuel 26:2, 7–9, 12–13, 22–23

The Lord put you in my power, but I would not raise my hand.

Saul set off and went down to the wilderness of Ziph, accompanied by three thousand men chosen from Israel to search for David in the wilderness of Ziph.

So in the dark David and Abishai made their way towards the force, where they found Saul asleep inside the camp, his spear stuck in the ground beside his head, with Abner and the troops lying round him.

The Abishai said to David, 'Today God has put your enemy in your power; so now let me pin him to the ground with his own spear. Just one stroke! I will not need to strike him twice.' David answered Abishai, 'Do not kill him, for who can lift his hand against the Lord's anointed and be without guilt?' David took the spear and the pitcher of water from beside Saul's head, and they made off. No one saw, no one knew, no one woke up; they were all asleep, for a deep sleep from the Lord had fallen on them.

David crossed to the other side and halted on the top of the mountain a long way off; there was a wide space between them. David then called out, 'Here is the king's spear. Let one of the soldiers come across and take it. The Lord repays everyone for his uprightness and loyalty. Today the Lord put you in my power, but I would not raise my hand against the Lord's anointed.'

The word of the Lord.
Thanks be to God.

RESPONSORIAL PSALM   Psalm 102:1–4, 8, 10, 12–13 response v 8

The Lord is compassion and love.

1 My soul, give thanks to the Lord,
   all my being, bless his holy name.
   My soul, give thanks to the Lord
   and never forget all his blessings.

2 It is he who forgives all your guilt,
   who heals every one of your ills,
   who redeems your life from the grave,
   who crowns you with love and compassion.

3 The Lord is compassion and love,
   slow to anger and rich in mercy.
   He does not treat us according to our sins
   nor repay us according to our faults.

4 As far as the east is from the west
so far does he remove our sins.
As a father has compassion on his sons,
the Lord has pity on those who fear him.

SECOND READING   *1 Corinthians 15:45–49*

We who have been modelled on the earthly man will be modelled on the heavenly man.

The first man, Adam, as scripture says, became a living soul; but the last Adam has become a life-giving spirit. That is, first the one with the soul, not the spirit, and after that, the one with the spirit. The first man, being from the earth, is earthly by nature; the second man is from heaven. As this earthly man was, so are we on earth; and as the heavenly man is, so are we in heaven. And we, who have been modelled on the earthly man, will be modelled on the heavenly man.

The word of the Lord.
Thanks be to God.

GOSPEL ACCLAMATION   *cf Acts 16:14*

Alleluia, alleluia!
Open our heart, O Lord,
to accept the words of your Son.
Alleluia!

or *John 13:34*

Alleluia, alleluia!
I give you a new commandment:
love one another,
just as I have loved you,
says the Lord.
Alleluia!

GOSPEL   *Luke 6:27–38*

The Lord be with you.
And with your spirit.

A reading from the holy Gospel according to Luke.
Glory to you, O Lord.

Be compassionate as your Father is compassionate.

Jesus said to his disciples: 'I say this to you who are listening: Love your enemies, do good to those who hate you, bless those who curse you, pray for those who treat you badly. To the man who slaps you on one cheek, present the other cheek too; to the man who takes your cloak from you, do not refuse your tunic. Give to everyone who asks you, and do not ask for your property back from the man who robs you. Treat others as you would like them to treat you. If you love those who love you, what thanks can you expect? Even sinners love those who love them. And if you do good to those who do good to you, what thanks can you expect? For even sinners do that much. And if you lend to those from whom you hope to receive, what thanks can you expect? Even sinners lend to sinners to get back the same amount. Instead, love your enemies and do good, and lend without any hope of return. You will have a great reward, and you will be sons of the Most High, for he himself is kind to the ungrateful and the wicked.

'Be compassionate as your Father is compassionate. Do not judge, and you will not be judged yourselves; do not condemn, and you will not be condemned yourselves; grant pardon, and you will be pardoned. Give, and there will be gifts for you: a full measure, pressed down, shaken together, and running over, will be poured into your lap; because the amount you measure out is the amount you will be given back.'

The Gospel of the Lord.
Praise to you, Lord Jesus Christ.

▷ *page 11*

PRAYER OVER THE OFFERINGS
As we celebrate your mysteries, O Lord,
with the observance that is your due,
we humbly ask you,
that what we offer to the honour of your majesty
may profit us for salvation.
Through Christ our Lord.　**Amen.**

▷ *page 15*

COMMUNION ANTIPHON　　*Psalm 9:2–3*
I will recount all your wonders,
I will rejoice in you and be glad,
and sing psalms to your name, O Most High.

or　*John 11:27*

Lord, I have come to believe that you are the Christ,
the Son of the living God, who is coming into this world.

▷ *page 58*

PRAYER AFTER COMMUNION
Grant, we pray, almighty God,
that we may experience the effects of the salvation
which is pledged to us by these mysteries.
Through Christ our Lord.　**Amen.**

▷ *page 59*

 ## EIGHTH SUNDAY IN ORDINARY TIME

ENTRANCE ANTIPHON　　*cf Psalm 17:19–20*
The Lord became my protector.
He brought me out to a place of freedom;
he saved me because he delighted in me.

▷ *page 7*

COLLECT
Grant us, O Lord, we pray,
that the course of our world
may be directed by your peaceful rule
and that your Church may rejoice,
untroubled in her devotion.
Through our Lord Jesus Christ, your Son,
who lives and reigns with you in the unity of the Holy Spirit,
one God, for ever and ever.　**Amen.**

FIRST READING   *Ecclesiasticus 27:4–7*

Do not praise a man before he has spoken.

In a shaken sieve the rubbish is left behind, so too the defects of a man appear in his talk. The kiln tests the work of the potter, the test of a man is in his conversation. The orchard where the tree grows is judged on the quality of its fruit, similarly a man's words betray what he feels. Do not praise a man before he has spoken, since this is the test of men.

The word of the Lord.
Thanks be to God.

RESPONSORIAL PSALM   *Psalm 91:2–3, 13–16 response cf v 2*

It is good to give you thanks, O Lord.

1   It is good to give thanks to the Lord
to make music to your name, O Most High,
to proclaim your love in the morning
and your truth in the watches of the night.

2   The just will flourish like the palm-tree
and grow like a Lebanon cedar.

3   Planted in the house of the Lord
they will flourish in the courts of our God
still bearing fruit when they are old,
still full of sap, still green,
to proclaim that the Lord is just.
In him, my rock, there is no wrong.

SECOND READING   *1 Corinthians 15:54–58*

He has given us the victory through our Lord Jesus Christ.

When this perishable nature has put on imperishability, and when this mortal nature has put on immortality, then the words of scripture will come true: Death is swallowed up in victory. Death, where is your victory? Death, where is your sting? Now the sting of death is sin, and sin gets its power from the Law. So let us thank God for giving us the victory through our Lord Jesus Christ.

Never give in then, my dear brothers, never admit defeat; keep on working at the Lord's work always, knowing that, in the Lord, you cannot be labouring in vain.

The word of the Lord.
Thanks be to God.

GOSPEL ACCLAMATION   *cf Acts 16:14*

**Alleluia, alleluia!
Open our heart, O Lord,
to accept the words of your Son.
Alleluia!**

or   *Philippians 2:15–16*

**Alleluia, alleluia!
You will shine in the world like bright stars
because you are offering it the word of life.
Alleluia!**

ORDINARY

GOSPEL   *Luke 6:39–45*

The Lord be with you.
And with your spirit.

A reading from the holy Gospel according to Luke.
Glory to you, O Lord.

A man's words flow out of what fills his heart.

Jesus told a parable to his disciples, 'Can one blind man guide another? Surely both will fall into a pit! The disciple is not superior to his teacher; the fully trained disciple will always be like his teacher. Why do you observe the splinter in your brother's eye and never notice the plank in your own? How can you say to your brother, "Brother let me take out the splinter that is in your eye," when you cannot see the plank in your own? Hypocrite! Take the plank out of your own eye first, and then you will see clearly enough to take out the splinter that is in your brother's eye.

'There is no sound tree that produces rotten fruit, nor again a rotten tree that produces sound fruit. For every tree can be told by its own fruit: people do not pick figs from thorns, nor gather grapes from brambles. A good man draws what is good from the store of goodness in his heart; a bad man draws what is bad from the store of badness. For a man's words flow out of what fills his heart.'

The Gospel of the Lord.
Praise to you, Lord Jesus Christ.

▷ *page 11*

PRAYER OVER THE OFFERINGS

O God, who provide gifts to be offered to your name
and count our oblations as signs
of our desire to serve you with devotion,
we ask of your mercy
that what you grant as the source of merit
may also help us to attain merit's reward.
Through Christ our Lord.   **Amen.**

▷ *page 15*

COMMUNION ANTIPHON   *cf Psalm 12:6*

I will sing to the Lord who has been bountiful with me,
sing psalms to the name of the Lord Most High.

or   *Matthew 28:20*

Behold, I am with you always,
even to the end of the age, says the Lord.

▷ *page 58*

PRAYER AFTER COMMUNION

Nourished by your saving gifts,
we beseech your mercy, Lord,
that by this same Sacrament
with which you feed us in the present age,
you may make us partakers of life eternal.
Through Christ our Lord.   **Amen.**

▷ *page 59*

LENT

ABOUT THE SEASON

The annual observance of Lent is the special season for the ascent to the holy mountain of Easter. Through its twofold theme of repentance and baptism, the season of Lent disposes both the catechumens and the faithful to celebrate the paschal mystery. Catechumens are led to the sacraments of initiation by means of the rite of election, the scrutinies, and catechesis. The faithful, listening more intently to the word of God and devoting themselves to prayer, are prepared through a spirit of repentance to renew their baptismal promises.

Ceremonial of Bishops n 249

ABOUT THE READINGS

The gospel readings are arranged as follows:

The first and second Sundays retain the accounts of the Lord's temptations and transfiguration, with readings, however, from all three Synoptics.

On the next three Sundays, the gospels about the Samaritan woman, the man born blind, and the raising of Lazarus have been restored in Year A. Because these gospels are of major importance in regard to Christian initiation, they may also be read in Year B and Year C, especially in places where there are catechumens.

Other texts, however, are provided for Year B and Year C: for Year B, a text from John about Christ's coming glorification through his cross and resurrection and for Year C, a text from Luke about conversion.

On Passion Sunday (Palm Sunday) the texts for the procession are selections from the Synoptic Gospels concerning the Lord's triumphal entrance into Jerusalem. For the Mass the reading is the account of the Lord's passion.

The Old Testament readings are about the history of salvation, which is one of the themes proper to the catechesis of Lent. The series of texts for each Year presents the main elements of salvation history from its beginning until the promise of the New Covenant.

The readings from the letters of the apostles have been selected to fit the gospel and the Old Testament readings and, to the extent possible, to provide a connection between them.

Introduction to the Lectionary n 97

LENT

COMMON RESPONSORIAL PSALMS FOR LENT

COMMON RESPONSE

Remember, O Lord, your faithfulness and love.

COMMON PSALM 1   *Psalm 50:3–6, 12–14, 17 response v 3*

Have mercy on us, Lord, for we have sinned.

1   Have mercy on me, God, in your kindness.
    In your compassion blot out my offence.
    O wash me more and more from my guilt
    and cleanse me from my sin.

2   My offences truly I know them;
    my sin is always before me.
    Against you, you alone, have I sinned:
    what is evil in your sight I have done.

3   A pure heart create for me, O God,
    put a steadfast spirit within me.
    Do not cast me away from your presence,
    nor deprive me of your holy spirit.

4   Give me again the joy of your help;
    with a spirit of fervour sustain me,
    O Lord, open my lips
    and my mouth shall declare your praise.

COMMON PSALM 2   *Psalm 90:1–2, 10–15 response cf v 15*

Be with me, Lord, in my distress.

1   He who dwells in the shelter of the Most High
    and abides in the shade of the Almighty
    says to the Lord: 'My refuge,
    my stronghold, my God in whom I trust!'

2   Upon you no evil shall fall,
    no plague approach where you dwell.
    For you has he commanded his angels,
    to keep you in all your ways.

3   They shall bear you upon their hands
    lest you strike your foot against a stone.
    On the lion and the viper you will tread
    and trample the young lion and the dragon.

4   His love he set on me, so I will rescue him;
    protect him for he knows my name.
    When he calls I shall answer: 'I am with you.'
    I will save him in distress and give him glory.

COMMON PSALM 3   *Psalm 129 response v 7*

**With the Lord there is mercy
and fullness of redemption.**

1   Out of the depths I cry to you, O Lord,
    Lord, hear my voice!
    O let your ears be attentive
    to the voice of my pleading.

2   If you, O Lord, should mark our guilt,
    Lord, who would survive?
    But with you is found forgiveness:
    for this we revere you.

3   My soul is waiting for the Lord,
    I count on his word.
    My soul is longing for the Lord
    more than watchman for daybreak.
    (Let the watchman count on daybreak
    and Israel on the Lord.)

4   Because with the Lord there is mercy
    and fullness of redemption,
    Israel indeed he will redeem
    from all its iniquity.

GOSPEL ACCLAMATIONS DURING LENT

During Lent, instead of *Alleluia*, one of the following phrases is used both before and after the Gospel Acclamation verse.

Praise to you, O Christ, king of eternal glory!
Praise and honour to you, Lord Jesus!
Glory and praise to you, O Christ!
Glory to you, O Christ, you are the Word of God!

ASH WEDNESDAY

In the course of today's Mass, ashes are blessed and distributed.
These are made from the olive branches or branches of other trees that were blessed the previous year.

INTRODUCTORY RITES

ENTRANCE ANTIPHON   *Wisdom 11:24, 25, 27*
You are merciful to all, O Lord,
and despise nothing that you have made.
You overlook people's sins, to bring them to repentance,
and you spare them, for you are the Lord our God.

The Penitential Act and Gloria are omitted, and the Distribution of Ashes takes its place after the homily.

COLLECT
Grant, O Lord, that we may begin with holy fasting
this campaign of Christian service,
so that, as we take up battle against spiritual evils,
we may be armed with weapons of self-restraint.
Through our Lord Jesus Christ, your Son,
who lives and reigns with you in the unity of the Holy Spirit,
one God, for ever and ever.

LITURGY OF THE WORD

FIRST READING   *Joel 2:12–18*

Let your hearts be broken, not your garments torn.

'Now, now – it is the Lord who speaks – come back to me with all your heart, fasting, weeping, mourning.' Let your hearts be broken, not your garments torn, turn to the Lord your God again, for he is all tenderness and compassion, slow to anger, rich in graciousness, and ready to relent. Who knows if he will not turn again, will not relent, will not leave a blessing as he passes, oblation and libation for the Lord your God? Sound the trumpet in Zion! Order a fast, proclaim a solemn assembly, call the people together, summon the community, assemble the elders, gather the children, even the infants at the breast. Let the bridegroom leave his bedroom and the bride her alcove. Between vestibule and altar let the priests, the ministers of the

Lord, lament. Let them say, 'Spare your people, Lord! Do not make your heritage a thing of shame, a byword for the nations. Why should it be said among the nations, "Where is their God?"'

Then the Lord, jealous on behalf of his land, took pity on his people.

The word of the Lord.
Thanks be to God.

RESPONSORIAL PSALM   *Psalm 50:3–6, 12–14, 17 response v 3*

Have mercy on us, O Lord, for we have sinned.

1   Have mercy on me, God, in your kindness.
     In your compassion blot out my offence.
     O wash me more and more from my guilt
     and cleanse me from my sin.

2   My offences truly I know them;
     my sin is always before me.
     Against you, you alone, have I sinned:
     what is evil in your sight I have done.

3   A pure heart create for me, O God,
     put a steadfast spirit within me.
     Do not cast me away from your presence,
     nor deprive me of your holy spirit.

4   Give me again the joy of your help;
     with a spirit of fervour sustain me,
     O Lord, open my lips
     and my mouth shall declare your praise.

SECOND READING   *2 Corinthians 5:20–6:2*

Be reconciled to God... now is the favourable time.

We are ambassadors for Christ; it is as though God were appealing through us, and the appeal that we make in Christ's name is: be reconciled to God. For our sake God made the sinless one into sin, so that in him we might become the goodness of God. As his fellow workers, we beg you once again not to neglect the grace of God that you have received. For he says: At the favourable time, I have listened to you; on the day of salvation I came to your help. Well, now is the favourable time; this is the day of salvation.

The word of the Lord.
Thanks be to God.

GOSPEL ACCLAMATION   *Psalm 50:12, 14*

**Praise to you, O Christ, king of eternal glory!
A pure heart create for me, O God,
and give me again the joy of your help.
Praise to you, O Christ, king of eternal glory!**

or   cf Psalm 94:8

**Praise to you, O Christ, king of eternal glory!
Harden not your hearts today,
but listen to the voice of the Lord.
Praise to you, O Christ, king of eternal glory!**

GOSPEL   *Matthew 6:1–6, 16–18*

The Lord be with you.
And with your spirit.

A reading from the holy Gospel according to Matthew.
Glory to you, O Lord.

Your Father who sees all that is done in secret will reward you.

Jesus said to his disciples: 'Be careful not to parade your good deeds before men to attract their notice; by doing this you will lose all reward from your Father in heaven. So when you give alms, do not have it trumpeted before you; this is what the hypocrites do in the synagogues and in the streets to win men's admiration. I tell you solemnly, they have had their reward. But when you give alms, your left hand must not know what your right is doing; your almsgiving must be secret, and your Father who sees all that is done in secret will reward you.

'And when you pray, do not imitate the hypocrites: they love to say their prayers standing up in the synagogues and at the street corners for people to see them. I tell you solemnly, they have had their reward. But when you pray, go to your private room and, when you have shut your door, pray to your Father who is in that secret place, and your Father who sees all that is done in secret will reward you.

'When you fast do not put on a gloomy look as the hypocrites do: they pull long faces to let men know they are fasting. I tell you solemnly, they have had their reward. But when you fast, put oil on your head and wash your face, so that no one will know you are fasting except your Father who sees all that is done in secret; and your Father who sees all that is done in secret will reward you.'

The Gospel of the Lord.
Praise to you, Lord Jesus Christ.

HOMILY

BLESSING AND DISTRIBUTION OF ASHES

After the Homily, the Priest says:

Dear brethren (brothers and sisters), let us humbly ask God our Father
that he be pleased to bless with the abundance of his grace
these ashes, which we will put on our heads in penitence.

After a brief prayer in silence he continues:

O God, who are moved by acts of humility
and respond with forgiveness to works of penance,
lend your merciful ear to our prayers
and in your kindness pour out the grace of your ✠ blessing
on your servants who are marked with these ashes,
that, as they follow the Lenten observances,
they may be worthy to come with minds made pure
to celebrate the Paschal Mystery of your Son.
Through Christ our Lord.   **Amen.**

An alternative prayer is given overleaf.

or

O God, who desire not the death of sinners,
but their conversion,
mercifully hear our prayers
and in your kindness be pleased to bless ✠ these ashes,
which we intend to receive upon our heads,
that we, who acknowledge we are but ashes
and shall return to dust,
may, through a steadfast observance of Lent,
gain pardon for sins and newness of life
after the likeness of your Risen Son.
Who lives and reigns for ever and ever.   **Amen.**

He sprinkles the ashes with holy water.

All who wish to receive ashes then come forward. As the Priest places ashes on the head each person, he says:

or
　　　　　Repent, and believe in the Gospel.

　　　　　Remember that you are dust, and to dust you shall return.

Meanwhile, the following, or other appropriate chant(s) are sung:

ANTIPHON 1
Let us change our garments to sackcloth and ashes,
let us fast and weep before the Lord,
that our God, rich in mercy, might forgive us our sins.

ANTIPHON 2   *cf Joel 2:17; Esther 4:17*
Let the priests, the ministers of the Lord,
stand between the porch and the altar and weep and cry out:
Spare, O Lord, spare your people;
do not close the mouths of those who sing your praise, O Lord.

ANTIPHON 3   *Psalm 50:3*
Blot out my transgressions, O Lord.
This may be repeated after each verse of Psalm 50 (Have mercy on me, O God).

RESPONSORY   *cf Baruch 3:2; Psalm 78:9*
R　　　Let us correct our faults which we have committed in ignorance, let us not
　　　　be taken unawares by the day of our death, looking in vain for leisure to repent.
　　　　* Hear us, O Lord, and show us your mercy, for we have sinned against you.
V　　　Help us, O God our Saviour; for the sake of your name, O Lord, set us free.
　　　　* Hear us, O Lord...

The Profession of Faith is not said and the Mass continues with the Prayer of the Faithful. ▷ page 13

PRAYER OVER THE OFFERINGS
As we solemnly offer
the annual sacrifice for the beginning of Lent,
we entreat you, O Lord,
that, through works of penance and charity,
we may turn away from harmful pleasures
and, cleansed from our sins, may become worthy
to celebrate devoutly the Passion of your Son.
Who lives and reigns for ever and ever. **Amen.** ▷ page 15

Preface III or IV of Lent, p 71.

COMMUNION ANTIPHON   *cf Psalm 1:2–3*
He who ponders the law of the Lord day and night
will yield fruit in due season.

▷ *page 58*

PRAYER AFTER COMMUNION
May the Sacrament we have received sustain us, O Lord,
that our Lenten fast may be pleasing to you
and be for us a healing remedy.
Through Christ our Lord.   **Amen.**

▷ *page 59*

PRAYER OVER THE PEOPLE
For the dismissal, the Priest stands facing the people and, extending his hands over them, says this prayer:

Pour out a spirit of compunction, O God,
on those who bow before your majesty,
and by your mercy may they merit the rewards you promise
to those who do penance.
Through Christ our Lord. **Amen.**

FIRST SUNDAY OF LENT

ENTRANCE ANTIPHON   *cf Psalm 90:15–16*
When he calls on me, I will answer him;
I will deliver him and give him glory,
I will grant him length of days.

▷ *page 7*

The Gloria is omitted.

COLLECT
Grant, almighty God,
through the yearly observances of holy Lent,
that we may grow in understanding
of the riches hidden in Christ
and by worthy conduct pursue their effects.
Through our Lord Jesus Christ, your Son,
who lives and reigns with you in the unity of the Holy Spirit,
one God, for ever and ever.   **Amen.**

FIRST READING   *Deuteronomy 26:4–10*
The creed of the chosen people.

Moses said to the people: 'The priest shall take the pannier from your hand and lay it before the altar of the Lord your God. Then, in the sight of the Lord your God, you must make this pronouncement: "My father was a wandering Aramaean. He went down into Egypt to find refuge there, few in numbers; but there he became a nation, great, mighty, and strong. The Egyptians ill-treated us, they gave us no peace and inflicted harsh slavery on us. But we called on the

Lord, the God of our fathers. The Lord heard our voice and saw our misery, our toil and our oppression; and the Lord brought us out of Egypt with mighty hand and outstretched arm, with great terror, and with signs and wonders. He brought us here and gave us this land, a land where milk and honey flow.

Here then I bring the first-fruits of the produce of the soil that you, Lord, have given me." You must then lay them before the Lord your God, and bow down in the sight of the Lord your God.'

The word of the Lord.

Thanks be to God.

RESPONSORIAL PSALM   *Psalm 90:1–2, 10–15 response v 15*

Be with me, O Lord, in my distress.

1   He who dwells in the shelter of the Most High
      and abides in the shade of the Almighty
      says to the Lord: 'My refuge,
      my stronghold, my God in whom I trust!'

2   Upon you no evil shall fall,
      no plague approach where you dwell.
      For you has he commanded his angels,
      to keep you in all your ways.

3   They shall bear you upon their hands
      lest you strike your foot against a stone.
      On the lion and the viper you will tread
      and trample the young lion and the dragon.

4   His love he set on me, so I will rescue him;
      protect him for he knows my name.
      When he calls I shall answer: 'I am with you.'
      I will save him in distress and give him glory.

SECOND READING   *Romans 10:8–13*

The creed of the Christian.

Scripture says: The word, that is the faith we proclaim, is very near to you, it is on your lips and in your heart. If your lips confess that Jesus is Lord and if you believe in your heart that God raised him from the dead, then you will be saved. By believing from the heart you are made righteous; by confessing with your lips you are saved. When scripture says: those who believe in him will have no cause for shame, it makes no distinction between Jew and Greek: all belong to the same Lord who is rich enough, however many ask for help, for everyone who calls on the name of the Lord will be saved.

The word of the Lord.

Thanks be to God.

GOSPEL ACCLAMATION   *Matthew 4:4*

Praise to you, O Christ, king of eternal glory!
Man does not live on bread alone,
but on every word that comes from the mouth of God.
Praise to you, O Christ, king of eternal glory!

GOSPEL   *Luke 4:1–13*

The Lord be with you.
And with your spirit.

A reading from the holy Gospel according to Luke.
Glory to you, O Lord.

Jesus was led by the Spirit through the wilderness and was tempted there.

Filled with the Holy Spirit, Jesus left the Jordan and was led by the Spirit through the wilderness, being tempted there by the devil for forty days. During that time he ate nothing and at the end he was hungry. Then the devil said to him, 'If you are the Son of God, tell this stone to turn into a loaf.' But Jesus replied, 'Scripture says: Man does not live on bread alone.'

Then leading him to a height, the devil showed him in a moment of time all the kingdoms of the world and said to him, 'I will give you all this power and the glory of these kingdoms, for it has been committed to me and I give it to anyone I choose.

Worship me, then, and it shall all be yours.' But Jesus answered him, 'Scripture says:

'You must worship the Lord your God, and serve him alone.'

Then he led him to Jerusalem and made him stand on the parapet of the Temple. 'If you are the Son of God,' he said to him 'throw yourself down from here, for scripture says: He will put his angels in charge of you to guard you, and again: They will hold you up on their hands in case you hurt your foot against a stone.' But Jesus answered him, 'It has been said: You must not put the Lord your God to the test.' Having exhausted all these ways of tempting him, the devil left him, to return at the appointed time.

The Gospel of the Lord.
Praise to you, Lord Jesus Christ.

▷ *page 11*

PRAYER OVER THE OFFERINGS

Give us the right dispositions, O Lord, we pray,
to make these offerings,
for with them we celebrate the beginning
of this venerable and sacred time.
Through Christ our Lord.   **Amen.**

▷ *page 15*

Preface: The Temptation of the Lord, p 71.

COMMUNION ANTIPHON   *Matthew 4:4*
One does not live by bread alone,
but by every word that comes forth from the mouth of God.
or   cf Psalm 90:4

The Lord will conceal you with his pinions,
and under his wings you will trust.

▷ *page 58*

PRAYER AFTER COMMUNION
Renewed now with heavenly bread,
by which faith is nourished, hope increased,
and charity strengthened,
we pray, O Lord,
that we may learn to hunger for Christ,
the true and living Bread,
and strive to live by every word
which proceeds from your mouth.
Through Christ our Lord.   **Amen.**

▷ *page 59*

PRAYER OVER THE PEOPLE
May bountiful blessing, O Lord, we pray,
come down upon your people,
that hope may grow in tribulation,
virtue be strengthened in temptation,
and eternal redemption be assured.
Through Christ our Lord.   **Amen.**

SECOND SUNDAY OF LENT

ENTRANCE ANTIPHON   *cf Psalm 26:8–9*
Of you my heart has spoken: Seek his face.
It is your face, O Lord, that I seek;
hide not your face from me.
or   cf Psalm 24:6, 2, 22

Remember your compassion, O Lord,
and your merciful love, for they are from of old.
Let not our enemies exult over us.
Redeem us, O God of Israel, from all our distress.

▷ *page 7*

The Gloria is omitted.

COLLECT

O God, who have commanded us
to listen to your beloved Son,
be pleased, we pray,
to nourish us inwardly by your word,
that, with spiritual sight made pure,
we may rejoice to behold your glory.
Through our Lord Jesus Christ, your Son,
who lives and reigns with you in the unity of the Holy Spirit,
one God, for ever and ever.   **Amen.**

FIRST READING   *Genesis 15:5–12, 17–18*

God enters into a Covenant with Abraham, the man of faith.

Taking Abram outside the Lord said, 'Look up to heaven and count the stars if you can. Such will be your descendants' he told him. Abram put his faith in the Lord, who counted this as making him justified.

'I am the Lord' he said to him 'who brought you out of Ur of the Chaldaeans to make you heir to this land.' 'My Lord, the Lord' Abram replied 'how am I to know that I shall inherit it?' He said to him, 'Get me a three-year-old heifer, a three-year-old goat, a three-year-old ram, a turtledove and a young pigeon.' He brought him all these, cut them in half and put half on one side and half facing it on the other; but the birds he did not cut in half. Birds of prey came down on the carcasses but Abram drove them off.

Now as the sun was setting Abram fell into a deep sleep, and terror seized him. When the sun had set and darkness had fallen, there appeared a smoking furnace and a fire-brand that went between the halves. That day the Lord made a Covenant with Abram in these terms:

'To your descendants I give this land, from the wadi of Egypt to the Great River.'

The word of the Lord.
Thanks be to God.

RESPONSORIAL PSALM   *Psalm 26:1, 7–9, 13–14 response v 1*

The Lord is my light and my help.

1   The Lord is my light and my help;
    whom shall I fear?
    The Lord is the stronghold of my life;
    before whom shall I shrink?

2   O Lord, hear my voice when I call;
    have mercy and answer.
    Of you my heart has spoken:
    'Seek his face."

3   It is your face, O Lord, that I seek;
    hide not your face.
    Dismiss not your servant in anger;
    you have been my help.

continued...

The Lord is my light and my help.

4 I am sure I shall see the Lord's goodness
in the land of the living.
Hope in him, hold firm and take heart.
Hope in the Lord!

SECOND READING *Philippians 3:17–4:1* *Shorter form (omitting oblique text): Philippians 3:20–4:1*
Christ will transfigure our bodies into copies of his glorious body.

My brothers, be united in following my rule of life. Take as your models everybody who is already doing this and study them as you used to study us. I have told you often, and I repeat it today with tears, there are many who are behaving as the enemies of the cross of Christ. They are destined to be lost. They make foods into their god and they are proudest of something they ought to think shameful; the things they think important are earthly things.

For us, our homeland is in heaven, and from heaven comes the saviour we are waiting for, the Lord Jesus Christ, and he will transfigure these wretched bodies of ours into copies of his glorious body. He will do that by the same power with which he can subdue the whole universe.

So then, my brothers and dear friends, do not give way but remain faithful in the Lord. I miss you very much, dear friends; you are my joy and my crown.

The word of the Lord.
Thanks be to God.

GOSPEL ACCLAMATION *Matthew 17:5*

**Glory and praise to you, O Christ!
From the bright cloud, the Father's voice was heard:
'This is my Son, the Beloved. Listen to him.'
Glory and praise to you, O Christ!**

GOSPEL *Luke 9:28–36*

The Lord be with you.
And with your spirit.

A reading from the holy Gospel according to Luke.
Glory to you, O Lord.

As Jesus prayed, the aspect of his face was changed.

Jesus took with him Peter and John and James and went up the mountain to pray. As he prayed, the aspect of his face was changed and his clothing became brilliant as lightning. Suddenly there were two men there talking to him; they were Moses and Elijah appearing in glory, and they were speaking of his passing which he was to accomplish in Jerusalem. Peter and his companions were heavy with sleep, but they kept awake and saw his glory and the two men standing with him. As these were leaving him, Peter said to Jesus, 'Master, it is wonderful for us to be here; so let us make three tents, one for you, one for Moses and one for Elijah.' He did not know what he was saying. As he spoke, a cloud came and covered them with shadow; and when they went into the cloud the disciples were afraid. And a voice came from the cloud saying, 'This is my Son, the Chosen One. Listen to him.' And after the voice had spoken, Jesus was found alone. The disciples kept silence and, at that time, told no one what they had seen.

The Gospel of the Lord.
Praise to you, Lord Jesus Christ.

▷ page 11

PRAYER OVER THE OFFERINGS

May this sacrifice, O Lord, we pray,
cleanse us of our faults
and sanctify your faithful in body and mind
for the celebration of the paschal festivities.
Through Christ our Lord. **Amen.**

▷ page 15

Preface: The Transfiguration of the Lord, p 72.

COMMUNION ANTIPHON   *Matthew 17:5*

This is my beloved Son, with whom I am well pleased;
listen to him.

▷ page 58

PRAYER AFTER COMMUNION

As we receive these glorious mysteries,
we make thanksgiving to you, O Lord,
for allowing us while still on earth
to be partakers even now of the things of heaven.
Through Christ our Lord. **Amen.**

▷ page 59

PRAYER OVER THE PEOPLE

Bless your faithful, we pray, O Lord,
with a blessing that endures for ever,
and keep them faithful
to the Gospel of your Only Begotten Son,
so that they may always desire and at last attain
that glory whose beauty he showed in his own Body,
to the amazement of his Apostles.
Through Christ our Lord. **Amen.**

THIRD SUNDAY OF LENT (YEAR C)

This Mass is used when the First Scrutiny is not being celebrated.
Readings for Year A may be used with this Mass as an alternative (see p 164).

If the First Scrutiny is being celebrated today
the Ritual Mass for the Celebration of the First Scrutiny, with the readings for Year A is used (see p 163).

ENTRANCE ANTIPHON *cf Psalm 24:15–16*

My eyes are always on the Lord,
for he rescues my feet from the snare.
Turn to me and have mercy on me,
for I am alone and poor.

or *cf Ezechiel 36:23–26*

When I prove my holiness among you,
I will gather you from all the foreign lands;
and I will pour clean water upon you
and cleanse you from all your impurities,
and I will give you a new spirit, says the Lord.

▷ *page 7*

The Gloria is omitted.

COLLECT

O God, author of every mercy and of all goodness,
who in fasting, prayer and almsgiving
have shown us a remedy for sin,
look graciously on this confession of our lowliness,
that we, who are bowed down by our conscience,
may always be lifted up by your mercy.
Through our Lord Jesus Christ, your Son,
who lives and reigns with you in the unity of the Holy Spirit,
one God, for ever and ever. **Amen.**

The Readings for Year A may be used as an alternative *(see page 164).*

FIRST READING *Exodus 3:1–8, 13–15*

I Am has sent me to you.

Moses was looking after the flock of Jethro, his father-in-law, priest of Midian. He led his flock to the far side of the wilderness and came to Horeb, the mountain of God. There the angel of the Lord appeared to him in the shape of a flame of fire, coming from the middle of a bush. Moses looked; there was the bush blazing but it was not being burnt up. 'I must go and look at this strange sight,' Moses said 'and see why the bush is not burnt.' Now the Lord saw him go forward to look, and God called to him from the middle of the bush. 'Moses, Moses!' he said. 'Here I am' he answered. 'Come no nearer' he said. 'Take off your shoes, for the place on which you stand is holy ground. I am the God of your father,' he said 'the God of Abraham, the God of Isaac and the God of Jacob.' At this Moses covered his face, afraid to look at God.

And the Lord said, 'I have seen the miserable state of my people in Egypt.

I have heard their appeal to be free of their slave-drivers. Yes, I am well aware of their sufferings. I mean to deliver them out of the hands of the Egyptians and bring them up out of that land to a land rich and broad, a land where milk and honey flow.'

Then Moses said to God, 'I am to go, then, to the sons of Israel and say to them, "The God of your fathers has sent me to you." But if they ask me what his name is, what am I to tell them?' And God said to Moses, 'I Am who I Am.

This,' he added 'is what you must say to the sons of Israel: "I Am has sent me to you." And God also said to Moses, 'You are to say to the sons of Israel: "The Lord, the God of your fathers, the God of Abraham, the God of Isaac and the God of Jacob, has sent me to you." This is my name for all time; by this name I shall be invoked for all generations to come.'

The word of the Lord.
Thanks be to God.

RESPONSORIAL PSALM   *Psalm 102:1–4, 6–8, 11 response v 8*

The Lord is compassion and love.

1 My soul, give thanks to the Lord,
   all my being, bless his holy name.
   My soul, give thanks to the Lord
   and never forget all his blessings.

2 It is he who forgives all your guilt,
   who heals every one of your ills,
   who redeems your life from the grave,
   who crowns you with love and compassion.

3 The Lord does deeds of justice,
   gives judgement for all who are oppressed.
   He made known his ways to Moses
   and his deeds to Israel's sons.

4 The Lord is compassion and love,
   slow to anger and rich in mercy.
   For as the heavens are high above the earth
   so strong is his love for those who fear him.

SECOND READING   *1 Corinthians 10:1–6, 10–12*

The life of the people under Moses in the desert was written down to be a lesson for us.

I want to remind you, brothers, how our fathers were all guided by a cloud above them and how they all passed through the sea. They were all baptised into Moses in this cloud and in this sea; all ate the same spiritual food and all drank the same spiritual drink, since they all drank from the spiritual rock that

followed them as they went, and that rock was Christ. In spite of this, most of them failed to please God and their corpses littered the desert.

These things all happened as warnings for us, not to have the wicked lusts for forbidden things that they had. You must never complain: some of them did, and they were killed by the Destroyer.

All this happened to them as a warning, and it was written down to be a lesson for us who are living at the end of the age. The man who thinks he is safe must be careful that he does not fall.

The word of the Lord.
Thanks be to God.

GOSPEL ACCLAMATION   *Matthew 4:17*

> **Glory to you, O Christ, you are the Word of God!**
> **Repent, says the Lord,**
> **for the kingdom of heaven is close at hand.**
> **Glory to you, O Christ, you are the Word of God!**

GOSPEL   *Luke 13:1–9*

The Lord be with you.
And with your spirit.

A reading from the holy Gospel according to Luke.
Glory to you, O Lord.

Unless you repent you will all perish as they did.

Some people arrived and told Jesus about the Galileans whose blood Pilate had mingled with that of their sacrifices. At this he said to them, 'Do you suppose these Galileans who suffered like that were greater sinners than any other Galileans? They were not, I tell you. No; but unless you repent you will all perish as they did. Or those eighteen on whom the tower at Siloam fell and killed them? Do you suppose that they were more guilty than all the other people living in Jerusalem? They were not, I tell you. No; but unless you repent you will all perish as they did.'

He told this parable: 'A man had a fig tree planted in his vineyard, and he came looking for fruit on it but found none. He said to the man who looked after the vineyard, "Look here, for three years now I have been coming to look for fruit on this fig tree and finding none. Cut it down: why should it be taking up the ground?" "Sir," the man replied "leave it one more year and give me time to dig round it and manure it, it may bear fruit next year; if not, then you can cut it down."'

The Gospel of the Lord.
Praise to you, Lord Jesus Christ.

▷ *page 11*

PRAYER OVER THE OFFERINGS

Be pleased, O Lord, with these sacrificial offerings,
and grant that we who beseech pardon for our own sins,
may take care to forgive our neighbour.
Through Christ our Lord.   **Amen.**

▷ *page 15*

When Year C readings are used, Preface I or II of Lent is used, p 71.
When Year A readings are used, Preface: The Samaritan Woman is used, p 72.

COMMUNION ANTIPHON *for Year C readings* *cf Psalm 83:4–5*
The sparrow finds a home,
and the swallow a nest for her young:
by your altars, O Lord of hosts, my King and my God.
Blessed are they who dwell in your house,
for ever singing your praise.
or *for Year A readings: John 4:13–14*

For anyone who drinks it, says the Lord,
the water I shall give will become in him
a spring welling up to eternal life.

> *▷ page 58*

PRAYER AFTER COMMUNION
As we receive the pledge
of things yet hidden in heaven
and are nourished while still on earth
with the Bread that comes from on high,
we humbly entreat you, O Lord,
that what is being brought about in us in mystery
may come to true completion.
Through Christ our Lord. **Amen.**

> *▷ page 59*

PRAYER OVER THE PEOPLE
Direct, O Lord, we pray, the hearts of your faithful,
and in your kindness grant your servants this grace:
that, abiding in the love of you and their neighbour,
they may fulfil the whole of your commands.
Through Christ our Lord. **Amen.**

THIRD SUNDAY OF LENT (YEAR A) AND FIRST SCRUTINY

RITUAL MASS FOR THE CELEBRATION OF THE SCRUTINIES: FIRST SCRUTINY
This Mass is used when the First Scrutiny is being celebrated today.

ENTRANCE ANTIPHON *Ezekiel 36:23–26*
When I prove my holiness among you,
I will gather you from all the foreign lands
and I will pour clean water upon you
and cleanse you from all your impurities,
and I will give you a new spirit, says the Lord.
or *cf Isaiah 55:1*

Come to the waters, you who are thirsty, says the Lord;
you who have no money, come and drink joyfully.

> *▷ page 7*

The Gloria is omitted.

COLLECT

Grant, we pray, O Lord,
that these chosen ones may come worthily and wisely
to the confession of your praise,
so that in accordance with that first dignity
which they lost by original sin
they may be fashioned anew through your glory.
Through our Lord **Amen.**

These readings may be used in any year.

If the First Scrutiny is not celebrated today, the Mass prayers of the Third Sunday of Lent (Year C) are used, page 160.

FIRST READING   *Exodus 17:3–7*

Give the water to drink.

Tormented by thirst, the people complained against Moses. 'Why did you bring us out of Egypt?' they said. 'Was it so that I should die of thirst, my children too, and my cattle?' Moses appealed to the Lord. 'How am I to deal with this people?' he said. 'A little more and they will stone me!' The Lord said to Moses, 'Take with you some of the elders of Israel and move on to the forefront of the people; take in your hand the staff with which you struck the river, and go. I shall be standing before you there on the rock, at Horeb. You must strike the rock, and water will flow from it for the people to drink.' This is what Moses did, in the sight of the elders of Israel. The place was named Massah and Meribah because of the grumbling of the sons of Israel and because they put the Lord to the test by saying, 'Is the Lord with us, or not?'

The word of the Lord.
Thanks be to God.

RESPONSORIAL PSALM   *Psalm 94:1–2, 6–9 response v 9*

**O that today you would listen to his voice:
'Harden not your hearts.'**

1   Come, ring out our joy to the Lord;
    hail the rock who saves us.
    Let us come before him, giving thanks,
    with songs let us hail the Lord.

2   Come in; let us kneel and bend low,
    let us kneel before the God who made us
    for he is our God and we
    the people who belong to his pasture,
    the flock that is led by his hand.

3   O that today you would listen to his voice!
    'Harden not your hearts as at Meribah,
    as on that day at Massah in the desert
    when your fathers put me to the test;
    when they tried me, though they saw my work.'

SECOND READING   *Romans 5:1–2, 5–8*

The love of God has been poured into our hearts by the Holy Spirit which has been given us.

Through our Lord Jesus Christ by faith we are judged righteous and at peace with God, since it is by faith and through Jesus that we have entered this state of grace in which we can boast about looking forward to God's glory. This hope is not deceptive, because the love of God has been poured into our hearts by the Holy Spirit which has been given us. We were still helpless when at his appointed moment Christ died for sinful men. It is not easy to die even for a good man – though of course for someone really worthy, a man might be prepared to die – but what proves that God loves us is that Christ died for us while we were still sinners.

The word of the Lord.
Thanks be to God.

GOSPEL ACCLAMATION   *cf John 4:42, 15*

Glory to you, O Christ, you are the Word of God!
Lord, you are really the saviour of the world;
give me the living water, so that I may never get thirsty.
Glory to you, O Christ, you are the Word of God!

GOSPEL   *John 4:5–42*   *Shorter form (omitting oblique text): John 4:5–15, 19–26, 39–42*

The Lord be with you.
And with your spirit.

A reading from the holy Gospel according to John.
Glory to you, O Lord.

The water that I shall give will turn into a spring of eternal life.

Jesus came to the Samaritan town called Sychar, near the land that Jacob gave to his son Joseph. Jacob's well is there and Jesus, tired by the journey, sat straight down by the well. It was about the sixth hour. When a Samaritan woman came to draw water, Jesus said to her, 'Give me a drink.' His disciples had gone into the town to buy food. The Samaritan woman said to him, 'What? You are a Jew and you ask me, a Samaritan, for a drink?' – Jews, in fact, do not associate with Samaritans. Jesus replied: 'If you only knew what God is offering and who it is that is saying to you: Give me a drink, you would have been the one to ask, and he would have given you living water.' 'You have no bucket, sir,' she answered, 'and the well is deep: how could you get this living water? Are you a greater man than our father Jacob who gave us this well and drank from it himself with his sons and his cattle?' Jesus replied: 'Whoever drinks this water will get thirsty again; but anyone who drinks the water that I shall give will never be thirsty again: the water that I shall give will turn into a spring inside him, welling up to eternal life.' 'Sir,' said the woman 'give me some of that water, so that I may never get thirsty and never have to come here again to draw water.' *'Go and call your husband' said Jesus to her 'and come back here.' The woman answered, 'I have no husband.' He said to her, 'You are right to say, "I have no husband"; for although you have had five, the one you have now is not your husband. You spoke the truth there.'* 'I see you are a prophet, sir' said the woman. 'Our fathers worshipped on this mountain, while you say that Jerusalem is the place where one ought to worship.'

Jesus said: 'Believe me, woman, the hour is coming when you will worship the Father neither on this mountain nor in Jerusalem. You worship what you do not know; we worship what we do know; for salvation comes from the Jews. But the hour will come – in fact it is here already – when true worshippers will worship the Father in spirit and truth: that is the kind of worshipper the Father wants. God is spirit, and those who worship must worship in spirit and truth.'

The woman said to him, 'I know that Messiah – that is, Christ – is coming; and when he comes he will tell us everything.' 'I who am speaking to you,' said Jesus 'I am he.'

At this point his disciples returned, and were surprised to find him speaking to a woman, though none of them asked, 'What do you want from her?' or, 'Why are you talking to her?' The woman put down her water jar and hurried back to the town to tell the people, 'Come and see a man who has told me everything I ever did; I wonder if he is the Christ?' This brought people out of the town and they started walking towards him.

Meanwhile, the disciples were urging him, 'Rabbi, do have something to eat;' but he said, 'I have food to eat that you do not know about.' So the disciples asked one another, *'Has someone been bringing him food?' But Jesus said:*

'My food is to do the will of the one who sent me, and to complete his work. Have you not got a saying: Four months and then the harvest? Well, I tell you: Look around you, look at the fields; already they are white, ready for harvest! Already the reaper is being paid his wages, already he is bringing in the grain for eternal life, and thus sower and reaper rejoice together. For here the proverb holds good: one sows, another reaps; I sent you to reap a harvest you had not worked for. Others worked for it; and you have come into the rewards of their trouble.'

Many Samaritans of that town had believed in him on the strength of the woman's testimony when she said, 'He told me all I have ever done,' so, when the Samaritans came up to him, they begged him to stay with them. He stayed for two days, and when he spoke to them many more came to believe; and they said to the woman, 'Now we no longer believe because of what you told us; we have heard him ourselves and we know that he really is the saviour of the world.'

The Gospel of the Lord.

Praise to you, Lord Jesus Christ.

HOMILY

After the readings, and guided by them, the minister explains the meaning of the First Scrutiny in the light of the Lenten liturgy and of the spiritual journey of the elect.

FIRST SCRUTINY

INVITATION TO SILENT PRAYER

After the homily, the elect with their godparents come forward and stand before the celebrant.

The celebrant first addresses the assembly of the faithful, inviting them to pray in silence and to ask that the elect will be given a spirit of repentance, a sense of sin, and the true freedom of the children of God. The celebrant then addresses the elect, inviting them also to pray in silence and suggesting that as a sign of their inner spirit of repentance they bow their heads or kneel; he concludes his remarks with the following or similar words.

Elect of God, bow your heads [kneel down] and pray.

The elect bow their heads or kneel, and all pray for some time in silence. After the period of silent prayer, the community and the elect stand for the intercessions.

INTERCESSIONS FOR THE ELECT

During the intercessions, the godparents stand with their right hand on the shoulder of the elect.

Each intercession for the elect concludes:

Let us pray to the Lord
Lord, hear our prayer

If the Prayer of the Faithful is to be omitted, intercessions for the Church and the whole world are added to the intercessions for the elect.

EXORCISM

A prayer of exorcism is said, to which all reply:

Amen.

Then, if this can be done conveniently, the celebrant lays hands on each one of the elect.
Then with hands outstretched over the elect he says a prayer over the elect, to which all respond:

Amen.

An appropriate song may now be sung

DISMISSAL OF THE ELECT

The elect are normally dismissed in order to continue their reflection on the Scripture readings and on the scrutiny.

The celebrant dismisses the elect in these or similar words:

Dear elect, go in peace,
and join us again at the next scrutiny.
May the Lord remain with you always.

or

My dear friends,
this community now sends you forth
to reflect more deeply on the word of God which you have shared with us today.
Be assured of our loving support and prayers for you.
We look forward to the day when you will share fully in the Lord's Table.

If for serious reasons the elect cannot leave and must remain with the baptised, they are to be instructed that though they are present at the eucharist, they cannot take part as the baptised do. They may be reminded of this in these or similar words.

Although you cannot yet participate fully in the Lord's eucharist,
stay with us as a sign of our hope
that all God's children will eat and drink with the Lord
and work with his Spirit to re-create the face of the earth.

PRAYER OF THE FAITHFUL AND PROFESSION OF FAITH

Intercessory prayer is resumed with the usual Prayer of the Faithful for the needs of the Church and the whole world; then, if required, the Profession of Faith is said. But for pastoral reasons, the Prayer of the Faithful and the Profession of Faith may be omitted.

▷ *page 13*

PRAYER OVER THE OFFERINGS

May your merciful grace prepare your servants, O Lord,
for the worthy celebration of these mysteries,
and lead them to it by a devout way of life.
Through Christ our Lord.   **Amen.**

▷ *page 15*

LENT

EUCHARISTIC PRAYER

Preface: The Samaritan Woman is used, p 72.
In Eucharistic Prayers I, II and III, proper forms of certain sections are used:

EUCHARISTIC PRAYER I

Memento, Domine
(Remember, Lord, your servants):
Remember, Lord, your servants
who are to present your chosen ones
for the holy grace of your Baptism,
Here the names of the godparents are read out
and all gathered here,
whose faith and devotion are known to you...

Hanc igitur (Therefore, Lord, we pray):
Therefore, Lord, we pray:
graciously accept this oblation
which we make to you for your servants,
whom you have been pleased
to enrol, choose and call for eternal life
and for the blessed gift of your grace.
(Through Christ our Lord. Amen.)

EUCHARISTIC PRAYER II

After the words 'and all the clergy,'
the following is added:
Remember also, Lord, your servants
who are to present these chosen ones
at the font of rebirth.

EUCHARISTIC PRAYER III

After the words 'the entire people you have gained for
your own', the following is added:
Assist your servants with your grace,
O Lord, we pray,
that they may lead these chosen ones by
   word and example
to new life in Christ, our Lord.

COMMUNION ANTIPHON   *cf John 4:13–14*
For anyone who drinks it, says the Lord,
the water I shall give will become in him a spring
welling up to eternal life.

▷ *page 58*

PRAYER AFTER COMMUNION
Give help, O Lord, we pray,
by the grace of your redemption
and be pleased to protect and prepare
those you are to initiate
through the Sacraments of eternal life.
Through Christ our Lord.   **Amen.**

▷ *page 59*

FOURTH SUNDAY OF LENT (YEAR C)

This Mass is used when the Second Scrutiny is not being celebrated.
Readings for Year A may be used with this Mass as an alternative (see p 172).

If the Second Scrutiny is being celebrated today
the Ritual Mass for the Celebration of the Second Scrutiny, with the readings for Year A is used (see p 172).

ENTRANCE ANTIPHON   *cf Isaiah 66:10–11*
Rejoice, Jerusalem, and all who love her.
Be joyful, all who were in mourning;
exult and be satisfied at her consoling breast.

▷ *page 7*

The Gloria is omitted.

COLLECT

O God, who through your Word
reconcile the human race to yourself in a wonderful way,
grant, we pray,
that with prompt devotion and eager faith
the Christian people may hasten
toward the solemn celebrations to come.
Through our Lord Jesus Christ, your Son,
who lives and reigns with you in the unity of the Holy Spirit,
one God, for ever and ever. **Amen.**

The Readings for Year A may be used as an alternative *(see page 172).*

FIRST READING *Joshua 5:9–12*

The People of God keep the Passover on their entry into the promised land.

The Lord said to Joshua 'Today I have taken the shame of Egypt away from you.'

The Israelites pitched their camp at Gilgal and kept the Passover there on the fourteenth day of the month, at evening in the plain of Jericho. On the morrow of the Passover they tasted the produce of that country, unleavened bread and roasted ears of corn, that same day. From that time, from their first eating of the produce of that country, the manna stopped falling. And having manna no longer, the Israelites fed from that year onwards on what the land of Canaan yielded.

The word of the Lord.
Thanks be to God.

RESPONSORIAL PSALM *Psalm 33:2–7, response v 9*

Taste and see that the Lord is good.

1 I will bless the Lord at all times,
   his praise always on my lips;
   in the Lord my soul shall make its boast.
   The humble shall hear and be glad.

2 Glorify the Lord with me.
   Together let us praise his name.
   I sought the Lord and he answered me;
   from all my terrors he set me free.

3 Look towards him and be radiant;
   let your faces not be abashed.
   This poor man called; the Lord heard him
   and rescued him from all his distress.

SECOND READING *2 Corinthians 5:17–21*

God reconciled us to himself through Christ.

For anyone who is in Christ, there is a new creation; the old creation has gone, and now the new one is here. It is all God's work. It was God who reconciled us to himself through Christ and gave us the work of handing on this reconciliation. In other words, God in Christ was reconciling the world to himself, not holding men's faults against them, and he has entrusted to us the news that they are reconciled. So we are ambassadors for Christ; it is as though God were appealing through us, and the appeal that we make in Christ's name is: be reconciled to God. For our sake God made the sinless one into sin, so that in him we might become the goodness of God.

The word of the Lord.
Thanks be to God.

GOSPEL ACCLAMATION   *Luke 15:18*

**Praise and honour to you, Lord Jesus!
I will leave this place and go to my father and say:
'Father, I have sinned against heaven and against you.'
Praise and honour to you, Lord Jesus!**

GOSPEL   *Luke 15:1–3, 11–32*

The Lord be with you.
And with your spirit.

A reading from the holy Gospel according to Luke.
Glory to you, O Lord.

Your brother here was dead and has come to life.

The tax collectors and the sinners were all seeking the company of Jesus to hear what he had to say, and the Pharisees and the scribes complained. 'This man' they said 'welcomes sinners and eats with them.' So he spoke this parable to them:

'A man had two sons. The younger said to his father, "Father, let me have the share of the estate that would come to me." So the father divided the property between them. A few days later, the younger son got together everything he had and left for a distant country where he squandered his money on a life of debauchery.

'When he had spent it all, that country experienced a severe famine, and now he began to feel the pinch, so he hired himself out to one of the local inhabitants who put him on his farm to feed the pigs. And he would willingly have filled his belly with the husks the pigs were eating but no one offered him anything. Then he came to his senses and said, "How many of my father's paid servants have more food than they want, and here am I dying of hunger! I will leave this place and go to my father and say: Father, I have sinned against heaven and against you; I no longer deserve to be called your son; treat me as one of your paid servants." So he left the place and went back to his father.

'While he was still a long way off, his father saw him and was moved with pity. He ran to the boy, clasped him in his arms and kissed him tenderly. Then his son said, "Father, I have sinned against heaven and against you. I no longer deserve to be called your son." But his father said to his servants, "Quick! Bring out the best robe and put it on him; put a ring on his finger and sandals on his feet. Bring the calf we have been fattening, and kill it; we are going to have a feast, a celebration, because this son of mine was dead and has come back to life; he was lost and is found." And they began to celebrate.

'Now the elder son was out in the fields, and on his way back, as he drew near the house, he could hear music and dancing. Calling one of the servants he asked what it was all about. "Your brother has come" replied the servant "and your father has killed the calf we had fattened because he has got him back safe and sound." He was angry then and refused to go in, and his father came out to plead with him; but he answered his father, "Look, all these years I have slaved for you and never once disobeyed your orders, yet you never offered me so much as a kid for me to celebrate with my friends. But, for this son of yours, when he comes back after swallowing up your property – he and his women – you kill the calf we had been fattening."

'The father said, "My son, you are with me always and all I have is yours. But it is only right we should celebrate and rejoice, because your brother here was dead and has come to life; he was lost and is found."'

The Gospel of the Lord.
Praise to you, Lord Jesus Christ.

▷ page 11

PRAYER OVER THE OFFERINGS
We place before you with joy these offerings,
which bring eternal remedy, O Lord,
praying that we may both faithfully revere them
and present them to you, as is fitting,
for the salvation of all the world.
Through Christ our Lord. **Amen.**

▷ page 15

When Year C readings are used, Preface I or II of Lent is used, p 70.
When Year A readings are used, Preface: The Man Born Blind is used, p 72.

COMMUNION ANTIPHON Year C readings Luke 15:32
You must rejoice, my son,
for your brother was dead and has come to life;
he was lost and is found.

Or *for Year A readings cf John 9:11, 38*

The Lord anointed my eyes: I went, I washed,
I saw and I believed in God.

▷ page 58

PRAYER AFTER COMMUNION
O God, who enlighten everyone who comes into this world,
illuminate our hearts, we pray,
with the splendour of your grace,
that we may always ponder
what is worthy and pleasing to your majesty
and love you in all sincerity.
Through Christ our Lord. **Amen.**

▷ page 59

PRAYER OVER THE PEOPLE

Look upon those who call to you, O Lord,
and sustain the weak;
give life by your unfailing light
to those who walk in the shadow of death,
and bring those rescued by your mercy from every evil
to reach the highest good.
Through Christ our Lord.

FOURTH SUNDAY OF LENT (YEAR A) AND SECOND SCRUTINY

RITUAL MASS FOR THE CELEBRATION OF THE SCRUTINIES: SECOND SCRUTINY
This Mass is used when the Second Scrutiny is being celebrated today.

ENTRANCE ANTIPHON   *cf Psalm 24:15–16*

My eyes are always on the Lord, for he rescues my feet from the snare.
Turn to me and have mercy on me, for I am alone and poor.

▷ *page 7*

The Gloria is omitted.

COLLECT

Almighty ever-living God,
give to your Church an increase in spiritual joy,
so that those once born of earth
may be reborn as citizens of heaven.
Through our Lord Jesus Christ, your Son,
who lives and reigns with you in the unity of the Holy Spirit,
one God, for ever and ever.   **Amen.**

These readings may be used in any year.

If the Second Scrutiny is not celebrated today, the Mass prayers of the Fourth Sunday of Lent (Year C) are used, page 168.

FIRST READING   *1 Samuel 16:1, 6–7, 10–13*
David is anointed king of Israel

The Lord said to Samuel, 'Fill your horn with oil and go. I am sending you to Jesse of Bethlehem, for I have chosen myself a king among his sons.' When Samuel arrived, he caught sight of Eliab and thought, 'Surely the Lord's anointed one stands there before him,' but the Lord said to Samuel, 'Take no notice of his appearance or his height for I have rejected him; God does not see as man sees; man looks at appearances but the Lord looks at the heart.' Jesse presented his seven sons to Samuel, but Samuel said to Jesse, 'The Lord has not chosen these'. He then asked Jesse, 'Are these all the sons you have?' He answered, 'There is still one left, the youngest; he is out looking after the sheep.' Then Samuel said to Jesse, 'Send for him; we will not sit down to eat until he comes.' Jesse had him sent for, a boy of fresh complexion, with fine eyes and pleasant bearing. The Lord said, 'Come, anoint him, for this is the one.' At this, Samuel took the horn of oil and anointed him where he stood with his brothers; and the spirit of the Lord seized on David and stayed with him from that day on.

The word of the Lord.
Thanks be to God.

RESPONSORIAL PSALM   *Psalm 22 response v 1*

> **The Lord is my shepherd;**
> **there is nothing I shall want.**

1 The Lord is my shepherd;
   there is nothing I shall want.
   Fresh and green are the pastures
   where he gives me repose.
   Near restful waters he leads me,
   to revive my drooping spirit.

2 He guides me along the right path;
   he is true to his name.
   If I should walk in the valley of darkness
   no evil would I fear.
   You are there with your crook and your staff;
   with these you give me comfort.

3 You have prepared a banquet for me
   in the sight of my foes.
   My head you have anointed with oil;
   my cup is overflowing.

4 Surely goodness and kindness shall follow me
   all the days of my life.
   In the Lord's own house shall I dwell
   for ever and ever.

SECOND READING   *Ephesians 5:8–14*

Rise from the dead and Christ will shine on you.

You were darkness once, but now you are light in the Lord; be like children of light, for the effects of the light are seen in complete goodness and right living and truth. Try to discover what the Lord wants of you, having nothing to do with the futile works of darkness but exposing them by contrast. The things which are done in secret are things that people are ashamed even to speak of; but anything exposed by the light will be illuminated and anything illuminated turns into light. That is why it is said:

Wake up from your sleep, rise from the dead, and Christ will shine on you.

The word of the Lord.
Thanks be to God.

GOSPEL ACCLAMATION   *John 8:12*

> **Glory to you, O Christ, you are the Word of God!**
> **I am the light of the world, says the Lord;**
> **anyone who follows me will have the light of life.**
> **Glory to you, O Christ, you are the Word of God!**

GOSPEL   *John 9:1–41   Shorter form (omitting oblique text): John 9:1, 6–9, 13–17, 34–38*

The Lord be with you.
And with your spirit.

A reading from the holy Gospel according to John.
Glory to you, O Lord.

The blind man went off and washed himself and came away with his sight restored

As Jesus went along, he saw a man who had been blind from birth. *His disciples asked him, 'Rabbi, who sinned, this man or his parents, for him to have been born blind?' 'Neither he nor his parents sinned,' Jesus answered 'he was born blind so that the works of God might be displayed in him.*

'As long as the day lasts I must carry out the work of the one who sent me; the night will soon be here when no one can work. As long as I am in the world I am the light of the world.'

Having said this, he spat on the ground, made a paste with the spittle, put this over the eyes of the blind man and said to him, 'Go and wash in the Pool of Siloam' (a name that means 'sent'). So the blind man went off and washed himself; and came away with his sight restored.

His neighbours and people who earlier had seen him begging said, 'Isn't this the man who used to sit and beg?' Some said, 'Yes, it is the same one.' Others said, 'No, he only looks like him.'The man himself said, 'I am the man.' *So they said to him, 'Then how do your eyes come to be open?' 'The man called Jesus' he answered 'made a paste, daubed my eyes with it and said to me, "Go and wash at Siloam"; so I went, and when I washed I could see.' They asked, 'Where is he?' 'I don't know' he answered.*

They brought the man who had been blind to the Pharisees. It had been a sabbath day when Jesus made the paste and opened the man's eyes, so when the Pharisees asked him how he had come to see, he said, 'He put a paste on my eyes, and I washed, and I can see.' Then some of the Pharisees said, 'This man cannot be from God: he does not keep the sabbath.' Others said, 'How could a sinner produce signs like this?' And there was disagreement among them. So they spoke to the blind man again, 'What have you to say about him yourself, now that he has opened your eyes?' 'He is a prophet' replied the man.

However, the Jews would not believe that the man had been blind and had gained his sight, without first sending for his parents and asking them, 'Is this man really your son who you say was born blind? If so how is it that he is now able to see?' His parents answered, 'We know he is our son and we know he was born blind, but we don't know how it is that he can see now, or who opened his eyes. He is old enough: let him speak for himself.' His parents spoke like this out of fear of the Jews, who had already agreed to expel from the synagogue anyone who should acknowledge Jesus as the Christ. This was why his parents said, 'He is old enough; ask him.'

So the Jews again sent for the man and said to him, 'Give glory to God! For our part, we know that this man is a sinner.' The man answered, 'I don't know if he is a sinner; I only know that I was blind and now I can see.' They said to him, 'What did he do to you? How did he open your eyes?' He replied, 'I have told you once and you wouldn't listen. Why do you want to hear it all again? Do you want to become his disciples too?' At this they hurled abuse at him: 'You can be his disciple,' they said 'we are disciples of Moses: we know that God spoke to Moses, but as for this man, we don't know where he comes from.' The man replied, 'Now here is an astonishing thing! He has opened my eyes and you don't know where he comes from! We know that God doesn't listen to sinners, but God does listen to men who are devout and do his will. Ever since the world began it is unheard of for anyone to open the eyes of a man who was born blind; if this man were not from God, he couldn't do a thing.' 'Are you trying to teach us,' they replied 'and you a sinner through and through, since you were born!' And they drove him away.

Jesus heard they had driven him away, and when he found him he said to him,

'Do you believe in the Son of Man?' 'Sir,' the man replied 'tell me who he is so that I may believe in him.' Jesus said, 'You are looking at him; he is speaking to you.' The man said, 'Lord, I believe', and worshipped him. *Jesus said:*

'It is for judgement that I have come into this world, so that those without sight may see and those with sight turn blind.'

Hearing this, some Pharisees who were present said to him, 'We are not blind, surely?' Jesus replied:

'Blind? If you were, you would not be guilty, but since you say, "We see", your guilt remains.'

The Gospel of the Lord.
Praise to you, Lord Jesus Christ.

HOMILY
After the readings, and guided by them, the minister explains the meaning of the Second Scrutiny in the light of the Lenten liturgy and of the spiritual journey of the elect.

SECOND SCRUTINY
The Second Scrutiny follows the same pattern as the First Scrutiny (p 166). An outline of the rite is given here for reference.

INVITATION TO SILENT PRAYER

INTERCESSIONS FOR THE ELECT
Let us pray to the Lord
Lord, hear our prayer

EXORCISM
After the exorcism and prayer over the elect, an appropriate song may now be sung.

DISMISSAL OF THE ELECT

PRAYER OF THE FAITHFUL AND PROFESSION OF FAITH
Intercessory prayer is resumed with the usual Prayer of the Faithful for the needs of the Church and the whole world; then, if required, the Profession of Faith is said. But for pastoral reasons, the Prayer of the Faithful and the Profession of Faith may be omitted.

▷ page 13

PRAYER OVER THE OFFERINGS
We place before you with joy these offerings,
which bring eternal remedy, O Lord,
praying that we may both faithfully revere them
and present them to you, as is fitting,
for those who seek salvation.
Through Christ our Lord.   **Amen.**

▷ page 15

LENT

EUCHARISTIC PRAYER
Preface: The Man Born Blind is used, p 72.
In Eucharistic Prayers I, II and III, proper forms of certain sections are used, see p 168.

COMMUNION ANTIPHON   *cf John 9:11, 38*
The Lord anointed my eyes; I went, I washed,
I saw and I believed in God.

▷ *page 58*

PRAYER AFTER COMMUNION
Sustain your family always in your kindness,
O Lord, we pray,
correct them, set them in order,
graciously protect them under your rule,
and in your unfailing goodness
direct them along the way of salvation.
Through Christ our Lord.   **Amen.**

▷ *page 59*

FIFTH SUNDAY OF LENT (YEAR C)

This Mass is used when the Third Scrutiny is not being celebrated.
Readings for Year A may be used with this Mass as an alternative (see p 180).

If the Third Scrutiny is being celebrated today
the Ritual Mass for the Celebration of the Third Scrutiny, with the readings for Year A is used (see p 179).

ENTRANCE ANTIPHON   *cf Psalm 42:1–2*
Give me justice, O God,
and plead my cause against a nation that is faithless.
From the deceitful and cunning rescue me,
for you, O God, are my strength.

▷ *page 7*

The Gloria is omitted.

COLLECT
By your help, we beseech you, Lord our God,
may we walk eagerly in that same charity
with which, out of love for the world,
your Son handed himself over to death.
Through our Lord Jesus Christ, your Son,
who lives and reigns with you in the unity of the Holy Spirit,
one God, for ever and ever.   **Amen.**

The Readings for Year A may be used as an alternative *(see below, page 180).*

FIRST READING   *Isaiah 43:16–21*

See, I am doing a new deed, and I will give my chosen people drink.

Thus says the Lord, who made a way through the sea, a path in the great waters; who put chariots and horse in the field and a powerful army, which lay there never to rise again, snuffed out, put out like a wick:

No need to recall the past, no need to think about what was done before. See, I am doing a new deed, even now it comes to light; can you not see it? Yes, I am making a road in the wilderness, paths in the wilds.

The wild beasts will honour me, jackals and ostriches, because I am putting water in the wilderness (rivers in the wild) to give my chosen people drink. The people I have formed for myself will sing my praises.

The word of the Lord.
Thanks be to God.

RESPONSORIAL PSALM   *Psalm 125 response v 3*

> **What marvels the Lord worked for us!**
> **Indeed we were glad.**

1   When the Lord delivered Zion from bondage,
    it seemed like a dream.
    Then was our mouth filled with laughter,
    on our lips there were songs.

2   The heathens themselves said: 'What marvels
    the Lord worked for them!'
    What marvels the Lord worked for us!
    Indeed we were glad.

3   Deliver us, O Lord, from our bondage
    as streams in dry land.
    Those who are sowing in tears
    will sing when they reap.

4   They go out, they go out, full of tears,
    carrying seed for the sowing:
    they come back, they come back, full of song,
    carrying their sheaves.

SECOND READING   *Philippians 3:8–14*

Reproducing the pattern of his death, I have accepted the loss of everything for Christ.

I believe nothing can happen that will outweigh the supreme advantage of knowing Christ Jesus my Lord. For him I have accepted the loss of everything, and I look on everything as so much rubbish if only I can have Christ and be given a place in him. I am no longer trying for perfection by my own efforts, the perfection that comes from the Law, but I want only the perfection that comes through faith in Christ, and is from God and based on faith. All I want is to know Christ and the power of his resurrection and to share his sufferings by reproducing the pattern of his death. That is the way I can hope to take my place in the resurrection of the dead. Not that I have become perfect yet: I have not yet won, but I am still

LENT

running, trying to capture the prize for which Christ Jesus captured me. I can assure you my brothers, I am far from thinking that I have already won. All I can say is that I forget the past and I strain ahead for what is still to come; I am racing for the finish, for the prize to which God calls us upwards to receive in Christ Jesus.

The word of the Lord.
Thanks be to God.

GOSPEL ACCLAMATION *cf Amos 5:14*

> Praise to you, O Christ, king of eternal glory!
> Seek good and not evil so that you may live,
> and that the Lord God of hosts may really be with you.
> Praise to you, O Christ, king of eternal glory!

or *Joel 2:12–13*

> Praise to you, O Christ, king of eternal glory!
> Now, now – it is the Lord who speaks –
> come back to me with all your heart,
> for I am all tenderness and compassion.
> Praise to you, O Christ, king of eternal glory!

GOSPEL *John 8:1–11*

The Lord be with you.
And with your spirit.

A reading from the holy Gospel according to John.
Glory to you, O Lord.

If there is one of you who has not sinned, let him be the first to throw a stone at her.

Jesus went to the Mount of Olives. At daybreak he appeared in the Temple again; and as all the people came to him, he sat down and began to teach them.

The scribes and Pharisees brought a woman along who had been caught committing adultery; and making her stand there in full view of everybody, they said to Jesus, 'Master, this woman was caught in the very act of committing adultery, and Moses has ordered us in the Law to condemn women like this to death by stoning. What have you to say?' They asked him this as a test, looking for something to use against him. But Jesus bent down and started writing on the ground with his finger.

As they persisted with their question, he looked up and said, 'If there is one of you who has not sinned, let him be the first to throw a stone at her.' Then he bent down and wrote on the ground again. When they heard this they went away one by one, beginning with the eldest, until Jesus was left alone with the woman, who remained standing there. He looked up and said, 'Woman, where are they? Has no one condemned you?' 'No one, sir', she replied. 'Neither do I condemn you,' said Jesus 'go away, and don't sin any more.'

The Gospel of the Lord.
Praise to you, Lord Jesus Christ.

▷ *page 11*

PRAYER OVER THE OFFERINGS

Hear us, almighty God,
and, having instilled in your servants
the teachings of the Christian faith,
graciously purify them
by the working of this sacrifice.
Through Christ our Lord.   **Amen.**

▷ *page 15*

When Year C readings are used, Preface I or II of Lent is used, p 70.
When Year A readings are used, Preface: Lazarus is used, p 72.

COMMUNION ANTIPHON   *for Year C readings   John 8:10–11*

Has no one condemned you, woman? No one, Lord.
Neither shall I condemn you. From now on, sin no more.

or   *for Year A readings: cf John 11:26*

Everyone who lives and believes in me
will not die for ever, says the Lord.

▷ *page 58*

PRAYER AFTER COMMUNION

We pray, almighty God,
that we may always be counted among the members of Christ,
in whose Body and Blood we have communion.
Who lives and reigns for ever and ever.

▷ *page 59*

PRAYER OVER THE PEOPLE

Bless, O Lord, your people,
who long for the gift of your mercy,
and grant that what, at your prompting, they desire
they may receive by your generous gift.
Through Christ our Lord.

FIFTH SUNDAY OF LENT (YEAR A) AND THIRD SCRUTINY

RITUAL MASS FOR THE CELEBRATION OF THE SCRUTINIES: THIRD SCRUTINY
This Mass is used when the Third Scrutiny is being celebrated today.

ENTRANCE ANTIPHON   *cf Psalm 17:5–7*

The waves of death rose about me;
the pains of the nether world surrounded me.
In my anguish I called to the Lord;
and from his holy temple he heard my voice.

▷ *page 7*

The Gloria is omitted.

COLLECT

Grant, O Lord, to these chosen ones
that, instructed in the holy mysteries,
they may receive new life at the font of Baptism
and be numbered among the members of your Church.
Through our Lord Jesus Christ, your Son,
who lives and reigns with you in the unity of the Holy Spirit,
one God, for ever and ever. **Amen.**

These readings may be used in any year.

If the Third Scrutiny is not celebrated today, the Mass prayers of the Fifth Sunday of Lent (Year C) are used, page 176.

FIRST READING   *Ezekiel 37:12–14*

I shall put my spirit in you, and you will live.

The Lord says this: I am now going to open your graves; I mean to raise you from your graves, my people, and lead you back to the soil of Israel. And you will know that I am the Lord, when I open your graves and raise you from your graves, my people. And I shall put my spirit in you, and you will live, and I shall resettle you on your own soil; and you will know that I, the Lord, have said and done this – it is the Lord God who speaks.

The word of the Lord.
Thanks be to God.

RESPONSORIAL PSALM   *Psalm 129 response v 7*

**With the Lord there is mercy
and fullness of redemption.**

1 Out of the depths I cry to you, O Lord,
Lord, hear my voice!
O let your ears be attentive
to the voice of my pleading.

2 If you, O Lord, should mark our guilt,
Lord, who would survive?
But with you is found forgiveness:
for this we revere you.

3 My soul is waiting for the Lord,
I count on his word.
My soul is longing for the Lord
more than watchman for daybreak.
(Let the watchman count on daybreak
and Israel on the Lord.)

4 Because with the Lord there is mercy
and fullness of redemption,
Israel indeed he will redeem
from all its iniquity.

SECOND READING   *Romans 8:8–11*

The Spirit of him who raised Jesus from the dead is living in you.

People who are interested only in unspiritual things can never be pleasing to God. Your interests, however, are not in the unspiritual, but in the spiritual, since the Spirit of God has made his home in you. In fact, unless you possessed the Spirit of Christ you would not belong to him. Though your body may be dead it is because of sin, but if Christ is in you then your spirit is life itself because you have been justified; and if the Spirit of him who raised Jesus from the dead is living in you, then he who raised Jesus from the dead will give life to your own mortal bodies through his Spirit living in you.

The word of the Lord.
Thanks be to God.

GOSPEL ACCLAMATION   *John 11:25, 26*

> **Glory and praise to you, O Christ!**
> **I am the resurrection and the life, says the Lord;**
> **whoever believes in me will never die.**
> **Glory and praise to you, O Christ!**

GOSPEL   *John 11:1–45   Shorter form (omitting oblique text): John 11:3–7, 17, 20–27, 33–45*

The Lord be with you.
And with your spirit.

A reading from the holy Gospel according to John.
Glory to you, O Lord.

I am the resurrection and the life.

There was a man named Lazarus who lived in the village of Bethany with the two sisters, Mary and Martha, and he was ill. It was the same Mary, the sister of the sick man Lazarus, who anointed the Lord with ointment and wiped his feet with her hair. The sisters sent this message to Jesus, 'Lord, the man you love is ill.' On receiving the message, Jesus said, 'This sickness will end not in death but in God's glory, and through it the Son of God will be glorified.'

Jesus loved Martha and her sister and Lazarus, yet when he heard that Lazarus was ill he stayed where he was for two more days before saying to the disciples, 'Let us go to Judaea.' *The disciples said, 'Rabbi, it is not long since the Jews wanted to stone you; are you going back again?' Jesus replied:*

'Are there not twelve hours in the day? A man can walk in the daytime without stumbling because he has the light of this world to see by; but if he walks at night he stumbles, because there is no light to guide him'.

He said that and then added, 'Our friend Lazarus is resting, I am going to wake him. *The disciples said to him 'Lord, if he is able to rest he is sure to get better.' The phrase Jesus used referred to the death of Lazarus, but they thought that by 'rest'* he meant 'sleep', so Jesus put it plainly, 'Lazarus is dead, and for your sake I am glad I was not there because now you will believe. But let us go to him.' Then Thomas – known as the Twin – said to the other disciples, 'Let us go too, and die with him.*

On arriving, Jesus found that Lazarus had been in the tomb for four days already. *Bethany is only about two miles from Jerusalem, and many Jews had come to Martha and Mary to sympathise with them over their brother.* When Martha heard that Jesus had come she went to meet him. Mary remained sitting in the house. Martha said to Jesus, 'If you had been here, my brother would not have died, but I know that, even now, whatever you ask of God, he will grant you.' 'Your brother' said Jesus to her 'will rise again.' Martha said, 'I know he will rise again at the resurrection on the last day.' Jesus said:

'I am the resurrection and the life. If anyone believes in me, even though he dies he will live, and whoever lives and believes in me will never die. Do you believe this?'

'Yes Lord,' she said 'I believe that you are the Christ, the Son of God, the one who was to come into this world.'

When she had said this, she went and

called her sister Mary, saying in a low voice, 'The Master is here and wants to see you.' Hearing this, Mary got up quickly and went to him. Jesus had not yet come into the village; he was still at the place where Martha had met him. When the Jews who were in the house sympathising with Mary saw her get up so quickly and go out, they followed her, thinking that she was going to the tomb to weep there.

Mary went to Jesus, and as soon as she saw him she threw herself at his feet, saying, 'Lord if you had been here, my brother would not have died.' At the sight of her tears, and those of the Jews who followed her, Jesus said in great distress, with a sigh that came straight from the heart, 'Where have you put him?' They said, 'Lord, come and see.' Jesus wept; and the Jews said, 'See how much he loved him!' But there were some who remarked, 'He opened the eyes of the blind man, could he not have prevented this man's death?' Still sighing, Jesus reached the tomb: it was a cave with a stone to close the opening. Jesus said, 'Take the stone away.' Martha said to him 'Lord by now he will smell; this is the fourth day.' Jesus replied 'Have I not told you that if you believe you will see the glory of God?' So they took away the stone. Then Jesus lifted up his eyes and said:

'Father, I thank you for hearing my prayer. I knew indeed that you always hear me. But I speak for the sake of all these who stand round me, so that they may believe it was you who sent me.'

When he had said this, he cried in a loud voice, 'Lazarus, here! Come out!' The dead man came out, his feet and hands bound with bands of stuff and a cloth round his face. Jesus said to them, 'Unbind him, let him go free.'

Many of the Jews who had come to visit Mary and had seen what he did believed in him.

The Gospel of the Lord.
Praise to you, Lord Jesus Christ.

HOMILY

After the readings, and guided by them, the minister explains the meaning of the Third Scrutiny in the light of the Lenten liturgy and of the spiritual journey of the elect.

THIRD SCRUTINY

The Third Scrutiny follows the same pattern as the First Scrutiny (see p 166).
An outline of the rite is given here for reference.

INVITATION TO SILENT PRAYER

INTERCESSIONS FOR THE ELECT
Let us pray to the Lord
Lord, hear our prayer

EXORCISM

After the exorcism and prayer over the elect, an appropriate song may now be sung.

DISMISSAL OF THE ELECT

PRAYER OF THE FAITHFUL AND PROFESSION OF FAITH

Intercessory prayer is resumed with the usual Prayer of the Faithful for the needs of the Church and the whole world; then, if required, the Profession of Faith is said. But for pastoral reasons, the Prayer of the Faithful and the Profession of Faith may be omitted.

▷ *page 13*

PRAYER OVER THE OFFERINGS

Hear us, almighty God,
and, having instilled in your servants
the first fruits of the Christian faith,
graciously purify them by the working of this sacrifice.
Through Christ our Lord. **Amen.**

▷ *page 15*

EUCHARISTIC PRAYER

Preface: Lazarus is used, p 72.
In Eucharistic Prayers I, II and III, proper forms of certain sections are used, see p 168.

COMMUNION ANTIPHON   *cf John 11:26*

Everyone who lives and believes in me
will not die for ever, says the Lord.

▷ *page 58*

PRAYER AFTER COMMUNION

May your people be at one, O Lord, we pray,
and in wholehearted submission to you
may they obtain this grace:
that, safe from all distress,
they may readily live out their joy at being saved
and remember in loving prayer those to be reborn.
Through Christ our Lord. **Amen.**

▷ *page 59*

PALM SUNDAY OF THE PASSION OF THE LORD

On this day the Church recalls the entrance of Christ the Lord into Jerusalem to accomplish his Paschal Mystery. Accordingly, the memorial of this entrance of the Lord takes place at all Masses.

There are three forms of commemoration of the Lord's entrance into Jerusalem:

1 Procession	page 184 (below)
2 Solemn Entrance	page 189
3 Simple Entrance	page 190

At the principal Mass of the day, one of the first two forms is used.
At other Masses, either the Second or Third Form is used.

If either of the first two forms is used, the Penitential Act is omitted and the Mass continues with the Collect.

COMMEMORATION OF THE LORD'S ENTRANCE INTO JERUSALEM
FIRST FORM: PROCESSION

The people gather outside the Church or a building other than the Church.
As the Priest an other ministers arrive the following antiphon or other appropriate chant is sung.

ANTIPHON *Matthew 21:9*

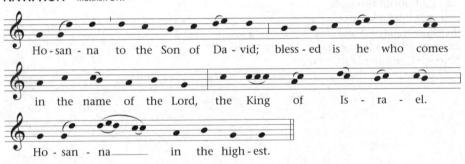

Ho-san-na to the Son of Da-vid; bless-ed is he who comes in the name of the Lord, the King of Is-ra-el. Ho-san-na in the high-est.

SIGN OF THE CROSS
All make the Sign of the Cross as the Priest says.

Priest: In the name of the Father, and of the Son, and of the Holy Spirit.
People: **Amen.**

GREETING

Priest: The grace of our Lord Jesus Christ,
and the love of God,
and the communion of the Holy Spirit
be with you all.

or

Priest: Grace to you and peace from God our Father
and the Lord Jesus Christ.

or

Priest: The Lord be with you.
People: **And with your spirit.**

A brief address is given, in which the faithful are invited to participate actively and consciously in the celebration of this day, in these or similar words:

Dear brethren (brothers and sisters),
since the beginning of Lent until now
we have prepared our hearts by penance and charitable works.
Today we gather together to herald with the whole Church
the beginning of the celebration
of our Lord's Paschal Mystery,
that is to say, of his Passion and Resurrection.
For it was to accomplish this mystery
that he entered his own city of Jerusalem.
Therefore, with all faith and devotion,
let us commemorate
the Lord's entry into the city for our salvation,
following in his footsteps,
so that, being made by his grace partakers of the Cross,
we may have a share also in his Resurrection and in his life.

After the address, the Priest says one of the following prayers with hands extended.
Let us pray.
Almighty ever-living God,
sanctify ✠ these branches with your blessing,
that we, who follow Christ the King in exultation,
may reach the eternal Jerusalem through him.
Who lives and reigns for ever and ever. **Amen.**

or

Increase the faith of those who place their hope in you, O God,
and graciously hear the prayers of those who call on you,
that we, who today hold high these branches
to hail Christ in his triumph,
may bear fruit for you by good works accomplished in him.
Who lives and reigns for ever and ever. **Amen.**

He sprinkles the branches with holy water without saying anything.

Then a Deacon or, if there is no Deacon, a Priest, proclaims the Gospel concerning the Lord's entrance.
The Deacon or Priest may use a different translation.

GOSPEL   *Luke 19:28–40*

The Lord be with you.
And with your spirit.

A reading from the holy Gospel according to Luke.
Glory to you, O Lord.

Blessed is he who comes in the name of the Lord.

Jesus went on ahead, going up to Jerusalem. When he drew near to Bethphage and Bethany, at the mount that is called Olivet, he sent two disciples, saying, 'Go into the village opposite, where on entering you will find a colt tied, on which no one has ever yet sat; untie it and bring it here. If anyone asks you, "Why are you untying it?" you shall say this, "The Lord has need of it"'. So those who were sent went away and found it as he had told them. And as they were untying the colt, its owners said to them, 'Why are you untying the colt?' And they said, 'The Lord has need of it'. And they brought it to Jesus, and throwing their garments on the colt they set Jesus upon it. And as he rode along, they spread their garments on the road. As he was drawing near, at the descent of the Mount of Olives, the whole multitude of the disciples began to rejoice and praise God with a loud voice for all the mighty works that they had seen, saying, 'Blessed is the King who comes in the name of the Lord! Peace in heaven and glory in the highest!' And some of the Pharisees in the multitude said to him, 'Teacher, rebuke your disciples'. He answered, 'I tell you, if these were silent, the very stones would cry out'.

The Gospel of the Lord.
Praise to you, Lord Jesus Christ.

HOMILY

A brief homily may be given.

PROCESSION

To begin the Procession, an invitation may be given by a Priest or a Deacon or a lay minister, in these or similar words:

Dear brethren (brothers and sisters),
like the crowds who acclaimed Jesus in Jerusalem,
let us go forth in peace.

or

Priest or Deacon: People:

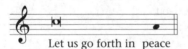

Let us go forth in peace   In the name of Christ. A-men.

As the Procession moves forward, the following or other suitable chants in honour of Christ the King are sung by the choir and people (see over).

Antiphon 1

The children of the Hebrews, carrying olive branches,
went to meet the Lord, crying out and saying:
Hosanna in the highest.

If appropriate, this antiphon is repeated between the strophes of the following Psalm.

Psalm 23

1   The LORD's is the earth and its fullness, *
the world, and those who dwell in it.
It is he who set it on the seas; *
on the rivers he made it firm.

The children of the Hebrews, carrying olive branches...

2   Who shall climb the mountain of the LORD? *
The clean of hands and pure of heart,
whose soul is not set on vain things, †
who has not sworn deceitful words. *

3   Blessings from the LORD shall he receive, *
and right reward from the God who saves him.
Such are the people who seek him, *
who seek the face of the God of Jacob.

4   O gates, lift high your heads, †
grow higher, ancient doors. *
Let him enter, the king of glory!
Who is this king of glory? *
The LORD, the mighty, the valiant;
the LORD, the valiant in war.

5   O gates, lift high your heads; †
grow higher, ancient doors. *
Let him enter, the king of glory!
Who is this king of glory? *
He, the LORD of hosts,
he is the king of glory.

Antiphon 2

The children of the Hebrews spread their garments on the road,
crying out and saying: Hosanna to the Son of David;
blessed is he who comes in the name of the Lord.

If appropriate, this antiphon is repeated between the strophes of the following Psalm.

Psalm 46

1   All peoples, clap your hands. *
Cry to God with shouts of joy!
For the LORD, the Most high, is awesome, *
the great king over all the earth.

The children of the Hebrews spread their garments...

2   He humbles peoples under us *
and nations under our feet.
Our heritage he chose for us, *
the pride of Jacob whom he loves.
God goes up with shouts of joy. *
The LORD goes up with trumpet blast.

3   Sing praise for God; sing praise! *
Sing praise to our king; sing praise!
God is king of all earth. *
Sing praise with all your skill.

4   God reigns over the nations. *
    God sits upon his holy throne.
    The princes of the peoples are assembled
    with the people of the God of Abraham. †
    The rulers of the earth belong to God, *
    who is greatly exalted.

Hymn to Christ the King

**Glory and honour and praise be to you, Christ, King and Redeemer,
to whom young children cried out loving Hosannas with joy.**

Israel's King are you, King David's magnificent offspring;
you are the ruler who come blest in the name of the Lord.

**Glory and honour and praise be to you, Christ, King and Redeemer,
to whom young children cried out loving Hosannas with joy.**

Heavenly hosts on high unite in singing your praises;
men and women on earth and all creation join in.

Bearing branches of palm, Hebrews came crowding to greet you;
see how with prayers and hymns we come to pay you our vows.

They offered gifts of praise to you, so near to your Passion;
see how we sing this song now to you reigning on high.

Those you were pleased to accept; now accept our gifts of devotion,
good and merciful King, lover of all that is good.

The following is a popular version of this hymn

**All glory, laud and honour,
To thee, Redeemer King,
To whom the lips of children
Made sweet hosannas ring.**

1   Thou art the King of Israel,
    Thou David's royal Son,
    Who in the Lord's name comest,
    The King and blessed one.

2   The company of angels
    Are praising thee on high,
    And mortal folk and all things
    Created make reply.

3   The people of the Hebrews
    With palms before thee went:
    Our praise and prayer and anthems
    Before thee we present.

4   To thee before thy passion
    They sang their hymns of praise;
    To thee now high exalted
    Our melody we raise.

5   Thou didst accept their praises,
    Accept the prayers we bring,
    Who in all good delightest,
    Thou good and gracious king.

As the procession enters the church, the following responsory
or another chant about the Lord's triumphal entry into Jerusalem is sung.

RESPONSORY

R   As the Lord entered the holy city, the children of the Hebrews proclaimed
     the resurrection of life.
     * Waving their branches of palm, they cried: Hosanna in the Highest.
V   When the people heard that Jesus was coming to Jerusalem,
     they went out to meet him.
     * Waving their branches...

The Mass continues with the Collect (see page 190).

SECOND FORM: SOLEMN ENTRANCE

When a procession outside the church cannot take place, the entrance of the Lord is celebrated inside the church by means of a Solemn Entrance before the principal Mass.

Holding branches in their hands, the faithful gather either outside, in front of the church door, or inside the church itself. The Priest and ministers and a representative group of the faithful go to a suitable place in the church outside the sanctuary, where at least the greater part of the faithful can see the rite.

As the Priest and other ministers arrive the following antiphon or other appropriate chant is sung.

ANTIPHON   *Matthew 21:9*

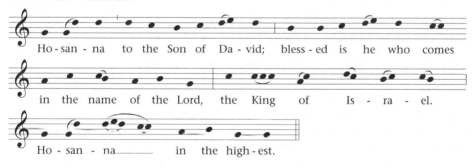

Ho-san-na to the Son of Da-vid; bless-ed is he who comes in the name of the Lord, the King of Is - ra - el. Ho - san - na in the high-est.

Then the blessing of branches and the proclamation of the Gospel of the Lord's entrance into Jerusalem take place as above (p 185).

After the Gospel, the Priest processes solemnly with the ministers and the representative group of the faithful through the church to the sanctuary, while the responsory 'As the Lord entered' (see above) or another appropriate chant is sung.

The Mass continues with the Collect (see page 190).

THIRD FORM: SIMPLE ENTRANCE

If the Simple Entrance is used, Mass begins in the usual way.

ENTRANCE ANTIPHON   *cf John 12:1, 12–13; Psalm 23:9–10*

Six days before the Passover,
when the Lord came into the city of Jerusalem,
the children ran to meet him;
in their hands they carried palm branches
and with a loud voice cried out:
* Hosanna in the highest!
Blessed are you, who have come in your abundant mercy!

O gates, lift high your heads;
grow higher, ancient doors.
Let him enter, the king of glory!
Who is this king of glory?
He, the Lord of hosts, he is the king of glory.
* Hosanna in the highest!
Blessed are you, who have come in your abundant mercy!

▷ *page 7*

The Gloria is omitted.

AT THE MASS

After the Procession or Solemn Entrance the Priest begins the Mass with the Collect.

COLLECT

Almighty ever-living God,
who as an example of humility for the human race to follow
caused our Saviour to take flesh and submit to the Cross,
graciously grant that we may heed his lesson of patient suffering
and so merit a share in his Resurrection.
Who lives and reigns with you in the unity of the Holy Spirit,
one God, for ever and ever.   **Amen.**

FIRST READING   *Isaiah 50:4–7*

*I did not cover my face against insult, I know I shall
not be shamed*

The Lord has given me a disciple's tongue. So that I may know how to reply to the wearied he provides me with speech. Each morning he wakes me to hear, to listen like a disciple. The Lord has opened my ear. For my part, I made no resistance, neither did I turn away. I offered my back to those who struck me, my cheeks to those who tore at my beard; I did not cover my face against insult and spittle. The Lord comes to my help, so that I am untouched by the insults. So, too, I set my face like flint; I know I shall not be shamed.

The word of the Lord.
Thanks be to God.

RESPONSORIAL PSALM   *Psalm 21:8–9, 17–20, 23–24 response v 2*

My God, my God, why have you forsaken me?

1   All who see me deride me.
They curl their lips, they toss their heads.
'He trusted in the Lord, let him save him;
let him release him if this is his friend.'

2   Many dogs have surrounded me,
a band of the wicked beset me,
They tear holes in my hands and my feet.
I can count every one of my bones.

3   They divide my clothing among them.
They cast lots for my robe.
O Lord, do not leave me alone,
my strength, make haste to help me!

4   I will tell of your name to my brethren
and praise you where they are assembled
'You who fear the Lord give him praise;
all sons of Jacob, give him glory.
Revere him, Israel's sons.'

SECOND READING   *Philippians 2:6–11*

He humbled himself; but God raised him high.

His state was divine, yet Christ Jesus did not cling to his equality with God but emptied himself to assume the condition of a slave, and became as men are; and being as all men are, he was humbler yet, even to accepting death, death on a cross. But God raised him high and gave him the name which is above all other names so that all beings in the heavens, on earth and in the underworld, should bend the knee at the name of Jesus and that every tongue should acclaim Jesus Christ as Lord, to the glory of God the Father.

The word of the Lord.
Thanks be to God.

GOSPEL ACCLAMATION   *Philippians 2:8–9*

**Praise to you, O Christ, king of eternal glory!
Christ was humbler yet,
even to accepting death,
death on a cross.
But God raised him high
and gave him the name which is above all names.
Praise to you, O Christ, king of eternal glory!**

LENT

GOSPEL   *Luke 22:14–23:56   Shorter form (omitting oblique text): Luke 23:1–49*

The narrative of the Lord's Passion is read without candles and without incense, with no greeting or signing of the book. It is read by a Deacon or, if there is no Deacon, by a Priest. It may also be read by readers, with the part of Christ, if possible, reserved to a Priest.
N = Narrator;   J = Jesus;   O = Other speaker;   C = Crowd, or more than one speaker

The passion of our Lord Jesus Christ according to Luke

N   When the hour came Jesus took his place at table, and the apostles with him. And he said to them,

J   I have longed to eat this passover with you before I suffer; because, I tell you, I shall not eat it again until it is fulfilled in the kingdom of God.

N   Then, taking a cup, he gave thanks and said,

J   Take this and share it among you, because from now on, I tell you, I shall not drink wine until the kingdom of God comes.

N   Then he took some bread, and when he had given thanks, broke it and gave it to them, saying,

J   This is my body which will be given for you; do this as a memorial of me.

N   He did the same with the cup after supper, and said,

J   This cup is the new covenant in my blood which will be poured out for you.

And yet, here with me on the table is the hand of the man who betrays me. The Son of Man does indeed go to his fate even as it has been decreed, but alas for that man by whom he is betrayed!

N   *And they began to ask one another which of them it could be who was to do this thing.*

A dispute arose also between them about which should be reckoned the greatest, but he said to them,

J   *Among pagans it is the kings who lord it over them, and those who have authority over them are given the title Benefactor. This must not happen with you. No; the greatest among you must behave as if he were the youngest, the leader as if he were the one who serves. For who is the greater: the one at table or the one who serves? The one at table, surely? Yet here am I among you as one who serves!*

You are the men who have stood by me faithfully in my trials; and now I confer a kingdom on you, just as my Father conferred one on me: you will eat and drink at my table in my kingdom, and you will sit on thrones to judge the twelve tribes of Israel.

Simon, Simon! Satan, you must know, has got his wish to sift you all like wheat; but I have prayed for you, Simon, that your faith may not fail, and once you have recovered, you in your turn must strengthen your brothers.

N   *He answered,*

O   *Lord, I would be ready to go to prison with you, and to death.*

N   *Jesus replied,*

J   *I tell you, Peter by the time the cock crows today you will have denied three times that you know me.*

N   *He said to them,*

J   *When I sent you out without purse or haversack or sandals, were you short of anything?*

N They answered,

C No.

N He said to them,

J But now if you have a purse, take it; if you have a haversack, do the same; if you have no sword, sell your cloak and buy one, because I tell you these words of scripture have to be fulfilled in me: He let himself be taken for a criminal. Yes, what scripture says about me is even now reaching its fulfilment.

N They said

C Lord, there are two swords here now.

N He said to them,

J That is enough!

N He then left the upper room to make his way as usual to the Mount of Olives, with the disciples following. When they reached the place he said to them,

J Pray not to be put to the test.

N Then he withdrew from them, about a stone's throw away, and knelt down and prayed, saying,

J Father, if you are willing, take this cup away from me. Nevertheless, let your will be done, not mine.

N Then an angel appeared to him, coming from heaven to give him strength. In his anguish he prayed even more earnestly, and his sweat fell to the ground like great drops of blood.

When he rose from prayer he went to the disciples and found them sleeping for sheer grief. He said to them,

J Why are you asleep? Get up and pray not to be put to the test.

N He was still speaking when a number of men appeared, and at the head of them the man called Judas, one of the Twelve, who went up to Jesus to kiss him. Jesus said,

J Judas, are you betraying the Son of Man with a kiss?

N His followers, seeing what was happening, said,

C Lord, shall we use our swords?

N And one of them struck out at the high priest's servant, and cut off his right ear. But at this Jesus spoke.

J Leave off! That will do!

N And touching the man's ear he healed him.

Then Jesus spoke to the chief priests and captains of the Temple guard and elders who had come for him. He said,

J Am I a brigand that you had to set out with swords and clubs? When I was among you in the Temple day after day you never moved to lay hands on me. But this is your hour; this is the reign of darkness.

N They seized him then and led him away, and they took him to the high priest's house. Peter followed at a distance. They had lit a fire in the middle of the courtyard and Peter sat down among them and as he was sitting there by the blaze a servant-girl saw him, peered at him, and said,

O This person was with him too.

N But he denied it saying,

O Woman, I do not know him.

N Shortly afterwards someone else saw him and said,

O You are another of them.

N But Peter replied,

O I am not, my friend.

N About an hour later another man insisted saying,

LENT

O This fellow was certainly with him. Why, he is a Galilean.

N Peter said,

O My friend, I do not know what you are talking about.

N At that instant, while he was still speaking, the cock crew, and the Lord turned and looked straight at Peter, and Peter remembered what the Lord had said to him. 'Before the cock crows today, you will have disowned me three times.' And he went outside and wept bitterly.

Meanwhile the men who guarded Jesus were mocking and beating him. They blindfolded him and questioned him, saying,

C Play the prophet. Who hit you then?

N And they continued heaping insults on him.

When day broke there was a meeting of the elders of the people, attended by the chief priests and scribes. He was brought before their council, and they said to him,

C If you are the Christ, tell us.

N He replied,

J If I tell you, you will not believe me, and if I question you, you will not answer. But from now on, the Son of Man will be seated at the right hand of the Power of God.

N Then they all said,

C So you are the Son of God then?

N He answered,

J It is you who say I am.

N They said,

C What need of witnesses have we now? We have heard it for ourselves from his own lips.

*N The whole assembly then rose, and they brought him before Pilate.

They began their accusation by saying,

C We found this man inciting our people to revolt, opposing payment of tribute to Caesar, and claiming to be Christ, a king.

N Pilate put to him this question,

O Are you the king of the Jews?

N He replied,

J It is you who say it.

N Pilate then said to the chief priests and the crowd,

O I find no case against this man.

N But they persisted,

C He is inflaming the people with his teaching all over Judaea; it has come all the way from Galilee, where he started, down to here.

N When Pilate heard this, he asked if the man were a Galilean; and finding that he came under Herod's jurisdiction he passed him over to Herod who was also in Jerusalem at that time.

Herod was delighted to see Jesus; he had heard about him and had been wanting for a long time to set eyes on him; moreover, he was hoping to see some miracle worked by him. So he questioned him at some length; but without getting any reply. Meanwhile the chief priests and the

---

* The shorter version of this reading begins:

N The elders of the people and the chief priests and scribes rose, and they brought Jesus before Pilate.

They began their accusation...

scribes were there, violently pressing their accusations. Then Herod, together with his guards, treated him with contempt and made fun of him; he put a rich cloak on him and sent him back to Pilate. And though Herod and Pilate had been enemies before, they were reconciled that same day.

Pilate then summoned the chief priests and the leading men and the people. He said,

O You brought this man before me as a political agitator. Now I have gone into the matter myself in your presence and found no case against the man in respect of all the charges you bring against him. Nor has Herod either, since he has sent him back to us. As you can see, the man has done nothing that deserves death, so I shall have him flogged and then let him go.

N But as one man they howled,

C Away with him! Give us Barabbas!

N This man had been thrown into prison for causing a riot in the city and for murder.

Pilate was anxious to set Jesus free and addressed them again, but they shouted back,

C Crucify him! Crucify him!

N And for the third time he spoke to them,

O Why? What harm has this man done? I have found no case against him that deserves death, so I shall have him punished and then let him go.

N But they kept on shouting at the top of their voices, demanding that he should be crucified. And their shouts were growing louder.

Pilate then gave his verdict: their demand was to be granted. He released the man they asked for, who had been imprisoned for rioting and murder, and handed Jesus over to them to deal with as they pleased.

As they were leading him away they seized on a man, Simon from Cyrene, who was coming in from the country, and made him shoulder the cross and carry it behind Jesus. Large numbers of people followed him, and of women too, who mourned and lamented for him. But Jesus turned to them and said,

J Daughters of Jerusalem, do not weep for me; weep rather for yourselves and for your children. For the days will surely come when people will say, 'Happy are those who are barren, the wombs that have never borne, the breasts that have never suckled!' Then they will begin to say to the mountains, 'Fall on us!'; to the hills, 'Cover us!' For if men use the green wood like this, what will happen when it is dry?

N Now with him they were also leading out two other criminals to be executed.

When they reached the place called The Skull, they crucified him there and the two criminals also, one on the right, the other on the left. Jesus said,

J Father, forgive them; they do not know what they are doing.

N Then they cast lots to share out his clothing. The people stayed there watching him. As for the leaders, they jeered at him, saying,

C He saved others, let him save himself if he is the Christ of God, the Chosen One.

N   The soldiers mocked him too, and when they approached to offer him vinegar they said,

C   If you are the king of the Jews, save yourself.

N   Above him there was an inscription: 'This is the King of the Jews.'

One of the criminals hanging there abused him, saying,

O   Are you not the Christ? Save yourself and us as well.

N   But the other spoke up and rebuked him.

O   Have you no fear of God at all? You got the same sentence as he did, but in our case we deserved it: we are paying for what we did. But this man has done nothing wrong. Jesus, remember me when you come into your kingdom.

N   He replied,

J   Indeed, I promise you, today you will be with me in paradise.

N   It was now about the sixth hour and, with the sun eclipsed, a darkness came over the whole land until the ninth hour. The veil of the Temple was torn right down the middle; and when Jesus had cried out in a loud voice, he said,

J   Father, into your hands I commit my spirit.

N   With these words he breathed his last.

All kneel and pause a moment.

N   When the centurion saw what had taken place, he gave praise to God and said,

O   This was a great and good man.

N   And when all the people who had gathered for the spectacle saw what had happened, they went home beating their breasts.

All his friends stood at a distance; so also did the women who had accompanied him from Galilee, and they saw all this happen.

Then a member of the council arrived, an upright and virtuous man named Joseph. He had not consented to what the others had planned and carried out. He came from Arimathaea, a Jewish town, and he lived in the hope of seeing the kingdom of God. This man went to Pilate and asked for the body of Jesus. He then took it down, wrapped it in a shroud and put him in a tomb which was hewn in stone in which no one had yet been laid. It was Preparation Day and the sabbath was imminent.

Meanwhile the women who had come from Galilee with Jesus were following behind. They took note of the tomb and of the position of the body.

Then they returned and prepared spices and ointments. And on the sabbath day they rested, as the Law required.

*The reading ends in silence
without any acclamation or response.*

HOMILY

After the narrative of the Passion, a brief homily should take place, if appropriate.
A period of silence may also be observed.

▷ *page 11*

PRAYER OVER THE OFFERINGS

Through the Passion of your Only Begotten Son, O Lord,
may our reconciliation with you be near at hand,
so that, though we do not merit it by our own deeds,
yet by this sacrifice made once for all,
we may feel already the effects of your mercy.
Through Christ our Lord.   **Amen.**

▷ *page 15*

Preface: The Passion of the Lord, see page 73.

COMMUNION ANTIPHON   *Matthew 26:42*

Father, if this chalice cannot pass without my drinking it,
your will be done.

▷ *page 58*

PRAYER AFTER COMMUNION

Nourished with these sacred gifts,
we humbly beseech you, O Lord,
that, just as through the death of your Son
you have brought us to hope for what we believe,
so by his Resurrection
you may lead us to where you call.
Through Christ our Lord.   **Amen.**

▷ *page 59*

PRAYER OVER THE PEOPLE

Look, we pray, O Lord, on this your family,
for whom our Lord Jesus Christ
did not hesitate to be delivered into the hands of the wicked
and submit to the agony of the Cross.
Who lives and reigns for ever and ever.   **Amen.**

LENT

SACRED PASCHAL TRIDUUM

ABOUT THE SEASON

Since Christ accomplished his work of human redemption and of the perfect glorification of God principally through his Paschal Mystery, in which by dying he has destroyed our death, and by rising restored our life, the sacred Paschal Triduum of the Passion and Resurrection of the Lord shines forth as the high point of the entire liturgical year.

Therefore the pre-eminence that Sunday has in the week, the Solemnity of Easter has in the liturgical year.

The Paschal Triduum of the Passion and Resurrection of the Lord begins with the evening Mass of the Lord's Supper, has its centre in the Easter Vigil, and closes with Vespers (Evening Prayer) of the Sunday of the Resurrection.

On Friday of the Passion of the Lord and, if appropriate, also on Holy Saturday until the Easter Vigil, the sacred Paschal Fast is everywhere observed.

The Easter Vigil, in the holy night when the Lord rose again, is considered the 'mother of all holy Vigils', in which the Church, keeping watch, awaits the Resurrection of Christ and celebrates it in the Sacraments. Therefore, the entire celebration of this sacred Vigil must take place at night, so that it both begins after nightfall and ends before the dawn on the Sunday.

Universal Norms on the Liturgical Year and the Calendar nn 18–21

ABOUT THE READINGS

On Holy Thursday at the evening Mass the remembrance of the supper preceding Christ's departure casts its own special light because of the Lord's example in washing the feet of his disciples and Paul's account of the institution of the Christian Passover in the eucharist.

On Good Friday the liturgical service has as its centre John's narrative of the passion of him who was portrayed in Isaiah as the Servant of the LORD and who became the one High Priest by offering himself to the Father.

On the holy night of the Easter Vigil there are seven Old Testament readings, recalling the wonderful works of God in the history of salvation. There are two New Testament readings, the announcement of the resurrection according to one of the Synoptic Gospels and a reading from St. Paul on Christian baptism as the sacrament of Christ's resurrection.

Introduction to the Lectionary n 99

MAUNDY THURSDAY

MASS OF THE LORD'S SUPPER

ENTRANCE ANTIPHON *cf Galatians 6:14*

We should glory in the Cross of our Lord Jesus Christ,
in whom is our salvation, life and resurrection,
through whom we are saved and delivered.

▷ *page 7*

The Gloria is sung during which bells are rung.
When it is finished, they remain silent until the Gloria of the Easter Vigil.

COLLECT

O God, who have called us to participate
in this most sacred Supper,
in which your Only Begotten Son,
when about to hand himself over to death,
entrusted to the Church a sacrifice new for all eternity,
the banquet of his love,
grant, we pray,
that we may draw from so great a mystery,
the fullness of charity and of life.
Through our Lord Jesus Christ, your Son,
who lives and reigns with you in the unity of the Holy Spirit,
one God, for ever and ever. **Amen.**

FIRST READING *Exodus 12:1–8, 11–14*

Instructions concerning the Passover meal.

The Lord said to Moses and Aaron in the land of Egypt, 'This month is to be the first of all the others for you, the first month of your year. Speak to the whole community of Israel and say, "On the tenth day of this month each man must take an animal from the flock, one for each family: one animal for each household. If the household is too small to eat the animal, a man must join with his neighbour, the nearest to his house, as the number of persons requires. You must take into account what each can eat in deciding the number for the animal. It must be an animal without blemish, a male one year old; you may take it from either sheep or goats. You must keep it till the fourteenth day of the month when the whole assembly of the community of Israel shall slaughter it between the two evenings. Some of the blood must then be taken and put on the two doorposts and the lintel of the houses where it is eaten. That night, the flesh is to be eaten, roasted over the fire; it must be eaten with unleavened bread and bitter herbs. You shall eat it like this: with a girdle round your waist, sandals on your feet, a staff in your hand. You shall eat it hastily: it is a Passover in honour of the Lord. That night, I will go through the land of Egypt and strike down all the first born in the land of Egypt, man and beast alike, and I shall deal out punishment to all the gods of Egypt, I am the Lord. The blood shall serve to mark the houses that you live

TRIDUUM

in. When I see the blood I will pass over you and you shall escape the destroying plague when I strike the land of Egypt. This day is to be a day of remembrance for you, and you must celebrate it as a feast in the Lord's honour. For all generations you are to declare it a day of festival, for ever."'

The word of the Lord.
Thanks be to God.

RESPONSORIAL PSALM   *Psalm 115:12–13, 15–18, response cf 1 Corinthians 10:16*

The blessing-cup that we bless
is a communion with the blood of Christ.

1 How can I repay the Lord
   for his goodness to me?
   The cup of salvation I will raise;
   I will call on the Lord's name.

2 O precious in the eyes of the Lord
   is the death of his faithful.
   Your servant, Lord, your servant am I;
   you have loosened my bonds.

3 A thanksgiving sacrifice I make:
   I will call on the Lord's name.
   My vows to the Lord I will fulfil
   before all his people.

SECOND READING   *1 Corinthians 11:23–26*

Every time you eat this bread and drink this cup, you are proclaiming the death of the Lord.

This is what I received from the Lord, and in turn passed on to you: that on the same night that he was betrayed, the Lord Jesus took some bread, and thanked God for it and broke it, and he said, 'This is my body, which is for you; do this as a memorial of me.' In the same way he took the cup after supper, and said, 'This cup is the new covenant in my blood. Whenever you drink it, do this as a memorial of me.' Until the Lord comes, therefore, every time you eat this bread and drink this cup, you are proclaiming his death.

The word of the Lord.
Thanks be to God.

GOSPEL ACCLAMATION   *John 13:34*

Paise and honour to you, Lord Jesus!
I give you a new commandment:
love one another just as I have loved you, says the Lord.
Praise and honour to you, Lord Jesus!

GOSPEL   *John 13:1–15*

The Lord be with you.
And with your spirit.

A reading from the holy Gospel according to John.
Glory to you, O Lord.

Now he showed how perfect his love was.

It was before the festival of the Passover, and Jesus knew that the hour had come for him to pass from this world to the Father. He had always loved those who were his in the world, but now he showed how perfect his love was. They were at supper, and the devil had already put it into the mind of Judas Iscariot son of Simon, to betray him. Jesus knew that the Father had put everything into his hands, and that he had come from God and was returning to God, and he got up from the table, removed his outer garment and, taking a towel, wrapped it round his waist; he then poured water into a basin and began to wash the disciples' feet and to wipe them with the towel he was wearing.

He came to Simon Peter, who said to him, 'Lord, are you going to wash my feet?' Jesus answered, 'At the moment you do not know what I am doing, but later you will understand.' 'Never!' said Peter 'You shall never wash my feet.' Jesus replied, 'If I do not wash you, you can have nothing in common with me.' 'Then, Lord,' said Simon Peter 'not only my feet, but my hands and my head as well!' Jesus said, 'No one who has taken a bath needs washing, he is clean all over. You too are clean, though not all of you are.' He knew who was going to betray him, that was why he said, 'though not all of you are.'

When he had washed their feet and put on his clothes again he went back to the table. 'Do you understand' he said 'what I have done to you? You call me Master and Lord, and rightly; so I am. If I, then, the Lord and Master, have washed your feet, you should wash each other's feet. I have given you an example so that you may copy what I have done to you.'

The Gospel of the Lord.
Praise to you, Lord Jesus Christ.

HOMILY

WASHING OF FEET

During the Washing of the Feet some of the following antiphons or other appropriate chants are sung.

ANTIPHON 1   *cf John 13:4, 5, 15*

After the Lord had risen from supper,
he poured water into a basin
and began to wash the feet of his disciples:
he left them this example.

ANTIPHON 2   *cf John 13:12, 13, 15*

The Lord Jesus, after eating supper with his disciples,
washed their feet and said to them:
Do you know what I, your Lord and Master, have done for you?
I have given you an example, that you should do likewise.

ANTIPHON 3   *John 13:6, 7, 8*

* Lord, are you to wash my feet? Jesus said to him in answer:
If I do not wash your feet, you will have no share with me.

V   So he came to Simon Peter and Peter said to him:
       * Lord...

V   What I am doing, you do not know for now,
       but later you will come to know.
       * Lord...

ANTIPHON 4   *cf John 13:14*

If I, your Lord and Master, have washed your feet,
how much more should you wash each other's feet?

ANTIPHON 5   *John 13:35*

* This is how all will know that you are my disciples:
if you have love for one another.

V   Jesus said to his disciples:
         * This is how...

ANTIPHON 6   *John 13:34*

I give you a new commandment,
that you love one another
as I have loved you, says the Lord.

ANTIPHON 7   *1 Corinthians 13:13*

* Let faith, hope and charity, these three, remain among you,
but the greatest of these is charity.

V   Now faith, hope and charity, these three, remain;
         but the greatest of these is charity.
         * Let faith...

The Profession of Faith is not said. The Mass continues with the Prayer of the Faithful.

▷ **page 13**

PREPARATION OF THE GIFTS

At the beginning of the Liturgy of the Eucharist, there may be a procession of the faithful in which gifts for the poor may be presented with the bread and wine.

Meanwhile the following, or another appropriate chant, is sung.

Ant   Where true charity is dwelling, God is present there.

V   By the love of Christ we have been brought together:
V   let us find in him our gladness and our pleasure;
V   may we love him and revere him, God the living,
V   and in love respect each other with sincere hearts.

Ant   Where true charity is dwelling, God is present there.
V   So when we as one are gathered all together,
V   let us strive to keep our minds free of division;
V   may there be an end to malice, strife and quarrels,
V   and let Christ our God be dwelling here among us.

Ant   Where true charity is dwelling, God is present there.
V   May your face thus be our vision, bright in glory,
V   Christ our God, with all the blessed Saints in heaven:
V   such delight is pure and faultless, joy unbounded,
V   which endures through countless ages world without end Amen.

PRAYER OVER THE OFFERINGS

Grant us, O Lord, we pray,
that we may participate worthily in these mysteries,
for whenever the memorial of this sacrifice is celebrated
the work of our redemption is accomplished.
Through Christ our Lord.   **Amen.**

▷ page 15

EUCHARISTIC PRAYER

Eucharistic Prayer I, II, or III may be used with Preface I of the Most Holy Eucharist, p 73.

When the Roman Canon (Eucharistic Prayer I) is used, the proper forms of the Communicantes (In communion with those), Hanc igitur (Therefore, Lord, we pray), and Qui pridie (On the day before he was to suffer) are said, pp 19–21.

COMMUNION ANTIPHON   1 Corinthians 11:24–25

This is the Body that will be given up for you;
this is the Chalice of the new covenant in my Blood, says the Lord;
do this, whenever you receive it, in memory of me.

▷ page 58

After the distribution of Communion, a ciborium with hosts for Communion on the following day is left on the altar.

PRAYER AFTER COMMUNION

Grant, almighty God,
that, just as we are renewed
by the Supper of your Son in this present age,
so we may enjoy his banquet for all eternity.
Who lives and reigns for ever and ever.   **Amen.**

THE TRANSFER OF THE MOST BLESSED SACRAMENT

After the Prayer after Communion, the Priest incenses the Blessed Sacrament. After this, a procession is formed in which the Blessed Sacrament, accompanied by torches and incense, is carried through the church to a place of repose.

Meanwhile a suitable eucharistic chant is sung. If the hymn Pange, lingua, gloriosi (Of the glorious body telling) is sung, the last two stanzas are reserved until the procession reaches the place of repose.

When the procession reaches the place of repose, the Priest, kneeling, incenses the Blessed Sacrament, while Tantum ergo Sacramentum (Therefore, we before him bending) or another eucharistic chant is sung.

After a period of adoration in silence, the Priest and ministers genuflect and return to the sacristy.

The faithful are invited to continue adoration before the Blessed Sacrament for a suitable length of time during the night, according to local circumstances, but after midnight the adoration should take place without solemnity.

TRIDUUM

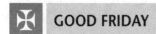 GOOD FRIDAY

CELEBRATION OF THE LORD'S PASSION

The celebration of the Lord's Passion consists of three parts

Liturgy of the Word

Adoration of the Cross

Holy Communion

The altar is bare: without a cross, without candles and without cloths.

The Priest and the Deacon, if a Deacon is present, go to the altar in silence and, after making a reverence to the altar, prostrate themselves or, if appropriate, kneel and pray in silence for a while.

All others kneel.

Then the Priest says one of the following prayers, omitting the invitation 'Let us pray'.

PRAYER

Remember your mercies, O Lord,
and with your eternal protection sanctify your servants,
for whom Christ your Son,
by the shedding of his Blood,
established the Paschal Mystery.
Who lives and reigns for ever and ever.   **Amen.**

or

O God, who by the Passion of Christ your Son, our Lord,
abolished the death inherited from ancient sin
by every succeeding generation,
grant that just as, being conformed to him,
we have borne by the law of nature
the image of the man of earth,
so by the sanctification of grace
we may bear the image of the Man of heaven.
Through Christ our Lord.   **Amen.**

FIRST PART: LITURGY OF THE WORD

FIRST READING   *Isaiah 52:13–53:12*

He was pierced through for our faults.

See, my servant will prosper, he shall be lifted up, exalted, rise to great heights.

As the crowds were appalled on seeing him – so disfigured did he look that he seemed no longer human – so will the crowds be astonished at him, and kings stand speechless before him; for they shall see something never told and witness something never heard before: 'Who could believe what we have heard, and to whom has the power of the Lord been revealed?'

Like a sapling he grew up in front of us, like a root in arid ground. Without beauty, without majesty (we saw him), no looks to attract our eyes; a thing despised and rejected by men, a man of sorrows and familiar with suffering, a man to make people screen their faces; he was despised and we took no account of him. And yet ours were the sufferings he bore, ours the sorrows he carried. But we, we thought of him as someone punished, struck by God, and brought low. Yet he was pierced through for our faults, crushed for our sins. On him lies a punishment that brings us peace, and through his wounds we are healed. We had all gone astray like sheep, each taking his own way, and the Lord burdened him with the sins of all of us. Harshly dealt with, he bore it humbly, he never opened his mouth, like a lamb that is led to the slaughterhouse, like a sheep that is dumb before its shearers never opening its mouth.

By force and by law he was taken; would anyone plead his cause? Yes, he was torn away from the land of the living; for our faults struck down in death. They gave him a grave with the wicked, a tomb with the rich, though he had done no wrong and there had been no perjury in his mouth. The Lord has been pleased to crush him with suffering. If he offers his life in atonement, he shall see his heirs, he shall have a long life and through him what the Lord wishes will be done.

His soul's anguish over he shall see the light and be content. By his sufferings shall my servant justify many, taking their faults on himself.

Hence I will grant whole hordes for his tribute, he shall divide the spoil with the mighty, for surrendering himself to death and letting himself be taken for a sinner, while he was bearing the faults of many and praying all the time for sinners.

The word of the Lord.

Thanks be to God.

RESPONSORIAL PSALM   *Psalm 30:2, 6, 12–13, 15–17, 25 response Luke 23:46*

Father, into your hands I commend my spirit.

1   In you, O Lord, I take refuge.
    Let me never be put to shame.
    In your justice, set me free.
    Into your hands I commend my spirit.
    It is you will redeem me, Lord.

2   In the face of all my foes
    I am a reproach,
    an object of scorn to my neighbours
    and of fear to my friends.

3   Those who see me in the street
    run far away from me.
    I am like a dead man, forgotten in men's hearts,
    like a thing thrown away.

4   But as for me, I trust in you, Lord,
    I say: 'You are my God.'
    My life is in your hands, deliver me
    from the hands of those who hate me.

5   Let your face shine on your servant.
    Save me in your love.
    Be strong, let your heart take courage,
    all who hope in the Lord.

SECOND READING   *Hebrews 4:14–16; 5:7–9*

He learnt to obey through suffering and became for all who obey him the source of eternal salvation.

Since in Jesus, the Son of God, we have the supreme high priest who has gone through to the highest heaven, we must never let go of the faith that we have professed. For it is not as if we had a high priest who was incapable of feeling our weaknesses with us; but we have one who has been tempted in every way that we are, though he is without sin. Let us be confident, then, in approaching the throne of grace, that we shall have mercy from him and find grace when we are in need of help.

During his life on earth, he offered up prayer and entreaty, aloud and in silent tears, to the one who had the power to save him out of death, and he submitted so humbly that his prayer was heard. Although he was Son, he learnt to obey through suffering; but having been made perfect, he became for all who obey him the source of eternal salvation.

The word of the Lord.

Thanks be to God.

GOSPEL ACCLAMATION   *Philippians 2:8–9*

> **Glory and praise to you, O Christ!**
> **Christ was humbler yet,**
> **even to accepting death, death on a cross.**
> **But God raised him high**
> **and gave him the name which is above all names.**
> **Glory and praise to you, O Christ!**

GOSPEL   *John 18:1–19:42*

The narrative of the Lord's Passion is read without candles and without incense, with no greeting or signing of the book. It is read by a Deacon or, if there is no Deacon, by a Priest. It may also be read by readers, with the part of Christ, if possible, reserved to a Priest.

N = Narrator;   J = Jesus;   O = Other speaker;   C = Crowd, or more than one speaker

The passion of our Lord Jesus Christ according to John

N Jesus left with his disciples and crossed the Kedron valley. There was a garden there, and he went into it with his disciples. Judas the traitor knew the place well, since Jesus had often met his disciples there, and he brought the cohort to this place together with a detachment of guards sent by the chief priests and the Pharisees, all with lanterns and torches and weapons. Knowing everything that was going to happen to him, Jesus then came forward and said,

J Who are you looking for?

N They answered,

C Jesus the Nazarene.

N He said,

J I am he.

N Now Judas the traitor was standing among them. When Jesus said, 'I am he', they moved back and fell to the ground. He asked them a second time,

J Who are you looking for?

N They said,

C Jesus the Nazarene.

N Jesus replied,

J I have told you that I am he. If I am the one you are looking for, let these others go.

N This was to fulfil the words he had spoken: 'Not one of those you gave me have I lost'.

Simon Peter, who carried a sword, drew it and wounded the high priest's servant, cutting off his right ear. The servant's name was Malchus. Jesus said to Peter,

J Put your sword back in its scabbard; am I not to drink the cup that the Father has given me?

N The cohort and its captain and the Jewish guards seized Jesus and bound him. They took him first to Annas, because Annas was the father-in-law of Caiaphas, who was high priest that year. It was Caiaphas who had suggested to the Jews, 'It is better for one man to die for the people'. Simon Peter, with another disciple, followed Jesus. This disciple, who was known to the high priest, went with Jesus into the high priest's palace, but Peter stayed outside the door. So the other disciple, the one known to the high priest, went out, spoke to the woman who was keeping the door and brought Peter in. The maid on duty at the door said to Peter,

O Aren't you another of that man's disciples?

N He answered,

O I am not.

N Now it was cold, and the servants and guards had lit a charcoal fire and were standing there warming themselves; so Peter stood there too, warming himself with the others The high priest questioned Jesus about his disciples and his teaching. Jesus answered,

J I have spoken openly for all the world to hear; I have always taught in the synagogue and in the Temple where all the Jews meet together: I have said nothing in secret. But why ask me? Ask my hearers what I taught: they know what I said.

N At these words, one of the guards standing by gave Jesus a slap in the face, saying,

O Is that the way to answer the high priest?

N Jesus replied,

J If there is something wrong in what I said, point it out; but if there is no offence in it, why do you strike me?

N Then Annas sent him, still bound, to Caiaphas, the high priest.

As Simon Peter stood there warming himself, someone said to him,

O Aren't you another of his disciples?

N He denied it saying,

O I am not.

N One of the high priest's servants, a relation of the man whose ear Peter had cut off, said,

O Didn't I see you in the garden with him?

N Again Peter denied it; and at once a cock crew.

They then led Jesus from the house of Caiaphas to the Praetorium. It was now morning. They did not go into the Praetorium themselves or they would be defiled and unable to eat the passover. So Pilate came outside to them and said,

O What charge do you bring against this man?

N They replied,

C If he were not a criminal, we should not be handing him over to you.

TRIDUUM

N Pilate said,

O Take him yourselves, and try him by your own Law.

N The Jews answered,

C We are not allowed to put a man to death.

N This was to fulfil the words Jesus had spoken indicating the way he was going to die.

So Pilate went back into the Praetorium and called Jesus to him, and asked,

O Are you the king of the Jews?

N Jesus replied,

J Do you ask this of your own accord, or have others spoken to you about me?

N Pilate answered,

O Am I a Jew? It is your own people and the chief priests who have handed you over to me: what have you done?

N Jesus replied,

J Mine is not a kingdom of this world; if my kingdom were of this world, my men would have fought to prevent me being surrendered to the Jews. But my kingdom is not of this kind.

N Pilate said,

O So you are a king then?

N Jesus answered,

J It is you who say it. Yes, I am a king. I was born for this, I came into the world for this; to bear witness to the truth, and all who are on the side of truth listen to my voice.

N Pilate said,

O Truth? What is that?

N And with that he went out again to the Jews and said,

O I find no case against him. But according to a custom of yours I should release one prisoner at the Passover; would you like me, then, to release the king of the Jews?

N At this they shouted:

C Not this man, but Barabbas.

N Barabbas was a brigand.

N Pilate then had Jesus taken away and scourged; and after this, the soldiers twisted some thorns into a crown and put it on his head, and dressed him in a purple robe. They kept coming up to him and saying,

C Hail, king of the Jews!

N and they slapped him in the face.

Pilate came outside again and said to them,

O Look, I am going to bring him out to you to let you see that I find no case.

N Jesus then came out wearing the crown of thorns and the purple robe. Pilate said,

O Here is the man.

N When they saw him the chief priests and the guards shouted,

C Crucify him! Crucify him!

N Pilate said,

O Take him yourselves and crucify him: I can find no case against him.

N The Jews replied,

C We have a Law, and according to the Law he ought to die, because he has claimed to be the son of God.

N When Pilate heard them say this his fears increased. Re-entering the Praetorium, he said to Jesus,

O Where do you come from?

N But Jesus made no answer. Pilate then said to him,

O Are you refusing to speak to me? Surely you know I have power to release you and I have power to crucify you?

N Jesus replied

J You would have no power over me if it had not been given you from above; that is why the one who handed me over to you has the greater guilt.

N From that moment Pilate was anxious to set him free, but the Jews shouted,

C If you set him free you are no friend of Caesar's; anyone who makes himself king is defying Caesar.

N Hearing these words, Pilate had Jesus brought out, and seated himself on the chair of judgement at a place called the Pavement, in Hebrew Gabbatha. It was Passover Preparation Day, about the sixth hour. Pilate said to the Jews,

O Here is your king.

N They said,

C Take him away, take him away. Crucify him!

N Pilate said,

O Do you want me to crucify your king?

N The chief priests answered,

C We have no king except Caesar.

N So in the end Pilate handed him over to them to be crucified. They then took charge of Jesus, and carrying his own cross he went out of the city to the place of the skull, or, as it was called in Hebrew, Golgotha, where they crucified him with two others, one on either side with Jesus in the middle. Pilate wrote out a notice and had it fixed to the cross; it ran: 'Jesus the Nazarene, King of the Jews.' This notice was read by many of the Jews, because the place where Jesus was crucified was not far from the city, and the writing was in Hebrew, Latin and Greek. So the Jewish chief priests said to Pilate,

C You should not write 'King of the Jews', but 'This man said: I am King of the Jews'.

N Pilate answered,

O What I have written, I have written.

N When the soldiers had finished crucifying Jesus they took his clothing and divided it into four shares, one for each soldier. His undergarment was seamless, woven in one piece from neck to hem; so they said to one another,

C Instead of tearing it, let's throw dice to decide who is to have it.

N In this way the words of scripture were fulfilled:

They shared out my clothing among them. They cast lots for my clothes.

This is exactly what the soldiers did.

Near the cross of Jesus stood his mother and his mother's sister, Mary the wife of Clopas, and Mary of Magdala. Seeing his mother and the disciple he loved standing near her, Jesus said to his mother,

J Woman, this is your son.

N Then to the disciple he said,

J This is your mother.

N And from that moment the disciple made a place for her in his home.

After this, Jesus knew that everything had now been completed, and to fulfil the scripture perfectly he said:

J I am thirsty.

N A jar full of vinegar stood there, so putting a sponge soaked in vinegar on a hyssop stick they held it up to his mouth. After Jesus had taken the vinegar he said,

TRIDUUM

J It is accomplished;

N and bowing his head he gave up the spirit.

All kneel and pause a moment.

N It was Preparation Day, and to prevent the bodies remaining on the cross during the sabbath – since that sabbath was a day of special solemnity – the Jews asked Pilate to have the legs broken and the bodies taken away. Consequently the soldiers came and broke the legs of the first man who had been crucified with him and then of the other. When they came to Jesus, they found that he was already dead, and so instead of breaking his legs one of the soldiers pierced his side with a lance; and immediately there came out blood and water. This is the evidence of one who saw it trustworthy evidence, and he knows he speaks the truth – and he gives it so that you may believe as well. Because all this happened to fulfil the words of scripture:

Not one bone of his will be broken, and again, in another place scripture says:

They will look on the one whom they have pierced.

After this, Joseph of Arimathaea, who was a disciple of Jesus – though a secret one because he was afraid of the Jews – asked Pilate to let him remove the body of Jesus. Pilate gave permission, so they came and took it away. Nicodemus came as well – the same one who had first come to Jesus at night-time – and he brought a mixture of myrrh and aloes, weighing about a hundred pounds. They took the body of Jesus and wrapped it with the spices in linen cloths, following the Jewish burial custom. At the place where he had been crucified there was a garden, and in the garden a new tomb in which no one had yet been buried. Since it was the Jewish Day of Preparation and the tomb was near at hand, they laid Jesus there.

The reading ends in silence
without any acclamation or response.

HOMILY

THE SOLEMN INTERCESSIONS

A Deacon or lay reader says or sings each invitation to pray.
All pray in silence for a while, then the Priest says or sings the prayer for that intention.

I For Holy Church

Let us pray, dearly beloved, for the holy Church of God,
that our God and Lord be pleased to give her peace,
to guard her and to unite her throughout the whole world
and grant that, leading our life in tranquillity and quiet,
we may glorify God the Father almighty.

Prayer in silence. Then the Priest says:

Almighty ever-living God,
who in Christ revealed your glory to all the nations,
watch over the works of your mercy,
that your Church, spread throughout all the world,
may persevere with steadfast faith in confessing your name.
Through Christ our Lord. **Amen.**

II   For the Pope

Let us pray also for our most Holy Father Pope N.,
that our God and Lord,
who chose him for the Order of Bishops,
may keep him safe and unharmed for the Lord's holy Church,
to govern the holy People of God.

Prayer in silence. Then the Priest says:

Almighty ever-living God,
by whose decree all things are founded,
look with favour on our prayers
and in your kindness protect the Pope chosen for us,
that, under him, the Christian people,
governed by you their maker,
may grow in merit by reason of their faith.
Through Christ our Lord.   **Amen.**

III   For all orders and degrees of the faithful

Let us pray also for our Bishop N. [1],
for all Bishops, Priests, and Deacons of the Church
and for the whole of the faithful people.

Prayer in silence. Then the Priest says:

Almighty ever-living God,
by whose Spirit the whole body of the Church
is sanctified and governed,
hear our humble prayer for your ministers,
that, by the gift of your grace,
all may serve you faithfully.
Through Christ our Lord.   **Amen.**

IV   For catechumens

Let us pray also for (our) catechumens,
that our God and Lord
may open wide the ears of their inmost hearts
and unlock the gates of his mercy,
that, having received forgiveness of all their sins
through the waters of rebirth,
they, too, may be one with Christ Jesus our Lord.

Prayer in silence. Then the Priest says:
Almighty ever-living God,
who make your Church ever fruitful with new offspring,
increase the faith and understanding of (our) catechumens,
that, reborn in the font of Baptism,
they may be added to the number of your adopted children.
Through Christ our Lord.   **Amen.**

TRIDUUM

---

1   Mention may be made here of the Coadjutor Bishop, or Auxiliary Bishops.

V   For the unity of Christians

Let us pray also for all our brothers and sisters who believe in Christ,
that our God and Lord may be pleased,
as they live the truth,
to gather them together and keep them in his one Church.

Prayer in silence. Then the Priest says:

Almighty ever-living God,
who gather what is scattered
and keep together what you have gathered,
look kindly on the flock of your Son,
that those whom one Baptism has consecrated
may be joined together by integrity of faith
and united in the bond of charity.
Through Christ our Lord.   **Amen.**

VI   For the Jewish people

Let us pray also for the Jewish people,
to whom the Lord our God spoke first,
that he may grant them to advance in love of his name
and in faithfulness to his covenant.

Prayer in silence. Then the Priest says:

Almighty ever-living God,
who bestowed your promises on Abraham and his descendants,
graciously hear the prayers of your Church,
that the people you first made your own
may attain the fullness of redemption.
Through Christ our Lord.   **Amen.**

VII   For those who do not believe in Christ

Let us pray also for those who do not believe in Christ,
that, enlightened by the Holy Spirit,
they, too, may enter on the way of salvation.

Prayer in silence. Then the Priest says:
Almighty ever-living God,
grant to those who do not confess Christ
that, by walking before you with a sincere heart,
they may find the truth
and that we ourselves, being constant in mutual love
and striving to understand more fully the mystery of your life,
may be made more perfect witnesses to your love in the world.
Through Christ our Lord.   **Amen.**

VIII   For those who do not believe in God

Let us pray also for those who do not acknowledge God,
that, following what is right in sincerity of heart,
they may find the way to God himself.

Prayer in silence.

Then the Priest says:

Almighty ever-living God,
who created all people
to seek you always by desiring you
and, by finding you, come to rest,
grant, we pray,
that, despite every harmful obstacle,
all may recognize the signs of your fatherly love
and the witness of the good works
done by those who believe in you,
and so in gladness confess you,
the one true God and Father of our human race.
Through Christ our Lord.   **Amen.**

IX   For those in public office
Let us pray also for those in public office,
that our God and Lord
may direct their minds and hearts according to his will
for the true peace and freedom of all.

Prayer in silence. Then the Priest says:

Almighty ever-living God,
in whose hand lies every human heart
and the rights of peoples,
look with favour, we pray,
on those who govern with authority over us,
that throughout the whole world,
the prosperity of peoples,
the assurance of peace,
and freedom of religion
may through your gift be made secure.
Through Christ our Lord.   **Amen.**

X   For those in tribulation
Let us pray, dearly beloved,
to God the Father almighty,
that he may cleanse the world of all errors,
banish disease, drive out hunger,
unlock prisons, loosen fetters,
granting to travellers safety, to pilgrims return,
health to the sick, and salvation to the dying.

Prayer in silence. Then the Priest says:

Almighty ever-living God,
comfort of mourners, strength of all who toil,
may the prayers of those who cry out in any tribulation
come before you,
that all may rejoice,
because in their hour of need
your mercy was at hand.
Through Christ our Lord.   **Amen.**

TRIDUUM

SECOND PART: ADORATION OF THE HOLY CROSS

The Holy Cross is shown three times to the assembly. This is done either by a progressive unveiling of the Cross at the front of the church, or by a procession through the church to the sanctuary.

After each showing, the Priest (assisted, if need be, by the Deacon or the choir) sings or says:

Priest / Deacon / Choir:

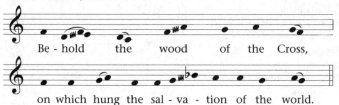

Be - hold the wood of the Cross,

on which hung the sal - va - tion of the world.

People:

Come, let us a - dore.

or

Priest / Deacon / Choir:

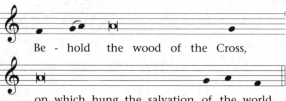

Be - hold the wood of the Cross,

on which hung the salvation of the world.

People:

Come, let us a - dore.

At the end of the singing, all kneel and for a brief moment adore in silence, while the Priest stands and holds the Cross raised.

THE ADORATION OF THE HOLY CROSS

The Cross is placed or held at the entrance to the sanctuary (or another suitable place), with candles placed on either side.

After the Priest Celebrant has venerated the Cross, other clergy, lay ministers, and the assembly approach in procession. They show reverence to the Cross by a simple genuflection or by some other appropriate sign, for example, by kissing the Cross.

If, because of the large number of people, it is not possible for all to approach individually, the Priest, after some of the clergy and faithful have adored, takes the Cross and, standing in the middle before the altar, invites the people in a few words to adore the Holy Cross and afterwards holds the Cross elevated higher for a brief time, for the faithful to adore it in silence.

SINGING DURING THE ADORATION OF THE HOLY CROSS

While the adoration of the Holy Cross is taking place, the following, or other suitable chants, are sung. During the singing, all who have already adored the Cross remain seated.

Ant.   We adore your Cross, O Lord,
we praise and glorify your holy Resurrection,
for behold, because of the wood of a tree
joy has come to the whole world.

May God have mercy on us and bless us;   *cf Psalm 66:2*
may he let his face shed its light upon us
and have mercy on us.

We adore your Cross...

Reproaches

– I –

Parts assigned to one of the two choirs separately are indicated by the numbers 1 (first choir) and 2 (second choir); parts sung by both choirs together are marked: 1 and 2. Some of the verses may also be sung by two cantors.

1 and 2	My people, what have I done to you? Or how have I grieved you? Answer me!
1	Because I led you out of the land of Egypt, you have prepared a Cross for your Saviour.

1	Hagios o Theos,
2	Holy is God,
1	Hagios Ischyros,
2	Holy and Mighty,
1	Hagios Athanatos, eleison himas.
2	Holy and Immortal One, have mercy on us.

1 and 2	Because I led you out through the desert forty years and fed you with manna and brought you into a land of plenty, you have prepared a Cross for your Saviour.
1	Hagios o Theos,
2	Holy is God,
1	Hagios Ischyros,
2	Holy and Mighty,
1	Hagios Athanatos, eleison himas.
2	Holy and Immortal One, have mercy on us.

1 and 2	What more should I have done for you and have not done? Indeed, I planted you as my most beautiful chosen vine and you have turned very bitter for me, for in my thirst you gave me vinegar to drink and with a lance you pierced your Saviour's side.

TRIDUUM

1	Hagios o Theos,
2	Holy is God,
1	Hagios Ischyros,
2	Holy and Mighty,
1	Hagios Athanatos, eleison himas.
2	Holy and Immortal One, have mercy on us.

– II –

Cantors:	I scourged Egypt for your sake with its firstborn sons, and you scourged me and handed me over.
1 and 2 repeat:	My people, what have I done to you? Or how have I grieved you? Answer me!
Cantors:	I led you out from Egypt as Pharoah lay sunk in the Red Sea, and you handed me over to the chief priests.
1 and 2 repeat:	My people...
Cantors:	I opened up the sea before you, and you opened my side with a lance.
1 and 2 repeat:	My people...
Cantors:	I went before you in a pillar of cloud, and you led me into Pilate's palace.
1 and 2 repeat:	My people...
Cantors:	I fed you with manna in the desert, and on me you rained blows and lashes.
1 and 2 repeat:	My people...
Cantors:	I gave you saving water from the rock to drink, and for drink you gave me gall and vinegar.
1 and 2 repeat:	My people...
Cantors:	I struck down for you the kings of the Canaanites, and you struck my head with a reed.
1 and 2 repeat:	My people...
Cantors:	I put in your hand a royal sceptre, and you put on my head a crown of thorns.
1 and 2 repeat:	My people...
Cantors:	I exalted you with great power, and you hung me on the scaffold of the Cross.
1 and 2 repeat:	My people...

Hymn

All:
Faithful Cross the Saints rely on,
Noble tree beyond compare!
Never was there such a scion,
Never leaf or flower so rare.
Sweet the timber, sweet the iron,
Sweet the burden that they bear!

Cantors:
Sing, my tongue, in exultation
Of our banner and device!
Make a solemn proclamation
Of a triumph and its price:
How the Saviour of creation
Conquered by his sacrifice!

All:
Faithful Cross the Saints rely on,
Noble tree beyond compare!
Never was there such a scion,
Never leaf or flower so rare.

Cantors:
For, when Adam first offended,
Eating that forbidden fruit,
Not all hopes of glory ended
With the serpent at the root:
Broken nature would be mended
By a second tree and shoot.

All:
Sweet the timber, sweet the iron,
Sweet the burden that they bear!

Cantors:
Thus the tempter was outwitted
By a wisdom deeper still:
Remedy and ailment fitted,
Means to cure and means to kill;
That the world might be acquitted,
Christ would do his Father's will.

All:
Faithful Cross the Saints rely on,
Noble tree beyond compare!
Never was there such a scion,
Never leaf or flower so rare.

Cantors:
So the Father, out of pity
For our self-inflicted doom,
Sent him from the heavenly city
When the holy time had come:
He, the Son and the Almighty,
Took our flesh in Mary's womb.

All:
Sweet the timber, sweet the iron,
Sweet the burden that they bear!

Cantors:
Hear a tiny baby crying,
Founder of the seas and strands;
See his virgin Mother tying
Cloth around his feet and hands;
Find him in a manger lying
Tightly wrapped in swaddling-bands!

All:
Faithful Cross the Saints rely on,
Noble tree beyond compare!
Never was there such a scion,
Never leaf or flower so rare.

Cantors:
So he came, the long-expected,
Not in glory, not to reign;
Only born to be rejected,
Choosing hunger, toil and pain,
Till the scaffold was erected
And the Paschal Lamb was slain.

All:
Sweet the timber, sweet the iron,
Sweet the burden that they bear!

Cantors:
No disgrace was too abhorrent:
Nailed and mocked and parched he died;
Blood and water, double warrant,
Issue from his wounded side,
Washing in a mighty torrent
Earth and stars and oceantide.

All:
Faithful Cross the Saints rely on,
Noble tree beyond compare!
Never was there such a scion,
Never leaf or flower so rare.

Cantors:
Lofty timber, smooth your roughness,
Flex your boughs for blossoming;
Let your fibres lose their toughness,
Gently let your tendrils cling;
Lay aside your native gruffness,
Clasp the body of your King!

All:
Sweet the timber, sweet the iron,
Sweet the burden that they bear!

Cantors:
Noblest tree of all created,
Richly jewelled and embossed:
Post by Lamb's blood consecrated;
Spar that saves the tempest-tossed;
Scaffold-beam which, elevated,
Carries what the world has cost!

All:
Faithful Cross the Saints rely on,
Noble tree beyond compare!
Never was there such a scion,
Never leaf or flower so rare.

The following conclusion is never to be omitted:

All:
Wisdom, power, and adoration
To the blessed Trinity
For redemption and salvation
Through the Paschal Mystery,
Now, in every generation,
And for all eternity. Amen.

THIRD PART: HOLY COMMUNION

The Altar is prepared.
As the Blessed Sacrament is brought to the Altar, all stand in silence.

ALL STAND

LORD'S PRAYER

Priest: At the Saviour's command
            and formed by divine teaching,
            we dare to say:

All: **Our Father, who art in heaven,**
            hallowed be thy name;
            thy kingdom come,
            thy will be done
            on earth as it is in heaven.
            Give us this day our daily bread,
            and forgive us our trespasses,
            as we forgive those who trespass against us;
            and lead us not into temptation,
            but deliver us from evil.

Priest: Deliver us, Lord, we pray, from every evil,
            graciously grant peace in our days,
            that, by the help of your mercy,
            we may be always free from sin
            and safe from all distress,
            as we await the blessed hope
            and the coming of our Saviour, Jesus Christ.

People: **For the kingdom,**
            the power and the glory are yours
            now and for ever.

INVITATION TO COMMUNION

The Priest then genuflects, takes a particle, and, holding it slightly raised over the ciborium, while facing the people, says aloud:

Priest: Behold the Lamb of God,
          behold him who takes away the sins of the world.
          Blessed are those called to the supper of the Lamb.

All: **Lord, I am not worthy**
          that you should enter under my roof,
          but only say the word
          and my soul shall be healed.

COMMUNION

During Communion, Psalm 21 or another appropriate chant may be sung.

PRAYER AFTER COMMUNION

Almighty ever-living God,
who have restored us to life
by the blessed Death and Resurrection of your Christ,
preserve in us the work of your mercy,
that, by partaking of this mystery,
we may have a life unceasingly devoted to you.
Through Christ our Lord.   **Amen.**

PRAYER OVER THE PEOPLE:

May abundant blessing, O Lord, we pray,
descend upon your people,
who have honoured the Death of your Son
in the hope of their resurrection:
may pardon come,
comfort be given,
holy faith increase,
and everlasting redemption be made secure.
Through Christ our Lord.   **Amen.**

After genuflecting to the Cross, all depart in silence.

HOLY SATURDAY

On Holy Saturday the Church waits at the Lord's tomb in prayer and fasting, meditating on his Passion and Death and on his Descent into Hell, and awaiting his Resurrection.

The Church abstains from the Sacrifice of the Mass, with the sacred table left bare, until after the solemn Vigil, that is, the anticipation by night of the Resurrection, when the time comes for paschal joys, the abundance of which overflows to occupy fifty days.

Some or all of the Preparation Rites for Baptism may be celebrated in a liturgy during the day:
Recitation of the Creed, Ephphetha Rite, Choosing a Baptismal Name, Anointing with the Oil of Catechumens.
(Rite of Christian Initiation of Adults nn 172–197)

EASTER TIME

ABOUT THE SEASON

The Easter Vigil, in the holy night when the Lord rose again, is considered the 'mother of all holy Vigils', in which the Church, keeping watch, awaits the Resurrection of Christ and celebrates it in the Sacraments. Therefore, the entire celebration of this sacred Vigil must take place at night, so that it both begins after nightfall and ends before the dawn on the Sunday.

The fifty days from the Sunday of the Resurrection to Pentecost Sunday are celebrated in joy and exultation as one feast day, indeed as one 'great Sunday'.

These are the days above all others in which the *Alleluia* is sung.

The Sundays of this time of year are considered to be Sundays of Easter and are called, after Easter Sunday itself, the Second, Third, Fourth, Fifth, Sixth, and Seventh Sundays of Easter. This sacred period of fifty days concludes with Pentecost Sunday.

The first eight days of Easter Time constitute the Octave of Easter and are celebrated as Solemnities of the Lord.

On the fortieth day after Easter the Ascension of the Lord is celebrated, except where, not being observed as a Holyday of Obligation, it has been assigned to the Seventh Sunday of Easter.

The weekdays from the Ascension up to and including the Saturday before Pentecost prepare for the coming of the Holy Spirit, the Paraclete.

Universal Norms on the Liturgical Year and the Calendar
nn 21–26

ABOUT THE READINGS

On the holy night of the Easter Vigil there are seven Old Testament readings, recalling the wonderful works of God in the history of salvation. There are two New Testament readings, the announcement of the resurrection according to one of the Synoptic Gospels and a reading from St. Paul on Christian baptism as the sacrament of Christ's resurrection.

The gospel reading for the Mass on Easter day is from John on the finding of the empty tomb. There is also, however, the option to use the gospel texts from the Easter Vigil or, when there is an evening Mass on Easter Sunday, to use the account in Luke of the Lord's appearance to the disciples on the road to Emmaus. The first reading is from Acts, which throughout the Easter season replaces the Old Testament reading. The reading from St. Paul concerns the living out of the paschal mystery in the Church.

The gospel readings for the first three Sundays recount the appearances of the risen Christ. The readings about the Good Shepherd are assigned to the Fourth Sunday. On the Fifth, Sixth, and Seventh Sundays, there are excerpts from the Lord's discourse and prayer at the last supper.

The first reading is from Acts, in a three-year cycle of parallel and progressive selections: material is presented on the life oft he primitive Church, its witness, and its growth.

For the reading from the apostles... Revelation [is used in] Year C... These are the texts that seem to fit in especially well with the spirit of joyous faith and sure hope proper to this season.

Introduction to the Lectionary nn 99–100

COMMON RESPONSORIAL PSALMS FOR EASTER TIME

COMMON RESPONSE

Alleluia! *(repeated two or three times)*

EASTER VIGIL — COMMON PSALM 1   *Psalm 135:1–3, 4–6, 7–9, 24–26*

In the two Common Psalms for the Easter Vigil, the response is sung after every line.

Great is his love, love without end.

1 O give thanks to the Lord for he is good.
Give thanks to the God of gods.
Give thanks to the Lord of lords.

3 It was he who made the great lights.
The sun to rule in the day.
The moon and the stars in the night.

2 He alone has wrought marvellous works.
Whose wisdom it was made the skies.
Who fixed the earth firmly on the seas.

4 And he snatched us away from our foes.
He gives food to all living things.
To the God of heaven give thanks.

EASTER VIGIL — COMMON PSALM 2   *Psalm 135:1, 3, 16, 21–26*

Great is his love, love without end. *(Sung after every line.)*

1 O give thanks to the Lord for he is good.
Give thanks to the Lord of lords.
Through the desert his people he led.

2 He let Israel inherit their land.
On his servant their land he bestowed.
He remembered us in our distress.

3 And he snatched us away from our foes.
He gives food to all living things.
To the God of heaven give thanks.

EASTER SEASON — COMMON PSALM 1   *Psalm 117:1–2, 16–17, 22–23 response v 24*

This day was made by the Lord;
we rejoice and are glad.

or   **Alleluia!** *(repeated two or three times)*

1 Give thanks to the Lord for he is good,
for his love has no end.
Let the sons of Israel say:
'His love has no end.'

2 The Lord's right hand has triumphed;
his right hand raised me up.
I shall not die, I shall live
and recount his deeds.

3 The stone which the builders rejected
has become the corner stone.
This is the work of the Lord,
a marvel in our eyes

EASTER SEASON — COMMON PSALM 2   *Psalm 65:1–7, 16, 20 response v 1*

Cry out with joy to God all the earth, alleluia!

1 Cry out with joy to God all the earth,
O sing to the glory of his name.
O render him glorious praise.
Say to God: 'How tremendous your deeds!'

continued…

EASTER

Cry out with joy to God all the earth, alleluia!

2 'Before you all the earth shall bow;
shall sing to you, sing to your name!'
Come and see the works of God,
tremendous his deeds among men.

3 He turned the sea into dry land,
they passed through the river dry-shod.
Let our joy then be in him;
he rules for ever by his might.

4 Come and hear, all who fear God.
I will tell what he did for my soul.
Blessed be God who did not reject my prayer
nor withhold his love from me.

COMMON PSALM — ASCENSION   *Psalm 46:2–3, 6–9 response v 6*

God goes up with shouts of joy.

1 All peoples, clap your hands,
cry to God with shouts of joy!
For the Lord, the Most High, we must fear,
great king over all the earth.

2 God goes up with shouts of joy;
the Lord goes up with trumpet blast.
Sing praise for God, sing praise,
sing praise to our king, sing praise.

3 God is king of all the earth.
Sing praise with all your skill.
God is king over the nations;
God reigns on his holy throne.

COMMON PSALM — PENTECOST SUNDAY   *Psalm 103:1, 24, 29–31, 34 response cf v 30*

**Send forth your spirit, O Lord,
and renew the face of the earth.**

1 Bless the Lord, my soul!
Lord God, how great you are.
How many are your works, O Lord!
The earth is full of your riches.

2 You take back your spirit, they die,
returning to the dust from which they came.
You send forth your spirit, they are created;
and you renew the face of the earth.

3 May the glory of the Lord last for ever!
May the Lord rejoice in his works!
May my thoughts be pleasing to him.
I find my joy in the Lord.

EASTER SUNDAY OF THE RESURRECTION OF THE LORD

Easter Sunday forms both the pinnacle of the Season of Triduum
and the fifty days of paschal rejoicing of Easter Time.

EASTER VIGIL IN THE HOLY NIGHT

The celebration of the Easter Vigil takes place after dark. The lights of the church are extinguished
and candles prepared for all who participate.

The Vigil consists of four parts:

Solemn Beginning of the Vigil or Lucernarium

Liturgy of the Word

Baptismal Liturgy

Liturgy of the Eucharist

FIRST PART: LUCERNARIUM

THE BLESSING OF THE FIRE AND PREPARATION OF THE CANDLE
A blazing fire is prepared outside the church. If circumstances require, a smaller fire is prepared inside the church entrance. When the people are gathered there, the Priest approaches with the ministers, one of whom carries the paschal candle.

All make the Sign of the Cross as the Priest says.
Priest: In the name of the Father, and of the Son, and of the Holy Spirit.
People: **Amen.**

The Priest greets the people in these or similar words

> Dear brethren (brothers and sisters),
> on this most sacred night,
> in which our Lord Jesus Christ
> passed over from death to life,
> the Church calls upon her sons and daughters,
> scattered throughout the world,
> to come together to watch and pray.
> If we keep the memorial
> of the Lord's paschal solemnity in this way,
> listening to his word and celebrating his mysteries,
> then we shall have the sure hope
> of sharing his triumph over death
> and living with him in God.

EASTER

The Priest blesses the fire:

Let us pray.
O God, who through your Son
bestowed upon the faithful the fire of your glory,
sanctify ✠ this new fire, we pray,
and grant that,
by these paschal celebrations,
we may be so inflamed with heavenly desires,
that with minds made pure
we may attain festivities of unending splendour.
Through Christ our Lord.   Amen.

After the blessing of the new fire, one of the ministers brings the paschal candle to the Priest, who cuts a cross into the candle with a stylus. Then he makes the Greek letter Alpha above the cross, the letter Omega below, and the four numerals of the current year between the arms of the cross, saying meanwhile:

Christ yesterday and today
the Beginning and the End
the Alpha
and the Omega
All time belongs to him
and all the ages
To him be glory and power
through every age and for ever. Amen

When the cutting of the cross and of the other signs has been completed, the Priest may insert five grains of incense into the candle in the form of a cross, meanwhile saying:

1	By his holy	1
2	and glorious wounds,	
3	may Christ the Lord	4 2 5
4	guard us	
5	and protect us. Amen.	3

The Priest lights the paschal candle from the new fire, saying:

May the light of Christ rising in glory
dispel the darkness of our hearts and minds.

PROCESSION

When the candle has been lit, the thurible is lit from the fire. Then the Deacon, standing at the door of the church, raises the candle and sings:

Deacon: All:

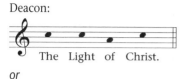   

The Light of Christ.   Thanks be to God.

or

Deacon: All:

Lu - men Chris - ti.   De - o grá - ti - as.

The Priest lights his candle from the flame of the paschal candle.

Then the Deacon moves forward to the middle of the church and, standing and raising up the candle, sings a second time:

Deacon: The Light of Christ.   *or*   Deacon: Lumen Christi.
All: **Thanks be to God.**   All: **Deo grátias.**

All light their candles from the flame of the paschal candle and continue in procession.

When the Deacon arrives before the altar, he stands facing the people, raises up the candle and sings a third time:

Deacon: The Light of Christ.   *or*   Deacon: Lumen Christi.
All: **Thanks be to God.**   All: **Deo grátias.**

Then the Deacon places the paschal candle on a large candlestand prepared next to the ambo or in the middle of the sanctuary.

And lights are lit throughout the church, except for the altar candles.

THE EASTER PROCLAMATION (EXSULTET)

If the Exsultet is sung by a lay cantor, the words in brackets are omitted.
(A shorter version of the Exsultet may be sung.)

Exult, let them exult, the hosts of heaven,
exult, let Angel ministers of God exult,
let the trumpet of salvation
sound aloud our mighty King's triumph!
Be glad, let earth be glad, as glory floods her,
ablaze with light from her eternal King,
let all corners of the earth be glad,
knowing an end to gloom and darkness.
Rejoice, let Mother Church also rejoice,
arrayed with the lightning of his glory,
let this holy building shake with joy,
filled with the mighty voices of the peoples.

EASTER

(Therefore, dearest friends,
standing in the awesome glory of this holy light,
invoke with me, I ask you,
the mercy of God almighty,
that he, who has been pleased to number me,
though unworthy, among the Levites,
may pour into me his light unshadowed,
that I may sing this candle's perfect praises).

Deacon: All:

(The Lord be with you.   And with your spir - it.)

Deacon/cantor: All:

Lift up your hearts.   We lift them up to the Lord.

Deacon/cantor: All:

Let us give thanks to the Lord our God.   It is right and just.

It is truly right and just,
with ardent love of mind and heart
and with devoted service of our voice,
to acclaim our God invisible, the almighty Father,
and Jesus Christ, our Lord, his Son, his Only Begotten.

Who for our sake paid Adam's debt to the eternal Father,
and, pouring out his own dear Blood,
wiped clean the record of our ancient sinfulness.

These then are the feasts of Passover,
in which is slain the Lamb, the one true Lamb,
whose Blood anoints the doorposts of believers.

This is the night,
when once you led our forebears, Israel's children,
from slavery in Egypt
and made them pass dry-shod through the Red Sea.

This is the night
that with a pillar of fire
banished the darkness of sin.

This is the night
that even now, throughout the world,
sets Christian believers apart from worldly vices

and from the gloom of sin,
leading them to grace
and joining them to his holy ones.

This is the night,
when Christ broke the prison-bars of death
and rose victorious from the underworld.

Our birth would have been no gain,
had we not been redeemed.
O wonder of your humble care for us!
O love, O charity beyond all telling,
to ransom a slave you gave away your Son!

O truly necessary sin of Adam,
destroyed completely by the Death of Christ!

O happy fault
that earned so great, so glorious a Redeemer!

O truly blessed night,
worthy alone to know the time and hour
when Christ rose from the underworld!

This is the night
of which it is written:
The night shall be as bright as day,
dazzling is the night for me,
and full of gladness.

The sanctifying power of this night
dispels wickedness, washes faults away,
restores innocence to the fallen, and joy to mourners,
drives out hatred, fosters concord, and brings down the mighty.

On this, your night of grace, O holy Father,
accept this candle, a solemn offering,
the work of bees and of your servants' hands,
an evening sacrifice of praise,
this gift from your most holy Church.

But now we know the praises of this pillar,
which glowing fire ignites for God's honour,
a fire into many flames divided,
yet never dimmed by sharing of its light,
for it is fed by melting wax,
drawn out by mother bees
to build a torch so precious.

O truly blessed night,
when things of heaven are wed to those of earth,
and divine to the human.

Therefore, O Lord,
we pray you that this candle,
hallowed to the honour of your name,
may persevere undimmed,
to overcome the darkness of this night.
Receive it as a pleasing fragrance,
and let it mingle with the lights of heaven.
May this flame be found still burning
by the Morning Star:
the one Morning Star who never sets,
Christ your Son,
who, coming back from death's domain,
has shed his peaceful light on humanity,
and lives and reigns for ever and ever.

All: **Amen.**

SECOND PART: LITURGY OF THE WORD

Wherever possible all the readings are read. However, in serious pastoral circumstances, a selection may be made of at least Old Testament readings, one of which must be the reading from Exodus 14.

After each reading, a Responsorial Psalm is sung, or this may be replaced by a sacred silence.

All set aside their candles, and sit.   **ALL SIT**

The Priest introduces the Liturgy of the Word in these or similar words:

Dear brethren (brothers and sisters),
now that we have begun our solemn Vigil,
let us listen with quiet hearts to the Word of God.
Let us meditate on how God in times past saved his people
and in these, the last days, has sent us his Son as our Redeemer.
Let us pray that our God may complete this paschal work of salvation
by the fullness of redemption.

FIRST READING   *Genesis 1:1–2:2   Shorter form (omitting oblique text): 1:1, 26–31)*
God saw all he had made, and indeed it was very good.

In the beginning God created the heavens and the earth. *Now the earth was a formless void, there was darkness over the deep, and God's spirit hovered over the water.*

God said, 'Let there be light.' and there was light. God saw that light was good, and God divided light from darkness. God called light 'day', and darkness he called 'night'. Evening came and morning came: the first day.

God said, 'Let there be a vault in the waters to divide the waters in two.' And so it was. God made the vault, and it divided the waters above the vault from the waters under the vault. God called the vault 'heaven'. Evening came and morning came: the second day.

God said, 'Let the waters under heaven come together into a single mass, and let dry land appear.' And so it was. God called the dry land 'earth' and the mass of waters 'seas', and God saw that it was good.

God said, 'Let the earth produce vegetation: seed-bearing plants, and fruit trees bearing fruit with their seed inside, on the earth.' And so it was. The earth produced vegetation, plants bearing seed in their several kinds, and trees bearing fruit with their seed inside in their several kinds. God saw that it was good. Evening came and morning came: the third day.

God said, 'Let there be lights in the vault of heaven to divide day from night, and let them indicate festivals, days and years. Let them be lights in the vault of heaven to shine on the earth.' And so it was. God made the two great lights: the greater light to govern the day, the smaller light to govern the night, and the stars. God set them in the vault of heaven to shine on the earth, to govern the day and the night and to divide light from darkness. God saw that it was good. Evening came and morning came: the fourth day.

God said, 'Let the waters teem with living creatures, and let birds fly above the earth within the vault of heaven.' And so it was. God created great sea-serpents and every kind of living creature with which the waters teem, and every kind of winged creature. God saw that it was good. God blessed them, saying 'Be fruitful, multiply, and fill the waters of the seas; and let the birds multiply upon the earth.' Evening came and morning came: the fifth day.

God said, 'Let the earth produce every kind of living creature: cattle, reptiles, and every kind of wild beast.' And so it was. God made every kind of wild beast, every kind of cattle, and every kind of land reptile. God saw that it was good.

God said, 'Let us make man in our own image, in the likeness of ourselves, and let them be masters of the fish of the sea, the birds of heaven, the cattle, all the wild beasts and all the reptiles that crawl upon the earth.'

God created man in the image of himself, in the image of God he created him, male and female he created them.

God blessed them, saying to them, 'Be fruitful, multiply, fill the earth and conquer it. Be masters of the fish of the sea, the birds of heaven and all living animals on the earth.' God said, 'See, I give you all the seed-bearing plants that are upon the whole earth, and all the trees with seed-bearing fruit; this shall be your food. To all wild beasts, all birds of heaven and all living reptiles on the earth I give all the foliage of plants for food.' And so it was. God saw all he had made, and indeed it was very good. Evening came and morning came: the sixth day.

Thus heaven and earth were completed with all their array. On the seventh day God completed the work he had been doing. He rested on the seventh day after all the work he had been doing.

The word of the Lord.
Thanks be to God.

RESPONSORIAL PSALM   Psalm 103:1–2, 5–6, 10, 12–14, 24, 35 response cf v 30

**Send forth your spirit, O Lord,
and renew the face of the earth.**

1   Bless the Lord, my soul!
Lord God, how great you are,
clothed in majesty and glory,
wrapped in light as in a robe!

continued...

**Send forth your spirit, O Lord,
and renew the face of the earth.**

2   You founded the earth on its base,
    to stand firm from age to age.
    You wrapped it with the ocean like a cloak;
    the waters stood higher than the mountains.

3   You make springs gush forth in the valleys:
    they flow in between the hills.
    On their banks dwell the birds of heaven;
    from the branches they sing their song.

4   From your dwelling you water the hills;
    earth drinks its fill of your gift.
    You make the grass grow for the cattle
    and the plants to serve man's needs.

5   How many are your works, O Lord!
    In wisdom you have made them all.
    The earth is full of your riches.
    Bless the Lord, my soul!

ALTERNATIVE RESPONSORIAL PSALM *Psalm 32:4–7, 12–13, 20, 22 response v 5*
The Lord fills the earth with his love.

1   The word of the Lord is faithful
    and all his works to be trusted.
    The Lord loves justice and right
    and fills the earth with his love.

2   By his word the heavens were made,
    by the breath of his mouth all the stars.
    He collects the waves of the ocean;
    he stores up the depths of the sea.

3   They are happy, whose God is the Lord,
    the people he has chosen as his own.
    From the heavens the Lord looks forth,
    he sees all the children of men.

4   Our soul is waiting for the Lord.
    The Lord is our help and our shield.
    May your love be upon us, O Lord,
    as we place all our hope in you.

PRAYER

ALL STAND

Let us pray.

Almighty ever-living God,
who are wonderful in the ordering of all your works,
may those you have redeemed understand
that there exists nothing more marvellous
than the world's creation in the beginning
except that, at the end of the ages,
Christ our Passover has been sacrificed.
Who lives and reigns for ever and ever.   **Amen.**

or

On the creation of man:
O God, who wonderfully created human nature
and still more wonderfully redeemed it,
grant us, we pray,
to set our minds against the enticements of sin,
that we may merit to attain eternal joys.
Through Christ our Lord.   **Amen.**

ALL SIT

SECOND READING   *Genesis 22:1–18   Shorter form (omitting oblique text): 22:1–2, 9–13, 15–18*

The sacrifice of Abraham, our father in faith.

God put Abraham to the test, 'Abraham, Abraham,' he called. 'Here I am' he replied. 'Take your son,' God said 'your only child Isaac, whom you love, and go to the land of Moriah. There you shall offer him as a burnt offering, on a mountain I will point out to you.'

Rising early next morning Abraham saddled his ass and took with him two of his servants and his son Isaac. He chopped wood for the burnt offering and started on his journey to the place God had pointed out to him. On the third day Abraham looked up and saw the place in the distance. Then Abraham said to his servants, 'Stay here with the donkey. The boy and I will go over there; we will worship and come back to you.'

Abraham took the wood for the burnt offering, loaded it on Isaac, and carried in his own hands the fire and the knife. Then the two of them set out together. Isaac spoke to his father Abraham, 'Father', he said. 'Yes, my son,' he replied. 'Look,' he said 'here are the fire and the wood, but where is the lamb for the burnt offering?' Abraham answered, 'My son, God himself will provide the lamb for the burnt offering.' Then the two of them went on together.

When they arrived at the place God had pointed out to him, Abraham built an altar there, and arranged the wood. Then he bound his son Isaac and put him on the altar on top of the wood. Abraham stretched out his hand and seized the knife to kill his son.

But the angel of the Lord called to him from heaven. 'Abraham, Abraham' he said. 'I am here' he replied. 'Do not raise your hand against the boy' the angel said. 'Do not harm him, for now I know you fear God. You have not refused me your son, your only son.' Then looking up, Abraham saw a ram caught by its horns in a bush. Abraham took the ram and offered it as a burnt offering in place of his son.

Abraham called this place 'The Lord provides', and hence the saying today: On the mountain the Lord provides.

EASTER

The angel of the Lord called Abraham a second time from heaven. 'I swear by my own self – it is the Lord who speaks – because you have done this, because you have not refused me your son, your only son, I will shower blessings on you, I will make your descendants as many as the stars of heaven and the grains of sand on the seashore. Your descendants shall gain possession of the gates of their enemies. All the nations of the earth shall bless themselves by your descendants, as a reward for your obedience.'

The word of the Lord.
Thanks be to God.

RESPONSORIAL PSALM   *Psalm 15:5, 8–11 response v 1*

Preserve me, God, I take refuge in you.

1 O Lord, it is you who are my portion and cup;
   it is you yourself who are my prize.
   I keep the Lord ever in my sight:
   since he is at my right hand, I shall stand firm.

2 And so my heart rejoices, my soul is glad;
   even my body shall rest in safety.
   For you will not leave my soul among the dead,
   nor let your beloved know decay.

3 You will show me the path of life,
   the fullness of joy in your presence,
   at your right hand happiness for ever.

PRAYER

`ALL STAND`

Let us pray.

O God, supreme Father of the faithful,
who increase the children of your promise
by pouring out the grace of adoption
throughout the whole world
and who through the Paschal Mystery
make your servant Abraham father of nations,
as once you swore,
grant, we pray,
that your peoples may enter worthily
into the grace to which you call them.
Through Christ our Lord. **Amen.**

`ALL SIT`

THIRD READING   *Exodus 14:15–15:1*

The sons of Israel went on dry ground right into the sea.

The Lord said to Moses, 'Why do you cry to me so? Tell the sons of Israel to march on. For yourself, raise your staff and stretch out your hand over the sea and part it for the sons of Israel to walk through the sea on dry ground. I for my part will make the heart of the Egyptians so stubborn that they will follow them. So shall I win myself glory at the expense of Pharaoh, of all his army, his chariots, his horsemen. And when I have won glory for myself, at the expense of Pharaoh and his chariots and his army, the Egyptians will learn that I am the Lord.'

Then the angel of the Lord, who marched at the front of the army of Israel, changed station and moved to their rear. The pillar of cloud changed station from the front to the rear of them, and remained there. It came between the camp of the Egyptians and the camp of Israel. The cloud was dark, and the night passed without the armies drawing any closer the whole night long. Moses stretched out his hand over the sea. The Lord drove back the sea with a strong easterly wind all night, and he made dry land of the sea. The waters parted and the sons of Israel went on dry ground right into the sea, walls of water to right and to left of them. The Egyptians gave chase: after them they went, right into the sea, all Pharaoh's horses, his chariots, and his horsemen. In the morning watch, the Lord looked down on the army of the Egyptians from the pillar of fire and of cloud, and threw the army into confusion. He so clogged their chariot wheels that they could scarcely make headway. 'Let us flee from the Israelites,' the Egyptians cried 'the Lord is fighting for them against the Egyptians!' 'Stretch out your hand over the sea,' the Lord said to Moses 'that the waters may flow back on the Egyptians and their chariots and their horsemen.' Moses stretched out his hand over the sea and, as day broke, the sea returned to its bed. The fleeing Egyptians marched right into it, and the Lord overthrew the chariots and the horsemen of Pharaoh's whole army, which had followed the Israelites into the sea; not a single one of them was left. But the sons of Israel had marched through the sea on dry ground, walls of water to right and to left of them. That day, the Lord rescued Israel from the Egyptians, and Israel saw the Egyptians lying dead on the shore. Israel witnessed the great act that the Lord had performed against the Egyptians, and the people venerated the Lord; they put their faith in the Lord and in Moses, his servant.

It was then that Moses and the sons of Israel sang this song in honour of the Lord:

The Responsorial Psalm begins immediately.

RESPONSORIAL PSALM *Exodus 15:1–6, 17–18 response v 1*

I will sing to the Lord, glorious his triumph!

1 I will sing to the Lord, glorious his triumph!
   Horse and rider he has thrown into the sea!
   The Lord is my strength, my song, my salvation.
   This is my God and I extol him,
   my father's God and I give him praise.

2 The Lord is a warrior! The Lord is his name.
   The chariots of Pharaoh he hurled into the sea,
   the flower of his army is drowned in the sea.
   The deeps hide them; they sank like a stone.

3 Your right hand, Lord, glorious in its power,
   your right hand, Lord, has shattered the enemy.
   In the greatness of your glory you crushed the foe.

EASTER

continued…

I will sing to the Lord, glorious his triumph!

4 You will lead your people and plant them on your mountain,
the place, O Lord, where you have made your home,
the sanctuary, Lord, which your hands have made.
The Lord will reign for ever and ever.

PRAYER

`ALL STAND`

Let us pray.

O God, whose ancient wonders
remain undimmed in splendour even in our day,
for what you once bestowed on a single people,
freeing them from Pharaoh's persecution
by the power of your right hand
now you bring about as the salvation of the nations
through the waters of rebirth,
grant, we pray, that the whole world
may become children of Abraham
and inherit the dignity of Israel's birthright.
Through Christ our Lord. **Amen.**

or

O God, who by the light of the New Testament
have unlocked the meaning
of wonders worked in former times,
so that the Red Sea prefigures the sacred font
and the nation delivered from slavery
foreshadows the Christian people,
grant, we pray, that all nations,
obtaining the privilege of Israel by merit of faith,
may be reborn by partaking of your Spirit.
Through Christ our Lord. **Amen.**

`ALL SIT`

FOURTH READING   *Isaiah 54:5–14*

With everlasting love the Lord your redeemer has taken pity on you.

Thus says the Lord:

Now your creator will be your husband, his name, the Lord of hosts; your redeemer will be the Holy One of Israel, he is called the God of the whole earth. Yes, like a forsaken wife, distressed in spirit, the Lord calls you back. Does a man cast off the wife of his youth? says your God.

I did forsake you for a brief moment, but with great love will I take you back. In excess of anger, for a moment I hid my face from you. But with everlasting love I have taken pity on you, says the Lord, your redeemer.

I am now as I was in the days of Noah when I swore that Noah's waters should never flood the world again. So now I swear concerning my anger with you and the threats I made against you; for the mountains may depart, the hills be shaken, but my love for you will never leave you and my covenant of peace with you will never be shaken, says the Lord who takes pity on you.

Unhappy creature, storm-tossed, disconsolate, see, I will set your stones on carbuncles and your foundations on sapphires. I will make rubies your battlements, your gates crystal, and your entire wall precious stones. Your sons will all be taught by the Lord. The prosperity of your sons will be great. You will be founded on integrity; remote from oppression, you will have nothing to fear; remote from terror, it will not approach you.

The word of the Lord.
Thanks be to God.

RESPONSORIAL PSALM   *Psalm 29:2, 4–6, 11–13 response v 2*

I will praise you, Lord, you have rescued me.

1   I will praise you, Lord, you have rescued me
     and have not let my enemies rejoice over me.
     O Lord, you have raised my soul from the dead,
     restored me to life from those who sink into the grave.

2   Sing psalms to the Lord, you who love him,
     give thanks to his holy name.
     His anger lasts but a moment; his favour through life.
     At night there are tears, but joy comes with dawn.

3   The Lord listened and had pity.
     The Lord came to my help.
     For me you have changed my mourning into dancing,
     O Lord my God, I will thank you for ever.

PRAYER   `ALL STAND`

Let us pray.

Almighty ever-living God,
surpass, for the honour of your name,
what you pledged to the Patriarchs by reason of their faith,
and through sacred adoption increase the children of your promise,
so that what the Saints of old never doubted would come to pass
your Church may now see in great part fulfilled.
Through Christ our Lord.   **Amen.**   `ALL SIT`

Alternatively, other prayers may be used from among those which follow the readings that have been omitted.

FIFTH READING   *Isaiah 55:1–11*

Come to me and your soul will live, and I will make an everlasting covenant with you.

Thus says the Lord:

Oh, come to the water all you who are thirsty; though you have no money, come! Buy corn without money, and eat, and, at no cost, wine and milk. Why spend money on what is not bread, your wages on what fails to satisfy? Listen, listen to me, and you will have good things to eat and rich food to enjoy. Pay attention, come to me; listen, and your soul will live.

With you I will make an everlasting covenant out of the favours promised to David. See, I have made of you a witness to the peoples, a leader and a master of the nations. See, you will summon a nation you never knew, those unknown will come hurrying to you, for the sake of the Lord your God, of the Holy One of Israel who will glorify you.

Seek the Lord while he is still to be found, call to him while he is still near. Let the wicked man abandon his way, the evil man his thoughts. Let him turn back to the Lord who will take pity on him, to our God who is rich in forgiving; for my thoughts are not your thoughts, my ways not your ways - it is the Lord who speaks.

Yes, the heavens are as high above earth as my ways are above your ways, my thoughts above your thoughts.

Yes, as the rain and the snow come down from the heavens and do not return without watering the earth, making it yield and giving growth to provide seed for the sower and bread for the eating, so the word that goes from my mouth does not return to me empty, without carrying out my will and succeeding in what it was sent to do.

The word of the Lord.
Thanks be to God.

RESPONSORIAL PSALM *Isaiah 12:2–6 response v 3*

With joy you will draw water from the wells of salvation.

1   Truly God is my salvation,
    I trust, I shall not fear.
    For the Lord is my strength, my song,
    he became my saviour.
    With joy you will draw water
    from the wells of salvation.

2   Give thanks to the Lord, give praise to his name!
    Make his mighty deeds known to the peoples,
    declare the greatness of his name.

3   Sing a psalm to the Lord
    for he has done glorious deeds,
    make them known to all the earth!
    People of Zion, sing and shout for joy
    for great in your midst is the Holy One of Israel.

PRAYER

ALL STAND

Let us pray.
Almighty ever-living God,
sole hope of the world,
who by the preaching of your Prophets
unveiled the mysteries of this present age,
graciously increase the longing of your people,
for only at the prompting of your grace
do the faithful progress in any kind of virtue.
Through Christ our Lord.   **Amen.**

ALL SIT

SIXTH READING   *Baruch 3:9–15, 32-4:4*

In the radiance of the Lord make your way to light.

Listen, Israel, to commands that bring life; hear, and learn what knowledge means, Why, Israel, why are you in the country of your enemies, growing older and older in an alien land, sharing defilement with the dead, reckoned with those who go to Sheol? Because you have forsaken the fountain of wisdom. Had you walked in the way of God, you would have lived in peace for ever. Learn where knowledge is, where strength, where understanding, and so learn where length of days is, where life, where the light of the eyes and where peace. But who has found out where she lives, who has entered her treasure house?

But the One who knows all knows her, he has grasped her with his own intellect, he has set the earth firm for ever and filled it with four-footed beasts, he sends the light – and it goes, he recalls it – and trembling it obeys; the stars shine joyfully at their set times: when he calls them, they answer, 'Here we are'; they gladly shine for their creator. It is he who is our God, no other can compare with him. He has grasped the whole way of knowledge, and confided it to his servant Jacob, to Israel his well beloved; so causing her to appear on earth and move among men.

This is the book of the commandments of God, the Law that stands for ever; those who desert her die. Turn back, Jacob, seize her, in her radiance make your way to light: do not yield your glory to another, your privilege to a people not your own. Israel, blessed are we: what pleases God has been revealed to us.

The word of the Lord.
Thanks be to God.

RESPONSORIAL PSALM   *Psalm 18:18–11 response John 6:68*

You have the message of eternal life, O Lord.

1 The law of the Lord is perfect,
   it revives the soul.
   The rule of the Lord is to be trusted,
   it gives wisdom to the simple.

2 The precepts of the Lord are right,
   they gladden the heart.
   The command of the Lord is clear,
   it gives light to the eyes.

3 The fear of the Lord is holy.
   abiding for ever.
   The decrees of the Lord are truth
   and all of them just.

4 They are more to be desired than gold,
   than the purest of gold
   and sweeter are they than honey,
   than honey from the comb.

PRAYER

Let us pray.
O God, who constantly increase your Church
by your call to the nations,
graciously grant
to those you wash clean in the waters of Baptism
the assurance of your unfailing protection.
Through Christ our Lord.   **Amen.**

ALL STAND

EASTER

ALL SIT

SEVENTH READING *Ezekiel 36:16–28*

I shall pour clean water over you, and I shall give you a new heart.

The word of the Lord was addressed to me as follows: 'Son of man, the members of the House of Israel used to live in their own land, but they defiled it by their conduct and actions. I then discharged my fury at them because of the blood they shed in their land and the idols with which they defiled it. I scattered them among the nations and dispersed them in foreign countries. I sentenced them as their conduct and actions deserved. And now they have profaned my holy name among the nations where they have gone, so that people say of them. "These are the people of the Lord; they have been exiled from his land." But I have been concerned about my holy name, which the House of Israel has profaned among the nations where they have gone. And so, say to the House of Israel, "The Lord says this: I am not doing this for your sake, House of Israel, but for the sake of my holy name, which you have profaned among the nations where you have gone. I mean to display the holiness of my great name, which has been profaned among the nations, which you have profaned among them. And the nations will learn that I am the Lord – it is the Lord who speaks – when I display my holiness for your sake before their eyes. Then I am going to take you from among the nations and gather you together from all the foreign countries, and bring you home to your own land. I shall pour clean water over you and you will be cleansed; I shall cleanse you of all your defilement and all your idols. I shall give you a new heart, and put a new spirit in you; I shall remove the heart of stone from your bodies and give you a heart of flesh instead. I shall put my spirit in you, and make you keep my laws and sincerely respect my observances. You will live in the land which I gave your ancestors. You shall be my people and I will be your God."'

The word of the Lord.
Thanks be to God.

RESPONSORIAL PSALM *Psalms 41:3, 5; 42:3, 4 response Psalm 41:2*

If a baptism takes place the Responsorial Psalm which follows the Fifth Reading is used, or Psalm 50 (see below)

**Like the deer that yearns for running streams,
so my soul is yearning for you, my God.**

1   My soul is thirsting for God,
the God of my life;
when can I enter and see
the face of God?

2   These things will I remember
as I pour out my soul:
how I would lead the rejoicing crowd
into the house of God,
amid cries of gladness and thanksgiving,
the throng wild with joy.

3   O send forth your light and your truth;
    let these be my guide.
    Let them bring me to your holy mountain
    to the place where you dwell.

4   And I will come to the altar of God,
    the God of my joy.
    My redeemer, I will thank you on the harp,
    O God, my God.

RESPONSORIAL PSALM   *Psalm 50:12–15, 18, 19 response verse 12*

If a baptism takes place either this Psalm or the Responsorial Psalm which follows the Fifth Reading is used.

A pure heart create for me, O God.

1   A pure heart create for me, O God,
    put a steadfast spirit within me.
    Do not cast me away from your presence,
    nor deprive me of your holy spirit.

2   Give me again the joy of your help;
    with a spirit of fervour sustain me,
    that I may teach transgressors your ways
    and sinners may return to you.

3   For in sacrifice you take no delight,
    burnt offering from me you would refuse,
    my sacrifice, a contrite spirit.
    A humbled, contrite heart you will not spurn.

PRAYER   `ALL STAND`

Let us pray.

O God of unchanging power and eternal light,
look with favour on the wondrous mystery of the whole Church
and serenely accomplish the work of human salvation,
which you planned from all eternity;
may the whole world know and see
that what was cast down is raised up,
what had become old is made new,
and all things are restored to integrity through Christ,
just as by him they came into being.
Who lives and reigns for ever and ever.   **Amen.**

EASTER

or

O God, who by the pages of both Testaments
instruct and prepare us to celebrate the Paschal Mystery,
grant that we may comprehend your mercy,
so that the gifts we receive from you this night
may confirm our hope of the gifts to come.
Through Christ our Lord.   **Amen.**

GLORIA

▷ *Music p 337*

After the last reading from the Old Testament with its Responsorial Psalm and its prayer, the altar candles are lit, and the Priest intones the hymn Gloria in excelsis Deo (Glory to God in the highest), which is taken up by all, while bells are rung, according to local custom.

COLLECT

Let us pray.

O God, who make this most sacred night radiant
with the glory of the Lord's Resurrection,
stir up in your Church a spirit of adoption,
so that, renewed in body and mind,
we may render you undivided service.
Through our Lord Jesus Christ, your Son,
who lives and reigns with you in the unity of the Holy Spirit,
one God, for ever and ever.   **Amen.**

ALL SIT

EPISTLE   *Romans 6:3–11*

Christ, having been raised from the dead, will never die again.

When we were baptised in Christ Jesus we were baptised in his death; in other words, when we were baptised we went into the tomb with him and joined him in death, so that as Christ was raised from the dead by the Father's glory, we too might live a new life. If in union with Christ we have imitated his death, we shall also imitate him in his resurrection. We must realise that our former selves have been crucified with him to destroy this sinful body and to free us from the slavery of sin. When a man dies, of course, he has finished with sin.

But we believe that having died with Christ we shall return to life with him: Christ, as we know, having been raised from the dead will never die again. Death has no power over him any more. When he died, he died, once for all, to sin, so his life now is life with God; and in that way, you too must consider yourselves to be dead to sin but alive for God in Christ Jesus.

The word of the Lord.
Thanks be to God.

After the Epistle has been read, all rise, then the Priest solemnly
intones the 'Alleluia' three times, raising his voice by a step each time,   **ALL STAND**
with all repeating it. If necessary, the psalmist intones the Alleluia.

RESPONSORIAL PSALM AND GOSPEL ACCLAMATION   *Psalm 117:1–2, 16–17, 22–23*

Alleluia, alleluia, alleluia!

1   Give thanks to the Lord for he is good,
　　for his love has no end.
　　Let the sons of Israel say:
　　'His love has no end.'

2   The Lord's right hand has triumphed;
　　his right hand raised me up.
　　I shall not die, I shall live
　　and recount his deeds.

3   The stone which the builders rejected
　　has become the corner stone.
　　This is the work of the Lord,
　　a marvel in our eyes,

GOSPEL   *Luke 24:1–12*

The Lord be with you.
And with your spirit.

A reading from the holy Gospel according to Luke.
Glory to you, O Lord.

Why look among the dead for someone who is alive?

On the first day of the week, at the first sign of dawn, the women went to the tomb with the spices they had prepared. They found that the stone had been rolled away from the tomb, but on entering discovered that the body of the Lord Jesus was not there. As they stood there not knowing what to think, two men in brilliant clothes suddenly appeared at their side. Terrified, the women lowered their eyes. But the two men said to them, 'Why look among the dead for someone who is alive? He is not here; he has risen. Remember what he told you when he was still in Galilee: that the Son of Man had to be handed over into the power of sinful men and be crucified, and rise again on the third day?' And they remembered his words.

When the women returned from the tomb they told all this to the Eleven and to all the others. The women were Mary of Magdala, Joanna, and Mary the mother of James. The other women with them also told the apostles, but this story of theirs seemed pure nonsense, and they did not believe them.

Peter, however, went running to the tomb. He bent down and saw the binding cloths, but nothing else; he then went back home, amazed at what had happened.

The Gospel of the Lord.
Praise to you, Lord Jesus Christ.

EASTER

HOMILY

THIRD PART: BAPTISMAL LITURGY

ELEMENTS OF THE BAPTISMAL LITURGY

The elements of the Baptismal Liturgy are printed in the order given below.
The table on the following page shows how the order may be altered
and some items omitted according to circumstances.

*Numbers refer to the Roman Missal, except oblique text which refers to the Rite of Christian Initiation of Adults
(RCIA). These numbers are also used in the text of the Baptismal Liturgy which follows.*

38	Calling forward of the candidates for baptism
41	Litany of Saints
43	Prayer over the candidates
44–47	Blessing of Baptismal Water
54	Blessing of Water
428	*Renunciation of sin by baptismal candidates*
429	*Renunciation of sin*
430	*Anointing with the Oil of Catechumens*
431	*Profession of Faith*
432	*Baptism*
434	*(Anointing After Baptism)*
435	*Clothing with a Baptismal Garment*
436	*Presentation of a Lighted Candle*
53	Celebration of Confirmation
54	Blessing of Water
441–443	*Reception of baptised Christians into the full communion of the Catholic Church*
(53	Celebration of Confirmation)
55	Renewal of Baptismal Promises
56	Sprinkling with Baptismal Water
58	Prayer of the Faithful

ARRANGEMENT OF THE BAPTISMAL LITURGY

In the following table, numbers refer to the Roman Missal, except oblique text which refers to the Rite of Christian Initiation of Adults (RCIA). These numbers are also used in the text of the Baptismal Liturgy which follows.

IF THERE IS BAPTISM

IF BAPTISM TAKES PLACE AT THE FONT	
38	Calling forward of the candidates for baptism
41	Procession to Font and Litany of Saints
40	Introductory Statement
43	Prayer over the candidates

IF BAPTISM TAKES PLACE IN THE SANCTUARY	
38	Calling forward of the candidates for baptism
40	Introductory Statement
41	Litany of Saints
43	Prayer over the candidates

44–47	Blessing of Baptismal Water
429	*Renunciation of sin*
430	*Anointing with the Oil of Catechumens*
431	*Profession of Faith*
432	*Baptism*
434	*(Anointing After Baptism)*
435	*Clothing with a Baptismal Garment*
436	*Presentation of a Lighted Candle*

IF THERE ARE NO CANDIDATES FOR RECEPTION INTO FULL COMMUNION	
53	Celebration of Confirmation
55	Renewal of Baptismal Promises
58	Prayer of the Faithful

IF THERE ARE CANDIDATES FOR RECEPTION INTO FULL COMMUNION	
55	Renewal of Baptismal Promises
56	Sprinkling with Baptismal Water
441–443	*Reception of baptised Christians into the full communion of the Catholic Church*
53	Celebration of Confirmation
58	Prayer of the Faithful

IF THERE IS NO BAPTISM

IF THE FONT IS TO BE BLESSED	
40	Introductory Statement
▷ 44–47	Blessing of Baptismal Water
55	Renewal of Baptismal Promises
58	Prayer of the Faithful

IF THE FONT IS NOT TO BE BLESSED	
▷ 54	Blessing of Water
55	Renewal of Baptismal Promises
58	Prayer of the Faithful

EASTER

37 *After the Homily the Baptismal Liturgy begins. The Priest goes with the ministers to the baptismal font, if this can be seen by the faithful. Otherwise a vessel with water is placed in the sanctuary.*

38 *Catechumens, if there are any, are called forward and presented by their godparents in front of the assembled Church or, if they are small children, are carried by their parents and godparents.*

39 *Then, if there is to be a procession to the baptistery or to the font, it forms immediately. A minister with the paschal candle leads off, and those to be baptized follow him with their godparents, then the ministers, the Deacon, and the Priest.*
During the procession, the Litany (n 43) is sung.

▷ page 245

When the Litany is completed, the Priest gives the address (n 40).

40 *If, however, the Baptismal Liturgy takes place in the sanctuary, the Priest immediately makes an introductory statement in these or similar words.*

INTRODUCTORY STATEMENT

If there are candidates to be baptized:
Dearly beloved,
with one heart and one soul, let us by our prayers
come to the aid of these our brothers and sisters in their blessed hope,
so that, as they approach the font of rebirth,
the almighty Father may bestow on them
all his merciful help.

If the font is to be blessed, but no one is to be baptized:
Dearly beloved,
let us humbly invoke upon this font
the grace of God the almighty Father,
that those who from it are born anew
may be numbered among the children of adoption in Christ.

LITANY OF SAINTS

41 *The Litany is sung by two cantors, with all standing (because it is Easter Time) and responding. If, however, there is to be a procession of some length to the baptistery, the Litany is sung during the procession; in this case, those to be baptized are called forward before the procession begins, and the procession takes place led by the paschal candle, followed by the catechumens with their godparents, then the ministers, the Deacon, and the Priest. The address should occur before the Blessing of Water.*

42 *If no one is to be baptized and the font is not to be blessed, the Litany is omitted, and the Blessing of Water (n 54) takes place at once.*

▷ page 250

43 *In the Litany the names of some Saints may be added, especially the Titular Saint of the church and the Patron Saints of the place and of those to be baptized.*

Cantors: All:

1. Lord, have mer - cy.   Lord, have mer - cy.
2. Christ, have mer - cy.   Christ, have mer - cy.
3. Lord, have mer - cy.   Lord, have mer - cy.

Cantors: All:

1. Holy Mary, Mother of God,   pray for us.
2. Saint Mich - ael,   pray for us.

Other verses follow, with the same response.

Cantors: All:

Lord, be mer - ci - ful,   Lord, de - li - ver us we pray.

From all evil   **Lord, deliver us, we pray.**
From every sin   **Lord, deliver us, we pray.**
From everlasting death   **Lord, deliver us, we pray.**
By your Incarnation   **Lord, deliver us, we pray.**
By your Death and Resurrection   **Lord, deliver us, we pray.**
By the outpouring of the Holy Spirit   **Lord, deliver us, we pray.**

Cantors: All:

Be merciful to us sin-ners,   Lord, we ask you hear our prayer.

If there are candidates to be baptized:
Bring these chosen ones to new birth
through the grace of baptism,   **Lord, we ask you, hear our prayer.**
or

If there is no one to be baptized:
Makes this font holy by your grace
for the new birth of your children,   **Lord, we ask you, hear our prayer.**

Jesus, Son of the living God,   **Lord, we ask you, hear our prayer.**

Cantors: All:

Christ, hear us.   Christ, hear us.

EASTER

Cantors: All:

Christ, gra-cious-ly hear us.   Christ, gra-cious-ly hear us.

PRAYER OVER THE CANDIDATES

If there are candidates to be baptized, the Priest, with hands extended, says the following prayer:

Almighty ever-living God,
be present by the mysteries of your great love
and send forth the spirit of adoption
to create the new peoples
brought to birth for you in the font of Baptism,
so that what is to be carried out by our humble service
may be brought to fulfilment by your mighty power.
Through Christ our Lord.   **Amen.**

BLESSING OF BAPTISMAL WATER

46   *The Priest then blesses the baptismal water, saying the following prayer:*

O God, who by invisible power
accomplish a wondrous effect
through sacramental signs
and who in many ways have prepared water, your creation,
to show forth the grace of Baptism;

O God, whose Spirit
in the first moments of the world's creation
hovered over the waters,
so that the very substance of water
would even then take to itself the power to sanctify;

O God, who by the outpouring of the flood
foreshadowed regeneration,
so that from the mystery of one and the same element of water
would come an end to vice and a beginning of virtue;

O God, who caused the children of Abraham
to pass dry-shod through the Red Sea,
so that the chosen people,
set free from slavery to Pharaoh,
would prefigure the people of the baptized;

O God, whose Son,
baptized by John in the waters of the Jordan,
was anointed with the Holy Spirit,
and, as he hung upon the Cross,
gave forth water from his side along with blood,
and after his Resurrection, commanded his disciples:
'Go forth, teach all nations, baptizing them
in the name of the Father and of the Son and of the Holy Spirit',
look now, we pray, upon the face of your Church
and graciously unseal for her the fountain of Baptism.

May this water receive by the Holy Spirit
the grace of your Only Begotten Son,
so that human nature, created in your image
and washed clean through the Sacrament of Baptism
from all the squalor of the life of old,
may be found worthy to rise to the life of newborn children
through water and the Holy Spirit.

*And, if appropriate, lowering the paschal candle into the water either once or three times,
he continues:*

May the power of the Holy Spirit,
O Lord, we pray,
come down through your Son
into the fullness of this font,

and, holding the candle in the water, he continues:

so that all who have been buried with Christ
by Baptism into death
may rise again to life with him.
Who lives and reigns with you in the unity of the Holy Spirit,
one God, for ever and ever.   **Amen.**

47   *Then the candle is lifted out of the water, as the people acclaim:*

All:

Springs of wa-ter, bless the Lord;   praise and exalt him above all for e - ver.

RENUNCIATION OF SIN BY BAPTISMAL CANDIDATES

48   *After the blessing of baptismal water and the acclamation of the people, the Priest, standing, puts
the prescribed questions to the adults and the parents or godparents of the children, as is set out
in the respective Rites of the Roman Ritual, in order for them to make the required renunciation.*

*The Priest questions the candidates for baptism together or individually. Godparents may answer
for candidates who are children The Priest then uses any of the three options A, B or C.*

429 **Option A**

Priest:	Do you reject sin so as to live in the freedom of God's children?
Candidates:	**I do.**
Priest:	Do you reject the glamour of evil and refuse to be mastered by sin?
Candidates:	**I do.**
Priest:	Do you reject Satan, father of sin and prince of darkness?
Candidates:	**I do.**

Option B

Priest:	Do you reject Satan,
	and all his works
	and all his empty promises?
Candidates:	**I do.**

Option C

Priest:	Do you reject Satan?
Candidates:	**I do.**

Priest:	And all his works?
Candidates:	**I do.**

Priest:	And all his empty promises?
Candidates:	**I do.**

430 ANOINTING WITH THE OIL OF CATECHUMENS

Unless it has taken place earlier in the day (see page 219), the anointing with the oil of catechumens takes place before the Profession of Faith. Where children are being baptized, the reply is given by their godparents.

Priest:	We anoint you with the oil of salvation
	in the name of Christ our Saviour.
	May he strengthen you with his power
	who lives and reigns for ever and ever.
Candidates	**Amen.**

The celebrant anoints each candidate with the oil of catechumens on both hands, on the breast, or, if this seems desirable, on other parts of the body.

PROFESSION OF FAITH BY BAPTISMAL CANDIDATES

431 *Then the Priest, informed again of each candidate's name by the godparents, questions each candidate individually. Each candidate is baptized immediately after his or her profession of faith.*

[If there are a great many to be baptized, the profession of faith may be made simultaneously by all together or group by group, then the baptism of each candidate follows.]

49 *Where many are to be baptized on this night, it is possible to arrange the rite so that, immediately after the response of those to be baptized and of the godparents and the parents, the Celebrant asks for and receives the renewal of baptismal promises of all present. In this case, the profession of faith on page 251 is used*

▷ *page 251*

Priest:	N., do you believe in God, the Father almighty,
	creator of heaven and earth?
Candidates:	**I do.**

Priest:	Do you believe in Jesus Christ, his only Son, our Lord, who was born of the Virgin Mary, was crucified, died, and was buried, rose from the dead, and is now seated at the right hand of the Father?
Candidates:	**I do.**

Priest:	Do you believe in the Holy Spirit, the holy Catholic Church, the communion of saints, the forgiveness of sins, the resurrection of the body, and the life everlasting?
Candidates:	**I do.**

BAPTISM

432   The celebrant baptizes each candidate either by immersion or the pouring of water. During the baptisms singing by the people is desirable or readings from Scripture or simply silent prayer.

Priest: N., I baptise you in the name of the Father,

The minister immerses the candidate or pours the water the first time.

and of the Son,

He immerses the candidate or pours the water the second time.

and of the Holy Spirit.

He immerses the candidate or pours the water the third time.

EXPLANATORY RITES

433   The following two rites may be celebrated according to circumstances.

Anointing After Baptism

434   If the confirmation of those baptized is separated from their baptism, the Priest anoints them with chrism immediately after their baptism.

Priest:	The God of power and Father of our Lord Jesus Christ has freed you from sin and brought you to new life through water and the Holy Spirit. He now anoints you with the chrism of salvation, so that, united with his people, you may remain for ever a member of Christ who is Priest, Prophet, and King.
Newly baptized:	**Amen.**

In silence, each of the newly-baptized is anointed with chrism on the crown of the head.

Clothing with a Baptismal Garment

435   The garment used in this rite may be white or of a colour that conforms to local custom. It is placed on the newly baptized by the godparents at the words 'Receive this baptismal garment'.

Priest: N. and N., you have become a new creation
                           and have clothed yourselves in Christ.

EASTER

Receive this baptismal garment
and bring it unstained to the judgement seat
of our Lord Jesus Christ,
so that you may have everlasting life.

Newly baptized: **Amen.**

PRESENTATION OF A LIGHTED CANDLE

436   The Priest takes the Easter candle in his hands, or touches it, saying:

Priest: Godparents, please come forward to give to the newly
                       baptized the light of Christ.

A godparent of each of the newly baptized goes to the celebrant, lights a candle from the Easter candle, then presents it to the newly baptized.

Then the celebrant says to the newly baptized:

Priest: You have been enlightened by Christ.
                       Walk always as children of the light
                       and keep the flame of faith alive in your hearts.
                       When the Lord comes, may you go out to meet him
                       with all the saints in the heavenly kingdom.

Newly baptized: **Amen.**

52   Afterwards, unless the baptismal washing and the other explanatory rites have occurred in the sanctuary, a procession returns to the sanctuary, formed as before, with the newly baptized or the godparents or parents carrying lighted candles. During this procession, the baptismal canticle Vidi aquam (I saw water) or another appropriate chant is sung (n 56).

▷ *page 253*

If the rite of Reception into Full Communion does not take place, Confirmation follows.

▷ *Confirmation page 254*

If the Rite of Reception into Full Communion is to take place, the newly baptized are confirmed with the newly received after the Rite of Reception.

▷ *Renewal of Baptismal Promises, page 251*

BLESSING OF WATER

54   If no one present is to be baptized and the font is not to be blessed, the Priest introduces the faithful to the blessing of water, saying:

Priest: Dear brothers and sisters,
              let us humbly beseech the Lord our God
              to bless this water he has created,
              which will be sprinkled upon us
              as a memorial of our Baptism.
              May he graciously renew us,
              that we may remain faithful to the Spirit
              whom we have received.

And after a brief pause in silence, he proclaims the following prayer:

Priest: Lord our God,
           in your mercy be present to your people
           who keep vigil on this most sacred night,
           and, for us who recall the wondrous work of our creation
           and the still greater work of our redemption,
           graciously bless this water.
           For you created water to make the fields fruitful
           and to refresh and cleanse our bodies.
           You also made water the instrument of your mercy:
           for through water you freed your people from slavery
           and quenched their thirst in the desert;
           through water the Prophets proclaimed the new covenant
           you were to enter upon with the human race;
           and last of all,
           through water, which Christ made holy in the Jordan,
           you have renewed our corrupted nature
           in the bath of regeneration.
           Therefore, may this water be for us
           a memorial of the Baptism we have received,
           and grant that we may share
           in the gladness of our brothers and sisters,
           who at Easter have received their Baptism.
           Through Christ our Lord.

All: **Amen.**

RENEWAL OF BAPTISMAL PROMISES

55 *When the Rite of Baptism (and Confirmation) has been completed or, if this has not taken place,*
   after the blessing of water, all stand, holding lighted candles in their hands, and renew the
   promise of baptismal faith, unless this has already been done together with those to be baptized
   *(cf no **49**).*

The Priest addresses the faithful in these or similar words:

Priest: Dear brethren (brothers and sisters), through the Paschal Mystery
           we have been buried with Christ in Baptism,
           so that we may walk with him in newness of life.
           And so, now that our Lenten observance is concluded,
           let us renew the promises of Holy Baptism,
           by which we once renounced Satan and his works
           and promised to serve God in the holy Catholic Church.
           And so I ask you:

Priest: Do you renounce Satan?
All: **I do.**

Priest: And all his works?
All: **I do.**

EASTER

Priest:	And all his empty show?
All:	**I do.**

or

Priest:	Do you renounce sin,
	so as to live in the freedom of the children of God?
All:	**I do.**

Priest:	Do you renounce the lure of evil,
	so that sin may have no mastery over you?
All:	**I do.**

Priest:	Do you renounce Satan,
	the author and prince of sin?
All:	**I do.**

If the situation warrants, this second formula may be adapted by Conferences of Bishops according to local needs.

Then the Priest continues:

Priest:	Do you believe in God,
	the Father almighty,
	Creator of heaven and earth?
All:	**I do.**

Priest:	Do you believe in Jesus Christ, his only Son, our Lord,
	who was born of the Virgin Mary,
	suffered death and was buried,
	rose again from the dead
	and is seated at the right hand of the Father?
All:	**I do.**

Priest:	Do you believe in the Holy Spirit,
	the holy Catholic Church,
	the communion of saints,
	the forgiveness of sins,
	the resurrection of the body,
	and life everlasting?
All:	**I do.**

And the Priest concludes:

Priest:	And may almighty God, the Father of our Lord Jesus Christ,
	who has given us new birth by water and the Holy Spirit
	and bestowed on us forgiveness of our sins,
	keep us by his grace,
	in Christ Jesus our Lord,
	for eternal life.
All:	**Amen.**

SPRINKLING WITH BAPTISMAL WATER

56 *The Priest sprinkles the people with the blessed water, while all sing the following antiphon, or another chant that is baptismal in character.*

Antiphon

I saw water flowing from the Temple,
from its right-hand side, alleluia;
and all to whom this water came were saved
and shall say: Alleluia, alleluia.

CELEBRATION OF RECEPTION

Invitation

441 *If baptism has been celebrated at the font, the celebrant, the assisting ministers, and the newly baptized with their godparents proceed to the sanctuary.*

As they do so the assembly may sing a suitable song.

In the following or similar words the celebrant invites the candidates for reception, along with their sponsors, to come into the sanctuary and before the community to make a profession of faith.

Priest: N. and N., of your own free will you have asked to be received into the full communion of the Catholic Church. You have made your decision after careful thought under the guidance of the Holy Spirit. I now invite you to come forward with your sponsors and in the presence of this community to profess the Catholic faith. In this faith you will be one with us for the first time at the Eucharistic table of the Lord Jesus, the sign of the Church's unity.

Profession by The Candidates

442 *The celebrant asks the candidates to make the following profession of faith. The candidates say:*

Candidates: I believe and profess all that the holy Catholic Church believes, teaches, and proclaims to be revealed by God.

Act of Reception

443 *Then the candidates with their sponsors go individually to the celebrant, who says to each candidate (laying his right hand on the head of any candidate who is not to receive confirmation):*

Priest: N., the Lord receives you into the Catholic Church. His loving kindness has led you here, so that in the unity of the Holy Spirit you may have full communion with us in the faith that you have professed in the presence of his family.

EASTER

CELEBRATION OF CONFIRMATION

444 Before the celebration of confirmation begins, the congregation may sing a suitable song.

Invitation

446 The celebrant first speaks briefly to the newly baptized and newly received in these or similar words.

My dear candidates for confirmation, by your baptism you have been born again in Christ and you have become members of Christ and of his priestly people. Now you are to share in the outpouring of the Holy Spirit among us, the Spirit sent by the Lord upon his apostles at Pentecost and given by them and their successors to the baptized.

The promised strength of the Holy Spirit, which you are to receive, will make you more like Christ and help you to be witnesses to his suffering, death, and resurrection. It will strengthen you to be active members of the Church and to build up the Body of Christ in faith and love.

(The Priests who will be associated with the celebrant as ministers of the sacrament now stand next to him) With hands joined, the celebrant next addresses the people:

My dear friends, let us pray to God our Father, that he will pour out the Holy Spirit on these candidates for confirmation to strengthen them with his gifts and anoint them to be more like Christ, the Son of God.

All pray briefly in silence.

Laying on of Hands

447 The celebrant holds his hands outstretched over the entire group of those to be confirmed and says the following prayer.

Priest: All-powerful God, Father of our Lord Jesus Christ,
by water and the Holy Spirit
you freed your sons and daughters from sin
and gave them new life.
Send your Holy Spirit upon them
to be their helper and guide.

Give them the spirit of wisdom and understanding,
the spirit of right judgment and courage,
the spirit of knowledge and reverence.
Fill them with the spirit of wonder and awe in your presence.

We ask this through Christ our Lord.

All: **Amen**

Anointing With Chrism

448   *Each candidate, with godparent or godparents, goes to the celebrant (or to an associated minister of the sacrament); or, if circumstances require, the celebrant (associated minister) may go to the candidates.*

Either or both godparents place the right hand on the shoulder of the candidate and either a godparent or the candidate gives the candidate's name to the minister of the sacrament. During the conferral of the sacrament a suitable song may be sung.

The minister of the sacrament dips his right thumb into the chrism and makes the sign of the cross on the forehead of the one to be confirmed as he says:

Priest: N., be sealed with the Gift of the Holy Spirit.
Newly confirmed: **Amen.**

The minister of the sacrament adds:

Priest: Peace be with you.
Newly confirmed: **And with your spirit.**

The newly baptized (and newly received) are led to their place among the faithful.

If Baptism has taken place, but no one has been received into full communion, the Renewal of Baptismal Promises now takes place.

▷ **Renewal of Baptismal Promises, page 251**

PRAYER OF THE FAITHFUL

The Priest returns to the chair.

The Profession of Faith is omitted and the Prayer of the Faithful begins immediately in which the newly baptized participate for the first time.

▷ *page 13*

FOURTH PART: LITURGY OF THE EUCHARIST

The Priest goes to the altar and begins the Liturgy of the Eucharist in the usual way.

It is desirable that the bread and wine be brought forward by the newly baptized or, if they are children, by their parents or godparents.

▷ *page 14*

EASTER

PRAYER OVER THE OFFERINGS

Accept, we ask, O Lord,
the prayers of your people
with the sacrificial offerings,
that what has begun in the paschal mysteries
may, by the working of your power,
bring us to the healing of eternity.
Through Christ our Lord.   **Amen.**

EUCHARISTIC PRAYER

Preface I of Easter: The Paschal Mystery (...on this night above all...), p 74.

When the Roman Canon is used, the proper form of the Hanc igitur (Therefore, Lord, we pray) is said, p 20. If there has been a baptism, proper forms of certain sections are used in Eucharistic Prayers I, II and III.

EUCHARISTIC PRAYER I
Memento, Domine
(Remember, Lord, your servants):

Remember, Lord, your servants
who have presented your chosen ones
for the holy grace of your Baptism,

Here the names of the godparents are read out.

and all gathered here,
whose faith and devotion are known to you...

EUCHARISTIC PRAYER II
*After the words 'and all the clergy,'
the following is added:*

Remember also, Lord, the newly baptized
who, through Baptism (and Confirmation),
have today been joined to your family,
that they may follow Christ, your Son,
with a generous heart and a willing spirit.
Remember also our brothers and sisters...

EUCHARISTIC PRAYER III
After the words 'whom you have summoned before you', the following is added:

Strengthen, we pray, in their holy purpose
your servants who by the cleansing waters of rebirth
(and the bestowing of the Holy Spirit)
have today been joined to your people
and grant that they may always walk in newness of life.
In your compassion, O merciful Father,
gather to yourself all your children
scattered throughout the earth.
To our departed brothers and sisters...

COMMUNION RITE

Before the 'Ecce Agnus Dei' ('Behold the Lamb of God'), the Priest may briefly address the newly baptized about receiving their first Communion and about the excellence of this great mystery, which is the climax of Initiation and the centre of the whole of Christian life.

It is desirable that the newly baptized receive Holy Communion under both kinds, together with their godfathers, godmothers, and Catholic parents and spouses, as well as their lay catechists.

Communion Antiphon   *1 Corinthians 5:7–8*
Christ our Passover has been sacrificed;
therefore let us keep the feast
with the unleavened bread of purity and truth, alleluia.

▷ *page 58*

Psalm 117 may appropriately be sung.

Prayer after Communion
Pour out on us, O Lord, the Spirit of your love,
and in your kindness make those you have nourished
by this paschal Sacrament
one in mind and heart.
Through Christ our Lord. **Amen.**

CONCLUDING RITES

SOLEMN BLESSING

Priest: May almighty God bless you
through today's Easter Solemnity
and, in his compassion,
defend you from every assault of sin.

All: **Amen.**

Priest: And may he, who restores you to eternal life
in the Resurrection of his Only Begotten,
endow you with the prize of immortality.

All: **Amen.**

Priest: Now that the days of the Lord's Passion have drawn to a close,
may you who celebrate the gladness of the Paschal Feast
come with Christ's help, and exulting in spirit,
to those feasts that are celebrated in eternal joy.

All: **Amen.**

Priest: And may the blessing of almighty God,
the Father, and the Son, ✠ and the Holy Spirit,
come down on you and remain with you for ever.

All: **Amen.**

The final blessing formula from the Rite of Baptism of Adults or of Children may also be used, according to circumstances.

DISMISSAL

*The following dismissal is used on Easter Sunday, the Octave of Easter,
and in the Mass during the day on Pentecost Sunday.*

Deacon/Priest:

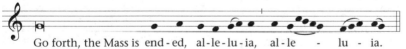

Go forth, the Mass is end-ed, al-le-lu-ia, al-le - lu - ia.

or

Deacon/Priest:

Go in peace, al-le-lu-ia, al-le - lu - ia.

All:

Thanks be to God, al-le-lu-ia, al-le - lu - ia.

EASTER SUNDAY — MASS DURING THE DAY

ENTRANCE ANTIPHON   *cf Psalm 138:18, 5–6*

I have risen, and I am with you still, alleluia.
You have laid your hand upon me, alleluia.
Too wonderful for me, this knowledge, alleluia, alleluia.

or   *Luke 24:34; cf Revelation 1:6*

The Lord is truly risen, alleluia.
To him be glory and power
for all the ages of eternity, alleluia, alleluia.

▷ *page 7*

COLLECT

O God, who on this day,
through your Only Begotten Son,
have conquered death
and unlocked for us the path to eternity,
grant, we pray, that we who keep
the solemnity of the Lord's Resurrection
may, through the renewal brought by your Spirit,
rise up in the light of life.
Through our Lord Jesus Christ, your Son,
who lives and reigns with you in the unity of the Holy Spirit,
one God, for ever and ever.   **Amen.**

FIRST READING   *Acts 10:34, 37–43*

We have eaten and drunk with him after his resurrection.

Peter addressed Cornelius and his household: 'You must have heard about the recent happenings in Judaea; about Jesus of Nazareth and how he began in Galilee, after John had been preaching baptism. God had anointed him with the Holy Spirit and with power, and because God was with him, Jesus went about doing good and curing all who had fallen into the power of the devil. Now I, and those with me, can witness to everything he did throughout the countryside of Judaea and in Jerusalem itself: and also to the fact that they killed him by hanging him on a tree, yet three days afterwards God raised him to life and allowed him to be seen, not by the whole people but only by certain witnesses God had chosen beforehand. Now we are those witnesses – we have eaten and drunk with him after his resurrection from the dead – and he has ordered us to proclaim this to his people and to tell them that God has appointed him to judge everyone, alive or dead. It is to him that all the prophets bear this witness: that all who believe in Jesus will have their sins forgiven through his name.'

The word of the Lord.
Thanks be to God.

RESPONSORIAL PSALM   *Psalm 117:1–2, 16–17, 22–23 response v 24*

> **This day was made by the Lord;**   *or*   **Alleluia, alleluia, alleluia!**
> **we rejoice and are glad.**

1 Give thanks to the Lord for he is good,
   for his love has no end.
   Let the sons of Israel say:
   'His love has no end.'

2 The Lord's right hand has triumphed;
   his right hand raised me up.
   I shall not die, I shall live
   and recount his deeds.

3 The stone which the builders rejected
   has become the corner stone.
   This is the work of the Lord,
   a marvel in our eyes.

SECOND READING   *Colossians 3:1–4*

You must look for he things that are in heaven, where Christ is.

Since you have been brought back to true life with Christ, you must look for the things that are in heaven, where Christ is, sitting at God's right hand. Let your thoughts be on heavenly things, not on the things that are on the earth, because you have died, and now the life you have is hidden with Christ in God. But when Christ is revealed – and he is your life – you too will be revealed in all your glory with him.

The word of the Lord.
Thanks be to God.

ALTERNATIVE SECOND READING
1 Corinthians 5:6–8

Get rid of the old yeast, and make yourselves into a completely new batch of bread.

You must know how even a small amount of yeast is enough to leaven all the dough, so get rid of all the old yeast, and make yourselves into a completely new batch of bread, unleavened as you are meant to be.

Christ, our Passover, has been sacrificed; let us celebrate the feast by getting rid of all the old yeast of evil and wickedness, having only the unleavened bread of sincerity and truth.

The word of the Lord.
Thanks be to God.

SEQUENCE
The Sequence is said or sung at all Masses.

Christians, to the Paschal Victim offer sacrifice and praise.
The sheep are ransomed by the Lamb;
and Christ, the undefiled,
hath sinners to his Father reconciled.
Death with life contended: combat strangely ended!
Life's own Champion, slain, yet lives to reign.
Tell us, Mary: say what thou didst see upon the way.
The tomb the Living did enclose;
I saw Christ's glory as he rose!
The angels there attesting;
shroud with grave-clothes resting.
Christ, my hope, has risen: he goes before you into Galilee.
That Christ is truly risen from the dead we know.
Victorious king, thy mercy show!

EASTER

GOSPEL ACCLAMATION   *1 Corinthians 5:7–8*

> Alleluia, alleluia!
> Christ, our Passover, has been sacrificed;
> let us celebrate the feast then, in the Lord.
> Alleluia!

Alternative Gospel Readings

As an alternative to the Gospel reading below, the Gospel of the Mass of the Easter Vigil may be read, p 241.
At an evening Mass, Luke 24:13–35 may be used as an alternative, see below.

GOSPEL   *John 20:1–9*

The Lord be with you.
And with your spirit.

A reading from the holy Gospel according to John.
Glory to you, O Lord.

He must rise from the dead.

It was very early on the first day of the week and still dark, when Mary of Magdala came to the tomb. She saw that the stone had been moved away from the tomb and came running to Simon Peter and the other disciple, the one Jesus loved. 'They have taken the Lord out of the tomb,' she said 'and we don't know where they have put him.'

So Peter set out with the other disciple to go to the tomb. They ran together, but the other disciple, running faster than Peter, reached the tomb first; he bent down and saw the linen cloths lying on the ground, but did not go in. Simon Peter who was following now came up, went right into the tomb, saw the linen cloths on the ground, and also the cloth that had been over his head; this was not with the linen cloths but rolled up in a place by itself. Then the other disciple who had reached the tomb first also went in; he saw and he believed. Till this moment they had failed to understand the teaching of scripture, that he must rise from the dead.

The Gospel of the Lord.
Praise to you, Lord Jesus Christ.

ALTERNATIVE GOSPEL FOR EVENING MASS   *Luke 24:13–35*

The Lord be with you.
And with your spirit.

A reading from the holy Gospel according to Luke.
Glory to you, O Lord.

They recognised Jesus at the breaking of the bread.

Two of the disciples of Jesus were on their way to a village called Emmaus, seven miles from Jerusalem, and they were talking together about all that had happened. Now as they talked this over, Jesus himself came up and walked by their side; but something prevented them from recognising him. He said to them, 'What matters are you discussing as you walk along?' They stopped short, their faces downcast.

Then one of them, called Cleopas, answered him, 'You must be the only person staying in Jerusalem who does not know the things that have been happening there these last few days'. 'What things?' he asked. 'All about Jesus of Nazareth', they answered, 'who proved he was a great prophet by the things he said and did in the sight of God and of the whole people; and how our chief priests and our leaders handed him over to be sentenced to death, and had him crucified. Our own hope had been that he would be the one to set Israel free. And this is not all: two whole days have gone by since it all happened; and some women from our group have astounded us: they went to the tomb in the early morning, and when they did not find the body, they came back to tell us they had seen a vision of angels who declared he was alive. Some of our friends went to the tomb and found everything exactly as the women had reported, but of him they saw nothing.'

Then he said to them, 'You foolish men! So slow to believe the full message of the prophets! Was it not ordained that the Christ should suffer and so enter into his glory?' Then, starting with Moses and going through all the prophets, he explained to them the passages throughout the scriptures that were about himself.

When they drew near to the village to which they were going, he made as if to go on; but they pressed him to stay with them. 'It is nearly evening,' they said, 'and the day is almost over'. So he went in to stay with them. Now while he was with them at table, he took the bread and said the blessing; then he broke it and handed it to them. And their eyes were opened and they recognised him; but he had vanished from their sight. Then they said to each other, 'Did not our hearts burn within us as he talked to us on the road and explained the scriptures to us?'

They set out that instant and returned to Jerusalem. There they found the Eleven assembled together with their companions, who said to them, 'Yes, it is true. The Lord has risen and has appeared to Simon.' Then they told their story of what had happened on the road and how they had recognised him at the breaking of bread.

The Gospel of the Lord.
Praise to you, Lord Jesus Christ.

▷ *page 11*

The Profession of Faith is said. However, in Easter Sunday Masses which are celebrated with a congregation, the rite of renewal of baptismal promises may take place after the homily, according to the text used at the Easter Vigil (p 251). In that case the Profession of Faith is omitted.

PRAYER OVER THE OFFERINGS
Exultant with paschal gladness, O Lord,
we offer the sacrifice
by which your Church
is wondrously reborn and nourished.
Through Christ our Lord.   **Amen.**

▷ *page 15*

Preface I of Easter, The Paschal Mystery, p 74. When the Roman Canon is used, the proper forms of the 'Communicantes '(In communion with those) and 'Hanc igitur' (Therefore, Lord, we pray) are said, p 20.

EASTER

COMMUNION ANTIPHON   *1 Corinthians 5:7–8*

Christ our Passover has been sacrificed, alleluia;
therefore let us keep the feast with the unleavened bread
of purity and truth, alleluia, alleluia.

▷ *page 58*

PRAYER AFTER COMMUNION

Look upon your Church, O God,
with unfailing love and favour,
so that, renewed by the paschal mysteries,
she may come to the glory of the resurrection.
Through Christ our Lord.   **Amen.**

A solemn blessing may be used.

▷ *page 59*

DISMISSAL

▷ *Music p 257*

Deacon or Priest: Go forth, the Mass is ended, alleluia, alleluia.
or
Deacon or Priest: Go in peace, alleluia, alleluia.
All: **Thanks be to God, alleluia, alleluia.**

 # SECOND SUNDAY OF EASTER

(OR OF DIVINE MERCY)

ENTRANCE ANTIPHON   *1 Peter 2:2*

Like newborn infants, you must long for the pure, spiritual milk,
that in him you may grow to salvation, alleluia.

or   *4 Esdras 2:36-37*

Receive the joy of your glory, giving thanks to God,
who has called you into the heavenly kingdom, alleluia.

▷ *page 7*

COLLECT

God of everlasting mercy,
who, in the very recurrence of the paschal feast
kindle the faith of the people you have made your own,
increase, we pray, the grace you have bestowed,
that all may grasp and rightly understand
in what font they have been washed,
by whose Spirit they have been reborn,
by whose Blood they have been redeemed.
Through our Lord Jesus Christ, your Son,
who lives and reigns with you in the unity of the Holy Spirit,
one God, for ever and ever.   **Amen.**

FIRST READING   Acts 5:12–6

The numbers of men and women who came to believe in the Lord increased steadily.

The faithful all used to meet by common consent in the Portico of Solomon. No one else ever dared to join them, but the people were loud in their praise and the numbers of men and women who came to believe in the Lord increased steadily. So many signs and wonders were worked among the people at the hands of the apostles that the sick were even taken out into the streets and laid on beds and sleeping-mats in the hope that at least the shadow of Peter might fall across some of them as he went past. People even came crowding in from the towns round about Jerusalem, bringing with them their sick and those tormented by unclean spirits, and all of them were cured.

The word of the Lord.
Thanks be to God.

RESPONSORIAL PSALM   *Psalm 117:2–4, 22–27 response v 1*

> **Give thanks to the Lord for he is good,**
> **for his love has no end.**

or

> **Alleluia, alleluia, alleluia!**

1 Let the sons of Israel say:
  'His love has no end.'
  Let the sons of Aaron say:
  'His love has no end.'
  Let those who fear the Lord say:
  'His love has no end.'

2 The stone which the builders rejected
  has become the corner stone.
  This is the work of the Lord,
  a marvel in our eyes.
  This day was made by the Lord;
  we rejoice and are glad.

3 O Lord, grant us salvation;
  O Lord, grant success.
  Blessed in the name of the Lord
  is he who comes.
  We bless you from the house of the Lord;
  the Lord God is our light.

SECOND READING   *Apocalypse 1:9–13, 17–19*

I was dead and now I am to live for ever and ever.

My name is John, and through our union in Jesus I am your brother and share your sufferings, your kingdom, and all you endure. I was on the island of Patmos for having preached God's word and witnessed for Jesus; it was the Lord's day and the Spirit possessed me, and I heard a voice behind me, shouting like a trumpet, 'Write down all that you see in a book.' I turned round to see who had spoken to me, and when I turned I saw seven golden lamp-stands and, surrounded by them, a figure like a Son of man, dressed in a long robe tied at the waist with a golden girdle.

When I saw him, I fell in a dead faint at his feet, but he touched me with his right hand and said, 'Do not be afraid; it is I, the First and the Last; I am the Living One. I was dead and now I am to live for ever and ever, and I hold the keys of death and of the underworld. Now write down all that you see of present happenings and things that are still to come.'

The word of the Lord.
Thanks be to God.

GOSPEL ACCLAMATION John 20:29

> **Alleluia, alleluia!**
> **Jesus said: 'You believe because you can see me.**
> **Happy are those who have not seen and yet believe.'**
> **Alleluia!**

GOSPEL John 20:19–31

The Lord be with you.
And with your spirit.

A reading from the holy Gospel according to John.
Glory to you, O Lord.

Eight days later, Jesus came.

In the evening of that same day, the first day of the week, the doors were closed in the room where the disciples were, for fear of the Jews. Jesus came and stood among them. He said to them, 'Peace be with you,' and showed them his hands and his side. The disciples were filled with joy when they saw the Lord, and he said to them again, 'Peace be with you.

As the Father sent me, so am I sending you.'

After saying this he breathed on them and said:

'Receive the Holy Spirit. For those whose sins you forgive, they are forgiven; for those whose sins you retain, they are retained.'

Thomas, called the Twin, who was one of the Twelve, was not with them when Jesus came. When the disciples said, 'We have seen the Lord', he answered, 'Unless I see the holes that the nails made in his hands and can put my finger into the holes they made, and unless I can put my hand into his side, I refuse to believe.' Eight days later the disciples were in the house again and Thomas was with them. The doors were closed, but Jesus came in and stood among them. 'Peace be with you' he said. Then he spoke to Thomas, 'Put your finger here; look, here are my hands. Give me your hand; put it into my side. Doubt no longer but believe.' Thomas replied, 'My Lord and my God!' Jesus said to him: 'You believe because you can see me. Happy are those who have not seen and yet believe.'

There were many other signs that Jesus worked and the disciples saw, but they are not recorded in this book. These are recorded so that you may believe that Jesus is the Christ, the Son of God, and that believing this you may have life through his name.

The Gospel of the Lord.
Praise to you, Lord Jesus Christ.

▷ page 11

PRAYER OVER THE OFFERINGS

Accept, O Lord, we pray,
the oblations of your people
(and of those you have brought to new birth),
that, renewed by confession of your name and by Baptism,
they may attain unending happiness.
Through Christ our Lord. **Amen.**

▷ *page 15*

Preface I of Easter (…on this day above all), p 74. When the Roman Canon is used, the proper forms of the Communicantes (In communion with those) and Hanc igitur (Therefore, Lord, we pray) are said, p 20.

COMMUNION ANTIPHON   *Cf John 20:27*

Bring your hand and feel the place of the nails,
and do not be unbelieving but believing, alleluia.

▷ *page 58*

PRAYER AFTER COMMUNION

Grant, we pray, almighty God,
that our reception of this paschal Sacrament
may have a continuing effect
in our minds and hearts.
Through Christ our Lord. **Amen.**

▷ *page 59*

A solemn blessing may be used.

DISMISSAL

▷ *Music p 257*

Deacon or Priest:	Go forth, the Mass is ended, alleluia, alleluia.
or	
Deacon or Priest:	Go in peace, alleluia, alleluia.
All:	**Thanks be to God, alleluia, alleluia.**

THIRD SUNDAY OF EASTER

EASTER

ENTRANCE ANTIPHON   *cf Psalm 65:1–2*

Cry out with joy to God, all the earth,
O sing to the glory of his name.
O render him glorious praise, alleluia.

▷ *page 7*

COLLECT

May your people exult for ever, O God,
in renewed youthfulness of spirit,
so that, rejoicing now in the restored glory of our adoption,
we may look forward in confident hope
to the rejoicing of the day of resurrection.
Through our Lord Jesus Christ, your Son,
who lives and reigns with you in the unity of the Holy Spirit,
one God, for ever and ever. **Amen.**

FIRST READING *Acts 5:27–32, 40–41*

We are witnesses of all this, we and the Holy Spirit.

The high priest demanded an explanation of the apostles. 'We gave you a formal warning,' he said 'not to preach in this name, and what have you done? You have filled Jerusalem with your teaching, and seem determined to fix the guilt of this man's death on us.' In reply Peter and the apostles said, 'Obedience to God comes before obedience to men; it was the God of our ancestors who raised up Jesus, but it was you who had him executed by hanging on a tree. By his own right hand God has now raised him up to be leader and saviour, to give repentance and forgiveness of sins through him to Israel. We are witnesses to all this, we and the Holy Spirit whom God has given to those who obey him,' They warned the apostles not to speak in the name of Jesus and released them. And so they left the presence of the Sanhedrin glad to have had the honour of suffering humiliation for the sake of the name.

The word of the Lord.
Thanks be to God.

RESPONSORIAL PSALM *Psalm 29:2, 4–6, 11–13 response v 2*

> **I will praise you, Lord,
> you have rescued me.**

or

> **Alleluia!** *(may be repeated two or three times)*

1   I will praise you, Lord, you have rescued me
   and have not let my enemies rejoice over me.
   O Lord, you have raised my soul from the dead,
   restored me to life from those who sink into the grave.

2   Sing psalms to the Lord, you who love him,
   give thanks to his holy name.
   His anger lasts but a moment; his favour through life.
   At night there are tears, but joy comes with dawn.

3   The Lord listened and had pity.
   The Lord came to my help.
   For me you have changed my mourning into dancing,
   O Lord my God, I will thank you for ever.

SECOND READING *Apocalypse 5:11–14*

The Lamb that was sacrificed is worthy to be given riches and power.

In my vision, I, John, heard the sound of an immense number of angels gathered round the throne and the animals and the elders; there were ten thousand times ten thousand of them and thousands upon thousands, shouting, 'The Lamb that was sacrificed is worthy to be given power, riches, wisdom, strength, honour, glory and blessing.' Then I heard all the living things in creation – everything that lives in the air, and on the ground, and under the ground, and in the sea, crying, 'To the One who is sitting on the throne and to the Lamb, be all praise, honour, glory and power, for ever and ever.' And the four animals said, 'Amen'; and the elders prostrated themselves to worship.

The word of the Lord.
Thanks be to God.

GOSPEL ACCLAMATION   *cf Luke 24:32*

Alleluia, alleluia!
Lord Jesus, explain the scriptures to us.
Make our hearts burn within us as you talk to us.
Alleluia!

or

Alleluia, alleluia!
Christ has risen: he who created all things,
and has granted his mercy to men.
Alleluia!

GOSPEL   *John 21:1–19*   *Shorter form (omitting oblique text): John 21:1–14*

The Lord be with you.
And with your spirit.

A reading from the holy Gospel according to John.
Glory to you, O Lord.

Jesus stepped forward, took the bread and gave it to them, and the same with the fish.

Jesus showed himself again to the disciples. It was by the Sea of Tiberias, and it happened like this: Simon Peter, Thomas called the Twin, Nathanael from Cana in Galilee, the sons of Zebedee and two more of his disciples were together. Simon Peter said, 'I'm going fishing.' They replied 'We'll come with you.' They went out and got into the boat but caught nothing that night.

It was light by now and there stood Jesus on the shore, though the disciples did not realise that it was Jesus. Jesus called out. 'Have you caught anything, friends?' And when they answered, 'No', he said, 'Throw the net out to starboard and you'll find something.' So they dropped the net, and there were so many fish that they could not haul it in. The disciple Jesus loved said to Peter, 'It is the Lord.' At these words 'It is the Lord', Simon Peter, who had practically nothing on, wrapped his cloak round him, and jumped into the water. The other disciples came on in the boat, towing the net and the fish; they were only about a hundred yards from land.

As soon as they came ashore they saw that there was some bread there, and a charcoal fire with fish cooking on it. Jesus said, 'Bring some of the fish you have just caught.' Simon Peter went aboard and dragged the net to the shore, full of big fish, one hundred and fifty-three of them; and in spite of there being so many the net was not broken. Jesus said to them, 'Come and have breakfast.' None of the disciples was bold enough to ask, 'Who are you?'; they knew quite well it was the Lord. Jesus then stepped forward, took the bread and gave it to them, and the same with the fish. This was the third time that Jesus showed himself to the disciples after rising from the dead.

After the meal Jesus said to Simon Peter. 'Simon son of John, do you love me more than these others do?' He answered. 'Yes, Lord, you know I love you.' Jesus said to him, 'Feed my lambs.' A second time he said to him, 'Simon son of John, do you love me?' He replied. 'Yes, Lord, you know I love you.' Jesus said to him, 'Look after my sheep.' Then he said to him a

EASTER

third time. 'Simon son of John, do you love me?' Peter was upset that he asked him the third time,' Do you love me?' and said, 'Lord, you know everything; you know I love you.' Jesus said to him, 'Feed my sheep.

'I tell you most solemnly, when you were young you put on your own belt and walked where you liked; but when you grow old you will stretch out your hands, and somebody else will put a belt round you and take you where you would rather not go.'

In these words he indicated the kind of death by which Peter would give glory to God. After this he said, 'Follow me.'

The Gospel of the Lord.
Praise to you, Lord Jesus Christ.

▷ *page 11*

PRAYER OVER THE OFFERINGS
Receive, O Lord, we pray,
these offerings of your exultant Church,
and, as you have given her cause for such great gladness,
grant also that the gifts we bring
may bear fruit in perpetual happiness.
Through Christ our Lord.   **Amen.**

▷ *page 15*

Preface of Easter, pp 74–75.

COMMUNION ANTIPHON   *Luke 24:35*
The disciples recognized the Lord Jesus
in the breaking of the bread, alleluia.

Optional for Year C: *Cf John 21:12–13*
Jesus said to his disciples: Come and eat.
And he took bread and gave it to them, alleluia.

▷ *page 58*

PRAYER AFTER COMMUNION
Look with kindness upon your people, O Lord,
and grant, we pray,
that those you were pleased to renew by eternal mysteries
may attain in their flesh
the incorruptible glory of the resurrection.
Through Christ our Lord.   **Amen.**

▷ *page 59*

A solemn blessing may be used.

FOURTH SUNDAY OF EASTER

ENTRANCE ANTIPHON   *cf Psalm 32:5–6*
The merciful love of the Lord fills the earth;
by the word of the Lord the heavens were made, alleluia.

▷ *page 7*

COLLECT

Almighty ever-living God,
lead us to a share in the joys of heaven,
so that the humble flock may reach
where the brave Shepherd has gone before.
Who lives and reigns with you in the unity of the Holy Spirit,
one God, for ever and ever.   **Amen.**

FIRST READING   *Acts 13:14, 43–52*

We must turn to the pagans.

Paul and Barnabas carried on from Perga till they reached Antioch in Pisidia. Here they went to synagogue on the sabbath and took their seats.

When the meeting broke up, many Jews and devout converts joined Paul and Barnabas, and in their talks with them Paul and Barnabas urged them to remain faithful to the grace God had given them.

The next sabbath almost the entire town assembled to hear the word of God. When they saw the crowds, the Jews, prompted by jealousy, used blasphemies and contradicted everything Paul said. Then Paul and Barnabas spoke out boldly. 'We had to proclaim the word of God to you first, but since you have rejected it, since you do not think yourselves worthy of eternal life, we must turn to the pagans. For this is what the Lord commanded us to do when he said: I have made you a light for the nations, so that my salvation may reach the ends of the earth.'

It made the pagans very happy to hear this and they thanked the Lord for his message; all who were destined for eternal life became believers. Thus the word of the Lord spread through the whole countryside.

But the Jews worked upon some of the devout women of the upper classes and the leading men of the city and persuaded them to turn against Paul and Barnabas and expel them from their territory. So they shook the dust from their feet in defiance and went off to Iconium; but the disciples were filled with joy and the Holy Spirit.

The word of the Lord.
Thanks be to God.

RESPONSORIAL PSALM   *Psalm 99:1–3, 5 response v 3*

We are his people, the sheep of his flock.

or

Alleluia! *(may be repeated two or three times)*

1   Cry out with joy to the Lord, all the earth.
 Serve the Lord with gladness.
 Come before him, singing for joy.

2   Know that he, the Lord, is God.
 He made us, we belong to him,
 we are his people, the sheep of his flock.

3   Indeed, how good is the Lord,
 eternal his merciful love.
 He is faithful from age to age.

EASTER

SECOND READING   *Apocalypse 7:9, 14–17*

The Lamb will be their shepherd and will lead them to springs of living water.

I, John, saw a huge number, impossible to count, of people from every nation, race, tribe and language; they were standing in front of the throne and in front of the Lamb, dressed in white robes and holding palms in their hands. One of the elders said to me, 'These are the people who have been through the great persecution, and because they have washed their robes white again in the blood of the Lamb, they now stand in front of God's throne and serve him day and night in his sanctuary; and the One who sits on the throne will spread his tent over them. They will never hunger or thirst again; neither the sun nor scorching wind will ever plague them, because the Lamb who is at the throne will be their shepherd and will lead them to springs of living water; and God will wipe away all tears from their eyes.'

The word of the Lord.
Thanks be to God.

GOSPEL ACCLAMATION   *John 10:14*

Alleluia, alleluia!
I am the good shepherd, says the Lord;
I know my own sheep and my own know me.
Alleluia!

GOSPEL   *John 10:27–30*

The Lord be with you.
And with your spirit.

A reading from the holy Gospel according to John.
Glory to you, O Lord.

I give eternal life to the sheep that belong to me.

Jesus said: 'The sheep that belong to me listen to my voice; I know them and they follow me. I give them eternal life; they will never be lost and no one will ever steal them from me. The Father who gave them to me is greater than anyone and no one can steal from the Father. The Father and I are one.'

The Gospel of the Lord.
Praise to you, Lord Jesus Christ.

▷ page 11

PRAYER OVER THE OFFERINGS

Grant, we pray, O Lord,
that we may always find delight in these paschal mysteries,
so that the renewal constantly at work within us
may be the cause of our unending joy.
Through Christ our Lord.   **Amen.**

▷ page 15

Preface of Easter, pp 74–75.

COMMUNION ANTIPHON

The Good Shepherd has risen,
who laid down his life for his sheep
and willingly died for his flock, alleluia.

▷ page 58

PRAYER AFTER COMMUNION
Look upon your flock, kind Shepherd,
and be pleased to settle in eternal pastures
the sheep you have redeemed
by the Precious Blood of your Son.
Who lives and reigns for ever and ever. **Amen.**

▷ *page 59*

A solemn blessing may be used.

FIFTH SUNDAY OF EASTER

ENTRANCE ANTIPHON   *cf Psalm 97:1–2*
O sing a new song to the Lord,
for he has worked wonders;
in the sight of the nations
he has shown his deliverance, alleluia.

▷ *page 7*

COLLECT
Almighty ever-living God,
constantly accomplish the Paschal Mystery within us,
that those you were pleased to make new in Holy Baptism
may, under your protective care, bear much fruit
and come to the joys of life eternal.
Through our Lord Jesus Christ, your Son,
who lives and reigns with you in the unity of the Holy Spirit,
one God, for ever and ever. **Amen.**

FIRST READING   *Acts 14:21–27*
They gave an account to the church of all that God had done with them.

Paul and Barnabas went back through Lystra and Iconium to Antioch. They put fresh heart into the disciples, encouraging them to persevere in the faith. 'We all have to experience many hardships 'they said 'before we enter the kingdom of God.' In each of these churches they appointed elders, and with prayer and fasting they commended them to the Lord in whom they had come to believe.

They passed through Pisidia and reached Pamphylia. Then after proclaiming the word at Perga they went down to Attalia and from there sailed for Antioch, where they had originally been commended to the grace of God for the work they had now completed.

On their arrival they assembled the church and gave an account of all that God had done with them, and how he had opened the door of faith to the pagans.

The word of the Lord.
Thanks be to God.

EASTER

RESPONSORIAL PSALM   *Psalm 144:8–13 response cf v 1*

> ## I will bless your name for ever, O God my King.

or

> ## Alleluia! *(may be repeated two or three times)*

1 The Lord is kind and full of compassion,
   slow to anger, abounding in love.
   How good is the Lord to all,
   compassionate to all his creatures.

2 All your creatures shall thank you, O Lord,
   and your friends shall repeat their blessing.
   They shall speak of the glory of your reign
   and declare your might, O God,
   to make known to men your mighty deeds
   and the glorious splendour of your reign.

3 Yours is an everlasting kingdom,
   your rule lasts from age to age.

SECOND READING   *Apocalypse 21:1–5*

God will wipe away all tears from their eyes.

I, John, saw a new heaven and a new earth; the first heaven and the first earth had disappeared now, and there was no longer any sea. I saw the holy city, and the new Jerusalem, coming down from God out of heaven, as beautiful as a bride all dressed for her husband. Then I heard a loud voice call from the throne, 'You see this city? Here God lives among men. He will make his home among them; they shall be his people, and he will be their God; his name is God-with-them. He will wipe away all tears from their eyes; there will be no more death, and no more mourning or sadness. The world of the past has gone.'

Then the One sitting on the throne spoke: 'Now I am making the whole of creation new' he said.

The word of the Lord.
Thanks be to God.

GOSPEL ACCLAMATION   *John 13:34*

> Alleluia, alleluia!
> Jesus said: 'I give you a new commandment:
> love one another, just as I have loved you.'
> Alleluia!

GOSPEL   *John 13:31–35*

The Lord be with you.
And with your spirit.

A reading from the holy Gospel according to John.
Glory to you, O Lord.

I give you a new commandment: love one another.

When Judas had gone Jesus said: 'Now has the Son of Man been glorified, and in him God has been glorified. If God has been glorified in him, God will in turn glorify him in himself, and will glorify him very soon. My little children, I shall not be with you much longer. I give you a new commandment: love one another; just as I have loved you, you also must love one another. By this love you have for one another, everyone will know that you are my disciples.'

The Gospel of the Lord.
Praise to you, Lord Jesus Christ.

▷ *page 11*

PRAYER OVER THE OFFERINGS

O God, who by the wonderful exchange effected in this sacrifice
have made us partakers of the one supreme Godhead,
grant, we pray,
that, as we have come to know your truth,
we may make it ours by a worthy way of life.
Through Christ our Lord.   **Amen.**

▷ *page 15*

Preface of Easter, pp 74–75.

COMMUNION ANTIPHON   *Cf John 15:1, 5*

I am the true vine and you are the branches, says the Lord.
Whoever remains in me, and I in him, bears fruit in plenty, alleluia.

▷ *page 58*

PRAYER AFTER COMMUNION

Graciously be present to your people, we pray, O Lord,
and lead those you have imbued with heavenly mysteries
to pass from former ways to newness of life.
Through Christ our Lord.   **Amen.**

▷ *page 59*

A solemn blessing may be used.

EASTER

SIXTH SUNDAY OF EASTER

ENTRANCE ANTIPHON   *cf Isaiah 48:20*

Proclaim a joyful sound and let it be heard;
proclaim to the ends of the earth:
The Lord has freed his people, alleluia.

COLLECT

Grant, almighty God,
that we may celebrate with heartfelt devotion these days of joy,
which we keep in honour of the risen Lord,
and that what we relive in remembrance
we may always hold to in what we do.
Through our Lord Jesus Christ, your Son,
who lives and reigns with you in the unity of the Holy Spirit,
one God, for ever and ever. **Amen.**

FIRST READING   Acts 15:1–2, 22–29

It has been decided by the Holy Spirit and by ourselves not to saddle you with any burden beyond these essentials.

Some men came down from Judaea and taught the brothers, 'Unless you have yourselves circumcised in the tradition of Moses you cannot be saved.' This led to disagreement, and after Paul and Barnabas had had a long argument with these men it was arranged that Paul and Barnabas and others of the church should go up to Jerusalem and discuss the problem with the apostles and elders.

Then the apostles and elders decided to choose delegates to send to Antioch with Paul and Barnabas; the whole church concurred with this. They chose Judas known as Barsabbas and Silas, both leading men in the brotherhood, and gave them this letter to take with them:

'The apostles and elders, your brothers, send greetings to the brothers of pagan birth in Antioch, Syria and Cilicia. We hear that some of our members have disturbed you with their demands and have unsettled your minds. They acted without any authority from us, and so we have decided unanimously to elect delegates and to send them to you with Barnabas and Paul, men we highly respect who have dedicated their lives to the name of our Lord Jesus Christ. Accordingly we are sending you Judas and Silas, who will confirm by word of mouth what we have written in this letter. It has been decided by the Holy Spirit and by ourselves not to saddle you with any burden beyond these essentials: you are to abstain from food sacrificed to idols, from blood, from the meat of strangled animals and from fornication. Avoid these, and you will do what is right. Farewell.'

The word of the Lord.
Thanks be to God.

RESPONSORIAL PSALM   Psalm 66:2–3, 5–6, 8 response v 4

Let the peoples praise you, O God;   or   **Alleluia!** *(may be repeated two or three times)*
let all the peoples praise you.

1   God, be gracious and bless us
    and let your face shed its light upon us.
    So will your ways be known upon earth
    and all nations learn your saving help.

2   Let the nations be glad and exult
    for you rule the world with justice.
    With fairness you rule the peoples,
    you guide the nations on earth.

3   Let the peoples praise you, O God;
    let all the peoples praise you.
    May God still give us his blessing
    till the ends of the earth revere him.

SECOND READING   *Apocalypse 21:10–14, 22–23*

He showed me the holy city coming down out of heaven.

In the spirit, the angel took me to the top of an enormous high mountain and showed me Jerusalem, the holy city, coming down from God out of heaven. It had all the radiant glory of God and glittered like some precious jewel of crystal-clear diamond. The walls of it were of a great height, and had twelve gates; at each of the twelve gates there was an angel, and over the gates were written the names of the twelve tribes of Israel; on the east there were three gates, on the north three gates, on the south three gates, and on the west three gates. The city walls stood on twelve foundation stones, each one of which bore the name of one of the twelve apostles of the Lamb.

I saw that there was no temple in the city since the Lord God Almighty and the Lamb were themselves the temple, and the city did not need the sun or the moon for light, since it was lit by the radiant glory of God and the Lamb was a lighted torch for it.

The word of the Lord.

Thanks be to God.

GOSPEL ACCLAMATION   *John 14:23*

> Alleluia, alleluia!
> Jesus said: 'If anyone loves me he will keep my word,
> and my Father will love him, and we shall come to him.'
> Alleluia!

GOSPEL   *John 14:23–29*

The Lord be with you.
And with your spirit.

A reading from the holy Gospel according to John.
Glory to you, O Lord.

The Holy Spirit will remind you of all I have said to you.

Jesus said to his disciples:

'If anyone loves me he will keep my word, and my Father will love him, and we shall come to him and make our home with him. Those who do not love me do not keep my words. And my word is not my own: it is the word of the one who sent me. I have said these things to you while still with you; but the Advocate, the Holy Spirit, whom the Father will send in my name, will teach you everything and remind you of all I have said to you. Peace I bequeath to you, my own peace I give you, a peace the world cannot give, this is my gift to you. Do not let your hearts be troubled or afraid. You heard me say: I am going away, and shall return. If you loved me you would have been glad to know that I am going to the Father, for the Father is greater than I. I have told you this now before it happens, so that when it does happen you may believe.'

The Gospel of the Lord.

Praise to you, Lord Jesus Christ.

EASTER

▷ *page 11*

PRAYER OVER THE OFFERINGS

May our prayers rise up to you, O Lord,
together with the sacrificial offerings,
so that, purified by your graciousness,
we may be conformed to the mysteries of your mighty love.
Through Christ our Lord.   **Amen.**

▷ *page 15*

Preface of Easter, pp 74–75.

COMMUNION ANTIPHON   *John 14:15–16*

If you love me, keep my commandments, says the Lord,
and I will ask the Father and he will send you another Paraclete,
to abide with you for ever, alleluia.

▷ *page 58*

PRAYER AFTER COMMUNION

Almighty ever-living God,
who restore us to eternal life in the Resurrection of Christ,
increase in us, we pray, the fruits of this paschal Sacrament
and pour into our hearts the strength of this saving food.
Through Christ our Lord.   **Amen.**

A solemn blessing may be used.

▷ *page 59*

ASCENSION OF THE LORD — VIGIL MASS

THURSDAY AFTER THE SIXTH SUNDAY OF EASTER
OR (if not a Holyday of Obligation) SEVENTH SUNDAY OF EASTER
This Mass is used on the evening of the day before the Solemnity.

ENTRANCE ANTIPHON   *Psalm 67:33, 35*

You kingdoms of the earth, sing to God;
praise the Lord, who ascends above the highest heavens;
his majesty and might are in the skies, alleluia.

▷ *page 7*

COLLECT

O God, whose Son today ascended to the heavens
as the Apostles looked on,
grant, we pray, that, in accordance with his promise,
we may be worthy for him to live with us always on earth,
and we with him in heaven.
Who lives and reigns with you in the unity of the Holy Spirit,
one God, for ever and ever.   **Amen.**

LITURGY OF THE WORD

The readings are as for the Mass During the Day. See page 278.

PRAYER OVER THE OFFERINGS

O God, whose Only Begotten Son, our High Priest,
is seated ever-living at your right hand to intercede for us,
grant that we may approach with confidence the throne of grace
and there obtain your mercy.
Through Christ our Lord. **Amen.**   ▷ *page 15*

Preface I or II of the Ascension, p 75.
When the Roman Canon is used, the proper form of the Communicantes (In communion with those) is said, p 20.

COMMUNION ANTIPHON   *cf Hebrews 10:12*

Christ, offering a single sacrifice for sins,
is seated for ever at God's right hand, alleluia.   ▷ *page 58*

PRAYER AFTER COMMUNION

May the gifts we have received from your altar, Lord,
kindle in our hearts a longing for the heavenly homeland
and cause us to press forward, following in the Saviour's footsteps,
to the place where for our sake he entered before us.
Who lives and reigns for ever and ever. **Amen.**   ▷ *page 59*

A solemn blessing may be used.

ASCENSION OF THE LORD — MASS DURING THE DAY

THURSDAY AFTER THE SIXTH SUNDAY OF EASTER
OR (IF NOT A HOLYDAY OF OBLIGATION) SEVENTH SUNDAY OF EASTER

ENTRANCE ANTIPHON   *Acts 1:11*

Men of Galilee, why gaze in wonder at the heavens?
This Jesus whom you saw ascending into heaven
will return as you saw him go, alleluia.   ▷ *page 7*

COLLECT

Gladden us with holy joys, almighty God,
and make us rejoice with devout thanksgiving,
for the Ascension of Christ your Son
is our exaltation,
and, where the Head has gone before in glory,
the Body is called to follow in hope.
Through our Lord Jesus Christ, your Son,
who lives and reigns with you in the unity of the Holy Spirit,
one God, for ever and ever. **Amen.**

An alternative Collect is found overleaf.

EASTER

ALTERNATIVE COLLECT

Grant, we pray, almighty God,
that we, who believe that your Only Begotten Son, our Redeemer,
ascended this day to the heavens,
may in spirit dwell already in heavenly realms.
Who lives and reigns with you in the unity of the Holy Spirit,
one God, for ever and ever.   **Amen.**

FIRST READING   *Acts 1:1–11*

He was lifted up while they looked on.

In my earlier work, Theophilus, I dealt with everything Jesus had done and taught from the beginning until the day he gave his instructions to the apostles he had chosen through the Holy Spirit, and was taken up to heaven. He had shown himself alive to them after his Passion by many demonstrations: for forty days he had continued to appear to them and tell them about the kingdom of God. When he had been at table with them, he had told them not to leave Jerusalem, but to wait there for what the Father had promised. 'It is,' he had said, 'what you have heard me speak about: John baptised with water but you, not many days from now, will be baptised with the Holy Spirit.'

Now having met together, they asked him, 'Lord, has the time come? Are you going to restore the kingdom to Israel?' He replied, 'It is not for you to know times or dates that the Father has decided by his own authority, but you will receive power when the Holy Spirit comes on you, and then you will be my witnesses not only in Jerusalem but throughout Judaea and Samaria, and indeed to the ends of the earth.'

As he said this he was lifted up while they looked on, and a cloud took him from their sight. They were still staring into the sky when suddenly two men in white were standing near them and they said, 'Why are you men from Galilee standing here looking into the sky? Jesus who has been taken from you into heaven, this same Jesus will come back in the same way as you have seen him go there.'

The word of the Lord.
Thanks be to God.

RESPONSORIAL PSALM   *Psalm 46:2–3, 6–9 response v 6*

**God goes up with shouts of joy;
the Lord goes up with trumpet blast.**

or

Alleluia! *(may be repeated two or three times)*

1   All peoples, clap your hands,
    cry to God with shouts of joy!
    For the Lord, the Most High, we must fear,
    great king over all the earth.

2   God goes up with shouts of joy;
    the Lord goes up with trumpet blast.
    Sing praise for God, sing praise,
    sing praise to our king, sing praise.

3   God is king of all the earth.
    Sing praise with all your skill.
    God is king over the nations;
    God reigns on his holy throne.

An alternative Second Reading is found below.

SECOND READING   *Ephesians 1:17–23*

He made him sit at his right hand in heaven.

May the God of our Lord Jesus Christ, the Father of glory, give you a spirit of wisdom and perception of what is revealed, to bring you to full knowledge of him. May he enlighten the eyes of your mind so that you can see what hope his call holds for you, what rich glories he has promised the saints will inherit and how infinitely great is the power that he has exercised for us believers. This you can tell from the strength of his power at work in Christ, when he used it to raise him from the dead and to make him sit at his right hand, in heaven, far above every Sovereignty, Authority, Power, or Domination, or any other name that can be named, not only in this age, but also in the age to come. He has put all things under his feet, and made him, as the ruler of everything, the head of the Church; which is his body, the fullness of him who fills the whole creation.

The word of the Lord.

Thanks be to God.

ALTERNATIVE SECOND READING   *Hebrews 9:24–28; 10:19–23*

Christ entered into heaven itself.

It is not as though Christ had entered a man-made sanctuary which was only modelled on the real one; but it was heaven itself, so that he could appear in the actual presence of God on our behalf. And he does not have to offer himself again and again, like the high priest going into the sanctuary year after year with the blood that is not his own, or else he would have had to suffer over and over again since the world began. Instead of that, he has made his appearance once and for all, now at the end of the last age, to do away with sin by sacrificing himself. Since men only die once, and after that comes judgement, so Christ, too, offers himself only once to take the faults of many on himself, and when he appears a second time, it will not be to deal with sin but to reward with salvation those who are waiting for him.

In other words, brothers, through the blood of Jesus we have the right to enter the sanctuary, by a new way which he has opened for us, a living opening through the curtain, that is to say, his body. And we have the supreme high priest over all the house of God. So as we go in, let us be sincere in heart and filled with faith, our minds sprinkled and free from any trace of bad conscience and our bodies washed with pure water. Let us keep firm in the hope we profess, because the one who made the promise is faithful.

The word of the Lord.

Thanks be to God.

GOSPEL ACCLAMATION   *Matthew 28:19, 20*

Alleluia, alleluia!
Go, make disciples of all the nations;
I am with you always; yes, to the end of time.
Alleluia!

EASTER

GOSPEL   *Luke 24:46–53*

The Lord be with you.
And with your spirit.

A reading from the holy Gospel according to Luke.
Glory to you, O Lord.

As he blessed them he was carried up to heaven.

Jesus said to his disciples: 'You see how it is written that the Christ would suffer and on the third day rise from the dead, and that, in his name, repentance for the forgiveness of sins would be preached to all the nations, beginning from Jerusalem. You are witnesses to this.

'And now I am sending down to you what the Father has promised. Stay in the city then, until you are clothed with the power from on high.'

Then he took them out as far as the outskirts of Bethany, and lifting up his hands he blessed them. Now as he blessed them, he withdrew from them and was carried up to heaven. They worshipped him and then went back to Jerusalem full of joy; and they were continually in the Temple praising God.

The Gospel of the Lord.
Praise to you, Lord Jesus Christ.

▷ *page 11*

PRAYER OVER THE OFFERINGS
We offer sacrifice now in supplication, O Lord,
to honour the wondrous Ascension of your Son:
grant, we pray,
that through this most holy exchange
we, too, may rise up to the heavenly realms.
Through Christ our Lord.   **Amen.**

▷ *page 15*

Preface I or II of the Ascension, p 75.
When the Roman Canon is used, the proper form of the Communicantes (In communion with those) is said, p 20.

COMMUNION ANTIPHON   *Matthew 28:20*
Behold, I am with you always,
even to the end of the age, alleluia.

▷ *page 58*

PRAYER AFTER COMMUNION
Almighty ever-living God,
who allow those on earth to celebrate divine mysteries,
grant, we pray,
that Christian hope may draw us onward
to where our nature is united with you.
Through Christ our Lord.   **Amen.**

▷ *page 59*

A solemn blessing may be used.

SEVENTH SUNDAY OF EASTER

Where the Solemnity of the Ascension is not to be observed as a Holyday of Obligation,
it replaces the Seventh Sunday of Easter.

ENTRANCE ANTIPHON *cf Psalm 26:7–9*

O Lord, hear my voice, for I have called to you;
of you my heart has spoken: Seek his face;
hide not your face from me, alleluia.

▷ *page 7*

COLLECT

Graciously hear our supplications, O Lord,
so that we, who believe that the Saviour of the human race
is with you in your glory,
may experience, as he promised,
until the end of the world,
his abiding presence among us.
Who lives and reigns with you in the unity of the Holy Spirit,
one God, for ever and ever. **Amen.**

FIRST READING *Acts 7:55–60*

I can see the Son of Man standing at the right hand of God.

Stephen, filled with the Holy Spirit, gazed into heaven and saw the glory of God, and Jesus standing at God's right hand. 'I can see heaven thrown open' he said 'and the Son of Man standing at the right hand of God.' At this all the members of the council shouted out and stopped their ears with their hands; then they all rushed at him, sent him out of the city and stoned him. The witnesses put down their clothes at the feet of a young man called Saul. As they were stoning him, Stephen said in invocation, 'Lord Jesus, receive my spirit.' Then he knelt down and said aloud, 'Lord, do not hold this sin against them'; and with these words he fell asleep.

The word of the Lord.
Thanks be to God.

RESPONSORIAL PSALM *Psalm 96:1–2, 6–7, 9 response vv 1, 9*

The Lord is king, most high above all the earth.

or

Alleluia! *(may be repeated two or three times)*

1 The Lord is king, let earth rejoice,
   the many coastlands be glad.
   His throne is justice and right.

2 The skies proclaim his justice;
   all peoples see his glory.
   All you spirits, worship him.

3 For you indeed are the Lord
   most high above all the earth
   exalted far above all spirits.

EASTER

SECOND READING   *Apocalypse 22:12–14, 16–17, 20*

Come, Lord Jesus!

I, John, heard a voice speaking to me: 'Very soon now, I shall be with you again, bringing the reward to be given to every man according to what he deserves. I am the Alpha and the Omega, the First and the Last, the Beginning and the End. Happy are those who will have washed their robes clean, so that they will have the right to feed on the tree of life and can come through the gates into the city.'

I, Jesus, have sent my angel to make these revelations to you for the sake of the churches. I am of David's line, the root of David and the bright star of the morning. The Spirit and the Bride say, 'Come.' Let everyone who listens answer, 'Come.' Then let all who are thirsty come; all who want it may have the water of life, and have it free.

The one who guarantees these revelations repeats his promise: I shall indeed be with you soon. Amen; come, Lord Jesus.

The word of the Lord.
Thanks be to God.

GOSPEL ACCLAMATION   *cf John 14:18*

Alleluia, alleluia!
I will not leave you orphans, says the Lord;
I will come back to you, and your hearts will be full of joy.
Alleluia!

GOSPEL   *John 17:20–26*

The Lord be with you.
And with your spirit.

A reading from the holy Gospel according to John.
Glory to you, O Lord.

May they be completely one.

Jesus raised his eyes to heaven and said:

'Holy Father, I pray not only for these, but for those also who through their words will believe in me. May they all be one. Father, may they be one in us, as you are in me and I am in you, so that the world may believe it was you who sent me. I have given them the glory you gave to me, that they may be one as we are one. With me in them and you in me, may they be so completely one that the world will realise that it was you who sent me and that I have loved them as much as you loved me. Father, I want those you have given me to be with me where I am, so that they may always see the glory you have given me because you loved me before the foundation of the world. Father, Righteous One, the world has not known you, but I have known you, and these have known that you have sent me. I have made your name known to them and will continue to make it known, so that the love with which you loved me may be in them, and so that I may be in them.'

The Gospel of the Lord.
Praise to you, Lord Jesus Christ.

▷ page 11

PRAYER OVER THE OFFERINGS

Accept, O Lord, the prayers of your faithful
with the sacrificial offerings,
that through these acts of devotedness
we may pass over to the glory of heaven.
Through Christ our Lord.   **Amen.**

▷ *page 15*

Preface of Easter, or of the Ascension, pp 74–75.

COMMUNION ANTIPHON   *John 17:22*

Father, I pray that they may be one
as we also are one, alleluia.

▷ *page 58*

PRAYER AFTER COMMUNION

Hear us, O God our Saviour,
and grant us confidence,
that through these sacred mysteries
there will be accomplished in the body of the whole Church
what has already come to pass in Christ her Head.
Who lives and reigns for ever and ever.   **Amen.**

▷ *page 59*

A solemn blessing may be used

Pentecost Sunday is found overleaf.

EASTER

PENTECOST SUNDAY — VIGIL MASS

The Vigil Mass may be celebrated in either an extended form (with or without the celebration of Evening Prayer I) or a simple form.

Here the Extended Form without the celebration of Evening Prayer I is printed, then the Simple Form. The tables below show how the Vigil Mass may be celebrated in other forms.

OUTLINE OF THE EXTENDED FORM

INCLUDING VESPERS (EVENING PRAYER I)

EITHER Introductory verse of Vespers
Hymn

OR Entrance Antiphon of the Mass
Procession
Greeting

Psalmody of Vespers with antiphons:

Prayer: 'Grant, we pray...'

WITHOUT VESPERS (EVENING PRAYER I)

Entrance Antiphon
Procession
Greeting
Penitential Act
Prayer: 'Grant, we pray...'

Introduction to the Liturgy of the Word

First Reading
Responsorial Psalm
Prayer

Second Reading
Responsorial Psalm
Prayer

Third Reading
Responsorial Psalm
Prayer

Fourth Reading
Responsorial Psalm
Prayer

Gloria

Collect: 'Almighty ever-living God...'

Epistle

then Mass continues in the usual way until...

INCLUDING VESPERS (EVENING PRAYER I)

Communion Antiphon

Holy Communion

Magnificat (with antiphon)

Prayer After Communion

then Mass continues in the usual way.

WITHOUT VESPERS (EVENING PRAYER I)

(As usual at Mass):

Communion Antiphon

Holy Communion

Prayer After Communion

Mass continues in the usual way.

OUTLINE OF THE SIMPLE FORM

Introductory Rites

The Introductory Rites of the Mass (including the Gloria) are celebrated in the usual way.
Either of the prayers, 'Almighty, ever-living God...' or 'Grant, we pray, almighty God...' may be said as the Collect.

Liturgy of the Word

One of the Old Testament Readings is chosen followed by the appropriate Responsorial Psalm.
This is followed by the Epistle, Gospel Acclamation and Gospel, in the usual way.

EXTENDED FORM

ENTRANCE ANTIPHON   *Romans 5:5; cf 8:11*

The love of God has been poured into our hearts
through the Spirit of God dwelling within us, alleluia.

The Mass begins in the usual way.   ▷ *page 7*
After the Kyrie (Lord, have mercy) the Priest says the following prayer

PRAYER

Grant, we pray, almighty God,
that the splendour of your glory
may shine forth upon us
and that, by the bright rays of the Holy Spirit,
the light of your light may confirm the hearts
of those born again by your grace.
Through our Lord Jesus Christ, your Son,
who lives and reigns with you in the unity of the Holy Spirit,
one God, for ever and ever.   **Amen.**

LITURGY OF THE WORD

Then the Priest may address the people in these or similar words:
Dear brethren (brothers and sisters),
we have now begun our Pentecost Vigil,
after the example of the Apostles and disciples,
who with Mary, the Mother of Jesus, persevered in prayer,
awaiting the Spirit promised by the Lord;
like them, let us, too, listen with quiet hearts to the Word of God.
Let us meditate on how many great deeds
God in times past did for his people
and let us pray that the Holy Spirit,
whom the Father sent as the first fruits for those who believe,
may bring to perfection his work in the world.

After each reading, a Responsorial Psalm is sung, or this may be replaced by a sacred silence.

EASTER

FIRST READING *Genesis 11:1–9*

It was named Babel because there the language of the whole earth was confused.

Throughout the earth men spoke the same language, with the same vocabulary. Now as they moved eastwards they found a plain in the land of Shinar where they settled. They said to one another, 'Come, let us make bricks and bake them in the fire.' – For stone they used bricks, and for mortar they used bitumen. – 'Come,' they said 'let us build ourselves a town and a tower with its top reaching heaven. Let us make a name for ourselves, so that we may not be scattered about the whole earth.'

Now the Lord came down to see the town and the tower that the sons of man had built. 'So they are all a single people with a single language!' said the Lord. 'This is but the start of their undertakings! There will be nothing too hard for them to do. Come, let us go down and confuse their language on the spot so that they can no longer understand one another.' The Lord scattered them thence over the whole face of the earth, and they stopped building the town. It was named Babel therefore, because there the Lord confused the language of the whole earth. It was from there that the Lord scattered them over the whole face of the earth.

The word of the Lord.
Thanks be to God.

RESPONSORIAL PSALM *Psalm 32:10–11, 12–13, 14–15 response v 12b*

Happy the people the Lord has chosen as his own.

1 He frustrates the designs of the nations,
   he defeats the plans of the peoples.
   His own designs shall stand for ever,
   the plans of his heart from age to age.

2 They are happy, whose God is the Lord,
   the people he has chosen as his own.
   From the heavens the Lord looks forth,
   he sees all the children of men.

3 From the place where he dwells he gazes
   on all the dwellers on the earth,
   he who shapes the hearts of them all
   and considers all their deeds.

PRAYER

Let us pray.
Grant, we pray, almighty God,
that your Church may always remain that holy people,
formed as one by the unity of Father, Son and Holy Spirit,
which manifests to the world
the Sacrament of your holiness and unity
and leads it to the perfection of your charity.
Through Christ our Lord. **Amen.**

SECOND READING   *Exodus 19:3–8, 16–20*

The Lord came down on the mountain of Sinai before all the people.

Moses went up to God, and the Lord called to him from the mountain, saying, 'Say this to the House of Jacob, declare this to the sons of Israel, 'You yourselves have seen what I did with the Egyptians, how I carried you on eagle's wings and brought you to myself. From this you know that now, if you obey my voice and hold fast to my covenant, you of all the nations shall be my very own, for all the earth is mine. I will count you a kingdom of priests, a consecrated nation.' Those are the words you are to speak to the sons of Israel.' So Moses went and summoned the elders of the people, putting before them all that the Lord had bidden him. Then all the people answered as one, 'All that the Lord has said, we will do.'

Now at daybreak on the third day there were peals of thunder on the mountain and lightning flashes, a dense cloud, and a loud trumpet blast, and inside the camp all the people trembled. Then Moses led the people out of the camp to meet God; and they stood at the bottom of the mountain. The mountain of Sinai was entirely wrapped in smoke, because the Lord had descended on it in the form of fire. Like smoke from a furnace the smoke went up, and the whole mountain shook violently. Louder and louder grew the sound of the trumpet. Moses spoke, and God answered him with peals of thunder. The Lord came down on the mountain of Sinai, on the mountain top, and the Lord called Moses to the top of the mountain.

The word of the Lord.
Thanks be to God.

An alternative Responsorial Psalm is found overleaf.

RESPONSORIAL PSALM   *Daniel: 3:52, 53, 54, 55, 56, response v 52b*

The response is sung after every line.

> **To you glory and praise for evermore.**

1 You are blest, Lord God of our fathers.
   To you glory and praise for evermore.
   Blest your glorious holy name.
   To you glory and praise for evermore.

2 You are blest in the temple of your glory.
   To you glory and praise for evermore.
   You are blest on the throne of your kingdom.
   To you glory and praise for evermore.

3 You are blest who gaze into the depths.
   To you glory and praise for evermore.
   You are blest in the firmament of heaven.
   To you glory and praise for evermore.

EASTER

ALTERNATIVE RESPONSORIAL PSALM   *Psalm 18:8, 9, 10, 11; response v 6:68c*

You have the message of eternal life, O Lord.

1 The law of the Lord is perfect,
  it revives the soul.
  The rule of the Lord is to be trusted,
  it gives wisdom to the simple.

2 The precepts of the Lord are right,
  they gladden the heart.
  The command of the Lord is clear,
  it gives light to the eyes.

3 The fear of the Lord is holy,
  abiding for ever.
  The decrees of the Lord are truth
  and all of them just.

4 They are more to be desired than gold,
  than the purest of gold
  and sweeter are they than honey,
  than honey from the comb.

PRAYER

Let us pray.
O God, who in fire and lightning
gave the ancient Law to Moses on Mount Sinai
and on this day manifested the new covenant
in the fire of the Spirit,
grant, we pray,
that we may always be aflame with that same Spirit
whom you wondrously poured out on your Apostles,
and that the new Israel,
gathered from every people,
may receive with rejoicing
the eternal commandment of your love.
Through Christ our Lord.   **Amen.**

THIRD READING   *Ezekiel 37:1–14*

Dry bones, I am going to make the breath enter you, and you will live.

The hand of the Lord was laid on me, and he carried me away by the spirit of the Lord and set me down in the middle of a valley, a valley full of bones. He made me walk up and down among them. There were vast quantities of these bones on the ground the whole length of the valley; and they were quite dried up. He said to me, 'Son of man, can these bones live?' I said, 'You know, Lord.' He said, 'Prophesy over these bones. Say, "Dry bones, hear the word of the Lord. The Lord says this to these bones: I am now going to make the breath enter you, and you will live. I shall put sinews on you, I shall make flesh grow on you, I shall cover you with skin and give you breath, and you will live; and you will learn that I am the Lord." ' I prophesied as I had been ordered. While I was prophesying, there was a noise, a sound of clattering; and the bones joined together. I looked, and saw that they were covered with sinews; flesh was growing on them and skin was covering them, but there was no breath in them. He said to me, 'Prophesy to the breath; prophesy, son of man. Say to the breath, "The Lord says this: Come from the four winds, breath; breathe on these dead; let them live!" ' I prophesied as he had ordered me, and the breath entered them; they came to life again and stood up on their feet, a great, an immense army.

Then he said, 'Son of man, these bones are the whole House of Israel. They keep saying, "Our bones are dried up, our hope has gone; we are as good as dead." So prophesy. Say to them, "The Lord says this: I am now going to open your graves; I mean to raise you from your graves, my people, and lead you back to the soil of Israel. And you will know that I am the Lord, when I open your graves and raise you from your graves, my people. And I shall put my spirit in you, and you will live, and I shall resettle you on your own soil; and you will know that I, the Lord, have said and done this – it is the Lord who speaks."'

The word of the Lord.
Thanks be to God.

RESPONSORIAL PSALM   *Psalm 106:2–3, 4–5, 6–7, 8–9; response v 1*

> **O give thanks to the Lord, for he is good;**
> **for his love has no end.**
>
> *or*
>
> **Alleluia!** *(repeated two or three times)*

1 Let them say this, the Lord's redeemed,
   whom he redeemed from the hand of the foe
   and gathered from far-off lands,
   from east and west, north and south.

2 Some wandered in the desert, in the wilderness,
   finding no way to a city they could dwell in.
   Hungry they were and thirsty;
   their soul was fainting within them.

3 Then they cried to the Lord in their need
   and he rescued them from their distress
   and he led them along the right way,
   to reach a city they could dwell in.

4 Let them thank the Lord for his love,
   for the wonders he does for men.
   For he satisfies the thirsty soul;
   he fills the hungry with good things.

PRAYER
Alternative prayers are to be found overleaf

Let us pray.
Lord, God of power,
who restore what has fallen
and preserve what you have restored,
increase, we pray, the peoples
to be renewed by the sanctification of your name,
that all who are washed clean by holy Baptism
may always be directed by your prompting.
Through Christ our Lord.   **Amen.**

ALTERNATIVE PRAYERS

O God, who have brought us to rebirth by the word of life,
pour out upon us your Holy Spirit,
that walking in oneness of faith,
we may attain in our flesh
the incorruptible glory of the resurrection.
Through Christ our Lord. **Amen.**

or

May your people exult for ever, O God,
in renewed youthfulness of spirit,
so that, rejoicing now in the restored glory of our adoption,
we may look forward in confident hope
to the rejoicing of the day of resurrection.
Through Christ Our Lord. **Amen.**

FOURTH READING *Joel 3:1-5*

I will pour out my spirit on all people.

Thus says the Lord:

'I will pour out my spirit on all mankind. Your sons and daughters shall prophesy, your old men shall dream dreams, and your young men see visions. Even on the slaves, men and women, will I pour out my spirit in those days. I will display portents in heaven and on earth, blood and fire and columns of smoke.'

The sun will be turned into darkness, and the moon into blood, before the day of the Lord dawns; that great and terrible day. All who call on the name of the Lord will be saved, for on Mount Zion there will be some who have escaped, as the Lord has said, and in Jerusalem some survivors whom the Lord will call.

The word of the Lord.
Thanks be to God.

RESPONSORIAL PSALM *Psalm 103:1–2, 24, 27–30, 35; response cf v 30*

Send forth your Spirit, O Lord, and renew the face of the earth.   *or*   **Alleluia!** *(repeated two or three times)*

1 Bless the Lord, my soul!
Lord God, how great you are,
clothed in majesty and glory,
wrapped in light as in a robe!

2 How many are your works, O Lord!
In wisdom you have made them all.
The earth is full of your riches.
Bless the Lord, my soul.

3 All of these look to you
to give them their food in due season.
You give it, they gather it up:
you open your hand, they have their fill.

4 You take back your spirit, they die,
returning to the dust from which they came.
You send forth your spirit, they are created;
and you renew the face of the earth.

PRAYER

Let us pray.
Fulfil for us your gracious promise,
O Lord, we pray, so that by his coming
the Holy Spirit may make us witnesses before the world
to the Gospel of our Lord Jesus Christ.
Who lives and reigns for ever and ever.   **Amen.**

GLORIA

The Priest intones the Gloria, and all take up the hymn.   ▷ *Music p 337*

COLLECT

Almighty ever-living God,
who willed the Paschal Mystery
to be encompassed as a sign in fifty days,
grant that from out of the scattered nations
the confusion of many tongues
may be gathered by heavenly grace
into one great confession of your name.
Through our Lord Jesus Christ, your Son,
who lives and reigns with you in the unity of the Holy Spirit,
one God, for ever and ever.   **Amen.**

EPISTLE   *Romans 8:22–27*

The Spirit himself expresses our plea in a way that could never be put into words.

From the beginning till now the entire creation, as we know, has been groaning in one great act of giving birth; and not only creation, but all of us who possess the first-fruits of the Spirit, we too groan inwardly as we wait for our bodies to be set free. For we must be content to hope that we shall be saved – our salvation is not in sight, we should not have to be hoping for it if it were – but, as I say, we must hope to be saved since we are not saved yet – it is something we must wait for with patience.

The Spirit too comes to help us in our weakness. For when we cannot choose words in order to pray properly, the Spirit himself expresses our plea in a way that could never be put into words, and God who knows everything in our hearts knows perfectly well what he means, and that the pleas of the saints expressed by the Spirit are according to the mind of God.

The word of the Lord.
Thanks be to God.

GOSPEL ACCLAMATION

Alleluia, alleluia!
Come, Holy Spirit, fill the hearts of your faithful,
and kindle in them the fire of your love.
Alleluia!

THE GOSPEL   *John 7:37–39*

The Lord be with you.
And with your spirit.

A reading from the holy Gospel according to John.
Glory to you, O Lord.

From his breast shall flow fountains of living water.

On the last day and the greatest day of the festival, Jesus stood there and cried out:

'If any man is thirsty, let him come to me! Let the man come and drink who believes in me!'

As scripture says: From his breast shall flow fountains of living water.

He was speaking of the Spirit which those who believed in him were to receive; for there was no Spirit as yet because Jesus had not yet been glorified.

The Gospel of the Lord.
Praise to you, Lord Jesus Christ.

▷ *page 11*

PRAYER OVER THE OFFERINGS

Pour out upon these gifts the blessing of your Spirit,
we pray, O Lord,
so that through them your Church may be imbued with such love
that the truth of your saving mystery
may shine forth for the whole world.
Through Christ our Lord.   **Amen.**

▷ *page 15*

Preface: The Mystery of Pentecost, p 76.
When the Roman Canon is used, the proper form of the Communicantes (In communion with those) is said, p 20.

COMMUNION ANTIPHON   *John 7:37*

On the last day of the festival, Jesus stood and cried out:
If anyone is thirsty, let him come to me and drink, alleluia.

▷ *page 58*

PRAYER AFTER COMMUNION

May these gifts we have consumed
benefit us, O Lord,
that we may always be aflame with the same Spirit,
whom you wondrously poured out on your Apostles.
Through Christ our Lord.   **Amen.**

A solemn blessing may be used.

DISMISSAL

▷ *Music p 257*

Deacon or Priest: Go forth, the Mass is ended, alleluia, alleluia.
or
Deacon or Priest: Go in peace, alleluia, alleluia.
People: **Thanks be to God, alleluia, alleluia.**

SIMPLE FORM

Introductory Rites

The Introductory Rites of the Mass (including the Gloria) are celebrated in the usual way.
Either of the prayers, 'Almighty, ever-living God...' or 'Grant, we pray, almighty God...' may be said as the Collect.

Liturgy of the Word

One of the Old Testament Readings is chosen followed by the appropriate Responsorial Psalm.
This is followed by the Epistle, Gospel Acclamation and Gospel, in the usual way.

ENTRANCE ANTIPHON   *Romans 5:5; cf 8:11*

The love of God has been poured into our hearts
through the Spirit of God dwelling within us, alleluia.

The Introductory Rites of the Mass (including the Gloria) are celebrated in the usual way.

▷ *page 7*

COLLECT

Almighty ever-living God,
who willed the Paschal Mystery
to be encompassed as a sign in fifty days,
grant that from out of the scattered nations
the confusion of many tongues
may be gathered by heavenly grace
into one great confession of your name.
Through our Lord Jesus Christ, your Son,
who lives and reigns with you in the unity of the Holy Spirit,
one God, for ever and ever.   **Amen.**
or

Grant, we pray, almighty God,
that the splendour of your glory
may shine forth upon us
and that, by the bright rays of the Holy Spirit,
the light of your light may confirm the hearts
of those born again by your grace.
Through our Lord Jesus Christ, your Son,
who lives and reigns with you in the unity of the Holy Spirit,
one God, for ever and ever.   **Amen.**

The readings for the Liturgy of the Word can be found starting on page 286.

One of the Old Testament Readings is chosen followed by the appropriate Responsorial Psalm.
This is followed by the Epistle, Gospel Acclamation and Gospel, in the usual way.

Following the Gospel, the Mass is celebrated as in the Extended form. See page 292.

EASTER

PENTECOST SUNDAY — MASS DURING THE DAY

ENTRANCE ANTIPHON *Wisdom 1:7*
The Spirit of the Lord has filled the whole world
and that which contains all things
understands what is said, alleluia.

or *Romans 5:5; cf 8:11*
The love of God has been poured into our hearts
through the Spirit of God dwelling within us, alleluia.

▷ *page 7*

COLLECT
O God, who by the mystery of today's great feast
sanctify your whole Church in every people and nation,
pour out, we pray, the gifts of the Holy Spirit
across the face of the earth
and, with the divine grace that was at work
when the Gospel was first proclaimed,
fill now once more the hearts of believers.
Through our Lord Jesus Christ, your Son,
who lives and reigns with you in the unity of the Holy Spirit,
one God, for ever and ever. **Amen.**

FIRST READING *Acts 2:1–11*

They were all filled with the Holy Spirit and began to speak.

When Pentecost day came round, the apostles had all met in one room, when suddenly they heard what sounded like a powerful wind from heaven, the noise of which filled the entire house in which they were sitting; and something appeared to them that seemed like tongues of fire; these separated and came to rest on the head of each of them. They were all filled with the Holy Spirit, and began to speak foreign languages as the Spirit gave them the gift of speech.

Now there were devout men living in Jerusalem from every nation under heaven, and at this sound they all assembled, each one bewildered to hear these men speaking his own language. They were amazed and astonished. 'Surely,' they said, 'all these men speaking are Galileans? How does it happen that each of us hears them in his own native language? Parthians, Medes and Elamites; people from Mesopotamia, Judaea and Cappadocia, Pontus and Asia, Phrygia and Pamphylia, Egypt and the parts of Libya round Cyrene; as well as visitors from Rome – Jews and proselytes alike – Cretans and Arabs; we hear them preaching in our own language about the marvels of God.'

The word of the Lord.
Thanks be to God.

RESPONSORIAL PSALM   *Psalm 103:1, 24, 29–31, 34 response cf v 30*

> **Send forth your Spirit, O Lord,**
> **and renew the face of the earth**
>
> *or*
>
> **Alleluia!** *(repeated two or three times)*

1   Bless the Lord, my soul!
    Lord God, how great you are,
    How many are your works, O Lord!
    The earth is full of your riches.

2   You take back your spirit, they die,
    returning to the dust from which they came.
    You send forth your spirit, they are created;
    and you renew the face of the earth.

3   May the glory of the Lord last for ever!
    May the Lord rejoice in his works!
    May my thoughts be pleasing to him.
    I find my joy in the Lord.

An alternative Second Reading is found below.

SECOND READING   *1 Corinthians 12:3–7, 12–13*

In the one Spirit we were all baptised.

No one can say, 'Jesus is Lord' unless he is under the influence of the Holy Spirit.

There is a variety of gifts but always the same Spirit; there are all sorts of service to be done, but always to the same Lord; working in all sorts of different ways in different people, it is the same God who is working in all of them. The particular way in which the Spirit is given to each person is for a good purpose.

Just as a human body, though it is made up of many parts, is a single unit because all these parts, though many, make one body, so it is with Christ. In the one Spirit we were all baptised, Jews as well as Greeks, slaves as well as citizens, and one Spirit was given to us all to drink.

The word of the Lord.
Thanks be to God.

ALTERNATIVE SECOND READING   *Romans 8:8–17*

Everyone moved by the Spirit is a son of God.

People who are interested only in unspiritual things can never be pleasing to God. Your interests, however, are not in the unspiritual, but in the spiritual, since the Spirit of God has made his home in you. In fact, unless you possessed the Spirit of Christ you would not belong to him. Though your body may be dead it is because of sin, but if Christ is in you then your spirit is life itself because you have been justified; and if the Spirit of him who raised Jesus from the dead is living in you, then he who raised Jesus from the dead will give life to your own mortal bodies through his Spirit living in you.

So then, my brothers, there is no necessity for us to obey our unspiritual selves or to live unspiritual lives. If you do live in that way, you are doomed to die; but if by the Spirit you put an end to the misdeeds of the body you will live.

EASTER

Everyone moved by the Spirit is a son of God. The spirit you received is not the spirit of slaves bringing fear into your lives again; it is the spirit of sons, and it makes us cry out, 'Abba, Father!' The Spirit himself and our spirit bear united witness that we are children of God. And if we are children we are heirs as well: heirs of God and coheirs with Christ, sharing his sufferings so as to share his glory.

The word of the Lord.
Thanks be to God.

SEQUENCE

The Sequence is said or sung at all Masses.

1   Holy Spirit, Lord of light,
From the clear celestial height,
Thy pure beaming radiance give.

2   Come, thou Father of the poor,
Come with treasures which endure;
Come, thou light of all that live!

3   Thou, of all consolers best,
Thou, the soul's delightful guest,
Dost refreshing peace bestow;

4   Thou in toil art comfort sweet;
Pleasant coolness in the heat;
Solace in the midst of woe.

5   Light immortal, light divine,
Visit thou these hearts of thine,
And our inmost being fill:

6   If thou take thy grace away,
Nothing pure in man will stay;
All his good is turned to ill.

7   Heal our wounds, our strength renew;
On our dryness pour thy dew;
Wash the stains of guilt away:

8   Bend the stubborn heart and will;
Melt the frozen, warm the chill;
Guide the steps that go astray.

9   Thou, on us who evermore
Thee confess and thee adore,
With thy sevenfold gifts descend:

10 Give us comfort when we die;
Give us life with thee on high;
Give us joys that never end.

GOSPEL ACCLAMATION

Alleluia, alleluia!
**Come, Holy Spirit, fill the hearts of your faithful,
and kindle in them the fire of your love.**
Alleluia!

An alternative Gospel reading is found opposite.

GOSPEL   *John 20:19–23*

The Lord be with you.
And with your spirit.

A reading from the holy Gospel according to John.
Glory to you, O Lord.

As the Father sent me, so am I sending you: receive the Holy Spirit.

In the evening of the first day of the week, the doors were closed in the room where the disciples were, for fear of the Jews. Jesus came and stood among them. He said to them, 'Peace be with you,' and showed them his hands and his side. The disciples were filled with joy when they saw the Lord, and he said to them again. 'Peace be with you.

As the Father sent me, so am I sending you.'

After saying this he breathed on them and said:

'Receive the Holy Spirit, for those whose sins you forgive, they are forgiven; for those whose sins you retain, they are retained.'

The Gospel of the Lord.
Praise to you, Lord Jesus Christ.

ALTERNATIVE GOSPEL   *John 14:15–16, 23–26*

The Lord be with you.
And with your spirit.

A reading from the holy Gospel according to John.
Glory to you, O Lord.

The Holy Spirit will teach you everything.

Jesus said to his disciples:

'If you love me you will keep my commandments. I shall ask the Father, and he will give you another Advocate to be with you for ever.

'If anyone loves me he will keep my word, and my Father will love him, and we shall come to him and make our home with him. Those who do not love me do not keep my words. And my word is not my own: it is the word of the one who sent me. I have said these things to you while still with you; but the Advocate, the Holy Spirit, whom the Father will send in my name, will teach you everything and remind you of all I have said to you.'

The Gospel of the Lord.
Praise to you, Lord Jesus Christ.

▷ *page 11*

PRAYER OVER THE OFFERINGS

Grant, we pray, O Lord,
that, as promised by your Son,
the Holy Spirit may reveal to us more abundantly
the hidden mystery of this sacrifice
and graciously lead us into all truth.
Through Christ our Lord.   **Amen.**

▷ *page 15*

Preface: The Mystery of Pentecost, p 76.
When the Roman Canon is used, the proper form of the Communicantes (In communion with those) is said, p 20.

COMMUNION ANTIPHON   *Acts 2:4, 11*

They were all filled with the Holy Spirit
and spoke of the marvels of God, alleluia.

▷ *page 58*

EASTER

PRAYER AFTER COMMUNION

O God, who bestow heavenly gifts upon your Church,
safeguard, we pray, the grace you have given,
that the gift of the Holy Spirit poured out upon her
may retain all its force
and that this spiritual food
may gain her abundance of eternal redemption.
Through Christ our Lord.   **Amen.**

A solemn blessing may be used.

▷ *page 59*

DISMISSAL

▷ *Music p 257*

Deacon or Priest: Go forth, the Mass is ended, alleluia, alleluia.
or
Deacon or Priest: Go in peace, alleluia, alleluia.
People: **Thanks be to God, alleluia, alleluia.**

Easter Time is now concluded.

PROPER OF SAINTS

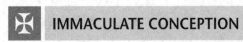

IMMACULATE CONCEPTION

IMMACULATE CONCEPTION OF THE BLESSED VIRGIN MARY
8 DECEMBER
If the Solemnity falls on a Sunday, it is transferred.

ENTRANCE ANTIPHON   *Isaiah 61:10*

I rejoice heartily in the Lord,
in my God is the joy of my soul;
for he has clothed me with a robe of salvation,
and wrapped me in a mantle of justice,
like a bride adorned with her jewels.

▷ *page 7*

The Gloria is sung (said).

COLLECT

O God, who by the Immaculate Conception of the Blessed Virgin
prepared a worthy dwelling for your Son,
grant, we pray,
that, as you preserved her from every stain
by virtue of the Death of your Son, which you foresaw,
so, through her intercession,
we, too, may be cleansed and admitted to your presence.
Through our Lord Jesus Christ, your Son,
who lives and reigns with you in the unity of the Holy Spirit,
one God, for ever and ever.   **Amen.**

FIRST READING   *Genesis 3:9–15, 20*

I will make you enemies of each other: your offspring and her offspring.

After Adam had eaten of the tree, the Lord God called to him. 'Where are you?' he asked. 'I heard the sound of you in the garden', he replied. 'I was afraid because I was naked, so I hid.' 'Who told you that you were naked?' he asked. 'Have you been eating of the tree I forbade you to eat?' The man replied, 'It was the woman you put with me; she gave me the fruit, and I ate it'. Then the Lord God asked the woman, 'What is this you have done?' The woman replied, 'The serpent tempted me and I ate'.

Then the Lord God said to the serpent, 'Because you have done this, 'Be accursed beyond all cattle, all wild beasts. You shall crawl on your belly and eat dust every day of your life. I will make you enemies of each other: you and the woman, your offspring and her offspring. It will crush your head and you will strike its heel.'

The man named his wife 'Eve' because she was the mother of all those who live.

The word of the Lord.
Thanks be to God.

RESPONSORIAL PSALM   *Psalm 97:1–4 response v 1*

**Sing a new song to the Lord
for he has worked wonders.**

1   Sing a new song to the Lord
for he has worked wonders.
His right hand and his holy arm
have brought salvation.

2   The Lord has made known his salvation;
has shown his justice to the nations.
He has remembered his truth and love
for the house of Israel.

3   All the ends of the earth have seen
the salvation of our God.
Shout to the Lord all the earth,
ring out your joy.

SECOND READING   *Ephesians 1:3–6, 11–12*

Before the world was made, God chose us in Christ.

Blessed be God the Father of our Lord Jesus Christ, who has blessed us with all the spiritual blessings of heaven in Christ. Before the world was made, he chose us, chose us in Christ, to be holy and spotless, and to live through love in his presence, determining that we should become his adopted sons, through Jesus Christ, for his own kind purposes, to make us praise the glory of his grace, his free gift to us in the Beloved. And it is in him that we were claimed as God's own, chosen from the beginning, under the predetermined plan of the one who guides all things as he decides by his own will; chosen to be, for his greater glory, the people who would put their hopes in Christ before he came.

The word of the Lord.
Thanks be to God.

GOSPEL ACCLAMATION   *cf Luke 1:28*

**Alleluia, alleluia!
Hail, Mary, full of grace; the Lord is with thee!
Blessed art thou among women.
Alleluia!**

GOSPEL   *Luke 1:26–38*

The Lord be with you.
And with your spirit.

A reading from the holy Gospel according to Luke.
Glory to you, O Lord.

Rejoice, so highly favoured! The Lord is with you.

The angel Gabriel was sent by God to a town in Galilee called Nazareth, to a virgin betrothed to a man named Joseph, of the House of David; and the virgin's name was Mary. He went in and said to her, 'Rejoice, so highly favoured! The Lord is with you.' She was deeply disturbed by these words and asked herself what this greeting could mean, but the angel said to her, 'Mary, do not be afraid; you have won God's favour. Listen! You are to conceive and bear a son, and you must name him Jesus. He will be great and will be called Son of the

SAINTS

Most High. The Lord God will give him the throne of his ancestor David; he will rule over the House of Jacob for ever and his reign will have no end.' Mary said to the angel, 'But how can this come about, since I am a virgin?' 'The Holy Spirit will come upon you' the angel answered 'and the power of the Most High will cover you with its shadow. And so the child will be holy and will be called Son of God. Know this too: your kinswoman Elizabeth has, in her old age, herself conceived a son, and she whom people called barren is now in her sixth month, for nothing is impossible to God.' 'I am the handmaid of the Lord', said Mary 'let what you have said be done to me.' And the angel left her.

The Gospel of the Lord.
Praise to you, Lord Jesus Christ.

▷ *page 11*

The Profession of Faith is said.

PRAYER OVER THE OFFERINGS
Graciously accept the saving sacrifice
which we offer you, O Lord,
on the Solemnity of the Immaculate Conception
of the Blessed Virgin Mary,
and grant that, as we profess her,
on account of your prevenient grace,
to be untouched by any stain of sin,
so, through her intercession,
we may be delivered from all our faults.
Through Christ our Lord.   **Amen.**

▷ *page 15*

Preface: The Mystery of Mary and the Church, p 76.

COMMUNION ANTIPHON
Glorious things are spoken of you, O Mary,
for from you arose the sun of justice,
Christ our God.

▷ *page 58*

PRAYER AFTER COMMUNION
May the Sacrament we have received,
O Lord our God,
heal in us the wounds of that fault
from which in a singular way
you preserved Blessed Mary in her Immaculate Conception.
Through Christ our Lord.   **Amen.**

▷ *page 59*

A solemn blessing may be used.

PRESENTATION OF THE LORD

2 FEBRUARY
If this feast falls on a Sunday, it replaces the Sunday in Ordinary Time.
When the feast is celebrated on a weekday there is only one reading before the Gospel.

THE BLESSING OF CANDLES AND THE PROCESSION
FIRST FORM: THE PROCESSION

The people gather outside the Church or a building other than the Church. Candles are prepared for all who participate. While the candles are being lit, the following antiphon or another appropriate chant is sung.

ANTIPHON
Behold, our Lord will come with power,
to enlighten the eyes of his servants, alleluia.

SIGN OF THE CROSS
All make the Sign of the Cross as the Priest says.
Priest: In the name of the Father, and of the Son, and of the Holy Spirit.
People: **Amen.**

GREETING
Priest: The grace of our Lord Jesus Christ,
                 and the love of God,
                 and the communion of the Holy Spirit
                 be with you all.
or
Priest: Grace to you and peace from God our Father
                 and the Lord Jesus Christ.
or
Priest: The Lord be with you.
People: **And with your spirit.**

INTRODUCTORY ADDRESS
The Priest gives an introductory address, encouraging the faithful to celebrate the rite of this feast day actively and consciously. He may use these or similar words:
Dear brethren (brothers and sisters),
forty days have passed since we celebrated the joyful feast
of the Nativity of the Lord.
Today is the blessed day
when Jesus was presented in the Temple by Mary and Joseph.
Outwardly he was fulfilling the Law,
but in reality he was coming to meet his believing people.
Prompted by the Holy Spirit,
Simeon and Anna came to the Temple.

Enlightened by the same Spirit,
they recognized the Lord
and confessed him with exultation.
So let us also, gathered together by the Holy Spirit,
proceed to the house of God to encounter Christ.
There we shall find him
and recognize him in the breaking of the bread,
until he comes again, revealed in glory.

BLESSING OF CANDLES

After the address the Priest blesses the candles, saying, with hands extended:

Let us pray.

O God, source and origin of all light,
who on this day showed to the just man Simeon
the Light for revelation to the Gentiles,
we humbly ask that,
in answer to your people's prayers,
you may be pleased to sanctify with your blessing ✠ these candles,
which we are eager to carry in praise of your name,
so that, treading the path of virtue,
we may reach that light which never fails.
Through Christ our Lord.   **Amen.**

or

O God, true light, who create light eternal,
spreading it far and wide,
pour, we pray, into the hearts of the faithful
the brilliance of perpetual light,
so that all who are brightened in your holy temple
by the splendour of these candles
may happily reach the light of your glory.
Through Christ our Lord.   **Amen.**

He sprinkles the candles with holy water without saying anything, and puts incense into the thurible for the procession.

PROCESSION

The Deacon, or Priest, sings:

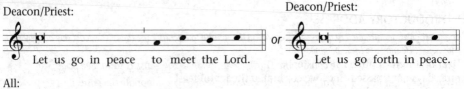

Deacon/Priest:

Let us go in peace   to meet the Lord.

or

Deacon/Priest:

Let us go forth in peace.

All:

In the name of Christ. A-men.

All carry lighted candles.
As the procession moves forward, one or other of the antiphons or another appropriate chant is sung.

Antiphon 1   *Luke 2:29–32*

Ant   A light for revelation to the Gentiles
       and the glory of your people Israel.

V   Lord, now you let your servant go in peace,
       in accordance with your word.

Ant   A light for revelation to the Gentiles...
V   For my eyes have seen your salvation.

Ant   A light for revelation to the Gentiles...
V   Which you have prepared in the sight of all peoples.

Ant   A light for revelation to the Gentiles...

Antiphon II

Sion, adorn your bridal chamber and welcome Christ the King; take Mary in your arms, who is the gate of heaven, for she herself is carrying the King of glory and new light. A Virgin she remains, though bringing in her hands the Son before the morning star begotten, whom Simeon, taking in his arms announced to the peoples as Lord of life and death and Saviour of the world.

ENTRANCE ANTIPHON

As the procession enters the church, the Entrance Antiphon of the Mass is sung. See p 306.

When the Priest has arrived at the altar, he venerates it and, if appropriate, incenses it. Then he goes to the chair, and Mass continues with the singing of the Gloria.

THE BLESSING OF CANDLES AND THE PROCESSION
SECOND FORM: THE SOLEMN ENTRANCE

Whenever a procession cannot take place, the faithful gather in church, holding candles in their hands.

The Priest, together with the ministers and a representative group of the faithful, goes to a suitable place, either in front of the church door or inside the church itself, where at least a large part of the faithful can conveniently participate in the rite.

All takes place in the same way as in the First Form, except that the procession is formed by only the Priest, the ministers and the representative group of the faithful

ENTRANCE ANTIPHON

As the procession enters the church, the Entrance Antiphon of the Mass is sung. See page 306.

When the Priest has arrived at the altar, he venerates it and, if appropriate, incenses it. Then he goes to the chair, and Mass continues with the singing of the Gloria.

SAINTS

AT THE MASS

ENTRANCE ANTIPHON *cf Psalm 47:10–11*

Your merciful love, O God,
we have received in the midst of your temple.
Your praise, O God, like your name,
reaches the ends of the earth;
your right hand is filled with saving justice.

The Penitential Act is omitted and the Gloria is now sung (said).

▷ *page 9*

▷ *Music p 337*

COLLECT

Almighty ever-living God,
we humbly implore your majesty
that, just as your Only Begotten Son
was presented on this day in the Temple
in the substance of our flesh,
so, by your grace,
we may be presented to you with minds made pure.
Through our Lord Jesus Christ, your Son,
who lives and reigns with you in the unity of the Holy Spirit,
one God, for ever and ever. **Amen.**

FIRST READING *Malachi 3:1–4*

The Lord you are seeking will suddenly enter his Temple.

The Lord God says this: Look, I am going to send my messenger to prepare a way before me. And the Lord you are seeking will suddenly enter his Temple; and the angel of the covenant whom you are longing for, yes, he is coming, says the Lord of hosts. Who will be able to resist the day of his coming? Who will remain standing when he appears? For he is like the refiner's fire and the fullers' alkali. He will take his seat as refiner and purifier; he will purify the sons of Levi and refine them like gold and silver, and then they will make the offering to the Lord as it should be made. The offering of Judah and Jerusalem will then be welcomed by the Lord as in former days, as in the years of old.

The word of the Lord.
Thanks be to God.

RESPONSORIAL PSALM *Psalm 23:7–10 response v 8*

**Who is the king of glory?
It is the Lord.**

1 O gates, lift up your heads;
   grow higher, ancient doors.
   Let him enter, the king of glory!

2 Who is the king of glory?
   The Lord, the mighty, the valiant,
   the Lord, the valiant in war.

3 O gates, lift high your heads;
   grow higher, ancient doors.
   Let him enter, the king of glory!

4 Who is he, the king of glory?
   He, the Lord of armies,
   he is the king of glory.

SECOND READING   *Hebrews 2:14–18*

It was essential that we should in this way become completely like his brother.

Since all the children share the same blood and flesh, Jesus too shared equally in it, so that by his death he could take away all the power of the devil, who had power over death, and set free all those who had been held in all their lives by the fear of death. For it was not the angels that he took to himself; he took to himself descent from Abraham. It was essential that he should in this way become completely like his brothers so that he could be a compassionate and trustworthy high priest of God's religion, able to atone for human sins. That is, because he has himself been through temptation he is able to help others who are tempted.

The word of the Lord.
Thanks be to God.

GOSPEL ACCLAMATION   *Luke 2:32*

Alleluia, alleluia!
The light to enlighten the Gentiles
and give glory to Israel, your people.
Alleluia!

GOSPEL   *Luke 2:22–40 Shorter form (omitting oblique text): Luke 2:22–32*

The Lord be with you.
And with your spirit.

A reading from the holy Gospel according to Luke.
Glory to you, O Lord.

My eyes have seen your salvation.

When the day came for them to be purified as laid down by the Law of Moses, the parents of Jesus took him up to Jerusalem to present him to the Lord – observing what stands written in the Law of the Lord: Every first-born male must be consecrated to the Lord – and also to offer in sacrifice, in accordance with what is said in the Law of the Lord, a pair of turtle doves or two young pigeons. Now in Jerusalem there was a man named Simeon. He was an upright and devout man; he looked forward to Israel's comforting and the Holy Spirit rested upon him. It had been revealed to him by the Holy Spirit that he would not see death until he had set eyes on the Christ of the Lord. Prompted by the Spirit he came to the Temple; and when the parents brought in the child Jesus to do for him what the Law required, he took him in his arms and blessed God; and he said:

'Now, Master, you can let your servant go in peace, just as you promised; because my eyes have seen the salvation which you have prepared for all nations to see, a light to enlighten the pagans and the glory of your people Israel.'

As the child's father and mother stood there wondering at the things that were being said about him, Simeon blessed them and said to Mary his mother, 'You see this child: he is destined for the fall and for the rising of many in Israel, destined to be a sign that is rejected – and a sword will pierce your own soul too – so that the secret thoughts of many may be laid bare.'

There was a prophetess also, Anna the daughter of Phanuel of the tribe of Asher.

SAINTS

She was well on in years. Her days of girlhood over, she had been married for seven years before becoming a widow. She was now eighty-four years old and never left the Temple, serving God night and day with fasting and prayer. She came by just at that moment and began to praise God; and she spoke of the child to all who looked forward to the deliverance of Jerusalem.

When they had done everything the Law of the Lord required, they went back to Galilee, to their own town of Nazareth. Meanwhile the child grew to maturity, and he was filled with wisdom; and God's favour was with him.

The Gospel of the Lord.
Praise to you, Lord Jesus Christilla.

▷ *page 11*

When this Feast falls on a Sunday, the Profession of Faith is said.

PRAYER OVER THE OFFERINGS
May the offering made with exultation by your Church
be pleasing to you, O Lord, we pray,
for you willed that your Only Begotten Son
be offered to you for the life of the world
as the Lamb without blemish.
Who lives and reigns for ever and ever.   **Amen.**

▷ *page 15*

Preface: The Mystery of the Presentation of the Lord, p 76.

COMMUNION ANTIPHON   Luke 2:30–31
My eyes have seen your salvation,
which you prepared in the sight of all the peoples.

▷ *page 58*

PRAYER AFTER COMMUNION
By these holy gifts which we have received, O Lord,
bring your grace to perfection within us,
and, as you fulfilled Simeon's expectation
that he would not see death
until he had been privileged to welcome the Christ,
so may we, going forth to meet the Lord,
obtain the gift of eternal life.
Through Christ our Lord.   **Amen.**

▷ *page 59*

SAINT PATRICK

In Ireland: Solemnity
In England and Scotland: Feast
In Wales: Optional Memorial

In Ireland, if 17 March falls on a Sunday, the Solemnity is transferred.

For Ireland, see below.   *For England, see page 314.*   *For Scotland, see page 316.*

FOR IRELAND

ENTRANCE ANTIPHON *Genesis 12:1–2*

Go from your country and your kindred and your father's house
        to the land that I will show you.
I will make of you a great nation, and I will bless you,
and make your name great, so that you will be a blessing.

▷ *page 7*

COLLECT

Lord, through the work of Saint Patrick in Ireland
we have come to acknowledge the mystery of the one true God
and give thanks for our salvation in Christ;
grant by his prayers
that we who celebrate this festival
may keep alive the fire of faith he kindled.
Through our Lord Jesus Christ, your Son,
who lives and reigns with you in the unity of the Holy Spirit,
one God, for ever and ever. **Amen.**

The Gloria is sung (said)

Alternative readings for use in Year C are found on page 311.

FIRST READING *Ecclesiasticus 39.6–10*

His memory will not disappear, generation after generation his name will live.

If it is the will of the great Lord, the scholar will be filled with the spirit of understanding, he will shower forth words of wisdom, and in prayer give thanks to the Lord. He will grow upright in purpose and learning, he will ponder the Lord's hidden mysteries. He will display the instruction he has received, taking his pride in the Law of the Lord's covenant. Many will praise his understanding, and it will never be forgotten. His memory will not disappear, generation after generation his name will live. Nations will proclaim his wisdom, the assembly will celebrate his praises.

The word of the Lord.
Thanks be to God.

SAINTS

RESPONSORIAL PSALM   *Psalm 115:12–19 response v 12*

How can I repay the Lord for his goodness to me?

1 How can I repay the Lord
   for his goodness to me?
   The cup of salvation I will raise;
   I will call on the Lord's name.

2 My vows to the Lord I will fulfil
   before all his people.
   O precious in the eyes of the Lord
   is the death of his faithful.

3 Your servant, Lord, your servant am I;
   you have loosened my bonds.
   A thanksgiving sacrifice I make;
   I will call on the Lord's name.

4 My vows to the Lord I will fulfil
   before all his people,
   in the courts of the house of the Lord,
   in your midst, O Jerusalem.

SECOND READING   *2 Timothy 4:1–8*

Refute falsehood, correct error, call to obedience – but do all with patience and with the intention of teaching.

Before God and before Christ Jesus who is to be judge of the living and the dead, I put this duty to you, in the name of his Appearing and of his kingdom: proclaim the message and, welcome or unwelcome, insist on it. Refute falsehood, correct error, call to obedience – but do all with patience and with the intention of teaching. The time is sure to come when, far from being content with sound teaching, people will be avid for the latest novelty and collect themselves a whole series of teachers according to their own tastes; and then, instead of listening to the truth, they will turn to myths. Be careful always to choose the right course; be brave under trials; make the preaching of the Good News your life's work, in thoroughgoing service.

As for me, my life is already being poured away as a libation, as the time has come for me to be gone. I have fought the good fight to the end; I have run the race to the finish; I have kept the faith; all there is to come now is the crown of righteousness reserved for me, which the Lord, the righteous judge, will give me on that Day; and not only to me but to all those who have longed for his Appearing.

The word of the Lord.
Thanks be to God.

GOSPEL ACCLAMATION   *James 1:21*

**Glory to you, O Christ, you are the Word of God!
Accept and submit to the word
which has been planted in you and can save your souls.
Glory to you, O Christ, you are the Word of God!**

GOSPEL   *Matthew 13:24–32*

The Lord be with you.
And with your spirit.

A reading from the holy Gospel according to Matthew.
Glory to you, O Lord.

It is the smallest of all the seeds, but when it has grown it is the greatest of shrubs.

Jesus put a parable before the crowds: 'The kingdom of heaven may be compared to a man who sowed good seed in his field. While everybody was asleep his enemy came, sowed darnel all among the wheat and made off. When the new wheat sprouted and ripened, the darnel appeared as well. The owner's servants went to him and said, "Sir, was it not good seed that you sowed in your field? If so, where does the darnel come from?" "Some enemy has done this," he answered. And the servants said, "Do you want us to go and weed it out?" But he said, "No, because when you weed out the darnel you might pull up the wheat with it. Let them both grow till the harvest; and at harvest time I shall say to the reapers: First collect the darnel and tie it in bundles to be burnt, then gather the wheat into my barn."'

He put another parable before them: 'The kingdom of heaven is like a mustard seed which a man took and sowed in his field. It is the smallest of all the seeds, but when it has grown it is the biggest of shrubs and becomes a tree, so that the birds of the air can come and shelter in its branches.'

The Gospel of the Lord.
Praise to you, Lord Jesus Christ.

▷ *page 11*

Readings for use *ad libitum* in Year C

FIRST READING   *Amos 7:12–15*

The Lord took me from following the flock.

Amaziah, the priest of Bethel, said to Amos, 'Go away, seer; get back to the land of Judah; earn your bread there, do your prophesying there. We want no more prophesying in Bethel; this is the royal sanctuary, the national temple.' 'I was no prophet, neither did I belong to any of the brotherhoods of prophets,' Amos replied to Amaziah. 'I was a shepherd, and looked after sycamores: but it was the Lord who took me from herding the flock, and the Lord who said, "Go, prophesy to my people Israel."'

The word of the Lord.
Thanks be to God.

RESPONSORIAL PSALM   *Psalm 138:1–3, 7–10, 13–14 response v 9–10*

**If I dwell at the sea's furthest end
even there you watch over me.**

1 O Lord, you search me and you know me,
   you know my resting and my rising,
   you discern my purpose from afar.
   You mark when I walk or lie down,
   all my ways lie open to you.

2 O where can I go from your spirit,
   or where can I flee from your face?
   If I climb the heavens, you are there.
   If I lie in the grave, you are there.

3 For it is you who created my being,
   knit me together in my mother's womb.
   I thank you for the wonders of my being,
   for the wonders of all your creation.

SAINTS

SECOND READING   *1 Thessalonians 2:2–8*

We never came with words of flattery or with a pretext for greed.

It was our God who gave us the courage to proclaim his Good News to you in the face of great opposition. We have not taken to preaching because we are deluded, or immoral, or trying to deceive anyone; it was God who decided that we were fit to be entrusted with the Good News, and when we are speaking, we are not trying to please men but God, who can read our inmost thoughts. You know very well, and we can swear it before God, that never at any time have our speeches been simply flattery, or a cover for trying to get money; nor have we ever looked for any special honour from men, either from you or anybody else, when we could have imposed ourselves on you with full weight, as apostles of Christ.

Instead, we were unassuming. Like a mother feeding and looking after her own children, we felt so devoted and protective towards you, and had come to love you so much, that we were eager to hand over to you not only the Good News but our whole lives as well.

The word of the Lord.
Thanks be to God.

GOSPEL ACCLAMATION   *Luke 4:18*

Glory to you, O Christ, you are the Word of God!
The Lord has sent me to bring good news to the poor,
to proclaim liberty to captives.
Glory to you, O Christ, you are the Word of God!

GOSPEL   *Luke 5:1–11*

The Lord be with you.
And with your spirit.

A reading from the holy Gospel according to Luke.
Glory to you, O Lord.

'Lord, I am a sinful man.' Jesus said, 'Do not be afraid.'

Jesus was standing one day by the Lake of Gennesaret , with the crowd pressing round him listening to the word of God, when he caught sight of two boats close to the bank. The fishermen had gone out of them and were washing their nets. He got into one of the boats – it was Simon's – and asked him to put out a little from the shore. Then he sat down and taught the crowds from the boat.

When he had finished speaking he said to Simon, 'Put out into deep water and pay out your nets for a catch.' 'Master,' Simon replied, 'we worked hard all night long and caught nothing, but if you say so, I will pay out the nets.' And when they had done this they netted such a huge number of fish that their nets began to tear, so they signalled to their companions in the other boat to come and help them; when these came, they filled the two boats to sinking point.

When Simon Peter saw this he fell at the knees of Jesus saying, 'Leave me, Lord; I am a sinful man.' For he and all his companions were completely overcome by the catch they had made; so also were

James and John, sons of Zebedee, who were Simon's partners. But Jesus said to Simon, 'Do not be afraid; from now on it is men you will catch.' Then bringing their boats back to the land, they left everything and followed him.

The Gospel of the Lord.
Praise to you, Lord Jesus Christ.

▷ page 11

The Profession of Faith is said.

PRAYER OVER THE OFFERINGS
Lord, accept this pure sacrifice
which, through the labours of Saint Patrick,
your grateful people make
to the glory of your name.
Through Christ our Lord.   **Amen.**

▷ page 15

Preface of Saint Patrick, p 77.

COMMUNION ANTIPHON   *cf Matthew 8:11*
Many will come from east and west
and sit down with Abraham, Isaac and Jacob
at the feast in the kingdom of heaven, says the Lord.

▷ page 58

PRAYER AFTER COMMUNION
Strengthen us, O Lord, by this sacrament
so that we may profess the faith taught by Saint Patrick
and to proclaim it in our way of living.
Through Christ our Lord.   **Amen.**

▷ page 59

SOLEMN BLESSING

Priest: May God the Father, who called us together
          to celebrate this feast of Saint Patrick,
          bless you, protect you and keep you faithful.
All: **Amen.**

Priest: May Christ the Lord, the High King of Heaven,
          be near you at all times and shield you from evil.
All: **Amen.**

Priest: May the Holy Spirit, who is the source of all holiness,
          make you rich in the love of God's people.
All: **Amen.**

Priest: And may the blessing of almighty God,
          the Father, and the Son, ✠ and the Holy Spirit,
          come down on you and remain for ever.
All: **Amen.**

SAINTS

IN ENGLAND

ENTRANCE ANTIPHON   *cf Psalm 95:2–3*
Proclaim the salvation of God day by day;
tell among the nations his glory.

▷ *page 7*

The Gloria is sung (said)

COLLECT
O God, who chose the Bishop Saint Patrick
to preach your glory to the peoples of Ireland,
grant through his merits and intercession,
that those who glory in the name of Christian
may never cease to proclaim your wondrous deeds to all.
Through our Lord Jesus Christ, your Son,
who lives and reigns with you in the unity of the Holy Spirit,
one God, for ever and ever.   **Amen.**

FIRST READING   *Jeremiah 1:4–9*
Go now to those to whom I send you.

The word of the Lord was addressed to me, saying,

'Before I formed you in the womb I knew you; before you came to birth I consecrated you; I have appointed you as prophet to the nations.'

I said, 'Ah, Lord; look, I do not know how to speak: I am a child!' But the Lord replied,

'Do not say, "I am a child". Go now to those to whom I send you and say whatever I command you. Do not be afraid of them, for I am with you to protect you – it is the Lord who speaks!'

Then the Lord put out his hand and touched my mouth and said to me:

'There! I am putting my words into your mouth.'

The word of the Lord.
Thanks be to God.

RESPONSORIAL PSALM   *Psalm 116 response Mark 16:15*

Go out to the whole world and tell the Good News.

1 O praise the Lord, all you nations,
   acclaim him all you peoples!

2 Strong is his love for us;
   he is faithful for ever.

SECOND READING   *Acts 13:46–49*
We must turn to the pagans.

Paul and Barnabas spoke out boldly to the Jews, 'We had to proclaim the word of God to you first, but since you have rejected it, since you do not think yourselves worthy of eternal life, we must turn to the pagans. For this is what the Lord commanded us to do when he said:

"I have made you a light for the nations, so that my salvation may reach the ends of the earth."'

It made the pagans very happy to hear this and they thanked the Lord for his message; all who were destined for eternal life became believers. Thus the word of the Lord spread through the whole countryside.

The word of the Lord.
Thanks be to God.

GOSPEL ACCLAMATION   *Luke 4:18*

Praise and honour to you, Lord Jesus!
The Lord sent me to bring Good News to the poor,
and freedom to prisoners.
Praise and honour to you, Lord Jesus!

GOSPEL   *Luke 10:1–12, 17–20*

The Lord be with you.
And with your spirit.

A reading from the holy Gospel according to Luke.
Glory to you, O Lord.

Your peace will rest on him.

The Lord appointed seventy-two others and sent them out ahead of him, in pairs, to all the towns and places he himself was to visit. He said to them, 'The harvest is rich but the labourers are few, so ask the Lord of the harvest to send labourers to his harvest. Start off now, but remember, I am sending you out like lambs among wolves. Carry no purse, no haversack, no sandals. Salute no one on the road. Whatever house you go into, let your first words be, "Peace to this house!" And if a man of peace lives there, your peace will go and rest on him; if not, it will come back to you. Stay in the same house, taking what food and drink they have to offer, for the labourer deserves his wages; do not move from house to house. Whenever you go into a town where they make you welcome, eat what is set before you. Cure those in it who are sick, and say. "The kingdom of God is very near to you." But whenever you enter a town and they do not make you welcome, go out into its streets and say, "We wipe off the very dust of your town that clings to our feet, and leave it with you. Yet be sure of this: the kingdom of God is very near." I tell you, on that day it will not go as hard with Sodom as with that town.'

The seventy-two came back rejoicing. 'Lord,' they said 'even the devils submit to us when we use your name.' He said to them, 'I watched Satan fall like lightning from heaven. Yes, I have given you power to tread underfoot serpents and scorpions and the whole strength of the enemy; nothing shall ever hurt you. Yet do not rejoice that the spirits submit to you; rejoice rather that your names are written in heaven.'

The Gospel of the Lord.
Praise to you, Lord Jesus Christ.

▷ *page 11*

PRAYER OVER THE OFFERINGS

Lord, accept this pure sacrifice
which, through the labours of Saint Patrick,
your grateful people make
to the glory of your name.
Through Christ our Lord.   **Amen.**

▷ *page 15*

SAINTS

COMMUNION ANTIPHON   *Luke 22:29–30*

I confer a kingdom on you
just as my Father has conferred one on me,
that you may eat and drink at my table in my kingdom, says the Lord.

▷ *page 58*

PRAYER AFTER COMMUNION

Strengthen us, O Lord, by this sacrament,
so that we may profess the faith taught by Saint Patrick
and proclaim it by our way of living.
Through Christ our Lord.   **Amen.**

▷ *page 59*

IN SCOTLAND

*In Scotland, the Antiphons, prayers and Readings are taken from the
Common of Pastors: For a Bishop.*

The following Collect is Proper.

COLLECT

O God, who chose the Bishop Saint Patrick
to preach your glory to the peoples of Ireland,
grant through his merits and intercession,
that those who glory in the name of Christian
may never cease to proclaim your wondrous deeds to all.
Through our Lord Jesus Christ, your Son,
who lives and reigns with you in the unity of the Holy Spirit,
one God, for ever and ever.   **Amen.**

The Gloria is sung (or said).

SAINT JOSEPH

SAINT JOSEPH, SPOUSE OF THE BLESSED VIRGIN MARY
19 MARCH

If 19 March falls on a Sunday, the Solemnity is transferred.

ENTRANCE ANTIPHON   *cf Luke 12:42*

Behold, a faithful and prudent steward,
whom the Lord set over his household.

▷ *page 7*

The Gloria is sung (said).

COLLECT

Grant, we pray, almighty God,
that by Saint Joseph's intercession
your Church may constantly watch over
the unfolding of the mysteries of human salvation,
whose beginnings you entrusted to his faithful care.
Through our Lord Jesus Christ, your Son,
who lives and reigns with you in the unity of the Holy Spirit,
one God, for ever and ever.   **Amen.**

FIRST READING   *2 Samuel 7:4–5, 12–14, 16*

The Lord God will give him the throne of his ancestor David.

The word of the Lord came to Nathan:

'Go and tell my servant David, "Thus the Lord speaks: When your days are ended and you are laid to rest with your ancestors, I will preserve the offspring of your body after you and make his sovereignty secure. (It is he who shall build a house for my name, and I will make his royal throne secure for ever.) I will be a father to him and he a son to me. Your House and your sovereignty will always stand secure before me and your throne be established forever." '

The word of the Lord.
Thanks be to God.

RESPONSORIAL PSALM   *Psalm 88:2–5, 27, 29 response v 37*

His dynasty shall last for ever.

1   I will sing for ever of your love, O Lord;
through all ages my mouth will proclaim your truth.
Of this I am sure, that your love lasts for ever,
that your truth is firmly established as the heavens.

2   'I have made a covenant with my chosen one;
I have sworn to David my servant:
I will establish your dynasty for ever
and set up your throne through all ages.'

continued...

SAINTS

His dynasty shall last for ever.

3 He will say to me: 'You are my father,
my God, the rock who saves me.'
I will keep my love for him always;
for him my covenant shall endure.

SECOND READING *Romans 4:13, 16–18, 22*
Though it seemed Abraham's hope could not be
fulfilled, he hoped and he believed.

The promise of inheriting the world was not made to Abraham and his descendants on account of any law but on account of the righteousness which consists in faith. That is why what fulfils the promise depends on faith, so that it may be a free gift and be available to all of Abraham's descendants, not only those who belong to the Law but also those who belong to the faith of Abraham who is the father of all of us. As scripture says: I have made you the ancestor of many nations – Abraham is our father in the eyes of God, in whom he put his faith, and who brings the dead to life and calls into being what does not exist.

Though it seemed Abraham's hope could not be fulfilled, he hoped and he believed, and through doing so he did become the father of many nations exactly as he had been promised: Your descendants will be as many as the stars. This is the faith that was 'considered as justifying him'.

The word of the Lord.
Thanks be to God.

GOSPEL ACCLAMATION *Psalm 83:5*

Glory and praise to you, O Christ.
They are happy who dwell in your house, O Lord,
for ever singing your praise.
Glory and praise to you, O Christ.

An alternative Gospel is found on page 319.

GOSPEL *Matthew 1:16, 18–21, 24*

The Lord be with you.
And with your spirit.

A reading from the holy Gospel according to Matthew.
Glory to you, O Lord.

Joseph did what the angel of the Lord had told him to do.

Jacob was the father of Joseph the husband of Mary; of her was born Jesus who is called Christ.

This is how Jesus Christ came to be born. His mother Mary was betrothed to Joseph; but before they came to live together she was found to be with child through the Holy Spirit. Her husband Joseph, being a man of honour and wanting to spare her publicity, decided to divorce her informally. He had made up his mind to do this when the angel of the Lord appeared to him in a dream and said 'Joseph son of David, do not be afraid to take Mary home as your wife, because she has conceived what is in her by the Holy Spirit. She will give birth to a son and you must name him Jesus, because he is the one who is to save his people from their sins.' When Joseph woke up he did what the angel of the Lord had told him to do.

The Gospel of the Lord.
Praise to you, Lord Jesus Christ.

ALTERNATIVE GOSPEL   *Luke 2:41–51*

The Lord be with you.
And with your spirit.

A reading from the holy Gospel according to Luke.
Glory to you, O Lord.

See how worried your father and I have been, looking for you.

Every year the parents of Jesus used to go to Jerusalem for the feast of the Passover. When he was twelve years old, they went up for the feast as usual. When they were on their way home after the feast, the boy Jesus stayed behind in Jerusalem without his parents knowing it. They assumed he was with the caravan, and it was only after a day's journey that they went to look for him among their relations and acquaintances. When they failed to find him they went back to Jerusalem looking for him everywhere.

Three days later, they found him in the Temple, sitting among the doctors, listening to them, and asking them questions; and all those who heard him were astounded at his intelligence and his replies. They were overcome when they saw him, and his mother said to him, 'My child, why have you done this to us? See how worried your father and I have been, looking for you.' 'Why were you looking for me?' he replied. 'Did you not know that I must be busy with my Father's affairs?' But they did not understand what he meant.

He then went down with them and came to Nazareth and lived under their authority.

The Gospel of the Lord.
Praise to you, Lord Jesus Christ.

▷ *page 11*

The Profession of Faith is said.

PRAYER OVER THE OFFERINGS

We pray, O Lord,
that, just as Saint Joseph served with loving care
your Only Begotten Son, born of the Virgin Mary,
so we may be worthy to minister
with a pure heart at your altar.
Through Christ our Lord.   **Amen.**

▷ *page 15*

SAINTS

PREFACE
THE MISSION OF SAINT JOSEPH

Priest: The Lord be with you.
People: **And with your spirit.**

Priest: Lift up your hearts.
People: **We lift them up to the Lord.**

Priest: Let us give thanks to the Lord our God.
People: **It is right and just.**

It is truly right and just, our duty and our salvation,
always and everywhere to give you thanks,
Lord, holy Father, almighty and eternal God,
and on the Solemnity of Saint Joseph
to give you fitting praise,
to glorify you and bless you.

For this just man was given by you
as spouse to the Virgin Mother of God
and set as a wise and faithful servant
in charge of your household,
to watch like a father over your Only Begotten Son,
who was conceived by the overshadowing of the Holy Spirit,
our Lord Jesus Christ.

Through him the Angels praise your majesty,
Dominions adore and Powers tremble before you.
Heaven and the Virtues of heaven and the blessed Seraphim
worship together with exultation.
May our voices, we pray, join with theirs
in humble praise, as we acclaim:

Holy, Holy, Holy Lord God of hosts...

COMMUNION ANTIPHON   *Matthew 25:21*
Well done, good and faithful servant.
Come, share your master's joy.

▷ page 58

PRAYER AFTER COMMUNION
Defend with unfailing protection,
O Lord, we pray,
the family you have nourished
with food from this altar,
as they rejoice at the Solemnity of Saint Joseph,
and graciously keep safe your gifts among them.
Through Christ our Lord.   **Amen.**

▷ page 59

ANNUNCIATION OF THE LORD

If 25 March falls on a Sunday or in Holy Week, the Solemnity is transferred.

ENTRANCE ANTIPHON *Hebrews 10:5, 7*
The Lord said, as he entered the world:
Behold, I come to do your will, O God.

▷ *page 7*

The Gloria is sung (said).

COLLECT
O God, who willed that your Word
should take on the reality of human flesh
in the womb of the Virgin Mary,
grant, we pray,
that we, who confess our Redeemer to be God and man,
may merit to become partakers even in his divine nature.
Who lives and reigns with you in the unity of the Holy Spirit,
one God, for ever and ever. **Amen.**

FIRST READING *Isaiah 7:10–14*
The maiden is with child.
The Lord spoke to Ahaz and said, 'Ask the Lord your God for a sign for yourself coming either from the depths of Sheol or from the heights above.' 'No', Ahaz answered 'I will not put the Lord to the test.'

Then Isaiah said:

Listen now, House of David: are you not satisfied with trying the patience of men without trying the patience of my God, too?

The Lord himself, therefore, will give you a sign. It is this: the maiden is with child and will soon give birth to a son whom she will call Emmanuel, a name which means 'God-is-with-us'.

The word of the Lord.
Thanks be to God.

RESPONSORIAL PSALM *Psalm 39:7–11 response vv 8, 9*

> **Here I am Lord!**
> **I come to do your will.**

1 You do not ask for sacrifice and offerings,
but an open ear.
You do not ask for holocaust and victim.
Instead, here am I.

2 In the scroll of the book it stands written
that I should do your will.
My God, I delight in your law
in the depth of my heart.

continued...

SAINTS

> Here I am Lord!
> I come to do your will.

3 Your justice I have proclaimed
  in the great assembly.
  My lips I have not sealed;
  you know it, O Lord.

4 I have not hidden your justice in my heart
  but declared your faithful help.
  I have not hidden your love and your truth
  from the great assembly.

SECOND READING   *Hebrews 10:4–10*

I was commanded in the scroll of the book, 'God, here I am! I am coming to obey your will.'

Bulls' blood and goats' blood are useless for taking away sins, and this is what Christ said, on coming into the world:

You who wanted no sacrifice or oblation, prepared a body for me.

You took no pleasure in holocausts or sacrifices for sin; then I said, just as I was commanded in the scroll of the book, 'God, here I am! I am coming to obey your will.'

Notice that he says first: You did not want what the Law lays down as the things to be offered, that is: the sacrifices, the oblations, the holocausts and the sacrifices for sin, and you took no pleasure in them; and then he says: Here I am! I am coming to obey your will. He is abolishing the first sort to replace it with the second. And this will was for us to be made holy by the offering of his body made once and for all by Jesus Christ.

The word of the Lord.
Thanks be to God.

GOSPEL ACCLAMATION DURING LENT   *John 1:14*

> Praise to you, O Christ, king of eternal glory!
> The Word was made flesh,
> he lived among us,
> and we saw his glory.
> Praise to you, O Christ, king of eternal glory!

GOSPEL ACCLAMATION OUTSIDE LENT   *John 1:14*

> Alleluia, alleluia!
> The Word was made flesh,
> he lived among us,
> and we saw his glory.
> Alleluia!

GOSPEL   *Luke 1:26–38*

The Lord be with you.
And with your spirit.

A reading from the holy Gospel according to Luke.
Glory to you, O Lord.

You are to conceive and bear a son.

The angel Gabriel was sent by God to a town in Galilee called Nazareth, to a virgin betrothed to a man named Joseph, of the House of David; and the virgin's name was Mary. He went in and said to her, 'Rejoice, so highly favoured! The Lord is with you.' She was deeply disturbed by these words and asked herself what this greeting could mean, but the angel said to her, 'Mary, do not be afraid; you have won God's favour. Listen! You are to conceive and bear a son, and you must name him Jesus. He will be great and will be called Son of the Most High. The Lord God will give him the throne of his ancestor David; he will rule over the House of Jacob for ever and his reign will have no end.'

Mary said to the angel, 'But how can this come about, since I am a virgin?' 'The Holy Spirit will come upon you,' the angel answered 'and the power of the Most High will cover you with its shadow. And so the child will be holy and will be called Son of God. Know this too: your kinswoman Elizabeth has, in her old age, herself conceived a son, and she whom people called barren is now in her sixth month, for nothing is impossible to God.' 'I am the handmaid of the Lord,' said Mary, 'let what you have said be done to me.' And the angel left her.

The Gospel of the Lord.
Praise to you, Lord Jesus Christ.

▷ *page 11*

PROFESSION OF FAITH
The Profession of Faith is said. All kneel at the words 'and by the Holy Spirit was incarnate.'

PRAYER OVER THE OFFERINGS
Be pleased, almighty God,
to accept your Church's offering,
so that she, who is aware that her beginnings
lie in the Incarnation of your Only Begotten Son,
may rejoice to celebrate his mysteries on this Solemnity.
Who lives and reigns for ever and ever.   **Amen.**

▷ *page 15*

SAINTS

PREFACE
THE MYSTERY OF THE INCARNATION

Priest: The Lord be with you.
People: **And with your spirit.**

Priest: Lift up your hearts.
People: **We lift them up to the Lord.**

Priest: Let us give thanks to the Lord our God.
People: **It is right and just.**

It is truly right and just,
    our duty and our salvation,
always and everywhere to give you thanks,
Lord, holy Father, almighty and eternal God,
through Christ our Lord.

For the Virgin Mary heard with faith
that the Christ was to be born among men
    and for men's sake
by the overshadowing power
    of the Holy Spirit.
Lovingly she bore him
    in her immaculate womb,

that the promises to the children of Israel
    might come about
and the hope of nations be accomplished
    beyond all telling.

Through him the host of Angels
    adores your majesty
and rejoices in your presence for ever.
May our voices, we pray, join with theirs
in one chorus of exultant praise,
    as we acclaim:

Holy, Holy, Holy Lord God of hosts...

COMMUNION ANTIPHON   *Isaiah 7:14*
Behold, a Virgin shall conceive and bear a son;
and his name will be called Emmanuel.

▷ *page 58*

PRAYER AFTER COMMUNION
Confirm in our minds the mysteries of the true faith,
we pray, O Lord,
so that, confessing that he who was conceived of the Virgin Mary
is true God and true man,
we may, through the saving power of his Resurrection,
merit to attain eternal joy.
Through Christ our Lord.   **Amen.**

▷ *page 59*

OTHER CELEBRATIONS

ANNIVERSARY OF DEDICATION OF A CHURCH

COMMON OF THE DEDICATION OF A CHURCH
ON THE ANNIVERSARY OF THE DEDICATION
I   IN THE CHURCH THAT WAS DEDICATED

ENTRANCE ANTIPHON   *Psalm 67:36*

Wonderful are you, O God in your holy place.
The God of Israel himself gives his people strength and courage.
Blessed be God! (*Easter Time:* alleluia).

▷ *page 7*

The Gloria is sung (or said).

COLLECT

O God, who year by year renew for us the day
when this your holy temple was consecrated,
hear the prayers of your people
and grant that in this place
for you there may always be pure worship
and for us, fullness of redemption.
Through our Lord Jesus Christ, your Son,
who lives and reigns with you in the unity of the Holy Spirit,
one God, for ever and ever.   **Amen.**

FIRST READING

The Lectionary notes that the pairings of Readings with Responsorial Psalms are suggestions only.
Any other suitable pairing may be used, having regard to the pastoral needs of the occasion.

Outside the Easter Season

One of the following readings is chosen:

1   1 Kings 8:22–23, 27–30
   Let your eyes watch over this house.

2   2 Chronicles 5:6–11, 13–6:2
   I have built you a dwelling place
   for you to live in for ever.

3   Isaiah 56:1, 6–7
   My house will be called a house of prayer
   for all the peoples.

4   Ezekiel 43:1–2, 4–7
   I saw the glory of the Lord fill the Temple.

5   Ezekiel 47:1–2, 8–9, 12
   I saw a stream of water coming from the
   Temple, bringing life to all wherever it
   flowed.

During the Easter Season

One of the following readings is chosen:

6   Acts: 7:44–50
   The Most High does not live in a house
   that human hands have built.

7   Apocalypse 21:1–5
   Here God lives among men.

8   Apocalypse 21:9–14
   I will show you the bride
   that the Lamb has married.

OTHER

RESPONSORIAL PSALM

One of the following Psalms is chosen:

FOR READING 5,

PSALM 45   *Psalm 45:2–3, 5–6, 8–9 response v 5*

> The waters of a river give joy to God's city
> the holy place where the Most High dwells.

FOR READING 1, 3 OR 7

PSALM 83   *Psalm 83:3–5, 10–11 response v 2, alternative response Apocalypse 21:3*

> How lovely is your dwelling place,
> Lord, God of hosts

or

> Here God lives among men.

FOR READING 6

PSALM 94   *Psalm 94:1–7 response v 2*

> Let us come before the Lord giving thanks

FOR READING 8

PSALM 121   *Psalm 121: 1–4, 8–9 response v 1*

> Let us go to God's house, rejoicing

FOR READING 2 OR 4

1 CHRONICLES 29   *1 Chronicles 29:10–12 response v 13*

> We praise your glorious name, O Lord

SECOND READING

One of the following readings is chosen:

1   1 Corinthians 3:9–11, 16–17

You are the temple of God.

2   Ephesians 2:19–22

All grow into one holy temple in the Lord.

3   Hebrews 12:18–19, 22–24

You have come to Mount Zion and to the city of the living God.

4   1 Peter 2:4–9

So that you too may be living stones making a spiritual house.

GOSPEL ACCLAMATION

The Lectionary notes that the pairings of each Gospel Acclamations with Gospel readings are suggestions only. Any other suitable pairing may be used, having regard to the pastoral needs of the occasion.

FOR GOSPEL 1   *Matthew 16:18*

> Alleluia, alleluia!
> You are Peter and on this rock I will build my Church.
> And the gates of the underworld can never hold out against it.
> Alleluia!

FOR GOSPEL 2   *cf Matthew 7:8*

> Alleluia, alleluia!
> In my house, says the Lord,
> the one who asks always receives;
> the one who searches always finds;
> the one who knocks will always have the door opened to him.
> Alleluia!

FOR GOSPEL 3   *2 Chronicles 7:16*

Alleluia, alleluia!
I have chosen and consecrated this house, says the Lord,
that my name may remain in it for all time.
Alleluia!

FOR GOSPEL 4   *Isaiah 66:1*

Alleluia, alleluia!
With heaven my throne
and earth my footstool,
what house could you build me? says the Lord.
Alleluia!

or   *Ezekiel 37:27*

Alleluia, alleluia!
I shall make my home among them, says the Lord;
I will be their God,
they shall be my people
Alleluia!

GOSPEL

One of the following readings is chosen:

1   Matthew 16:13–19

> *You are Peter; I will give you the keys
> of the kingdom of heaven.*

2   Luke 19:1–10

> *Today salvation has come to this house.*

3   John 2:13–22

> *He was speaking of the sanctuary
> that was his body.*

4   John 4:19–24

> *True worshippers will worship the Father
> in spirit and truth.*

▷ *page 11*

The Profession of Faith is said.

PRAYER OVER THE OFFERINGS

Recalling the day when you were pleased
to fill your house with glory and holiness, O Lord,
we pray that you may make of us
a sacrificial offering always acceptable to you.
Through Christ our Lord.   **Amen.**

▷ *page 15*

PREFACE

THE MYSTERY OF THE TEMPLE OF GOD, WHICH IS THE CHURCH.

Priest: The Lord be with you.
People: **And with your spirit.**

Priest: Lift up your hearts.
People: **We lift them up to the Lord.**

Priest: Let us give thanks to the Lord our God.
People: **It is right and just.**

OTHER

It is truly right and just, our duty and our salvation,
always and everywhere to give you thanks,
Lord, holy Father, almighty and eternal God,
through Christ our Lord.

For in this visible house that you have let us build
and where you never cease to show favour
to the family on pilgrimage to you in this place,
you wonderfully manifest and accomplish
the mystery of your communion with us.
Here you build up for yourself the temple that we are
and cause your Church, spread throughout the world,
to grow ever more and more as the Lord's own Body,
till she reaches her fullness in the vision of peace,
the heavenly city of Jerusalem.

And so, with the countless ranks of the blessed,
in the temple of your glory we praise you,
we bless you and proclaim your greatness, as we acclaim:

Holy, Holy, Holy Lord God of hosts...

COMMUNION ANTIPHON   *cf 1 Corinthians 3:16–17*
You are the temple of God, and the Spirit of God dwells in you.
The temple of God, which you are, is holy (*Easter Time:* alleluia).

▷ *page 58*

PRAYER AFTER COMMUNION
May the people consecrated to you, O Lord, we pray,
receive the fruits and joy of your blessing,
that the festive homage
they have offered you today in the body
may redound upon them as a spiritual gift.
Through Christ our Lord.   **Amen.**

BLESSING AT THE END OF MASS
Priest: May God, the Lord of heaven and earth,
            who has gathered you today
            in memory of the dedication of this church,
            make you abound in heavenly blessings.
All: **Amen.**

Priest: And may he, who has willed that all his scattered children
            be gathered together in his Son,
            grant that you may become his temple
            and the dwelling place of the Holy Spirit.
All: **Amen.**

Priest:	Thus, may you be made thoroughly clean,
	so that God may dwell within you
	and you may possess with all the Saints
	the inheritance of eternal happiness.
All:	**Amen.**

Priest:	And may the blessing of almighty God,
	the Father, and the Son, ✠ and the Holy Spirit,
	come down on you and remain with you for ever.
All:	**Amen.**

RCIA — RITE OF ACCEPTANCE

RITE OF CHRISTIAN INITIATION OF ADULTS
RITE OF ACCEPTANCE INTO THE ORDER OF CATECHUMENS

The Introductory Rites of the Mass are replaced by the act of Receiving the Candidates.

RECEIVING THE CANDIDATES

The candidates, their sponsors and a group of the faithful gather outside the church or at the church door (or elsewhere suitable to this rite).

The assembly may sing a Psalm or appropriate song.

GREETING

The Priest greets the candidates in a friendly manner. He speaks to them, their sponsors and all present about their journey of faith to this point.

He invites the sponsors and candidates to come forward.
As they take their places before the Priest, an appropriate song may be sung (for example Psalm 62:1–8).

OPENING DIALOGUE

The candidates may be introduced to the assembly, or their names called out. The Priest then asks the candidates their intentions

In asking the candidates about their intentions celebrant may use other words than those provided the and may let them answer in their own words for example, to the first question,

'What do you ask of the Church of God?' or 'What do you desire?' or 'For what reason have you come?',

he may receive such answers as 'The grace of Christ' or 'Entrance into the Church' or 'Eternal life' or other suitable responses. The celebrant then phrases his next question according to the answer received.

Priest:	What do you ask of God's Church?
Candidate:	**Faith.**

Priest:	What does faith offer you?
Candidate:	**Eternal life.**

OTHER

CANDIDATES' FIRST ACCEPTANCE OF THE GOSPEL

The the Priest addresses the candidates and then asks them about their acceptance of the Gospel.
His question may end in these or similar words:

Priest: ...Are you prepared to begin this journey
                             under the guidance of Christ?

Candidates: **I am.**

AFFIRMATION BY THE SPONSORS AND THE ASSEMBLY

The Priest then asks the sponsors and the assembly to commit themselves to support the candidates.
He uses these or similar words:

Priest: Sponsors, you now present these candidates to us; are you, and all who
              are gathered here with us, ready to help these candidates find and follow
              Christ?

All: **We are.**

Then the Priest says:

Priest: Father of mercy,
              we thank you for these your servants.
              You have sought and summoned them in many ways
              and they have turned to seek you.

              You have called them today
              and they have answered in your presence:
              we praise you, Lord, and we bless you.

All sing or say:

All: **We praise you, Lord, and we bless you.**

SIGNING OF THE CANDIDATES WITH THE CROSS

The catechists or sponsors sign the catechumens on the forehead as the Priest says:

Priest: N., receive the cross on your forehead.
              It is Christ himself who now strengthens you
              with this sign of his love.
              Learn to know him and follow him.

All say or sing this, or another suitable acclamation:

All: **Glory and praise to you, Lord Jesus Christ!**

Other parts of the body may also be signed with the Sign of the Cross. The catechists or sponsors sign
the catechumens on the appropriate part of the body as the Priest says each set of words.

Priest: Receive the sign of the cross on your ears,
              that you may hear the voice of the Lord.

All: **Glory and praise to you, Lord Jesus Christ!**

Priest: Receive the sign of the cross on your eyes,
              that you may see the glory of the Lord.

All: **Glory and praise to you, Lord Jesus Christ!**

Priest:	Receive the sign of the cross on your lips, that you may respond to the word of God.
All:	**Glory and praise to you, Lord Jesus Christ!**
Priest:	Receive the sign of the cross on your heart, that Christ may dwell there by faith.
All:	**Glory and praise to you, Lord Jesus Christ!**
Priest:	Receive the sign of the cross on your shoulders, that you may bear the gentle yolk of Christ.
All:	**Glory and praise to you, Lord Jesus Christ!**

Then the celebrant alone makes the sign of the cross over all the candidates at once:

Priest:	I sign you with the sign of eternal life in the name of the Father, and of the Son ✠ and of the Holy Spirit.
Catechumens:	**Amen.**

CONCLUDING PRAYER

Let us pray.

or

Lord,
we have signed these catechumens
with the sign of Christ's cross.
Protect them by its power,
so that, faithful to the grace which has
    begun in them,
they may keep your commandments
and come to the glory of rebirth in baptism.
We ask this through Christ our Lord.
Amen.

Almighty God,
by the cross and resurrection of your Son
you have given life to your people.
Your servants have received the sign of
    the cross:
make them living proof of its saving power
and help them to persevere in the footsteps
    of Christ.
We ask this through Christ our Lord.
Amen.

INVITATION TO THE CELEBRATION OF THE WORD OF GOD

The Priest invites the catechumens and their sponsors to enter the church, using these or similar words:

Priest:	N. and N., come into the church, to share with us at the table of God's word.

The catechumens and their sponsors enter the church to take their places among the assembly.

During the entry an appropriate song is sung, or the following antiphon may be used with Psalm 33:2, 3, 6, 9, 10, 11,16.

Ant. Come, my children, and listen to me;
    I will teach you the fear of the Lord.

OTHER

LITURGY OF THE WORD

INSTRUCTION

After the catechumens have taken their places among the assembly, the Priest speaks to them helping them understand the dignity of God's word which is proclaimed and heard in the church.

The Lectionary is carried in procession and placed with honour on the ambo, where it may be incensed.

READINGS

The readings may be chosen from any of the readings of the Lectionary for Mass that are suited to the new catechumens.

HOMILY

A homily follows that explains the readings.

PRESENTATION OF A BIBLE *(Optional)*

A book containing the gospels may be given to the catechumens by the celebrant; a cross may also be given, unless this has already been done as one of the additional rites.

INTERCESSIONS FOR THE CATECHUMENS

Each intercession for the catechumens concludes:

Let us pray to the Lord
Lord, hear our prayer

If the Prayer of the Faithful is to be omitted, intercessions for the Church and the whole world are added to the intercessions for the catechumens.

PRAYER OVER THE CATECHUMENS

After the intercessions, the celebrant, with hands outstretched over the catechumens, says one of the following prayers.

Let us pray.
[God of our forebears and] God of all creation,
we ask you to look favourably on your servants N. and N.;
make them fervent in spirit,
joyful in hope,
and always ready to serve your name.
Lead them, Lord, to the baptism of new birth,
so that, living a fruitful life in the company of your faithful,
they may receive the eternal reward that you promise.
We ask this in the name of Jesus the Lord.   **Amen.**

or

Almighty God,
source of all creation,
you have made us in your image.
Welcome with love those who come before you today.
They have listened among us to the word of Christ;
by its power renew them
and by your grace refashion them,
so that in time they may assume the full likeness of Christ,
who lives and reigns for ever and ever.   **Amen.**

DISMISSAL OF THE CATECHUMENS

If the eucharist is to be celebrated, the catechumens are normally dismissed at this point by use of option A; if the catechumens are to stay for the celebration of the eucharist, option B is used; if the eucharist is not to be celebrated, the entire assembly is dismissed by use of option C.

A   *The celebrant recalls briefly the great joy with which the catechumens have just been received and urges them to live according to the word of God they have just heard. After the dismissal formulary, the group of catechumens goes out but does not disperse. With the help of some of the faithful, the catechumens remain together to share their joy and spiritual experiences.*

Priest: Catechumens, go in peace,
                     and may the Lord remain with you always.
Catechumens: **Thanks be to God.**

Similar words may be used, for example:

Priest: My dear friends,
             this community now sends you forth
             to reflect more deeply on the word of God which you have shared with us today.
             Be assured of our loving support and prayers for you.
             We look forward to the day when you will share fully in the Lord's Table.

B   *If for serious reasons the catechumens cannot leave and must remain with the baptized, they are to be instructed that though they are present at the eucharist, they cannot take part in it as the baptized do. They may be reminded of this by the celebrant in these or similar words.*

Priest: Although you cannot yet participate fully in the Lord's eucharist,
             stay with us as a sign of our hope
             that all God's children will eat and drink with the Lord
             and work with his Spirit to re-create the face of the earth.

C   *The celebrant dismisses those present, using these or similar words.*

Priest: Go in peace, and may the Lord remain with you always.
All: **Thanks be to God.**

An appropriate song may conclude the celebration.

▷ page 13

PRAYER OF THE FAITHFUL AND PROFESSION OF FAITH

Intercessory prayer is resumed with the usual Prayer of the Faithful for the needs of the Church and the whole world; then, if required, the Profession of Faith is said. But for pastoral reasons, the Prayer of the Faithful and the Profession of Faith may be omitted.

Mass continues in the usual way, using the prayers proper to the day.

After the celebration of the Rite of Acceptance, the names of the catechumens are to be duly inscribed in the register of catechumens, along with the names of the sponsors and the minister and the date and place of the celebration...

...Joined to the Church, the catechumens are now part of the household of Christ, since the Church nourishes them with the word of God and by means of liturgical celebrations.

cf Rite of Christian Initiation of Adults n 46–47

OTHER

MUSIC FOR THE ORDER OF MASS

On occasion, music is not provided for the text which precedes the people's response. In this case a cue is given indicating the last note(s) sung before the response, as in the example opposite:

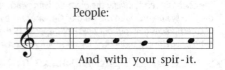

People:

And with your spir-it.

 ## INTRODUCTORY RITES

SIGN OF THE CROSS

All make the Sign of the Cross as the Priest sings:

Priest:

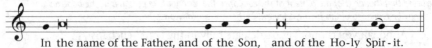

In the name of the Father, and of the Son,   and of the Ho-ly Spir-it.

People:

A-men.

GREETING

Priest: The grace of our Lord Jesus Christ,
           and the love of God,
           and the communion of the Holy Spirit
           be with you all.

or

Priest: Grace to you and peace from God our Father
           and the Lord Jesus Christ.

or

Priest: The Lord be with you.

A Bishop will say:

Bishop: Peace be with you.

People:

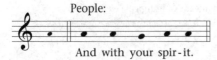

And with your spir-it.

PENITENTIAL ACT
Penitential Act B

Priest: People:

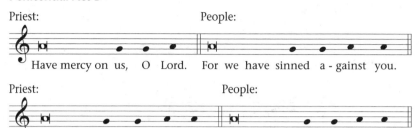

Have mercy on us, O Lord.   For we have sinned a - gainst you.

Priest: People:

Show us, O Lord, your mer - cy.   And grant us your sal - va - tion.

Penitential Act C

Priest or minister: You were sent to heal the contrite of heart:

Repeat after the Priest or minister:

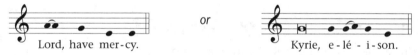

Lord, have mer-cy.   *or*   Kyrie, e - lé - i - son.

Priest or minister: You came to call sinners:

Repeat after the Priest or minister:

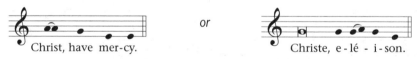

Christ, have mer-cy.   *or*   Christe, e - lé - i - son.

Priest or minister: You are seated at the right hand of the Father
                       to intercede for us:

Repeat after the Priest or minister:

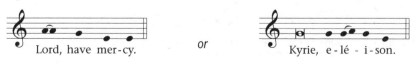

Lord, have mer-cy.   *or*   Kyrie, e - lé - i - son.

ABSOLUTION

The absolution by the Priest follows all of the options above

Priest:

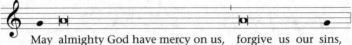

May almighty God have mercy on us,   forgive us our sins,

People:

and bring us to ever - last - ing life.   A - men.

KYRIE

V. Lord,   have mer - cy.   R. Lord,   have mer - cy.

V. Christ, have mer - cy.   R. Christ, have mer - cy.

V. Lord,   have mer - cy.   R. Lord,   have mer - cy.

or

V. Ky - ri - e,   e - lé - i - son.   R. Ky - ri - e,   e - lé - i - son.

V. Chri - ste,   e - lé - i - son.   R. Chri - ste,   e - lé - i - son.

V. Ky - ri - e,   e - lé - i - son.   R. Ky - ri - e,   e - lé - i - son.

or

R. Ky - ri - e,   e - lé - i - son.

GLORIA

Glo-ry to God in the high-est, and on earth peace to peo-ple of good will.

We praise you, we bless you, we a-dore you, we glo-ri-fy you,

we give you thanks for your great glo-ry, Lord God, heav-en-ly King,

O God, al-migh-ty Fa-ther. Lord Je-sus Christ,

On-ly Be-got-ten Son, Lord, God, Lamb of God, Son of the Fa-ther,

you take a-way the sins of the world, have mer-cy on us;

you take a-way the sins of the world, re-ceive our prayer;

you are seat-ed at the right hand of the Fa-ther, have mer-cy on us.

For you a-lone are the Ho-ly One, you a-lone are the Lord,

you a-lone are the Most High, Je-sus Christ, with the Ho-ly Spir-it,

in the glo-ry of God the Fa - ther. A - men.

MUSIC

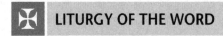

LITURGY OF THE WORD

FIRST READING

Acclamation at the end of the reading.

Reader: People:

The word of the Lord.   Thanks be to God.

SECOND READING

Acclamation at the end of the reading.

Reader: People:

The word of the Lord.   Thanks be to God.

GOSPEL

Dialogue at the beginning of the Gospel.

Deacon / Priest: People:

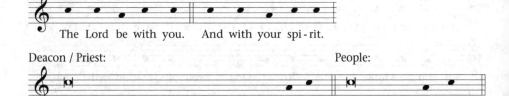

The Lord be with you.   And with your spi-rit.

Deacon / Priest: People:

A reading from the holy Gospel according to N.   Glory to you, O Lord.

Acclamation at the end of the Gospel.

Deacon / Priest: People:

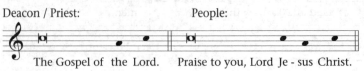

The Gospel of the Lord.   Praise to you, Lord Je-sus Christ.

PROFESSION OF FAITH

Niceno-Constantinopolitan Creed

I be-lieve in one God, the Fa-ther al-migh-ty, mak-er of heav-en

and earth, of all things vis - i - ble and in - vis - i - ble.

I be-lieve in one Lord Je-sus Christ, the Only Be - got-ten Son of God,

born of the Father be - fore all a - ges. God from God, Light from Light,

true God from true God, be - got-ten, not made, con-sub-stan-tial

with the Fa-ther; through him all things were made. For us men and for

At the words that follow, up to and

our sal - va-tion he came down from heav-en, and by the Ho-ly Spir-it

including 'and became man', all bow.

was in - car-nate of the Vir-gin Mar - y, and be-came man.

For our sake he was cru - ci - fied un - der Pon - tius Pi - late,

he suffered death and was bur - ied, and rose a-gain on the third day

MUSIC

in accordance with the Scrip - tures. He as - cen - ded in - to heav - en

and is seated at the right hand of the Fa - ther. He will come a - gain in glo - ry

to judge the living and the dead and his kingdom will have no end.

I be - lieve in the Ho - ly Spir - it, the Lord, the giv - er of life,

who pro - ceeds from the Father and the Son, who with the Fa - ther

and the Son is adored and glo - ri - fied, who has spoken

through the proph - ets. I be - lieve in one, ho - ly, cath - o - lic

and a - po - sto - lic Church. I con - fess one bap - tism

for the for - give - ness of sins and I look for - ward to the

res - ur - rec - tion of the dead and the life of the world to come.

A - - - men.

ORATE, FRATRES

ALL STAND

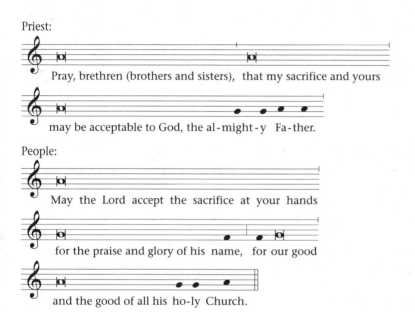

Priest:

Pray, brethren (brothers and sisters), that my sacrifice and yours

may be acceptable to God, the al-might-y Fa-ther.

People:

May the Lord accept the sacrifice at your hands

for the praise and glory of his name, for our good

and the good of all his ho-ly Church.

PREFACE DIALOGUE

Priest: / All:

The Lord be with you. And with your spir - it.

Priest. / All:

Lift up your hearts. We lift them up to the Lord.

Priest: / All:

Let us give thanks to the Lord our God. It is right and just.

MUSIC

SANCTUS

Ho - ly, Ho - ly, Ho - ly Lord God of hosts. Heav - en and earth are

full of your glo - ry. Ho - san - na in the high - est. Bles - sed is he

who comes in the name of the Lord. Ho - san - na in the high - est.

or

San - ctus, San - ctus, San - ctus Dó - mi - nus De - us Sá - ba - oth. Ple - ni sunt cae - li

et ter - ra gló - ri - a tu - a. Ho - sán - na in ex - cél - sis. Be - ne - dí - ctus

qui ven - it in nó - mi - ne Dó - mi - ni. Ho - sán - na in ex - cél - sis.

MEMORIAL ACCLAMATION

Priest:

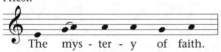

The mys - ter - y of faith.

Memorial Acclamation A

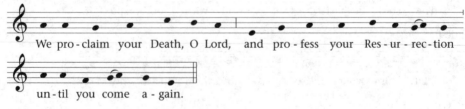

We pro - claim your Death, O Lord, and pro - fess your Res - ur - rec - tion

un - til you come a - gain.

Priest:

The mys - ter - y of faith.

Memorial Acclamation B

When we eat this Bread and drink this Cup, we pro-claim your

Death, O Lord, un - til you come a - gain.

Memorial Acclamation C

Save us, Sav - iour of the world, for by your Cross

and Res - ur - rec - tion you have set us free.

Memorial Acclamation D *for Ireland only*

My Lord and my God.

DOXOLOGY AND GREAT AMEN

Priest:

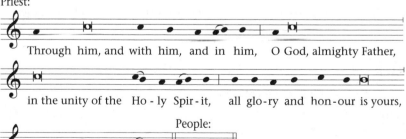

Through him, and with him, and in him, O God, almighty Father,

in the unity of the Ho - ly Spir - it, all glo-ry and hon-our is yours,

People:

for ev - er and ev - er. A - men.

MUSIC

LORD'S PRAYER

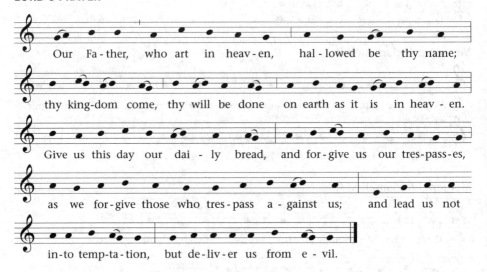

Our Fa-ther, who art in heav-en, hal-lowed be thy name;
thy king-dom come, thy will be done on earth as it is in heav-en.
Give us this day our dai-ly bread, and for-give us our tres-pass-es,
as we for-give those who tres-pass a-gainst us; and lead us not
in-to temp-ta-tion, but de-liv-er us from e-vil.

Priest   Deliver us, Lord, we pray, from every evil,
graciously grant peace in our days,
that, by the help of your mercy,
we may be always free from sin
and safe from all distress,
as we await the blessed hope
and the coming of our Saviour, Jesus Christ.

People:

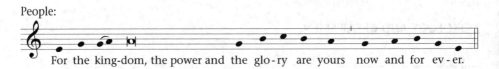

For the king-dom, the power and the glo-ry are yours now and for ev-er.

RITE OF PEACE

Priest: The peace of the Lord be with you always.

People:

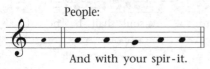

And with your spir-it.

BREAKING OF BREAD

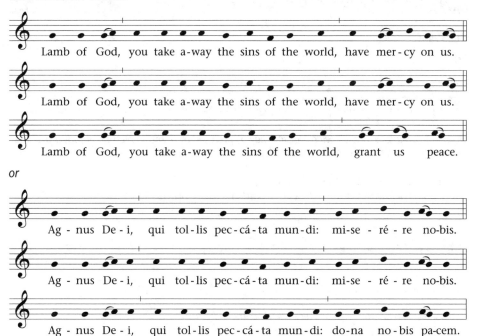

Lamb of God, you take a-way the sins of the world, have mer-cy on us.

Lamb of God, you take a-way the sins of the world, have mer-cy on us.

Lamb of God, you take a-way the sins of the world, grant us peace.

or

Ag - nus De - i, qui tol-lis pec-cá-ta mun-di: mi-se - ré - re no-bis.

Ag - nus De - i, qui tol-lis pec-cá-ta mun-di: mi-se - ré - re no-bis.

Ag - nus De - i, qui tol-lis pec-cá-ta mun-di: do-na no-bis pa-cem.

The invocation may be repeated several times if the Breaking of the Bread is prolonged.
The final time always ends 'grant us peace' ('dona nobis pacem').

INVITATION TO COMMUNION

Priest　　Behold the Lamb of God,
　　　　　behold him who takes away the sins of the world.
　　　　　Blessed are those called to the...

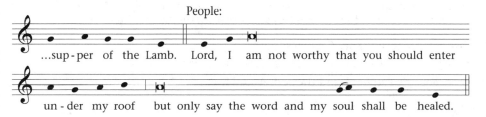

People:

...sup-per of the Lamb. Lord, I am not worthy that you should enter

un-der my roof but only say the word and my soul shall be healed.

MUSIC

CONCLUDING RITES

BLESSING

Priest: People:

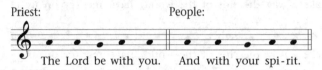

The Lord be with you.   And with your spi-rit.

On certain occasions, the following blessing may be preceded by a solemn blessing or prayer over the people. Then the Priest blesses the people, singing:

Priest: May almighty God bless you:
               the Father, and the Son, ✠ and the Holy Spirit.

Priest: People:

...Ho-ly Spi - rit.   A - men.

In a Pontifical Mass, the celebrant receives the mitre and sings:

Bishop: All:

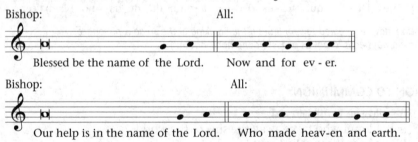

Blessed be the name of the Lord.   Now and for ev - er.

Bishop: All:

Our help is in the name of the Lord.   Who made heav-en and earth.

On certain occasions the following blessing may be preceded by a more solemn blessing or prayer over the people. Then the celebrant receives the pastoral staff, if he uses it, and sings:

Bishop: May almighty God bless you:
making the Sign of the Cross over the people three times, he adds:
               the Father, ✠ and the Son, ✠ and the...

Bishop: People:

...Ho - ly Spi - rit.   A - men.

If any liturgical action follows immediately, the rites of dismissal are omitted.

DISMISSAL

Deacon or Priest: Go forth, the Mass is ended.
or   Go and announce the Gospel of the Lord.
or   Go in peace, glorifying the Lord by your life.

Thanks be to God.

or

Go in peace. Thanks be to God.

The following dismissal is used on Easter Sunday, the Octave of Easter, and in the Mass during the day on Pentecost Sunday.

Deacon/Priest:

Go forth, the Mass is end-ed, al-le-lu-ia, al-le - lu - ia.

or

Deacon/Priest:

Go in peace, al-le-lu-ia, al-le - lu - ia.

All:

Thanks be to God, al-le-lu-ia, al-le - lu - ia.

THOUGHTS AND PRAYERS

Prayer Before a Crucifix

Behold, O kind and most sweet Jesus,
I cast myself on my knees in your sight,
and with the most fervent desire of my soul,
I pray and beseech you
that you would impress upon my heart
lively sentiments of faith, hope and charity,
with a true repentance for my sins
and a firm desire of amendment,
while with deep affection and grief of soul
I ponder within myself
and mentally contemplate
your five most precious wounds,
having before my eyes
that which David spoke in prophecy of you,
O good Jesus:
'They have pierced my hands and my feet;
they have numbered all my bones.'

On Silence

We need to find God, and he cannot be found in noise and restlessness,
God is the friend of silence.
See how nature – trees, flowers, grass – grow in silence;
see the stars, the moon and sun, how they move in silence.
Is not our mission to give God to the poor in the slums?
Not a dead God, but a living, loving God.
The more we receive in silent prayer, the more we can give in our active life.
We need silence to be able to touch souls.
The essential thing is not what we say, but what God says to us and through us.
All our words will be useless unless they come from within –
words which do not give the light of Christ increase the darkness.

Mother Teresa

Prayers to Mary

The Memorare

Remember, O most loving Virgin Mary,
that it is a thing unheard of,
that anyone ever had recourse to your protection,
implored your help,
or sought your intercession,
and was left forsaken.
Filled therefore with confidence in your goodness
I fly to you, O Mother, Virgin of virgins.
To you I come, before you I stand,
a sorrowful sinner.
Despise not my poor words,
O Mother of the Word of God,
but graciously hear and grant my prayer.

Hail, Holy Queen

Hail, holy Queen, mother of mercy:
hail, our life, our sweetness, and our hope!
To you do we cry,
poor banished children of Eve.
To you do we send up our sighs,
mourning and weeping
in this vale of tears.
Turn then, most gracious advocate,
your eyes of mercy towards us;
and after this our exile,
show to us
the blessed fruit of your womb, Jesus.
O clement,
O loving,
O sweet Virgin Mary.
Pray for us, O holy Mother of God.
That we may be made worthy
    of the promises of Christ.

Anima Christi
Soul of Christ, sanctify me.
Body of Christ, save me.
Blood of Christ, inebriate me.
Water from the side of Christ, wash me.
Passion of Christ, strengthen me.

Jesus, hear me.
Hide me in your wounds,
that I may never leave your side
and never let me be parted from you.
From the malicious enemy defend me.

In the hour of my death call me,
and tell me come unto you,
that with your saints I may praise you
through all eternity,
for ever and ever. Amen

O Sacrum Convivium
O Sacred Banquet,
in which Christ is received,
and the memory of his Passion is renewed;
where the soul is filled with grace,
and a pledge of future glory is given to us.

PRAYERS AFTER MASS

Prayer of Saint Ignatius
Teach us, good Lord,
to serve you as you deserve;
to give and not to count the cost;
to fight and not to heed the wounds;
to toil, and not to seek for rest;
to labour and to ask for no reward,
save that of knowing
that we do your will;
through Jesus Christ our Lord.

Jesus, Our Brother
Dear Lord,
I believe that Holy Communion joins us all
together in union with you and in union
with one another.

As we all received you together at the
Holy Table, let us remember that we are all
members of one family.

Let us help one another and forgive one
another, bearing one another's burdens.

You have said that if we do not love our
neighbour, whom we can see, how can we
love God, whom we cannot see?

Make me careful, therefore, not to despise
anyone, as if they were beneath me; not
to bear a grudge against anyone who may
have done me wrong.

Whenever there is any work to be done for
the good of the parish, make me overcome
my laziness and my pride and give me the
desire to help.

Let me be a good example, not a stumbling
block, to those around me.

Prayer of Saint Francis
Lord, make me an instrument of your peace.

Where there is hatred let me sow peace;
where there is injury, pardon;
where there is doubt, let me sow faith;
where there is despair, let me give hope;
where there is darkness, let me give light;
where there is sadness, let me give joy.

O Divine Master, grant that I may not seek
to be comforted, but to comfort;
to be understood, but to understand;
to be loved, but to love.

For it is in giving that we receive,
it is in forgiving that we are forgiven,
and it is in dying
    that we are born to eternal life.

Prayer of St Richard
O dear Lord,
three things I pray:
to see thee more clearly,
love thee more dearly,
and follow thee more nearly,
day by day.

A Thought on Thanksgiving
It is very easy to pray to God
    when we are in trouble;
even people who do not think
    they believe in God
may utter a short prayer in times of crisis.
Fewer people thank God
    for the good things which we are given.
Remember how often Jesus said,
'Father, I thank you...'

Etta Gullick